William O´Connor Morris

Great commanders of Modern Times

The campaign of 1815

William O´Connor Morris

Great commanders of Modern Times
The campaign of 1815

ISBN/EAN: 9783337815844

Printed in Europe, USA, Canada, Australia, Japan

Cover: Foto ©ninafisch / pixelio.de

More available books at **www.hansebooks.com**

GREAT COMMANDERS
OF MODERN TIMES

AND

THE CAMPAIGN OF 1815.

.

BY

WILLIAM O'CONNOR MORRIS.

Reprinted from the
"ILLUSTRATED NAVAL AND MILITARY MAGAZINE."

" Faites la guerre offensive comme Alexandre, Annibal, César, Gustave Adolphe,. Turenne, le Prince Eugène et Fredéric; lisez, relisez l'histoire de leurs quatre vingt trois campagnes; modelez vous sur eux."—NAPOLEON.

LONDON: W. H. ALLEN AND CO., LIMITED,
AND AT CALCUTTA.

1891.

LONDON:
PRINTED BY W. H. ALLEN AND CO., LIMITED,
13, WATERLOO PLACE.

CONTENTS.

GREAT COMMANDERS OF MODERN TIMES.

THE CAMPAIGN OF 1815.

LIST OF
MAPS, PLANS, AND ILLUSTRATIONS.

PREFACE.

THIS volume consists of a series of essays on Great Commanders of Modern Times, and of two papers on the Campaign of 1815. I have to thank the Editor of *The Illustrated Naval and Military Magazine*, in which these studies originally appeared, for thinking them worthy of republication; and my acknowledgments are due to the press for many favourable notices. The text has been revised and slips of the pen corrected; but I have made no substantial change in what I had at first written.

A civilian, who attempts to treat of military affairs, ought to bear in mind the remark of Hannibal to the Greek sophist—" It is pretty, but it is all nonsense." Yet it is with the art of war as with lesser arts; the unprofessional inquirer can attain knowledge of leading truths, though he may not be able to master technical details. Thucydides was perhaps not a soldier, but he observed this principle, and his narrative of the siege of Syracuse is a masterpiece. An ordinary writer is not worthy to unloose the shoe latchet of Thucydides; but he may, in this matter, imitate the method of the great Athenian; and if he has fair intelligence, works hard, and devotes laborious hours to reflecting on the exploits of great captains, he may become, in some measure, a sound military critic. These essays are not, I trust, wholly devoid of the only merits I claim for them.

The papers on the Campaign of 1815, though only sketches, are the least fugitive pieces of any in this volume. I have formed my conclusions after a careful study of nearly every valuable authority on the subject; and I have had the advantage of some special information not yet given to the public. I have described Napoleon as easily superior, as a strategist, to his adversaries; while I have done justice to the great qualities displayed by Wellington and Blücher, as soldiers, I have dwelt on the grave strategic mistakes they committed. This will not gratify national vanity; but, in my judgment, it is the verdict which History will pronounce, nay, is already pronouncing, upon the questions raised by this mighty conflict, after a full and dispassionate investigation of the evidence.

My short account of the Battle of Waterloo may be flatly contradicted, or sharply criticized, in two particulars. I have described La Haye Sainte as having been captured at about 4 P.M. on the 18th of June; and I have left it to be inferred that only one column of the Imperial Guard actually reached the British line. It would take too long to explain why I have made these statements; I shall merely remark that the testimony in their favour seems to me greatly to preponderate.

Gartnamona, Tullamore,
September 1890.

GREAT COMMANDERS OF MODERN TIMES.

GREAT COMMANDERS

OF

MODERN TIMES.

INTRODUCTION.

BY A SOLDIER.

It will doubtless appear to some that this is a trite subject whose interest has long ago evaporated, exhausted by the numerous and competent pens which have treated it. The soldier, at all events, will judge otherwise, and conclude that the careers of that small group of demi-gods, commonly known as " great generals," afford matter for consideration which can never tire, and which gains in interest the more it is analysed. As we vary our point of view, so the prospect grows upon us and the more we admire its details. Again, passing from select readers to the multitude, we have the sanction of a most sagacious observer of mankind for retracing the ground which has been so often trodden aforetime.

> Difficile est proprie communia dicere ; tuque
> Rectius Iliacum carmen deducis in actus,
> Quam si proferres ignota indictaque primus.

This being so, a concise summary like this of the campaigns of the most eminent of these great military leaders will not prove devoid of novelty and interest, as coming from the pen of one whom a civil career has left free from professional prejudice, and the study of law has trained to weigh

1

conflicting evidence. These biographical summaries include the following names :—

1. Turenne.
2. Marlborough.
3. Frederick the Great.
4. Napoleon.
5. Wellington.
6. Moltke.

If in any particular we are at variance with the writer, it is that he hardly attaches sufficient importance to the influence of Turenne's predecessor, Gustavus Adolphus, in the development of the military art. We ourselves agree with Gfrörer, his German biographer, that the Swedish king was the father of modern strategy, and the first really great general since Julius Cæsar. As Judge O'Connor Morris points out, many great soldiers lived during this long interval of time, but in our opinion (and it is in accord with Napoleon's) it was the campaigns of the Swedish hero, and notably the Thirty Years' War, which first revealed the dawn of that science which in later days was brought to such perfection by his successors. The tactical improvements introduced by Gustavus were extensive, though cavalry still played too exclusive a *rôle* in his engagements ; his reforms in the armament and equipment of his troops were remarkable ; nor is the military historian oblivious of his services to good discipline and morality by the Articles of War which he compiled and promulgated.

Gustavus Adolphus, when he ascended the throne at the tender age of seventeen, found his realm engaged in hostilities with Denmark, Russia, and Poland. His successor, Charles XII., curiously enough, was similarly entangled, but promptitude and good fortune in each case enabled the monarch to assail his enemies in succession and beat them in detail. The Danes already occupied the southern provinces of Sweden and, in the spring of 1612, they advanced in two columns, intending to move on Stockholm by the routes east and west of the Wettern Lake which give access to the capital. This afforded the boy-king an opportunity for signalizing his latent military talent. Posting his forces at Jönköping, at the southernmost extremity of the lake, he struck alternately at the divided columns of the Danish army till he thrust them in disorderly retreat back to the sea-coast. Thus early was the leading idea which governed the defence of France in 1814 foreshadowed amid the rocks and lakes of Sweden. Peace with Denmark resulted in 1613, and through the mediation of James I. of England.

Russia was next assailed. Semi-barbarous at the time, that State was in the throes of revolution brought about by the extinction of the House of Ruric; and a project was actually on foot for her dismemberment, one half to go to Sweden, the other to Poland. But Muscovite patriotism defeated its execution. Michael Románoff was, in 1613, elected Tsar. Gustavus at the same time landed in Esthonia, but effected little beyond the capture of Gdoff, and in 1617 concluded peace, again through the good offices of England. The Thirty Years' War was looming in the distance; the diplomacy of the Protestant Powers tended towards a union against the Papacy. Thus both dynastic and religious considerations recommended an attack on Poland to the judgment of Gustavus. Sigismund III., her king, was both a bigoted Catholic and the rightful though dethroned King of Sweden. Nothing could be effected in Germany leaving such an active and embittered foe in flank and rear. At first the King operated from Riga as a base, with the Dwina as his line of operations; but experience soon taught that, to effect his purpose, he must strike vigorously home at the heart of the adversary's power. The theatre of war was therefore transferred to West Prussia, then directly subject to Poland, where he proceeded to establish a solid base on the coast, by making himself master of the fortresses of Frauenburg, Elbing, Marienburg, Stuhm, Mewe, Dirschau, and Oliva. Dantzig was besieged to facilitate communication with Sweden and, in this case, the line chosen by him for an eventual advance into the interior was the river Vistula. In all of his campaigns we find Gustavus keeping up his communications with the coast by means

1 *

of a great river; he lived in times when railways were not dreamt of and even roads could scarcely be said to exist. A commodious port on the Baltic was also necessary for safe communication with Sweden, and to serve as a depôt for stores. Thus his strategy was far in advance of the practice of his renowned successors Charles X. and Charles XII., who, great soldiers as they were, relapsed into pre-Gustavus methods, though they had both the King's example and that of Turenne before them.

During this " Prussian War," as the Swedish historians designate the struggle with Poland, Gustavus, involved himself in the Thirty Years' War by sending troops to succour the hard-pressed garrison of Stralsund, then besieged by Wallenstein. This affront quickly brought a division of 10,000 Imperialists to the fields of Poland. Nevertheless, the belligerents concluded, in 1629, an armistice for the space of six years, which enabled Gustavus to turn his attention to the horrible struggle which was deluging Germany with blood, while securing his recent acquisitions on the Baltic. In one particular, however, he had persistently infringed the rules of conduct which should guide the great Commander : he had recklessly exposed his life during this Prussian campaign. During an action at Dirschau, the Swedes were on the point of victory when a bullet struck their chief in the shoulder, and he was borne insensible from the field. The action was stopped in consequence, and it was this wound which ever afterwards made it irksome for him to wear a cuirass, the absence of which probably occasioned his death on the field of Lützen. On several other occasions he escaped death or capture by a hair's breadth. But it is only on critical occasions that the leader of a host ought to risk his life. The interests committed to his charge ought to be paramount in his estimation. Cæsar and Napoleon both well knew when such a course seemed necessary.

We now approach the crowning enterprize of this " Lion of the North," his intervention in the Thirty Years' War, with the glories which were compressed into the short span of life which yet remained to him : an enterprize which he had long dreamed of in secret, and the fatal termination of which he probably only too plainly foresaw.

He landed on the island of Usedom on the 26th June 1630. Separated from the mainland by a narrow arm of the sea, it was admirably suited for the purpose of a maritime base of operations. Gustavus, the first who leaped ashore, sank on his knees, gave thanks to God, and, this done, seized a spade and began to dig the trenches. The island of Wollin was next subjugated, and the command of the mouth of the Oder by this means secured. Tilly was absent, dancing attendance on the Diet at Regensburg; Torquato Conti, his lieutenant, seemed paralyzed by the emergency; Wallenstein had justly been deposed from the supreme command. Embarking on the Stettiner Haff, the " Snow King," as his enemies contemptuously nick-named him, seized possession of Stettin in July. In September he invaded the duchy of Mecklenburg, thus extending his area of supply and acquiring a broad and solid base for operating in relief of beleaguered Magdeburg. He drove Schaumburg, Conti's successor, as far as Frankfort-on-the-Oder, and by the close of the year all the Pomeranian strong-holds except Colberg, Greifswald, and Demmin, were in his possession. Thus much to prove how systematic was his system of warfare, and to show how carefully he fortified his base before venturing into the interior of Germany.

It must be noted that Gustavus continued active operations throughout the winter, in contrast to the habits of the age. In January 1631 his troops, clothed in sheep-skins, quitted Stettin, and New Brandenburg, Loitz, Malchin, and Demmin fell to their arms. These successes brought Tilly raging with fury on their track. Traversing Brandenburg amid blood and flame, he captured New Brandenburg by assault. Gustavus had skilfully concentrated his forces to protect the town at Friedland and at Pasewalk, but was informed by his lieutenants that the troops were so demoralized by the idea of encountering Tilly's terrible bands that they were not to be relied on! In this desperate emergency the genius of the Swede stood by him. While Horn disputed the passage of the Peene and Trebel by the Imperialists, the King ascended the Oder with the bulk of his forces, and, taking post at Schwedt, menaced the enemy's right and rear so that Tilly rapidly retraced his steps, and, finding the Swedish position impregnable, continued his retreat to Magdeburg. When the field was clear, Gustavus, dashing out of his camp, appeared before Frankfort-on-the-Oder. On the 3rd April the assault was sounded, the gates were blown open by his petards, and the fortress succumbed amid great slaughter. Shortly afterwards Landsberg encountered a similar fate.

In May the fall of Magdeburg startled the civilized world—a disaster to be ascribed to the obstinacy and timidity of the Saxon and Brandenburg electors, who hesitated to afford Gustavus their support. In plain words, the King resolutely declined to advance to the city's relief till he had safe-guarded his line of retreat in conformity with the maxims of what we now-a-days call strategy, but with him was merely martial instinct. Possession of the fortresses which secured his line of retreat was deliberately withheld from him by these Protestant potentates until too late. But the bestial fury of the Imperialist soldiery robbed Tilly of the fruits of victory. Instead of acquiring a pivot whence to dominate North Germany, he was constrained to slink back into Thuringia and the banks of the Unstruth.

The indignation aroused by this massacre throughout the Protestant world enabled Gustavus to coerce his brother-in-law of Berlin ; a treaty of alliance signed and sealed safeguarded the Swedish rear, and the King was in a position to execute a general advance across the Elbe which placed his strategic front in a direction parallel to his base. Having effected the passage near Tangermünde, he pitched his camp at Werben, near the confluence of the Havel and Elbe, across which he constructed a bridge. Immediately on receipt of the news, Tilly, uniting with Pappenheim at Magdeburg, flew to the assault, but soon experienced his opponent's mettle. The King surprised the Imperialist advance-guard by night near Burgstall, and destroyed 2,000 of their cavalry. Tilly reconnoitred the works at Werben, but, not liking their aspect, retired to Eisleben. He had lost one quarter of his numbers, but was there raised to 30,000 men by the arrival of troops, liberated from Italy by the treaty of Cherasco, under Count von Fürstenberg, so that he was in a position to enforce the Imperial summons that the Saxon Elector should surrender his army and revenues for Catholic purposes. The insolent demand drove that Prince into the arms of Sweden, and a convention was signed which placed his army together with Wittenburg at the disposition of Gustavus. Leipzig capitulated to Tilly and the Swedes crossed the Elbe, effecting a junction with the Saxons on the banks of the Mulda. Two days later (the 7th September) was fought the battle of Leipzig, which justified all the plans and precautions of the Swedish strategist.

Into the details of that great conflict it is not our business here to inquire. The splendid tactical *coup d'œil* of Gustavus has never been called into question. Let us rather consider how he profited by this amazing triumph. While the adversary withdrew into Thuringia, Gustavus struck right across his communications with Bavaria, pressing along the "Priest's Lane," the rich string of ecclesiastical principalities which then lined the banks of the Main—that march which is mentioned with admiration by the present biographer of Turenne. He thus provided himself with a new and fertile base for operating against the heart of the Empire at the expense of the Catholic party, while the Saxons invested Leipzig and defended the line of the Elbe from the enemy in Silesia. The Swedish King jealously guarded his communications with the sea, which were demarked by the rivers Saale and Elbe. Thuringia was garrisoned by Weimar troops; Halle by those of the Prince of Anhalt; Banér invested Magdeburg, while Tott held Mecklenburg in subjection.

On the 26th September the King's army, leaving Erfurt, began to ascend the Main, and on the 10th October they took the episcopal fortress of Würtzburg by assault. This calamity drew Tilly in hot haste to the south. Towards the end of October his army, 40,000 strong, was bivouacked along the Tauber, where, on the night of the 23rd, Gustavus again cut up three Imperialist cavalry regiments which had bivouacked in an exposed position.

After a futile demonstration against Ochsenfurt, where he lost heart on discovering the Swedes drawn up beyond the Main, Tilly retreated in the direction of Nuremberg, when Gustavus, leaving Horn to observe his movements, sped along that river to Frankfort, into which capital he made his triumphal entry on the 17th November 1631. Meanwhile his antagonist, as if crushed in spirit by the swift ruin which had overtaken his fortunes, raided about Franconia at random, and seemed utterly incapable of arriving at any fixed determination. Finally he imagined the assault of Nuremberg; but a Protestant soldier, applying a slow-match to his store of gunpowder, blew it into the air together with the projects of his chief, who forthwith left Nuremberg and cantoned his troops in winter quarters around Nördlingen. The Swede, however, was more energetic, and crossing the Rhine at Oppenheim in defiance of the troops of Spain, gained possession of the great fortress of Mentz as the reward of his valour and activity. Here Gustavus spent Christmas with his Queen and Chancellor, Oxenstierna, who had come from Sweden to meet him. He was at the high pitch of his prosperity, courted by the petty princes of Germany and by the envoys of more considerable Powers. He was dreaming, it was said, of a Protestant Empire. But France, his ally, had taken umbrage at his successes. Richelieu endeavoured to arrange a pacification, but the sagacity or ambition of Gustavus impelled him to decline these overtures.

Early in 1632, Tilly, advancing from Nördlingen, surprised Horn at Bamberg, forcing him down the valley of the Main till he was supported by the King with 40,000 men. The Imperialists then retreated in their turn, and Gustavus, suddenly crossing the river, nearly succeeded in cutting them off from the Danube and Ingolstadt. Having entered Nuremberg in triumph, he continued the pursuit, and turned the line of the Danube by seizing, at Donauwörth, the only bridge left intact by Tilly between Neuburg and Ulm. Tilly hurried his troops from Ingolstadt to the Lech, in order to dispute the passage of the stream. Dissuaded from attacking by his generals, who urged that Wallenstein's army in Bohemia was threatening his communications with the Baltic,

Gustavus persisted in his intention, replying that a demoralized enemy should be crushed without allowing him a respite for recovery: his own retreat by Donauwörth on Mentz was safe. He was out-voted in council, but acted on his own opinion, and his able dispositions were crowned with perfect success. The passage of the rapid current was forced. Tilly, like Turenne, was slain by an unlucky round-shot. Gustavus did not pursue vigorously— that art seems to have been invented by Napoleon—but Augsburg formed a substantial prize for the victor. Here was the cradle of the Protestant faith, and in days of religious bigotry this solemn entry into the city must have caused rapturous sensations in Lutheran hearts. Munich likewise received him with open gates.

While repressing a revolt of the peasantry the King was suddenly apprised that Wallenstein, having seized the Pass of Eger, had entered Franconia, seeking to force the Thuringian defiles, and opened communication with the Bavarians at Regensburg. This was the contingency foreseen by those who had condemned the passage of the Lech. Wallenstein, careless about his own communications or the interests of the Empire he served, and desirous only of fixing his own authority in North Germany while living at free-quarters, had thrust himself between the Swedes and the Baltic Sea. In June therefore the King, hurriedly retracing his steps, crossed the Danube at Donauwörth in the endeavour to cut off the Bavarians in their march northwards to join Wallenstein. In this he failed, but narrowly. The enemy had given him the slip by requisitioning carts for their conveyance. He entrenched himself at Nuremberg, was followed thither by Wallenstein, and a terrible drama of slaughter, disease, and starvation, which seemed to typify all the plagues of Egypt, was enacted around that city. It resulted in a drawn battle; and the martial reputation of the Swedish king suffered proportionate diminution. He had been withstood successfully; nay, more, he had been the first to withdraw from it. For this his moral nature was perhaps responsible. He could no longer endure the pandemonium of human suffering which was in progress around him, while to the cynical Wallenstein all this was a matter of indifference. Strangely enough the Imperialists retreated north, the Protestants southwards. Wallenstein swept through Saxony with his ravenous, ruthless hordes; Gustavus once more subjected Bavaria to his requisitions. War was to be made to support war; but let us bear in mind that it was the fond hope of Wallenstein to establish an empire for himself in North Germany; while it is surmised that his adversary held not dissimilar views, though with nobler aspirations; at all events his strategic base at this time was the city of Mentz and the fertile valley of the Rhine in its proximity. But the inhuman atrocities of the Imperialists in Saxony were again too much for the sensitive nature of Gustavus; in addition to which, the statesman will note that the Elector, a dubious ally, was likely to make terms with the oppressor, and this would signify a permanent severance from Sweden which could not be acquiesced in. On the 11th October, the King directed his army north *via* Donauwörth in two columns, and by the end of the month was able to review them reunited at Erfurt. Unfortunately his allies, the Saxons and Lüneburgers were still beyond the Elbe, and a flank march in front of the concentrated Imperialists became indispensible in order to effect a junction; for Wallenstein and Pappenheim had judiciously united their forces near Leipzig, while George of Lüneburg had disobeyed the King's orders, which enjoined him to rendezvous in Thuringia, and the Saxon Elector, as if paralysed by dread of Wallenstein, was still in the depths of Silesia. Grimma was the point indicated for concentration, thus well within striking distance of the enemy; and Gustavus left Naumburg in this direction on the 5th November. On the march, however, an intercepted letter was placed in his hand. He learnt that Wallenstein, deeming the campaign ended for that year, had permitted Pappenheim with 10,000 men to depart on a raid into Westphalia, and had cantoned the remainder of his forces in and around Lützen. At this sudden crisis, Gustavus proved his title to a niche among the " demigods " of war. Instantly wheeling his columns to the left, he advanced to the attack across the vast plain which leads to the town of Lützen. But " Man proposes, God disposes," an adage which is peculiarly applicable to warlike enterprize. The passage of the Rippach stream, strenuously defended by Isolani's Croats, stopped the Swedes till nightfall, a delay which enabled Wallenstein to assemble his scattered forces; while a dense fog next morning, which did not lift till 11 o'clock, prevented the attack taking place at an early hour, and so afforded time for Pappenheim to return with his troops to the field ere the close of the battle. But by this time the great King had breathed his last, and Pappenheim roamed the field in vain in order to cross swords with him. After a desperate struggle, the Catholics suffered defeat, but the loss of the Protestant champion converted disaster into a victory for their faith.

In the long struggle which followed after his death, and lasted no less than sixteen years, the name of TURENNE first became known to fame.

CHAPTER I.

TURENNE.

I REMEMBER hearing a soldier of promise remark that war had so completely changed that it was useless to study the campaigns of Napoleon. This foolish paradox represents ideas too common among military men of late; and is about as true as an old notion, rudely exploded on the great day of Austerlitz, that Frederick's usual method of giving battle was so infallible, under all circumstances, that a long flank march under the guns of an enemy in position is scientific strategy. An opinion is abroad that German genius has wrought such a revolution in the art of war, that all that has gone before is obsolete; that Moltke is a faultless commander, whose exploits surpass those of all chiefs; nay, that mechanism and organization are the best means of assuring success to armies in the field. It is time to expose the perilous errors, mixed with particles of truth, in these shallow statements. The subordinate methods and rules of war have been largely changed, in the progress of the age, and especially through its material inventions; but the higher parts of the art can never vary, for they have their origin in the faculties of man, as grandly developed in Cæsar and Hannibal as in the great captains of modern times; and the exhibition of these, whatever may be the conditions of time and other accidents, will always be matter of fruitful study. As for the "faultlessness" of Moltke, that distinguished man would be the first to admit that, like all generals, he has made grave and palpable errors. Extraordinary,

TURENNE.

indeed, as have been his achievements, his campaigns in Bohemia and France show that his strategic and tactical mistakes were many; and though he is a real chief of the Napoleonic school, he has done nothing that can be compared to the movements round Mantua in 1796, to the Alpine march that led to Marengo, to the manœuvres that immured Mack in Ulm, to the last swoop on Belgium in 1815. That mechanism and organization count for much, is a truth as old as the days of the Legions; but the genius of leaders in directing armies has always been the chief element of success in war; and, so far from this being less the case at the present day than it has been of old, this influence is now more than ever decisive. It is obvious, in fact, that the powers of the chief will have increasingly greater effect as armies have grown to immense proportions, and military movements have become more complex, more extended, and, above all, more rapid; and if a mere tactician will, perhaps, do less, on a given field, than a century ago, victory in a campaign will, in this age, in the main, depend on superior strategy.

I purpose, in this and subsequent articles, to endeavour to illustrate the main principles and permanent lessons of the art of war in brief sketches of the lives and the deeds of famous commanders of modern times; and I shall try to dispel the notions that military history before Sadowa is a mere old almanack, and that the exclusive study of modern Prussian routine is the best education of the accomplished soldier. For authority, I need only refer to Napoleon.* "Tactics," wrote that master of war, "manœuvres, the science of the engineer and of the artillerist, can be learned in treatises, like geometry; but knowledge of the high parts of war can be acquired only by study of the history of war, and of the battles of great captains, and by experience."

I have placed Turenne at the head of my list, not only because he comes first in time, but because the art of war made immense progress during the long career of this illustrious chief, was greatly improved by his powerful genius, and gradually acquired a modern

---

* *Napoleon Correspondence,* vol. xxxi., p. 365.

aspect. Before I attempt, however, to sketch his exploits, I would say a word on the condition of the art before it passed into his master hand. The leading maxims of war were fully understood; and great commanders had, in many a contest, shown what the qualities are which ensure success in the strife of opposing armies. That a general in a campaign should have a distinct object, that he should steadily endeavour to carry it out, and that he should so combine his means as to promote his ends, were recognised and approved principles; and the value of intelligence in great movements, of energy and skill in the direction of troops and of careful administration in military affairs, had been illustrated by fine examples. Passing, too, from these universal truths, the principal rules of strategic science had been ascertained in their main outlines, and ably brought to the test of experience; nay, war had exhibited grand instances of strategy, whether of offence or defence, which, founded as it is on the peculiar character and faculties of individual men, had never perhaps more noted champions than Hannibal and the Roman Fabius. The advantage, for instance, of having the possession of interior lines on a field of manœuvre had been clearly perceived by Guébriant, and was repeatedly seen in the Thirty Years' War; Gustavus had shown what could be accomplished by rapid and well concerted movements against the communications of a hostile army; and Wallenstein had proved how great could be the power of firmness, endurance, and patient skill in resisting even the most able enemy.

The art, however, owing to many causes, had not as yet been nearly developed, and had not even approached its present perfection. Fine movements, indeed, were occasionally made; the march of Gustavus, for example, down "the Priests' Lane," which carried him into the heart of the Empire, and some of the marches of Parma, in an earlier age, remain noble specimens of audacious genius. But strategy was still, so to speak, cramped and limited by all kinds of obstacles, and it could not attain the freedom and grandeur which it has exhibited in the wars of this century. On every theatre of war, from Vienna to Brussels, the state of husbandry was backward in the extreme; there were immense wastes of morass and forest; and even the plain country was not half cultivated. The roads, too, were comparatively few, and even the main roads were, for the most part, bad; the great rivers had but few bridges, and minor streams were not bridged at all; and the passes across the chief mountain ranges were mere paths and tracks, intricate and difficult. The natural impediments to the march of armies were, therefore, many and often formidable; and these were greatly increased by the numerous fortresses which had grown up since the feudal age, and which, covering frontiers and main approaches, and barring the way to an invader's progress, could not easily be passed by even a daring enemy. In addition to this, the means of supply and of transport possessed by modern armies, either did not exist or were very scanty; magazines, trains, and the many appliances that enable troops of this day to live and move, were quite in an embryonic state; and a general was often compelled to rely on plunder and rapine to support his soldiery. In these circumstances, the rapid manœuvres and the grand movements leading to decisive battles which belong to the age of Napoleon and Moltke, could be witnessed only on a small scale, and occurred only in rare instances. War, as a rule, had a contracted aspect; and its ends were often different from those of our time. Beset by impediments, even the greatest chiefs were frequently unable to make long marches, or to attempt anything like audacious strategy; and though Gustavus had fully seen that the main object of a campaign was to cripple an adversary in pitched battles, this was not yet an accepted principle. The art of war still largely consisted in wearing out an enemy in petty combats, in devastation, and wrecking a country, in incursions attended by partial success; and the aim of commanders often was, not so much to defeat a hostile army as to find good quarters in an unravaged province. Campaigns were late, slow, and had small results; as a rule, winter campaigns were rare. Above all, it had become a maxim that before invading an enemy's country it was necessary first to reduce its fortresses; months, and even years, were taken up in sieges; and the art, it has been said, " seemed to flit around strong places." In short, owing to the local accidents and peculiarities of the seventeenth century, strategy, though in existence and in a state of progress, was still quite immature and imperfect.

The science of Tactics had at this period made less progress than that of Strategy. It had become recognized that the three arms should act in concert, and support each other ; and a distinct unity was seen in battles, unlike the desultory combats of the Middle Ages. But one great principle of modern tactics, that an army should be arrayed on the ground, not according to any unchanging method but so that each arm should turn to account the character and local features of the spot, had scarcely entered the minds of men ; it certainly had not been fully established. An army took its position in a settled order : the cavalry always on either wing, the infantry in the centre, and the guns in front. There usually was a considerable reserve ; and the importance, for instance, of so placing cavalry that it could fall on an enemy from under cover, or of so distributing guns that they could enfilade infantry, or throw a concentrated or plunging fire, was as yet little, if at all, understood. In these circumstances the marked diversity which is a characteristic of modern battles, which makes no one exactly resemble the other, and in consequence of which the tactical skill of a chief in command is taxed to the utmost, existed only to a small extent. There was a distinct sameness in the battles of the age, and these usually consisted in a contest between the hostile footmen and guns in the centre—a mere partial engagement without manœuvres—until the success of the cavalry on either side enabled it to assail the flank or the rear of the enemy. The tactics, therefore, of this period were very different from those of our own ; and this difference was made greater through the change in the relations of the three arms, and in the efficiency and the power of infantry, which has taken place since the seventeenth century. At this period, cavalry was by far the most important and capable arm ; it was, in fact, the manœuvring force in the field. The value of artillery was still unknown, for guns were comparatively few and ill served ; and footmen, often inferior in numbers to horsemen, were a combined array of musketeers and pikemen, invariably marshalled in dense masses, unequal to quick and difficult movements, and utterly inferior to the infantry of this day in relative strength, in the efficacy of fire, in ability either to attack or defend, and in evolutions and manœuvres in the field.

Under these conditions, a general gave his chief attention to his most powerful arm; artillery and foot played a subordinate part; and, as I have said, the event of battles was usually decided by a charge of horsemen launched against an exposed side of a hostile army. But if the tactics of those days were unlike ours, it is a mistake to suppose that they did not afford full scope to superior skill and genius. The front of battles was comparatively small; a general's eye could command the whole field, and victory usually depended on the inspiration of the chief, who, with ready design, and at the fitting moment, could direct his cavalry in collected force against a hesitating and already shaken enemy. This was the distinctive gift of the famed Condé, and of that born master of tactics, Cromwell; it was conspicuously proved at Rocroy and Marston Moor; and it is a gift of the very highest order, if it does not exactly resemble the faculties which prepared Ramillies, Leuthen, and Austerlitz. For the rest, an army of this period, considered as a whole, was very different from an army of the nineteenth century; and this, too, affected the art of Tactics. In numbers, it was comparatively small; 30,000 men would be a very large army. It was deficient in unity and combined strength, for it was a mere array of battalions and squadrons; divisions and corps were as yet unknown, and a general-in-chief did not possess the supreme authority now entrusted to him. The discipline, too, and the organization of such an army was still far from good; the troops did not even wear a uniform, and were more akin to a feudal militia than to regular and trained soldiers; the muster rolls were always incomplete, owing to the Falstaffian tricks of officers, as yet subject to little control, and mutiny and insubordination were too common. Such an army, from the nature of the case, would be a weak and uncertain instrument of war; and this alone made the tactics of the day less decisive, as a general rule, in results, than those of later great masters of war.

The art of war at this time, in short, has been happily compared

2

to a bird, which eagerly spreads its wings for a flight, but is held, checked by restraints, to the ground. I pass on to the great captain whose life and career I attempt to illustrate. Turenne was born in 1611, a scion of the princely *noblesse* of France, his father being Sovereign Lord of Sedan, his mother a daughter of William the Silent, who largely transmitted the high qualities of the House of Nassau to her renowned offspring. As has happened with other famous warriors—with Luxemburg, William III., and Wellington— the future master of war was a sickly child ; but from the earliest age he showed strength of character. He was educated with remarkable care ; and though, unlike Condé, he was not a preco- cious genius—he remained heavy and dull in exterior through life— still, even in those years, the assiduous care with which he studied the campaigns of Cæsar, and followed Alexander in his march to the Indus, revealed the natural tendencies of the coming strategist. Turenne entered the service of the Seven Provinces as a private soldier at the age of fourteen ; and under the care of his maternal uncle, Maurice of Nassau, and his successor Henry, he took part in the long wars of sieges which marked the conflict with Spain in the Low Countries. He fought his way steadily up from the ranks ; he seems to have owed little to birth or to favour ; but, though he gained distinction at the siege of Bois-le-Duc, this was not the natural bent of his genius, and the value to him of these essays in arms was probably to teach him the important truth, which he illustrated in many striking instances, that " in war you should march and not besiege," that you should rather out- manœuvre and defeat your enemy than waste months in attacking fortresses which fall of themselves after success in the field.

In 1630, when twenty years old, Turenne obtained a regiment from Louis XIII. He addressed himself with untiring diligence to the discipline and the training of his men ; and, like Wellington—in matters like this he had much in common with our great country- man—he was soon known as a capable officer, and could justify his boast that his " corps was equal to the best troops of the King's household." The young colonel, however, made no way at Court ; its frivolity and luxury were distasteful to a mind singularly

modest and sedate; its licentious recklessness shocked a nature
formed by the rigid tenets of Calvin; and while Condé was already
a star at the Louvre, Turenne, taciturn and awkward, was scarcely
noticed. The future great chief of the armies of France served for
many years in a subordinate rank; he passed, in fact, through all
inferior grades, though his merits were recognized by good judges;
but if this term of probation was unduly long, its experience, he
has said, was most precious, for it "fully taught him a soldier's
calling." Long before the close of the Thirty Years' War,
Turenne was known as an able man, though his great powers had
not yet been developed. He was singled out for honours at the
great siege of Breisach; he showed remarkable skill and firmness
in covering a disastrous retreat from the Sarre; and he had won
the praise of La Valette and Saxe Weimar for his singular
steadiness and coolness in the field, and for the paternal care he
took of his troops, a quality in which his comrades of the *noblesse*,
brave, but unreflecting, were as a rule wanting. The chief point,
however, of permanent interest in this early part of the career of
Turenne is the evidence it affords of the dawn of those powers for
which he was to be proudly eminent. He occasionally had an
independent command, and in this position he never failed to
display the gifts of a true strategist. In 1636 he made a forced
march, by which he surprised and routed Gallas. He captured
Maubeuge, combining his movements with those of his chief with
remarkable skill. At the siege of Turin, in 1640, he out-manœuvred
and baffled his enemy, and kept away the relieving army; in 1643
he made a feint against Alessandria, which deceived his adversary,
and enabled him to seize the fortress of Trino.

In 1643, as the Thirty Years' War was nearing its end, Turenne
received the staff of a Marshal of France. His achievements
during the next two years will repay a careful reader's attention;
but I can only glance at them in this sketch, for they scarcely
reveal his peculiar genius. He took part, under the Grand Condé,
in the desperate combats around Fribourg, marked by the daring
and vigour of his chief, but, in Napoleon's judgment, worse than
useless; we see proof of his strategic powers in his operations

2 *

between divided enemies in the Palatinate at the close of 1644;
and I cannot doubt but that the fine march of Condé down the
Rhine, after the fall of Philippsbourg, which made the French
masters of Landau, Mayence, and other cities on the German
bank, was due to the inspiration of Turenne. In 1645, having
advanced to the Tauber, and overrun the Franconian lowlands, the
marshal was surprised and routed by Mercy—a Lorraine chief,
little known to fame, but a great captain of the Thirty Years' War;
and we can gather from this and other instances that the genius
of Turenne, rather profound than quick, made him less admirable
in the sphere of tactics than he was in the higher parts of war.
He was soon again under the command of Condé, and he led the
left wing of the French army in the terrible struggle around
Nördlingen; but though he contributed to the success of the day,
the glory of the victory, doubtful as it was, belongs wholly to his
renowned chief, whose tenacity, boldness, and insight on the field,
plucked safety and even a triumph from danger. The campaign
of 1646 distinctly brought out for the first time the special
gifts of Turenne in full relief, and to this day is a strategic
master-piece. The Marshal was on the French bank of the
Rhine, near Mayence, as the year opened, and Mazarin had
directed him to remain in his camps trusting to a pledge that the
Duke of Bavaria would not send aid to the Imperial forces. The
Duke, however, broke faith and marched against the Swedes,
hoping to defeat them as they moved into Westphalia, and to join
hands with the Archduke Leopold, advancing in force from
Western Austria; and had success attended this operation France
would have probably lost her best ally. Turenne made up his
mind at once; without waiting for a word from his Government,
he broke up from Mayence, moved down the Rhine in a march of
astonishing speed for those days, and, having crossed the river as
far north as Wesel, he effected his junction with the Swedish
chief, Wrangel, on the Lahn, having forestalled his enemy by a
movement of singular skill and daring.

Turenne and Wrangel were now at the head of an army of more
than 20,000 men; the hostile force, about equally strong, fell back

THEATRE OF WAR
IN
GERMANY

English Miles

Landau

Wetzlar
Limburg
Friedberg
Frankfurt
lich
Baccarach
Mayence
Main
Aschaff
Kreutznach
Darmstadt
Oppenheim
Meisenheim
Worms
Marienthal
Kaiserslantern
Heidelberg
Mannheim
Neustadt
Spire
Germersheim
Neckar
bruck
Landau
Philippsberg
Bitche
Weissenburg
Haguenau
Saverne
Neuenburg

to Friedberg, north of the Main ; and the Archduke, clinging to his communications, began to retreat to the Danube by an exterior line, through Schweinfurth and Nuremberg, towards the Bavarian plains. Turenne seized the occasion with the eye of genius ; holding the chord of the arc, he advanced through Franconia by forced marches, and attained Dönauworth, and while his adversary was toiling on his eccentric movement, he crossed the Danube, pushed on to the Lech, and boldly assailed the great place of Augsburg.* He failed in this siege, having been persuaded by his Swedish colleague to attack Rain, a little fortress of no importance; but his subsequent operations were marked by genius and constancy of the highest order. The Archduke, after weeks of delay, had crossed the Danube and approached the Allies, and he took a strong position from Landsberg to Memmingen, in order at once to cover Bavaria and to threaten the communications of his audacious foes, who had advanced into the heart of Germany, far from the Danube and even from the Rhine. It was now November, and an ordinary chief would have fallen back to seek winter quarters, foregoing the gains of the whole campaign ; but Turenne resolved to take the bolder course, and, against the advice of all his lieutenants, he made a feint on Memmingen, and then, moving rapidly, seized the communications of the Archduke at Landsberg and forced him, baffled behind the Inn. This splendid campaign—a game of manœuvres in which decisive success was gained without the risk of a single battle, which shows the highest parts of a master of war, and in which Napoleon, a draconic critic, can detect only a small mistake, the weakening the attack on Augsburg to besiege Rain—detached Bavaria finally from the Imperial cause, and, in truth, all but closed the Thirty Years' War.

The campaign of 1647, in which Turenne overcame a dangerous mutiny of the German auxiliaries in the French army, is one of the many instances of the strength of his character. That of 1648, the last of the Thirty Years' War, is a repetition of that of 1646, but scarcely gives proof of equal genius ; it is chiefly re-

* Compare this with the movement, described on p. 8, which was made by Gustavus Adolphus in pursuit of Tilly.

markable as the first occasion in which Montecuculi, a worthy antagonist, and a friend of Turenne in after years, exhibited his capacity in the field. I pass rapidly over the next three years—an unhappy passage in the career of Turenne—for they saw the most illustrious captain of France in arms against the State and the National Government. Strong affection for a despoiled brother, and the artful wiles of a beautiful siren—this was a weak point in the warrior's nature—caused Turenne to join the rebels of the Fronde; but though excuses may be made for him, history has justly condemned his conduct, and, like Marlborough but much less worthy of blame, Turenne is an instance how revolution can pervert even the noblest faculties. Turenne showed his strategic gifts in the contest; he proposed to advance to Paris and to dictate peace, but he was overruled by his Spanish colleagues, and he was soon afterwards beaten by Du Plessis Praslin, in a pitched battle not far from Réthel, a point of capital importance in the wars of that age. Turenne's tactics, Napoleon remarks on this occasion, were faulty and slow—this, in truth, was his least perfect part; but Turenne, and even Condé, never displayed that pre-eminence in war when opposed to France which they exhibited when in command of Frenchmen.

Turenne made his peace with Mazarin in 1652. Though naturally distrusted by a Court he had betrayed, he soon made his extraordinary powers felt, and in a few months he obtained the supreme direction of military affairs in the war of the Second Fronde. Civil war is never an attractive subject, but in this contest Turenne was opposed to the Great Condé and the forces of Spain, and events have great and peculiar interest. Turenne's splendid faculties strategic insight, skill in large manœuvres, judgment and constancy were never perhaps more grandly seen. He proved himself far superior to his brilliant rival, though it is but fair to say that the genius of Condé was repeatedly baffled by Spanish obstinacy, and Turenne was justly hailed as the Saviour of France and of the House of Bourbon when in the extreme of danger. He out-manœuvred Condé at Blêneau, near the Loire, in a passage-of-arms singled out by Napoleon, as a marvellous instance of military skill; and he would probably have brought the war to an end had Mazarin followed his sagacious counsels to march straight on Paris in 1652. When he was compelled to obey the too cautious minister, and to undertake the siege of Etampes—a timid half measure of no avail—he raised the siege at a moment's notice, with the decision that belongs to great captains only, at the intelligence of the approach of Charles of Lorraine; and the stand he made against the Duke's army, which prevented its junction with that of Condé, very probably saved the royal cause. Turenne distinguished himself in the murderous fight of St. Antoine, under the walls of Paris, and in the subsequent game of manœuvres with Condé; and his commanding genius was again seen when a double Spanish and Lorraine army marched towards the capital to assist Condé, and threatened the Government with utter ruin. The Regent and Mazarin, in the extreme of peril, wished to abandon Paris, and to fly to Lyons; but Turenne saw that this precipitate retreat would prove fatal to the Bourbon cause. He insisted on keeping his army on the spot, and, standing in the path of his divided enemies, he baffled the Spaniards on the line of the Somme, held the Duke of Lorraine successfully at bay, and prevented either foe from joining hands with Condé. The results of this generalship, not unworthy of the unrivalled captain of 1814, were magical and completely decisive. Condé and his troops were forced to leave Paris; the foreign invaders fell back to the frontier; the young King and the Court entered the capital, to the joy of the citizens; the Government was replaced in its seat, and Turenne read in the nation's eyes how he had closed the civil war and restored the throne. In this remarkable contest he had given proof, from first to last, of the highest faculties; but those, perhaps, which most deserve notice are his insight in perceiving that Paris was the centre on which to direct all efforts; his firmness in compelling the Court to cling to the capital at any risk, and his astonishing skill in repelling the enemies converging against him in greatly superior force.

Though Mazarin had been replaced in power, Spain, in 1653, was still able to send a larger force into the field than France. Turenne conducted a Fabian campaign on the Oise, baffling the

Archduke—his foe in 1646—and taking care to avoid Condé; and he exhibited once more what Napoleon has called " the divine side of the art of war," in making a stand in a strong position, where Condé had all but brought him to bay, and imposing upon the cowed Spanish chiefs.   In 1654 the reviving strength of France began to prevail over Spain in decline.   Turenne appeared at the head of a large army, and he successfully raised the seige of Arras, the capital of Burgundian Artois, in a night attack of remarkable daring, in which he surprised the Austrian chief and kept skilfully away from Condé's lines.   This was one of his greatest exploits in the field, and France acquired a marked ascendency over her enemies along her northern frontier.   I can only refer to the next three campaigns, in which the strategic gifts of Turenne and his admirable firmness were again made manifest.   True to his maxim, then a revelation in war—"always march rather than make sieges "—he gradually advanced to the Scheldt and the Lys, turning their fortresses by operations in the field, and sitting down before them as seldom as possible; and in less than three years he had overcome barriers* which hitherto had been deemed invincible, and which had been theatres of war for centuries without great or decisive 'results, a feat of generalship which astounded Europe. The genius of Condé more than once shone out in his efforts to avert Fate.   He destroyed a part of Turenne's army, in the hands of an incapable colleague, at Valenciennes, in 1656; and he brilliantly raised the siege of Cambray, an exploit marked out for praise by Napoleon.

The arms of France, however, directed by Turenne, made steady progress despite these checks, and the fine campaign of 1658 brought the contest with Spain to a glorious close.   By this time Turenne had secured his position in Spanish Flanders, and was formidably strong.   The England of Cromwell was in a league with France, and the allies resolved to attack Dunkirk, the strongest place on the seaboard of Flanders, and long a seat of piracy against British commerce.   The fortress was difficult in the extreme to master, not so

* French armies had before this taken many of these fortresses, but they had been retaken on the first turn of fortune.

much owing to its works and defences as to the obstacles formed
by the sea, the marshes, the woods, and the canals which girdled
it round; and it was protected by a large Spanish force in
observation not far from Yprés. Turenne crossed the inunda-
tion let loose by the garrison, threw lines of investment round
the fortress, and blocked up the approaches along the coast.
An English fleet closed the port from the sea, and 5,000 of the
renowned Ironsides were disembarked to support the French.
These operations, rapid in the extreme for the age, surprised
and disconcerted the Spanish chiefs, and they hastily advanced to
relieve Dunkirk with an army inferior in force to the enemy, and
not possessing a single gun. Turenne broke up from his lines
to attack; his left, the English contingent, rested on the sea,
covered by the batteries of the English squadron; his centre and
right formed a semi-circle, extending to the great canal of Furnes;
and as his troops advanced, Condé, it is said, exclaimed to the
young Duke of Gloucester that "all was lost." The battle was
almost at once decided; Condé, on the Spanish left, did indeed
wonders; but the Ironsides, backed by the fire of the fleet—they
were praised by Turenne in the highest terms--annihilated the
Spanish right in one charge, and the whole Spanish army, deprived
of artillery, lost heart and became a mere mass of fugitives. The
place fell, and was handed over to England. Turenne, breaking
up from his camps, took Bergues and Gravelines, and overran the
country, and he only stopped his victorious march at Oudenarde,
Spanish Flanders lying as it were at his feet. Napoleon, however, contends that the marshal ought to have done more, and
pushed on to Brussels, success which would have brought the war
to an end; and this may be an instance, perhaps, in which
Turenne's powerful, but somewhat slow intellect erred on the side
of too prudent caution. Yet we must bear in mind that the
strategy of the seventeenth could not be that of the nineteenth
century. Turenne certainly contemplated this very step, but declared that it was not practicable; and, as it was, the campaign
was a splendid triumph which soon brought about the Peace of
the Pyrenees.

During the next twelve years France enjoyed repose, broken only by a brief contest with Spain, caused by the claims of Louis XIV. on the Low Countries in right of his consort. Turenne commanded the royal army, captured Lille, and overran Flanders; but it is unnecessary to dwell on these easy triumphs. The marshal was now the first subject of France and admittedly the first soldier of Europe; and he played a part of no small importance in the able French diplomacy of the time. He gave much attention also to civil affairs, was a disciple of the renowned Colbert, drew up reports on the condition of France which showed real insight and marked sagacity, and proved that he possessed administrative powers of the highest order in provincial government. Like nearly all the highest *noblesse* of France, he renounced the Calvinist creed of his fathers—the will of the King was supreme in this—but, like the illustrious Villars at a later day he condemned the wrongs already done to the Huguenots, and ventured to utter a weighty protest. His great work, however, at this period, was the reorganization of the military power of France; and though Louvois had a large share in this, Turenne is perhaps entitled to the chief merit. His reforms were thorough and yet practical; he did not change everything, and break with the past; but he so improved what he found existing as to bring it to a high state of excellence, and the French army, in his constructive hands, became a mighty instrument of war.

Turenne's method was to leave the army still largely in the hands of the *noblesse*, and to allow it to retain a half feudal character; but he not the less made it the force of the Crown, the disciplined array of an all-powerful monarchy; and he so transformed its institutions and spirit, and increased its strength, as to make it by far the most formidable organization for war in Europe. The *noblesse* were allowed to retain their charges, and to raise their levies as in former days; but they were subjected to the strictest inspection; incapable officers were summarily dismissed, and " men in buckram " and false returns were no longer permitted to exist. While the feudal militia still remained, every inducement was offered to encourage the men to enter the ranks of the regular troops; the temporary disbanding of regiments ceased;

and select corps—need we name the Maison du Roi, the brilliant victors on many a field ?—were carefully formed, and inspired the army as a whole with their gallant and martial spirit. These were great reforms if they stood alone, but the process of improvement went much further. The hierarchy of the service had its rules changed ; the general-in-chief was made supreme in everything; the three arms and their chiefs were placed under his immediate control in all respects, and discipline and subordination to one head were thus secured for the first time. Unity of command caused unity in lower spheres ; the comparatively loose formations, indeed, of battalions and squadrons were not changed, but every regiment was clad in uniform ; and care was taken that all weapons should be constructed and fashioned on the same patterns. Strenuous efforts, again, which reveal the strategist, were made to accelerate movements in war ; the arrays of trains and carriages were greatly increased ; the system of magazines, of depôts of food, and of field hospitals was immensely improved, and the mechanism of the army attained a degree of perfection never witnessed before. Yet the greatest change of all remains to be noticed—a change, Napoleon remarks, which made this period a new era in war. A master of his art, Turenne had perceived that infantry, hitherto kept in the background, was naturally the most important of the arms ; it could accomplish more in his wars of marches, even in that age, than the more prized cavalry ; and Turenne trebled its force in the French service, reducing horse to much less significance, though cavalry still, no doubt, retained its superiority in the shock of battle. As for artillery, Turenne went with the age ; the proportion of guns, though comparatively small as regards the other arms for modern times, was gradually but distinctly increased.

Through these immense reforms, the army of France became, for many years, the terror of Europe ; and, except that the changes wrought in formations by the discovery of the bayonet were as yet unknown, it had acquired a really modern aspect. An opportunity arose, in 1672, to prove this tremendous instrument of war. Louis XIV. invaded the Dutch Republic; the French army and

that of his allies exceeded 130,000 men, a force never seen since
the fall of Rome; and while Turenne and Condé, now restored to
France, advanced along the Sambre and crossed the Meuse, the
allied contingent under Luxemburg moved down the Rhine by
Mayence and Cologne. True to his strategic genius, Turenne
insisted, against the advice even of the audacious Condé, on
"masking" Maastricht and pressing forward; the operations of
the invading host were marked by a celerity hitherto unknown,
and in less than two months the hostile armies had crossed the
Rhine near the Waal, had attained the Yssel and had moved into
the heart of the Seven Provinces. When the victorious French
had approached Amsterdam, Condé, always great on a field of
manœuvre, entreated the King to seize the dykes, which formed
the last defence of the capital of the States; and, had this been
done, the fortunes of Europe might have taken a wholly different
turn. The golden occasion was, however, lost; time and men
were wasted in taking fortresses; and William of Orange, a sickly
youth, then for the first time seen on the stage of history, saved
the Commonwealth by cutting the dykes and letting loose floods
which made Amsterdam an island in the midst of a submerged
country, and effectually baffled the French commanders.

This bad generalship was due to Louvois, and, it is said, was
inspired by the King, never capable in operations in the field; but
Turenne must, at least, have assented, and Napoleon severely condemns the Marshal for giving his sanction to unwise counsels
which he scarcely could have approved in his heart. This possibly
may be another instance in which Turenne was somewhat slow and
too cautious; but probably he shrank from opposing the will of a
sovereign, then almost an idol, and a minister already hostile to
him; and it is scarcely to be supposed that a chief of his powers,
in full possession of the state of affairs, would have committed a
palpable strategic error. Be this as it may, he soon had an occasion to exhibit once more his great capacity. The invasion of the
States, and the success of Louis, had alarmed Europe and aroused
Germany; Austria and Prussia joined hands for the first time in
war; and two German armies of superior strength were marched

THEATRE OF WAR
IN
THE LOW COUNTRIES

English Miles
0   10   20   30   40   50

NORTH

SEA

Friesland

Groningen

ZUIDER ZEE

Amsterdam
Muiden
The Hague
Rhine
Utrecht
Lek
Maas
Bommel
Breda
Bois le Duc
Bergen op Zoom
Antwerp

Rijssen
Deventer
Zutphen
Arghem
Nimeguen
Wesel

Venlo
Rhine

Ostende
Neuport
Bruges
Dunkirk
Dixmunde
Cassel
Ypres
Lille
Tournai
Lens
Donai
Valenciennes
Arras
Bouchain
Cambrai
Guise

Scheldt
Lys
Courtray
Oudenarde
Brussels
Ath
Mons
St Ghislain
Binche
Maubeuge
Sambre
Le Quesnoy
Landrecies
Avesnes
Rocroi
La Capelle

Maeseyck
Maastricht
Vise
Aix la Chapelle
Liege

Charleroi
Namur
Huy
Dinant
Philippeville
Sedan
Mouzon
Rethel
Stenay
Meuse

Wittlich

Luxemburg
Treves

towards the Rhine and threatened Alsace. Louis abandoned
Holland and his rapid conquests ; Condé was despatched to defend
the Rhine, and Turenne was placed at the head of an army
intended to confront the Germans on the Main. The Marshal
had soon seen through the projects of his foes ; he judged rightly
that their real purpose was to unite on the Meuse with William of
Orange, not to venture alone to enter Alsace, and he took his
course with characteristic skill. Moving into the region around
Trèves, he established himself in the valley of the Moselle, and when
the Germans, as he expected, sought to cross the Palatinate from
Mayence, he successfully kept them for weeks at bay, held back
the army of the States on the Meuse, and completely frustrated
the intended junction. This fine strategy probably saved France
from an invasion upon her weakest frontier.

Louvois had now openly broken with Turenne ; the King, irritated
at the reverse in Holland, took part with the imperious minister,
underrating the Marshal's last achievement, and Turenne found
little favour at court. It was impossible, however, to question his
genius ; he directed the general plan of the campaign of 1673,
and he held supreme command on the German frontier. As the
Austrians and Prussians fell back from the Moselle, they began to
diverge towards the Elbe and the Danube ; Turenne saw his
advantage, and crossed the Rhine, and venturing on a winter
campaign, despite the remonstrances even of the King, he advanced to the Weser, defeated the Prussians, and drove the
Austrians far beyond the Main. Prussia abandoned the Coalition
for a time, but the Emperor refused to give up the contest, and
Turenne, for the first and last time, was outgeneralled on the
theatre of war by an antagonist not unworthy of him. Montecuculi, at the head of an Imperial army, had advanced into the
Franconian lowlands, eluding Turenne, who was on the Tauber ;
he gained over one of the prince bishops, made a forced march
and got over the Main, and then having made a feint on Alsace,
he embarked with his troops upon the Rhine, effected his junction
with William of Orange at Bonn, and quickly reduced that important fortress. This, Napoleon has said, is " the darkest

cloud on the reputation of this great captain;" but the glory
of Turenne was not long in eclipse; and he surpassed himself
in the campaign of 1674, the most striking instance, perhaps,
of his powers. The success of Montecuculi had again roused
Germany; Prussia and the Lesser States took part with the
Emperor, and France was threatened with a more formidable
League than she had ever encountered before. Turenne directed
operations once more; with admirable wisdom he neglected the
North, and urged the King to invade Franche Comté, an enterprise
crowned with complete success; and he took again his station on
the Rhine, watching the masses of foes collected against him.

Every movement he made in the contest that followed is a masterpiece of a great strategist. Turenne, crossing the Rhine, advanced
to the Neckar, threw himself between the armies converging against
him; and, having routed the Austrians near Sinsheim, turned
boldly against the Northern Germans, marching from the Elbe
and the plains of Brandenburg. To gain time and to check their
progress, he ravaged the Palatinate with unflinching sternness; and
though history condemns the act, and Turenne only once adopted
this course, it was justified by the laws of war of the age—nay, by
those of a much later period. The Germans had reached Mayence
by the end of August, and before long had entered Alsace; the
Imperial army was close at hand, and it was the purpose of the
Imperial chiefs to invade France with the combined forces, when
the Prussian contingent had come into line. Turenne saw the
danger, and did not hesitate; with an energy worthy of the youthful Bonaparte, he fell on his foes before their junction, and he
defeated them in a fierce fight at Entzheim, a day memorable if
it were for this only—that Marlborough served on the marshal's
staff, and received the thanks of his chief for his conduct. This
reverse, however, only checked the enemy; the Great Elector
brought up his army. Turenne was obliged to fall back to the
Vosges, and a huge wave of Teutonic conquest seemed about to
overflow the plains of Champagne. Had the Germans pushed on
they might have reached Paris, where confusion and terror already
reigned; but they paused at the decisive moment. They seem to

have dreaded the strokes of Turenne, who had skilfully taken a position on their flank, and they methodically settled in winter quarters in Alsace, having let a grand opportunity pass. The subsequent operations of their great adversary, in conception at least, were of the highest order. Deceiving his enemy and scorning the hardships of winter among the Alsatian hills, Turenne feigned to retreat into Lorraine; he then counter-marched with remarkable quickness, defiled behind the Vosges with a devoted army which appreciated the admirable skill of its chief, and, having screened the movement by the mountain barrier, broke in through the gap of Belfort on the astounded Germans, and surprised them completely divided and scattered. The effects of this masterly stroke were immense; the Great Elector was routed at Turckheim, Turenne pressed forward and threatened Strasbourg, and the horde of invaders, baffled and humbled, were only too glad to get across the Rhine.

The movement behind the Vosges of Turenne which surprised the Germans and caused their defeat has a certain resemblance, it will be perceived, to the march of Napoleon, screened by the Alps, which after Marengo gave him Italy. Turenne, however, the reader will note, fell on his enemy, when he had reached him, in front, and his triumph though great was not overwhelming; Napoleon descended on the rear of Mélas, and, though he ran many risks, he completely conquered. Turenne, the Emperor insists, would have achieved more had he crossed the Vosges in the middle of the chain, and struck the flank and rear of the Germans; in that event, the invaders, perhaps, would have never been able to attain the Rhine. This criticism is, in theory, perfect; but though Napoleon, in the place of Turenne, would probably have played the more daring game, the Vosges in those days were most difficult to pass; the operation would have been very hazardous, and the two movements, in fact, illustrate the difference between the natures of the two men.

I have reached the last campaign of Turenne, a long game of manœuvre between two great strategists, in which the marshal perished on the very edge of victory. The League

against France, though shattered, still held together; and faulty
generalship having been the cause of the signal discomfiture of
1674, Montecuculi was sent, in 1675, to cope with Turenne,
still upon the Rhine.   The Imperial commander, having
threatened Philipsburg, crossed the river near Spires and
invaded Alsace; but Turenne, instead of attacking his foe,
crossed the river near Strasbourg, and, reaching Wilstedt, struck
at the communications of the hostile army; and this forced
his adversary to recross the Rhine.   Turenne, having gained this
strategic advantage, and carried the war into German territory,
took a position between Strasbourg and Ottenheim, the place where
he had bridged the Rhine; but Ottenheim is at some distance from
Strasbourg, and the French army was very much divided.   Montecuculi approached the Marshal's camps, and missed a grand
opportunity to strike, which, Napoleon remarks, Condé would have
seized; Turenne, perceiving the danger, raised his bridge, placed it
near Strasbourg, and drew in his forces; and Montecuculi, again
baffled, descended the Rhine and occupied Freistett, his object
being to cross the Rhine at that point by means of a bridge, to
be sent down from Strasbourg—then, it will be borne in mind, an
Imperial city—and his ultimate end being to re-enter Alsace.
Turenne, however, barred the course of the Rhine, by redoubts
and batteries carefully placed; and having thus prevented the
passage of the bridge, he, for the third time, out-manœuvred his
enemy and kept him bound with his army to Germany.   The
antagonists now held their camps for some months, each watching
the other, and seeking a chance; but Turenne was the first to
move.   He crossed the Rench by an undefended ford; and this
movement compelled his enemy to retreat, for it threatened his
communications, and almost reached his flank.   Montecuculi,
utterly foiled and out-generalled, abandoned at once the valley of
the Rhine, and made for the defiles of Würtemberg.   Turenne,
hanging on his foe, pursued; and, by the close of July, he had
attained the Sassbach, assured that he would triumph in a great
and decisive battle.   Fate, however, withheld from Turenne a
victory justly earned by his most able strategy.   He was struck

down by a shot from a hostile battery, and Montecuculi escaped from the toils which had been admirably laid around him. The Imperial chief, indeed—a remarkable man, and in this campaign he was suffering from disease—when apprised of the death of his renowned adversary, at once boldly resumed the offensive. The French army, deprived of the genius which had led it to victory for many years, was soon in full retreat on the Rhine ; and having fallen into the hands of incapable chiefs, it was nearly involved in a crushing disaster. The history of war has few more striking instances of what a commander is to his troops than the reverses which, after the fall of Turenne, followed the course of his steady success before it ; and the passionate cry of his defeated soldiery, to the worthless men who stood in his place, " Give us Magpie "— the warrior's charger—" to lead us ! " is only an exaggeration of a substantial truth. Montecuculi's eulogy on Turenne is well-known; but the offensive return which he made with confidence and victoriously after his great rival's death is a more expressive and a finer epitaph.

Sorrowing Ilium mourned her mighty shade ; the remains of Turenne were borne to St. Denis, and laid in the tombs of the Kings of France, an honour never again conferred on a subject. They were spared even by the Jacobin hands which violated the royal abodes of death in the madness of Paris in 1793; and they now fitly rest beside those of Napoleon. A word on the place of this great man among the masters of the noblest of arts. The peculiar gifts of Turenne were a far-sighted and calm intelligence, sagacity of the finest kind, and admirable constancy and force of character, and these made him one of the first of generals, though he did not possess, in the highest degree, the dazzling imagination, the power of thought and of calculation, and the astonishing energy which distinguish Napoleon and, perhaps, Hannibal. These qualities made him a consummate strategist, few chiefs have ever moved on a theatre of war with the perfect skill and success of Turenne ; few have known how to make grand manœuvres with as certain results, and with equal brilliancy ; and his great wars of marches, replacing sieges, were an inspiration of most striking genius. As for special illustration of his strategic powers, Turenne has been surpassed by Napoleon alone in the art of reaching the communications of a foe, and of operating between separate hostile masses; and he was safer than Napoleon in these efforts, though he did not accomplish such marvels of war. Considering the state of the art in his time, no chief perhaps has ever achieved more than Turenne by scientific movements; he triumphed in several campaigns by mere marches without fighting a single battle, and yet his success was complete and decisive, as was specially seen in 1646 and 1675. In fact, strategy made little progress for many years after this great captain; and yet Turenne did not quite attain the highest rank among modern strategists, for his intellect was somewhat wanting in quickness, and his nature in what is called the sacred fire; he let grand opportunities slip, and in three great instances, at least, he did not do what probably might have been accomplished by him.

These defects—and genius is never perfect—made him a tactician of the second order only; he had not Condé's inspired thought on the field; and for a commander of extraordinary gifts, he suffered defeat in many instances. Yet the decision and firmness which were among his qualities stood him in good stead, even in the conduct of troops; no general has ever known better how to make a bold stand, and to impose on an enemy; and it was one of his special characteristics that he could overcome defeat, and that he was most formidable after a reverse of fortune. For the rest, Turenne, like most great captains, had administrative powers of the highest order; he, usually, even in his long marches, contrived to have his army in good condition; he remodelled the military organisation of France, and made it by far the best in Europe; and, as an administrator, he had this distinctive merit—that he was in advance of the ideas of his time. I must add a word on the relations between this illustrious chief and the armies he led. Turenne had a truly chivalrous nature; he was singularly considerate to his lieutenants, and though he could be stern and severe when needful, he made the largest allowance for mere errors, and never blamed others for shortcomings of his own. No general has ever had more devoted officers; and this magnanimous character was admired and recognized by every chief who was opposed to him, by Leopold, Montecuculi, and even the arrogant Condé. As for his troops, Turenne was most chary of their blood, resembling Wellington in this respect; and, like Wellington too— a regimental officer, versed in the details of professional work— Turenne knew their wants and gave much attention to them. As has always happened with real chiefs, Turenne fashioned his soldiers to his own nature; they were not rapid and vehement in in his hands as they were in those of Condé and Villars; but he made them steady, enduring, bold, but tenacious; and their phrase, "our father," shows how he was beloved by them. Except for one unhappy lapse, the career of Turenne does "honour to humanity," to quote the words of his ablest adversary and yet sympathetic friend.

CHAPTER II.

Marlborough.

A THOROUGH estimate of Marlborough would fill a volume, and I must confine myself to the military career of one described by a great historian as "a prodigy of turpitude," who "combined the genius of Richelieu with the genius of Turenne." John Churchill was born in 1650, the offspring of parents who ranked among the landed gentry of Devon and Dorset, and who, without apparent gifts of their own, transmitted supreme ability to two descendants. Little is known about the first years of the boy; but the attachment he felt through life for the Church of England was probably more due to his Cavalier birth than to the assiduous care of a clerical tutor; and, unlike the Great Condé, Turenne, and Villars, he was not trained to arms by constant practice and study. It is, perhaps, mere gossip that he owed his first commission to the shame of a sister, Arabella Churchill, the mother of Berwick by James II.; and we might pass over his amour with Barbara Palmer, if it did not bring out, at an early age, proof of the love of money, which was a master vice of his richly endowed but most complex nature. He first saw war in an admirable school, having been placed on the staff of Turenne; he served under that great commander in the memorable campaigns of 1672 and 1674; soon attracted the special notice of his chief as an officer of extraordinary promise, and was publicly thanked by him on the field of Entzheim for the cool intrepidity which was one of his distinctive qualities. It is impossible to doubt that this experience was of the greatest advantage to the future warrior; and though there is a difference in the genius of

MARLBOROUGH.

the men, we may, I think, trace the example of Turenne in more than one of the great feats of Marlborough. The young, but already distinguished, soldier in 1678 married Sarah Jennings, then a beauty of Grammont, but long afterwards to become the Atossa of Pope's vengeance, and the marriage, which led to a domestic history of a most strange and eventful kind, had a decisive effect on the fortunes alike of Churchill, of England, and even of Europe. The pair flourished at the little Court of the Duke of York, held in his provincial capital; and it is unnecessary to tell how the wife became Lady of the Bedchamber to the Princess Anne, and acquired an ascendency over the future Queen which was to be followed by the most momentous results. During these years, Churchill first gave proof of the diplomatic skill which, at a later time, was to make him the master of the Grand Alliance. He negotiated some of the underhand bargains of Charles II. with Louis XIV., designed to make England a vassal of France, and for this and other services he obtained the reward of a Scotch, then akin to an Irish, peerage.

At the accession of James II. to the throne, Lord Churchill was made again an agent to obtain a bribe from the great Bourbon Sovereign; but though he was raised to the English Peerage, and he really crushed the rising of Monmouth by his direction of the Royal troops at Sedgemoor, he was left rather in the shade during the trying time when the King was carrying out his fatal policy against the laws, the liberties, and the Church of England. I do not justify his desertion of James, when at the head of his men, at a critical moment, but his guilt was shared by the first men of the time; and if self-interest, perhaps, was his ruling motive, the strong sympathy he certainly felt for the Church in part, I belive, determined his conduct. He participated in the Revolution and its spoils, was made Earl of Marlborough, and was given a seat at the Council of Nine, which ruled England, under Mary, in the absence of William; and he again gave proof of his military gifts in a sharp combat in the Low Countries, in his admirable conduct of the war in Ireland, and in his always able and successful advice. He was already the foremost of English soldiers, and his genius and promise had been recognized by more than one of the King's veterans; but he was never really liked by William III., and the great captain who, had he been in command, would have changed the fortunes of Steenkirk and Landen, was usually kept at home in a subordinate place. Marlborough betrayed and abandoned William in turn. I shall not attempt to excuse the act; but soaring ambition, wounded to the quick, and the scorn of inferior men raised over his head, had probably more to do with his conduct than alarm at the prospect of the return of James, or a desire to place the Princess Anne on the throne; and in judging these things, we must never forget that many of his peers and colleagues were no less to blame, and that Revolution had destroyed loyalty, divided allegiance, and blighted good faith in the hearts of three-fourths of our leading statesmen. At this conjuncture, however, one act of Marlborough stands out marked as a foul deed of shame; he treacherously disclosed the descent on Brest, caused the death of an honoured companion-in-arms, and involved a large British force in destruction; and, corrupt and bad as the age was, had the crime and its author become known, the head of the criminal would, no doubt, have justly fallen on the block at Tower Hill. Marlborough, in fact, could not endure his late disgrace; he feared for his life, and made up his mind to come to terms at St. Germains, at any risk, and he sacrificed Talmash, without scruple, in order to weaken a detested Government, and to promote his own selfish ends.

The treason of Marlborough, in the affair of Brest, was unsuspected by the men of his time; but it is characteristic of a revolutionary age that William ere long turned to him again, though in merited disgrace for other offences. His ability, in fact, was necessary to the State, and politicians had few scruples; and the diplomatist who had shown skill and tact in the negotiations of the Stuarts with Louis XIV. was employed, and with marked success, by the King in cementing the Grand Alliance against the Bourbon Monarchy. On the death of William, Marlborough received the command of the English forces destined for the contest with France, and through the influence of Heinsius, the great Dutch

Minister, he was placed at the head of the armies of the States. His reputation, already eminent, entitled him to this high position; but almost from the first he gained an ascendency in the direction of the military affairs of England which no other British general has possessed. This, as is well known, was due to the complete control his wife exercised over the Queen; Mrs. Freeman governed Mrs. Morley, and practically nearly guided the State; and Marlborough enjoyed more real authority than belonged to William, in England at least, until near the end of the war of the Spanish Succession. On the other hand, the English commander was by this time in his fifty-second year; he had never conducted war on a great scale, though he had proved himself to be a most able soldier, and it seemed scarcely probable that he could cope, with success, with the trained and experienced generals of France, brought up amidst the traditions of Turenne and Condé. No one dreamed, when Marlborough assumed his command, that Blenheim and Ramillies were not distant; and though the Allies had some advantages which they did not possess in previous contests, France had hitherto confronted Europe with success; and, as Spain and Bavaria were now on her side, the chances seemed to be in the main in her favour.

I must glance at the state of the military art at the beginning of the war of the Spanish Succession. Since the invasion of Holland in 1672, war had assumed ample and even vast dimensions; very large armies had appeared in the field, and the contest which had closed at the Peace of Ryswick had extended from the Shannon to the far wilds of Hungary. The obstacles, to the march of troops, which had existed in the preceding age, had been, to a certain extent, lessened; roads and agriculture had slightly improved; and owing to the great development of the efficacy of the attack, due to the engineering genius of Vauban, the power of fortresses had much declined, and they could scarcely ever offer a prolonged resistance, or permanently shield an endangered frontier. Strategy ought, therefore, to have made distinct progress; but exactly the contrary had been the case. No genius had appeared to turn to account the advantages offered by the new conditions, and the art had retrograded; for while all that belongs to what is material in it conduced to its advance, the intelligence which it requires to give it grandeur, and to rule matter, had been largely wanting. The operations of war during the thirty years before Marlborough emerged on the scene had been comparatively timid and slow; vast as were the masses arrayed in the field, we see scarcely a single great combination, a remarkable march, or a decisive battle, except in the case of the Turkish hordes; campaigns were feebly directed and had few results; and though sieges took much less time than formerly, armies seldom ventured to pass fortresses, or to make daring attempts at invasion. The reason simply was, there were no consummate chiefs; William III., Câtinat, Louis of Baden, Luxemburg, each with special and real merits of his own, were all generals of the second order, and the "sublime part of the art," in Napoleon's language, had had no masters to bring out its splendours since the grave had closed on Turenne and Condé. One peculiarity of the strategy of the time deserves the attention of the careful student, and it exhibits a marked backward tendency. The generals of the first half of the seventeenth century had made considerable use of great defensive lines; but Turenne had nearly exploded this system, and his triumphs were mainly due to his masterly movements. During the period that followed, inferior men went back to the routine of the past; as fortresses became of less importance, huge barriers were raised to cover frontiers, and whole campaigns were spent in manœuvres to turn or to force these artificial obstacles. This indicates a decline in the art, though the value of these lines was often great, and* it has, perhaps, been underrated in our time.

While strategy had thus, for a moment, declined, a change had passed over the art of tactics. Armies had continued to grow in numbers, and infantry—its importance becoming recognized—was now the arm of greatest force on a field of battle. The bayonet, too, had been invented, and this invention, almost a revolution

* Napoleon never made use of lines of this kind, but nothing escaped him, and he had the example of Torres Vedras; at St. Helena he made admirable observations on this system of defence.

in itself, by degrees largely modified the old formations of the age of Gustavus, Turenne, and Condé. The masses of pikemen and musketeers arrayed in dense squares and close columns, were gradually replaced by extended lines of infantry, whose weapon combined the powers of the musket and pike; and though these lines were still deep and serried, foot, owing to the change, covered far more ground on a given field than had been the case formerly. The general result of these two circumstances was that, in almost all instances, the front of battles was enlarged to an immense extent; instead of occupying a few hundred yards, armies about to engage filled vast spaces, and as these could scarcely ever be open plains, and usually presented local features, such as woods, streams, hills, and folds of the ground, it became of increased importance to turn to account these peculiarities in any impending conflict. Skill in tactics, accordingly, began to consist less in seizing an opportunity to throw cavalry upon infantry exposed or broken than in so arranging the three arms, and employing them as to derive advantage from the special characteristics of the field; and the old order of battle, horse on either wing, foot in the centre, and guns in front, as a fixed system, became obsolete; and each arm began to be so disposed as to be made most effective, having regard to the actual situation and its accidents of place. This change, though slow, had become manifest; it had been conspicuously seen on the great day of Zenta, where the powers of Eugene were first displayed; and battles, though very different from what they are now, had assumed an essentially modern aspect, troops acting in concert, by no method of routine, but so as always best to support each other, and to make use of the ground with this object in view.

The tactics, however, of this age, in what may be called their subordinate parts, had little in common with those of a later period. Cavalry was still considered the most active arm, and far the most efficient in the shock of battle; the proportion of horsemen to foot was still much larger than it has become in the present century, and a general still mainly relied on cavalry for the decisive movements that assured victory. Though infantry, too, had greatly increased in numbers, and its power in action had been largely multiplied, it was still deemed rather an arm to support, to defend, and to cover the ground, than to strike; the old traditions still clung to it; its lines, four deep at least, were clumsy and heavy, and did not furnish sufficient fire; it often was formed in dense columns, and it had never yet decided a battle by its own special and unaided efforts. As for artillery, guns were still few, and the days of horse artillery had not come; and though the power of the arm had been much augmented, and its true uses had been partly ascertained, it was still in an undeveloped state. The tactics of the day, therefore, so far as regards the handling of the three arms, were still immature; and one of the methods of these, the blending together in single or in successive lines of horsemen and footmen, in an offensive movement, though often witnessed, is now obsolete. For the rest, armies were still loosely formed; they were still arrays of battalions and squadrons, and they were as yet without that complete unity which has made them more perfect instruments of war. As for discipline and equipment, little had been changed since the grand reforms of Louvois and Turenne; armies had become bodies of regular troops with officers, as a rule, of a noble class; and the system of magazines, of depôts of supplies, and of trains remained what it had been, strategic science having made no progress. The organization of the French army was still decidedly the best in Europe; but it had been imitated with more or less success by more than one of the Continental armies; and the difference in this respect was probably less than it had been thirty years previously. As for the British army, it already possessed fine regiments, of unsurpassed worth; but, as has always happened, it was badly organized, and its organization, such as it was, owed much to the care of William III.

I must pass rapidly over the two first campaigns, in which Marlborough held supreme command. The theatre of the war was the Low Countries as, indeed, was usually the case with him; and, as Spain was now in alliance with France, the French armies occupied the Belgian provinces from the mouths of the Scheldt to the Lower Meuse. Either from over-confidence, however, or perhaps, because the incapable Chamillart had become his minister, Louis XIV., at the beginning of the war, paid little attention to this frontier; and Marlborough was largely superior in force when the campaign of 1702 opened. The object of the British commander was to master the course of the Meuse, with a view to gain a base for more decisive efforts; though hampered already by the Dutch deputies, and the many impediments of a coalition, his march was a series of easy triumphs; Venloo, Liège, and other places fell, with Kaiserwerth on the Middle Rhine; and, if Boufflers made a gallant resistance, he was compelled to fall back to the Upper Meuse. Marlborough received a dukedom for these services. The recompense now appears extravagant, and was, doubtless, largely due to the favour of the Queen; but we must recollect that the arms of France had scarcely ever been checked before, and for half a century had been deemed invincible.

The operations of the campaign of 1703 first distinctly brought out the powers of Marlborough in designing great combinations of war, and should be studied by those who deny that he possessed the gift of strategic genius. The French had been forced back to the Upper Meuse, but they still held most of the Belgian strongholds, and they occupied a vast system of defensive lines, formed by the rivers and forests of an intricate country, and extending from the Mehaigne, not far from Namur, to the verge of Antwerp, and thence to Ostend. Marlborough aiming, as he always did, at a vital point, and seeking to carry the war to the frontier of France, but knowing the difficulties of a direct attack, resolved to turn and pass this great obstacle, and thence to advance to the French seaboard; and the measures he took to accomplish his "great design," as he called it, in perfectly true language, were in the highest degree admirable. The French, largely reinforced, held the lines and the fortresses with probably*

---

* Every real student of the wars of the seventeenth and eighteenth centuries knows the difficulty of forming anything like a just estimate of the numbers of the armies in conflict. This is mainly due to the systematic practice of enumeration by battalions and squadrons, bodies always in a state of change; and besides, national pride and interest have obscured the truth. I have taken some pains to collate the authorities, and to arrive at an estimate approximately correct.

130,000 men; the strength of the allies was not 100,000, but Marlborough possessed the immense advantage, ever to be borne in mind by an English chief, of the mastery of the movable base of the sea, and he clearly saw how to turn this to account. His plan, simple alike and excellent, was to hold Boufflers, now supported by Villeroy, in check himself with the bulk of his forces; in the meantime the lines were to be assailed by Cohorn and Opdam with the Dutch army, and this attack was to be combined with a descent on the coast, to be made to the south by an English fleet, in order to harass and perplex the enemy. This grand project which, in its conception, reveals the genius of a great captain, and which ought to have sent the allied armies past the French lines to the Upper Lys, was frustrated by the errors of the Dutch commanders, and by the jealousies and intrigues too common in a league. Cohorn neglected his mission to ravage a province; Opdam made a false and premature movement, and before Marlborough had his grasp on his enemy, Boufflers, leaving Villeroy in Marlborough's front, and making a forced march with conspicuous skill, anticipated Opdam as he approached Antwerp, and defeated him with heavy loss at Eckeren. The "great design" had thus been revealed and baffled; but Marlborough believed it could yet be accomplished, and moving on Antwerp with the mass of his army, he proposed to force the French to fight a great battle, hoping, if successful, to get across their lines. Timid and divided counsels, however, prevailed; the Dutch commanders refused to second their colleague, and Marlborough, bitterly vexed, returned to the Meuse. The capture of the small place of Huy was the only fruit of the campaign of 1703, and Marlborough was so indignant at the conduct of the Dutch that he was on the point of throwing up his command.

Happily for the Grand Alliance, ambition and interest diverted Marlborough from this hasty purpose; and the memorable campaign of 1704 was to be the most renowned of his triumphs. Bavaria had joined France in 1703; a real chief, the illustrious Villars, had overcome Louis of Baden on the Rhine, had marched into the Swabian lowlands, and had defeated a German

THEATRE OF THE

CAMPAIGN

of 1704.

Scale of Miles

force on the Danube; and had the Elector of Bavaria followed his counsels, and his colleagues in Italy given him aid, he would have anticipated the campaign of 1805, and have ended the war by a march on Vienna. Villars, however, was disliked at Munich and Versailles, and, unlike Marlborough, had an unhappy temper; he was recalled for a squabble with the Elector; and his place was filled by the incompetent Marsin, who could not even comprehend his strategy. Yet the situation of the Empire remained most critical; a combined French and Bavarian army threatened the capital from the Iller and the Inn; the insurrection of Hungary raged in the East; and Austria might be overrun and even subdued if the grand project of Villars were ably carried out. Eugene, the first of the Imperialist chiefs, perceived the danger and sought to avert it; he addressed himself, not in vain, to Marlborough; and a plan of operations was agreed between them, which, it was hoped, would detach Bavaria from France, and at least prevent an advance on Vienna.

The situation of the belligerent armies on the theatre of war shows that it was difficult in the extreme to give effect to any combination of the kind. Marlborough commanded the principal force of the allies; but he was on the Meuse far away from the Danube, and was held in check, as it appeared, by Villeroy, with an army that ought to have sufficed for the purpose; Tallard, at the head of a powerful army, was on the Rhine, confronting a much weaker enemy—the contingent, in fact, defeated by Villars—drawn within the well-known lines of Stolhoffen, formed to prevent an attack from Alsace; and the Elector and Marsin were in Swabia, greatly superior in force to Louis of Baden, who held the approaches from the Black Forest. For Marlborough to attain the heart of the Empire, through these masses of surrounding enemies, seemed to be almost an impossible task; but he encountered the risk, and adopted a project which, I am convinced, was a thought of Eugene's, for it bears the mark of his peculiar genius, in which grandeur was combined with rashness. Breaking up from the Lower Meuse, on the 19th of May, at the head of, perhaps, 70,000 men, increased as he advanced, by German contingents, he crossed the Rhine and made for Mayence ; he then pressed forward to the Main and the Neckar, and having traversed the Franconian plains, he reached the Danube near Ulm on the 22nd of June, and joined hands with Louis of Baden, a movement resembling the best of Turenne's as regards its admirable speed and decision. His despatches prove that he was fully aware of the peril of this audacious march, with Villeroy in his rear and Tallard on his flank ; but possibly no other course was open ; and, as always happened with him, he did not hesitate, and he executed his task with consummate skill. Marlborough and Baden were now immensely superior in force to the Elector and Marsin, who, on being informed of the approach of Marlborough, had advanced from the Iller, and attained the Danube ; and the allied chiefs did not lose an instant in turning their present advantage to account. Leaving a considerable force to restrain the enemy, they moved down the Danube quickly to Donauwörth ; and after a fierce and well-contested struggle stormed the heights of the Schellenberg covering the town, and became masters of the course of the river. Within a few days, the victorious army was overrunning the Bavarian plains and harrying them, after the fashion of the age, in order to force the Elector to yield ; Marlborough having completely transformed the situation for a time by operations which had astounded Europe.

While Marlborough had thus attained and overcome the Danube, what had been the conduct of the French commanders he had left behind on the Meuse and the Rhine ? Villeroy had nearly 40,000 men in hand ; the army of Tallard, even allowing for a detachment sent in the spring to Marsin, must have been about 45,000 strong; and had these chiefs been capable men, they ought to have prevented Marlborough's movement, though, it is fair to remark, they were bound and hampered by injudicious orders from Versailles. Had they combined their armies and crossed the Rhine, they ought easily to have carried the lines of Stolhoffen—these did not stop Villars a few years afterwards—and crushed the feeble army of defence ; and they then ought to have been able to have forestalled Marlborough, in what was a strategic flank march of extreme risk, to have at least fallen on his communications between the Neckar, the Main, and the Danube, and to have perhaps compelled him to fight in positions where the loss of a battle would have been ruinous. Villeroy and Tallard, however, were not great chiefs; they marched and countermarched, lost many weeks, and allowed their enemy to pass them by; and it was only in July, when Marlborough and Baden were, we have seen, in the heart of Bavaria, that they took anything like a decided course. Their armies, before united, were now again divided; Villeroy crossed the Rhine to observe the lines of Stolhoffen, occupied now by Eugene, at the head of, perhaps, 30,000 men; and Tallard made for the Black Forest, with a force probably 35,000 strong, in order to join hands with the Elector and Marsin.

The junction was effected on the 4th of August, not far from the central town of Augsburg, and the collected armies must have formed a mass of nearly 70,000 men at least, for the most part troops of the best quality. Meanwhile, Villeroy had altogether failed to hold Eugene along the Rhine in check; that great captain, when aware of the movement of Tallard, resolved to give support to Marlborough and Baden, already menaced by the combined enemies; and he broke up from his lines and flew to the Danube, with a force of about 15,000 men, having left a detachment to keep back Villeroy, and having baffled that most worthless commander. He was at Höchstedt on the 8th of August—the scene of the victory gained by Villars—and, leaving his small force on the northern bank, he crossed the Danube to confer with Marlborough, at the time at Aichach, to the north-east of Augsburg. A grand opportunity was offered again to the French, who, in this campaign, seemed always to miss the occasion. The combined Bavarian and French armies were, at this moment, quite near Höchstedt; and had they made a rapid and decisive movement, they might have crushed the isolated wing of Eugene, and have placed Marlborough, who had been left by Baden, in order to make the siege of Ingoldstadt, in a position of the most critical kind, in a hostile country, with an enemy on his flank, and separated from his base on the Danube. Tallard, Marsin, and the Elector, however, paused; they crossed the Danube, indeed, at

Lauingen; but they did not attempt to fall on Eugene; and Marlborough, meanwhile—he clearly saw his danger—marched with extraordinary speed from Aichach, and came into line with his daring colleague, west of Donauwörth on the 11th of August. The allied chiefs decided to attack the enemy, who, by this time, was in a strong position, in a region of marsh and forest, where the stream of the Nebel falls into the Danube through a plain bounded by the villages of Lützingen and Blenheim. Less confident men would hardly have run the risk, for the hostile army already threatened the line of their communications northwards; and a serious defeat might have been destruction.

I can only describe in faint outline the great and decisive battle that followed. By the early dawn of the 13th of August, the allied army had passed the defiles which lead through Dapfheim into the plain of the Nebel, and began to take up its positions for attack. Marlborough and Eugene had hoped to surprise the enemy, and Tallard and Marsin were really unprepared; in fact, with the Elector, they thought that the allies were falling back on Nördlingen, on the line of their communications with the Main. The French and Bavarians, however, were soon ready; but some hours passed before the hostile armies had joined in the actual shock of battle. Each was from 55,000 to 60,000 strong; but the French and Bavarian army, a veteran force, was probably a better instrument of war than the composite masses of many races collected under the allied standards. The dispositions, however, of the French marshals were essentially bad, and gave the great commanders opposed to them a distinct advantage. Tallard and Marsin seem to have been convinced that the Nebel, which ran across their front, was impassable or could be passed only by an enemy with extreme difficulty; and that if Lützingen and Blenheim, with the neighbouring village of Oberglau, were held in strong force, the allies, should they advance on the Nebel, would be stopped at the centre by a powerful obstacle, and on either wing could be easily repelled. They divided their army accordingly into two masses, each, it would seem, of nearly equal force; and while they crowded their right wing at Blenheim, and placed large bodies of men at Oberglau, and at Lützingen on their left wing, their extended centre was weakly occupied by a long line of cavalry only, supported by an insignificant body of footmen. This conception was altogether ill-founded; the obstacle of the Nebel was not very great, and were it once forced it would fare ill with the thin and ill-guarded French centre, and even with the wings— with the right especially, cooped up in Blenheim and close to the Danube. The vice of the arrangement, there is reason to believe, was perceived by Marlborough almost at once; the masses of the allied army were so arrayed as to be ready to assail the hostile centre; and Tallard, who commanded the French right, when he saw this, it is said, asked Marsin, who was in command of the French left, to send reinforcements to the threatened point, but only received an angry refusal.

The battle began at about 9 A.M., Marlborough attacking Blenheim from the allied left, while Eugene made a circuitous march on the right; and the attack on Blenheim—which, I conceive, was a feint only to deceive the enemy—was repulsed with no inconsiderable loss. At about noon, when he had been made aware that Eugene was engaged with Marsin, Marlborough made a first great effort against the French centre; and a mass of cavalry, formed in two lines, with a mass of infantry in their front and their rear, was launched forward to cross the Nebel. The French horsemen, however, were not wanting to themselves; they fell with terrible effect on the hostile array as it was entangled and confused in the passage; and though part of Marlborough's troops succeeded in the attempt, they were held to the spot and made no progress. Meanwhile, a secondary allied attack on Oberglau had altogether failed; and though Marlborough's presence restored the contest, it has been thought that had Tallard and Marsin co-operated at this moment in a counter-attack, the French and Bavarian army might have won a victory. Eugene, however, who, with an inferior force, had held Marsin in check by prodigious efforts, sent a detachment to the aid of his colleague, and about 4 P.M. Marlborough was once more free to strike what he had seen from the first was the vulnerable point in the hostile position. Massing footmen and

4

horsemen once more together, he hurled them against the French centre; and though the French cavalry fought to the last, their weak support of infantry gave way, and the centre yielded to the overwhelming pressure. The victorious army, with Marlborough at its head, was now master of the whole position of its foes; and turning in full force against the French right, shut up in Blenheim and pressed against the Danube, it compelled it, almost at once, to surrender. Marsin and the Elector, who, unlike Eugene, had done nothing to aid a companion in arms, contrived to effect their retreat in safety; but an accident only averted their ruin. The loss of the victors was, probably, from 11,000 to 12,000 men; that of the French and Bavarians was 40,000; and the routed army was, in fact, destroyed.

This splendid campaign, decisive as it was, cannot be deemed a strategic masterpiece. The project of the march from the Meuse to the Danube, with Villeroy in the rear and Tallard on the Rhine, was too hazardous to deserve high praise;* and Eugene, I repeat, was, I think, its author, though Marlborough is, of course, responsible for it. Had Condé been in the place of Villeroy, and Turenne held the staff of Tallard, Marlborough, I believe, would not have attained Donauwörth, and the great campaign of 1704 would have probably had a different issue. Remarkable, too, as was the skill of Eugene in eluding Villeroy, and pushing on to the Danube, in order to join his colleague, he ought not to have left an isolated detachment in little force within reach of an enemy fourfold in strength; and had Tallard and Marsin been real chiefs, they would have crushed Eugene and have placed Marlborough in extreme peril, when he stood alone and inferior in force in his camp at† Aichach. Apart, however, from these risks and mistakes, Eugene and Marlborough, especially the last, carried out their plans with

---

* This march, in fact, strongly resembles Eugene's famous march up the Po in 1706, described by Napoleon as "a marvellous piece of audacity," but it was far more perilous.

† Coxe, though a dull is a conscientious writer, and occasionally he had good military assistance. Alone, as far as I know, of commentators on the campaign of 1704, he points out the risk to which, at this juncture, Eugene and Marlborough were exposed. Napoleon wrote on Marlborough, but his observations have never been published; it would be most interesting to know his judgment on this passage in the campaign.

consummate ability. The march from the Meuse, by the Main, to the Danube, was a prodigy of execution for the age ; the advance to the Schellenberg was rapid and brilliant; and the forced march from Aichach to join Eugene was admirable for its quickness and boldness. The decision, too, to give battle at Blenheim was characteristic of great captains ; it was hazardous, but a retreat would have lost the whole fruits of a successful campaign, and very probably would have been fatal.

Nevertheless, it is upon the field of Blenheim that Marlborough's genius becomes most manifest. With that perfect insight which never failed him, he at once perceived what was false and defective in the disposition of the hostile army. He concentrated his forces against the one weak point; and though he was beaten back and even placed in danger, he never relaxed his efforts, carrying out his purpose with inflexible constancy and calm firmness until he had pierced the enemy's centre, and made a decisive victory certain. Here we see the development of what we may call the new tactics in full perfection. Tallard and Marsin did not comprehend the ground, and unskilfully arrayed their troops upon it. Marlborough took in the situation at a glance, and so conducted the battle that an overwhelming mass was brought to bear on the decisive spot. Nothing, too, could have been more admirable than the loyalty of Eugene to his colleague ; but for his support Marlborough might have lost the battle ; and the result of Blenheim was, in fact, due to the unrivalled tactics of the one chief and the chivalrous and unselfish zeal of the other. As for the French Marshals, the arrangements they made might have succeeded against inferior men ; but, if formidable in appearance they were radically bad ; though Tallard of the two is the least to blame, for he understood the mistake that was made ; and Marsin deserves the severest censure for disregarding Tallard's advice, and for neglecting all through to send him assistance—a too characteristic fault of the warriors of France. The conduct of the allied army was such as great chiefs almost always obtain from the troops they lead. English, Austrians, and Prussians fought like heroes ; but the French and Bavarians had perhaps the better army—and the

4 *

French cavalry made magnificent efforts, if the surrender at
Blenheim betrays the weakness of the French soldier in the hour
of defeat.   Blenheim, in truth, was a general's not a soldier's
battle; the triumph of genius in command, not of mere valour.

Blenheim saved the Empire, and set Germany free; and the
defeated army, a shattered wreck, reaching the Rhine in fragments, fled into Alsace.   Having cleared the German bank of the
river, the Allies sat down before the great place of Landau, which
covered the approaches to the French frontier; but, though the
fortress made an heroic resistance, Marlborough had entered the
Palatinate by the close of autumn, had seized the important points
of Traerbach and Trêves, and had secured a base for the invasion
of France.   Everything, he hoped, would be ready by the early
spring—armies still seldom held the field in winter—and his purpose was to advance into Lorraine by the valleys of the Moselle
and the Sarre, with an army of 100,000 men formed of contingents
of many nations, the line long afterwards marked out by Gneisenau,
and followed by Moltke in 1870.   This indicates a true strategic
eye; and, in fact, in strategy as well as in tactics Marlborough
always detected the fault in the cuirass, and seized the vulnerable
point on the scene before him.   The great Englishman, however,
had not the good fortune of the renowned Dane many years afterwards.   Marlborough was not seconded as Moltke was.   Louis of
Baden, who on the field of manœuvre held the place of the Crown
Prince of Prussia in August 1870, refused to move even a man
from the Rhine; and though Marlborough advanced to the
Moselle, in the early summer of 1705, in order to force the hand
of his colleague, he had not sufficient force to make a decisive
movement.   Marlborough, too, had a very different man to cope
with from Napoleon III.; his antagonist was Villars, already
proved to be incomparably the greatest of living French chiefs, and
destined to justify the proud title of "Invincible," given by a
grateful Sovereign.   The operations of Villars were able in the
extreme; assailing the heads of Marlborough's columns, but
taking care to cover his own flanks, he retreated to the well known
position of Sierk, resting on the Moselle and a chain of heights,

and he calmly awaited the victor of Blenheim. The hostile armies were each about 50,000 strong—the Memoirs of Villars are incorrect in making out that his foe had 80,000 men; but Marlborough, deprived of the support of Baden, did not venture to risk an attack, and, after waiting some days, he recoiled, baffled, and fell back to the country round Trêves. He was so angry that he sent a message to Villars to explain the cause of his retreat; but though his colleague was wholly to blame, Villars had gained his object and had saved France from an invasion which might have ended the war.

Marlborough was ere long recalled to the theatre which had been the scene of his first exploits. Villeroy by this time had returned to the Meuse with an army greatly strengthened since the year before, and, at the head of about 70,000 men, he had retaken Huy, advanced down the Meuse, and seized the important town of Liège. Terror now prevailed in the councils of the States; their chief commander, Auverquerque, had been defeated; and Marlborough was compelled to break up from Trêves, to abandon the hope of invading France, and to try to restore the war in the Low Countries. He had joined Auverquerque by the first week of July, and he instantly assumed a bold offensive at the head of about 60,000 men. Villeroy, a noisy braggart and an incapable chief, was out-manœuvred and lost Huy; and he had soon fallen back to the great French lines extending across Belgium from the Mehaigne to the sea, which had been the scene of operations in 1703. Marlborough, despite a protest of the Dutch deputies—they hampered him in all his great movements—resolved, to master and pass the obstacle; he marched across the well-known field of Landen, which had witnessed Luxemburg's brilliant triumph, and deceiving Villeroy by well-designed feints, he forced the lines near Tirlemont on the Gheete, winning a bloody combat, and taking many prisoners. The beaten army fell back to the Dyle, in the hope of covering Louvain and Brussels, but Marlborough crossed the stream at Genappe; and on the 18th of August he was about to assail the French in position not far from Waterloo—a village then wholly unknown to fame—when once more Dutch fears and jealousies prevented his fighting a decisive battle. He was again so indignant that he wrote to England, declaring that he would leave his command ; and his operations, in truth, had been shamefully thwarted. Deserted by Baden in the beginning of the year, he had failed in his project of invading France; crossed by the Generals and Commissioners of the States, he had not been able to bring Villeroy to bay, and the only result of the campaign of 1705, which might have seen the Allies on the Marne and the Seine, was the capture of the French lines in Belgium, a result important indeed, but not very remarkable.

Marlborough spent the winter of 1705-6 in visiting crowned heads of the Grand Alliance; a master of diplomacy as well as of war, he threw the spell of commanding genius over the King of Denmark and the King of Prussia, and secured pledges of support for the ensuing campaign. He had been so ill-treated by the States that he wished to invade the South of France in 1706, in concert with his loyal colleague, Eugene ; and it would be a curious specu-lation whether this effort, which failed in his absence in 1706–7, and has never yet been attended with success, would have succeeded had Marlborough been in command. He was, however, induced to return to the Low Countries, and he advanced towards the Meuse to threaten Namur, a great strategic point for a march into France, with an army of about 60,000 men. With the infa-tuation that befalls despots, Louis XIV. still had faith in Villeroy, and though deprived of the protection of the lines, the Marshal was ordered to take the offensive. Villeroy was advancing towards Leuwe with an army equal in numbers, at least, to that of his foe, when he met Marlborough on his march southwards, in a country of marsh, woodland, and low hills, between the Mehaigne and the lesser Gheete, crowned by the insignificant village of Ramillies.

A few words must suffice to trace the incidents of the great battle that followed. On the 23rd of May 1706, the French army, with a Bavarian wing—the Elector still clung to the fortunes of France —was seen arrayed on a range of upland, extending from near the course of the Mehaigne to beyond the little Gheete, on the hill of St. André, the villages of Ramillies and Autre Eglise, and a morass formed by the Gheete and its feeders, covering the position across

THEATRE OF
THE
CAMPAIGNS
in
Belgium and North of France.

Scale of Miles

0   10   20   30   40   50   60

North   Sea

Groningen
Leeuwarden
Texel
R. Kuinde
Assen
Hoorn
Genemuiden
ZUIDER
R. Vecht
Zwolle
ZEE
AMSTERDAM
Harderwyk
Deventer
Utrecht
Old Rhine
Rotterdam
River
Rhine
Mouths of the Scheldt Meuse & Rhine
Boio le Duo
Bergen op Zoom
R. Domme
Venloo
R. Meuse
Ostend
Rhermunde
Antwerp
Lokeren
Ghent
R. Nemen
Louvain
R. Lys
Oudenarde
Tirlemont
R. Scheldt
BRUSSELS
Boulogne
R. Dender
Anzein
R. Senne
R. Dyle
Ramillies
Lille
R. Veurne
Leuze
Genappe
Huy
Liege
Aire
Tournay
Luwe
Bethune
Douay
Namur
Artois
Marchiennes
Mons
Malplaquet
R. Sambre
R. Scarpe
Denain
Bouchain
R. Ourthe
Cambray
Landrecies
Amiens
River Somme
St Quentin

three-fourths of its front. Villeroy had formed his army into two masses, his right nearly upon the Mehaigne, but strongly occupying an old Roman road which led across the plain in a line with the river, his centre and left along the marshes of the Gheete ; and he held Ramillies and Autre Eglise as fortified outposts. The position seemed formidable, as at Blenheim, but the eagle eye of Marlborough saw at a glance that his enemy's arrangements had two marked defects, and that able manœuvring would assure him victory. Villeroy's centre and left, especially the left, covered by an impassable swamp, was not assailable; but neither could he attack that side ; and Marlborough held the chord of the arc in front of the French Marshal's position. Marlborough prepared his battle with that unerring judgment which scarcely ever forsook him in war ; and the result was a splendid and complete triumph. The English chief began by a feint against the French left, which, of course, was repelled without difficulty ; but it had the effect which Marlborough hoped for ; Villeroy detached from his right to support his left, weakening thus his army at the real point of attack. Marlborough fell once more on the French left, in order to distract the attention of his foe ; and then, turning his shorter line to account, and moving rapidly a great body of troops unseen by Villeroy, behind a hill and a wood, he struck the French right in overwhelming force, his men three-fold in numbers, at the critical point, pressing forward along the Roman causeway into the very heart of the hostile position. The French centre and left, held bound to the spot, and scarcely able to move, saw the battle lost, and made few efforts to avert defeat ; and though the French right fought well for a time, the resistance was not like that at Blenheim, for the French soldier had lost the moral power of success. The villages of Ramillies and Autre Eglise were quickly stormed, without heavy loss ; and the French right was ere long overpowered, and fled from the field in despair and rout. Villeroy's centre and left, being not assailable, drew off for a time in fair order ; but the contagion of defeat soon affected the men, and his whole army became a horde of fugitives, abandoning guns and standards, and were captured by thousands. Marlborough followed up his victory with the strokes of a master; he was free to act and he achieved wonders; and in a few days at most the whole of Belgium and its fortresses had become his spoils. Brussels, Ghent, Antwerp, and even Ostend fell with a rapidity for that age surprising; the French, hopelessly demoralized, made no stand, and, before the autumn had closed, the allied standards had been carried to the Lys and the Scheldt, and waved ominously near the frontier of France.

I would select Ramillies as the most distinctive and character-istic of Marlborough's battles. Eugene shares the honours of Blenheim with him, and the issue hung in suspense at Blenheim; but Ramillies was a masterpiece all his own, and the victory was never for a moment doubtful. The day was won by a single stroke of tactics; and here again we see the peculiar excellence of Marl-borough in the highest perfection, his genius in taking advantage of the ground, and in turning to account the faults of his enemy. France seemed fallen after the campaign of 1706, marked, not only by this immense disaster, but by Eugene's grand campaign on the Po, through which the French were expelled from Italy; yet the exhausted nation suddenly made one of those prodigious and heroic efforts which have so often astounded Europe. Berwick, a nephew of Marlborough, and in war a Churchill, reconquered Spain in the great fight of Almanza; and an attempt to invade Provence and to besiege Toulon, though conducted by Eugene, completely failed. Mean-while Louis XIV., taught at last by misfortune, had replaced Villeroy in his command by Vendôme, a man of many gifts and many evil qualities; and the King strained the resources of his realm to the utmost to make head against his foes in the Low Countries. Ven-dôme took the field with about 100,000 men; Marlborough certainly was inferior in force; and the campaign of 1707 was spent in manœu-vres between the Lys, the Scheldt, and the Sambre, with little results.

I shall only glance at the campaign of 1708, for though Marlborough gained a succession of triumphs, it was less marked, perhaps, by his peculiar genius than by the fatal dissensions of the French chiefs, and the profound demoralization of the French army. Vendôme recovered Ghent, and the line of the

Lys; he even passed the Scheldt, and advanced to the Dender,
and though he failed to capture Oudenarde, he held a favourable
position when he confronted Marlborough on the Dender, in the
first days of July. He was embarrassed, however, by a fatal burden; the Duke of Burgundy, rather a monk than a soldier, shared
with him an ill-defined command; and the Duke insisted on falling
back to the Scheldt, renouncing the initiative with timid weakness.
Marlborough by this time had been joined by Eugene, who had
moved from the Moselle into Belgium; and the two chiefs advanced
to the relief of Oudenarde, resolved, if possible, to fight a great
battle. The march of the French had been extremely slow, owing
to the bickerings of the Duke and Vendôme; but they were collected
upon the Scheldt near Gaveren; and they ought to have made the
Allies rue an audacious attempt to cross the river. The divided
chiefs, however, sent forward only a weak detachment to dispute
the passage. This was cut to pieces after a short struggle; and
Marlborough and his colleague bridged the Scheldt under the
beard, so to speak, of the ill-directed enemy. The hostile armies
met, on the 11th of July, in a region of plain and forest outside Oudenarde. Each was probably about 70,000 strong; and the
fortunes of France were once more marred by timidity and divided
counsels. Marlborough had gained ground on the French right,
when Vendôme wished to attack from his left, but the Duke of
Burgundy had resolved to fall back; and though the retreat began
in good order, the French troops, hard pressed and wretchedly led,
broke up by degrees in ignominious flight. The defeated army was
unable to rally until it had found a refuge near Ghent; and Marlborough and Eugene, pressing boldly forward, overran the country
between the Lys and the Scheldt, and sate down before the vast
stronghold of Lille. I cannot dwell on the great siege that
followed, the most remarkable of the whole contest. Lille was a
place of extraordinary strength. It was defended by Boufflers with
a large garrison; it was surrounded by neighbouring friendly fortresses, and it had the support of the army that had fought at
Oudenarde, and of another army of relief which, under Berwick,
had followed the steps of Eugene from the Moselle. To capture

such a stronghold appeared impossible—Vendôme ridiculed the very
notion, and yet Marlborough and Eugene accomplished the task,
though Boufflers made an heroic resistance. This undoubtedly
was in a great measure due to the ability and daring of the allied
chiefs. Eugene clung to the fortress with tenacious constancy.
and Marlborough gave proof of extraordinary resource in covering
the siege and in maintaining his communications open through all
kinds of obstacles. Yet Lille would probably not have fallen but
for the animosities of the French commanders. Vendôme openly
quarrelled with the Duke of Burgundy, and Berwick sullenly stood
aloof from both ; and the two armies of relief did almost nothing.
The moral power, too, of the French soldiery was fatally injured
by these disputes and failures ; and when Lille fell, the war seemed
about to close in a triumphant march of the Allies on Paris.

At this crisis, indeed, the condition of France was such as might
have made even men like Richelieu and Turenne begin to despair.
The convulsive effort of 1707 had failed ; the Allies were on the
verge of Artois ; and the Monarchy in decline, and the exhausted
nation seemed unable to confront the mass of their enemies.
Yet Louis XIV. did not lose heart ; he refused the insolent proposals of the Dutch to take up arms against his own grandson,
and he appealed, not in vain, to an heroic people. Recruits
flocked in thousands to defend the lilies ; the misery, in truth,
and the prostration of France, increased the numbers that joined her
armies ; but everything that constitutes organized force—supplies,
depôts, and magazines, were wanting. The King, however, throwing prejudice aside, at last confided the army on his northern
frontier to the one commander who had never failed in the
calamitous war of the Spanish Succession. History and gossip
have alike been unjust to Villars ; he was ridiculed in England and
hated at Versailles, but he was a general of extraordinary powers,
for he combined almost in the highest degree the great faculties
of Turenne and Condé. Yet when Villars, in the spring of 1709,
assumed the command of his master's army, he was almost
appalled at the prospect before him ; he was at the head of
perhaps 100,000 men, but he was so ill supplied that he could

make no movement. It is on occasions like these that French soldiers, when ably directed, show at their best. Villars in a few weeks had obtained the means of operating with some hope of success, and he had breathed into his troops that extreme self-confidence which was one of his most distinctive qualities. By the early summer he was in positions of formidable strength, in the space between the heads of the Lys and the Scheldt, and covering the low ranges overlooking Artois; and he had protected himself with defensive lines that extended almost from the feeders of the Scheldt to the sea. Marlborough and Eugene were now at the head of from 110,000 to 120,000 men, and Marlborough, with true strategic insight, proposed to turn the French lines by the coast, combining the attack with a descent on Boulogne, supported by British troops and a fleet, and then, passing the Somme and masking its fortresses, to press forward boldly to the capital of France. This was a recurrence to the "great design" of 1703, and worthy of a chief of supreme genius; and it is an additional proof that Marlborough perceived, with perfect clearness, the immense importance to an English army of the command of the sea. The Dutch deputies, however, refused to sanction a movement they doubtless could not understand; and Eugene, I believe, agreed with them, for, as we shall see, he had formed a plan of quite a different kind to invade France. The Allies had now "to take the bull by the horns," and to enter France through the network of fortresses, of rivers, canals, and intricate woodland, which still covers her northern frontier; and issuing from Lille in great strength, they proceeded to invest the stronghold of Tournay, in order to secure and widen their base. The place fell after a weak resistance, and Marlborough and Eugene now turned against Mons, still pursuing the same methodical warfare, and hoping to master the line of the Sambre. This was too much for Villars, who would have been placed in extreme difficulty had the Allies gained the heads of the Sambre without a contest. He issued from his lines in the first week of September, and by the 10th he had taken a strong position in a wide opening between two masses of woodland, not far from the beleaguered fortress, which overlook the heathy plain and the hamlet of Malplaquet, ever since a great name. He fortified ground, naturally perilous to attack, with all the resources of the art of the engineer; and he boldly awaited the advance of the enemy.

The allied chiefs had meant to attack Villars before he had made these formidable lines; but, as usual, they were crossed by the deputies of the States, and the result proved how disastrous had been their meddling. In the early dawn of the 11th of September, Marlborough and Eugene put their army in motion, and the French army was soon descried holding a position which has been aptly described as " an infernal gulf surrounded by fire." The French right and left were respectively covered by the woods of Lanière and of Taisnière, which crescent-like converged towards each other; the wood of Sart spread beyond that of Taisnière; and the French centre holding the space between, in the opening that leads to the plain of Malplaquet, was massed behind a triple line of entrenchments, with apertures to allow the free use of cavalry. The position, in short, was of extraordinary strength, and it was held by troops who, under the spell of Villars, ably seconded by the gallant Boufflers, who had volunteered to assist his colleague, were animated by heroic ardour. Yet Marlborough and Eugene did not hesitate; and they marshalled their forces for the most desperate and best contested struggle of the war, in which princely soldiers from all the lands of Europe took part, like knights in a tournament to the death. The numbers on each side were not far from equal,* the Allies having a slight advantage—about 100,000 to 90,000 men; but, prodigiously strong as its position was, the French army, crowded with rude levies, could not be compared as an efficient force with the victorious legions of many campaigns, and the allied chiefs possibly trusted too much to an inferiority repeatedly proved.

The plan of Eugene and Marlborough seems to have been to turn the French left and to force the left centre, making only a secondary effort against the right; and Eugene, after

---

* It is more difficult to arrive at an estimate of the strength of the contending armies in the case of Malplaquet than in that of any other great battle of the war. I think my calculation is fairly accurate.

a prolonged contest, fairly expelled the enemy from the wood of Sart. The Prince, supported by Marlborough in force, now advanced upon the wood of Taisnière, and a murderous struggle kept fortune in suspense, until Villars, drawing a body of troops from his centre, drove back Eugene in a furious onslaught, conspicuous for the valour of the Irish exiles,* "ever and everywhere, true" to the Bourbon lilies. The situation of the Allies was now critical, when a wound deprived the French of the genius of their chief; and as the detachment made by Villars had weakened their line to a considerable extent—he was hurrying to the endangered point when he fell—Marlborough, seizing the occasion with his wonted judgment, made a tremendous attack on the enemy's centre. The first range of entrenchments was ere long carried, but the obstacles presented by the lines behind, and the heroism of the defence, kept the issue doubtful. A magnificent effort made by the household troops of France for a time forced the assailants back; and even when the inner entrenchments were won the French centre prolonged the still undecided battle. Meanwhile the false attack on the French right had been turned into an attack in full force. The Prince of Orange, carried away by excitement, advanced along the wood of Lanière, and tried to storm the hostile entrenchments in front, and his troops were literally mown down in thousands by enemies who suffered little loss. The battle was raging until 3 P.M., when a flank movement, most skilfully made by Eugene, outside the verge of the wood of Taisnière, began to endanger the French left, and threatened the only line of retreat; and this caused Boufflers, now in supreme command, to draw gradually off from the scene of carnage. The Allies, utterly worn out, and cruelly stricken, made no attempt to molest the enemy, and the French fell back a few miles only, in perfect order, and not the least disheartened. Villars, it is said, exclaimed from his litter, that "he expected his army to fight again, as soon as it had had a moment of repose."

Marlborough and Eugene won this terrible battle, the greatest

---

* "*Semper et ubique fideles*" was the proud and well-merited device on the flag of the Irish brigade.

by far of the eighteenth century, in what may be called a military sense; for the French army retired from the field, and Mons fell a few weeks afterwards. But it was not an inconsiderate boast of Villars that Malplaquet was truly a Pyrrhic victory; the Allies lost fully 20,000 men, the French probably not half that number; the Dutch contingent never recovered from the fight; and the frightful slaughter of the allied soldiery provoked angry discontent in England, and sent a thrill of alarm through the enemies of France. Eugene and Marlborough, in the actual battle, displayed as usual their great powers; but the whole enterprise was, perhaps, too hazardous; and if, as has been alleged, Marl- · borough chose to fight in order to keep up the war party at home, he was justly punished for an unprincipled act, for Malplaquet shook the Grand Alliance to its base. Villars showed admirable skill in choosing his ground, and strengthening a naturally strong position, and in arranging his troops upon it; he, too, was a master of the new tactics, and he would not improbably have repulsed his foes had he not been disabled at a critical moment. As it is, Malplaquet does him the highest honour; it is a proof of his extraordinary gifts, that, with an army inferior in every respect, he should have inflicted losses on the allied army at least two-fold greater than that of his own, and that he successfully stemmed the tide of misfortune which had for years set in against France.

I shall merely refer to the two campaigns of 1710 and 1711, for Marlborough is not their real hero, and his great qualities, though seen in them, do not appear in their accustomed splendour, owing to adverse circumstances which combined against him. He was supported by Eugene in the first of these years; and the allied chiefs, in the absence of Villars, forced the lines he had made the year before, and invested and took the place of Douay, on the second line of the French fortresses of the north. Villars, however, though still suffering from his wound, was in command by the end of May, and he constructed a new great defensive barrier, extending from the Scarpe to the neighbourhood of Boulogne, and adding enormously to the many obstacles of a region already protected by nature and art. The Allies reached the lines, and Eugene, as was his wont, for a daring exploit, gave his voice for an attack in force; but the Dutch, remembering Malplaquet, held back; Marlborough, it is believed, agreed with them, and the two great captains had to content themselves with taking Bethune, St. Vénant, and Aire, little places around the head of the Lys, which cost them thousands of their best soldiers. Villars, meanwhile, showed little sign of life; but he kept on extending his lines until they formed an immense position of defence, spreading from the coast to the heads of the Sambre; and he boasted, not, we shall see, in vain, that the enemy should advance no further. In 1711 Marlborough had not Eugene with him, but he was at the head of a very large army; and the campaign was spent in a game of manœuvres, in which Villars and he were fairly matched. The Englishman succeeded at last in forcing the lines, which were too long to be covered at all points; but the capture of the insignificant place of Bouchain was the only prize of immense efforts; and though the wits of Versailles and St. James's cried scorn at the *ne plus ultra* of Villars, that great chief had really attained his object, and had successfully shielded the French frontier. These campaigns, in fact, have been misdescribed by English partisans in Marlborough's interest. The true victor was, beyond dispute, Villars; he had compelled the Allies to waste their strength in sieges, which simply had no results; he had proved himself to be a master in defence, as remarkable as he had been in attack; and, combining genius in politics and war, he had gained for France what she needed, time to dissolve the Grand Alliance already weakened. It would be unfair, however, to say that Marlborough was wanting to himself in this contest; as a military exploit, his forcing the lines of Villars was an admirable feat; but, in truth, he was circumscribed and baffled by the turn which affairs had for some time been taking in England and upon the Continent. He had for years been almost supreme in England, and had had full control over her resources for war; but Sarah Jennings and Anne Stuart had quarrelled; Mrs. Masham had crept to the ear of the Queen; Malplaquet had aroused a storm in England; the Ministers in

power sought means to destroy him ; he received no real support
from the Whigs ; and he had become the object of grave charges,
partly the clamours of faction, but, in part, well founded.   On the
other hand, France had triumphed in Spain ; the success of
Villars had saved her in the north ; the Dutch and the English
had had enough of war; and the Grand Alliance was being broken
up largely owing to the rapacity of the House of Austria.   In 1710
and 1711, Marlborough had no scope for his commanding genius ;
he was no longer able to make great efforts ; he knew that his
splendid career was drawing to a close.

Before the beginning of 1712, Marlborough had been deprived of
all his military commands, dismissed from office amidst shouts of
obloquy, and threatened with impeachment for crimes against the
State.   He was not brought to a public trial ; and some of the
accusations heaped upon him were certainly false, and now seem
ridiculous.   But he wisely left England with his disgraced wife ;
and though he was not convicted of malversation and fraud, the
unscrupulous ambition and avaricious greed which were perhaps
his most distinctive vices were dragged into light by a great deal
of evidence.   It is remarkable, too, though no commander has
ever been more beloved by his troops, that he was distrusted by
some of his best officers ; and if his treason at Brest remained
unknown, he was disliked and suspected by both Whigs and Tories.

The value, however, of his genius in war, was conspicuously
proved, in an indirect way, in the memorable campaign of 1712.
England had now withdrawn from the Grand Alliance, but the Emperor still maintained the struggle; and Eugene, who hated Louis
XIV., and had confirmed his master in his warlike purpose, was
placed at the head of a great army intended to invade and to subdue
France.   He was now in possession of most of the fortresses which
cover the northern French frontier, and his position was so formidable that Louis XIV., when he gave Villars once more the army
of the North, and bade the warrior farewell at Versailles, exclaimed that, should fortune prove adverse, " the King and the
Marshal would perish together."   The plan of Eugene, his base
now secure, was to capture the strongholds near the heads of the

Oise, and then marching down the open valley of the stream, the path followed for ages by the House of Austria and its generals in assailing France, to pass by the fortified lines of the Somme, and to finish the war by an advance on the capital. He sate down to invest Landrecies, now almost the only obstacle in his way, and his army was so confident in itself and its chief that it called its lines "the approaches to Paris." This resembled, in some respects, the daring march on Turin in 1706; but Eugene had made a strategic mistake; arguing from what he thought was the timid attitude of Villars, in the campaign of 1710, he believed that the Marshal would never attack, and he spread his army, in ill-connected posts, from Landrecies to near Marchiennes on the frontier, leaving a detachment to guard a weak point at Denain. The Prince had to deal with a different foe from the chiefs he had routed in 1706; his adversary was a man of genius, full of resource and thought, in execution admirable. Villars by this time was in his lines near Cambray; he quickly detected Eugene's error, and he took advantage of it with consummate skill. Breaking up from his camps, he made a forced march as though he was trying to relieve Landrecies; he ostentatiously gave out that this was his purpose, and then, screening the movement with perfect art, and countermarching with extreme rapidity, he fell in full force on the communications of his foe, and attacked Denain in largely superior numbers. The results of this fine strategy were almost marvellous; the detachment guarding Denain was destroyed; a large body of troops, hurried up by Eugene to join in the defence, was utterly routed, and the whole army of invasion, smitten in the flank, and losing its communications, was compelled to retreat, and to fall back, baffled, behind the frontier. Villars made the very most of this splendid success; the siege of Landrecies was instantly raised; the French fortresses, which had been the prizes of many campaigns, were soon retaken, and the standards of France were ere long seen waving in triumph along the course of the Sambre. France was finally saved by this grand feat of arms, and before a year had passed, Villars was in the heart of Germany, had driven Eugene beyond the Rhine, and had compelled the Emperor to sue for peace. France had never such an awakening again until, rescuing her from defeat and anarchy, Napoleon won the great fight of Marengo.

In the Revolution which followed the death of Queen Anne, Marlborough was placed again in command of the army; but he was disliked by George I. and his ministers; and it is significant that he never regained anything like his old authority in the State. The last years of his life were somewhat obscure; he gradually survived his splendid faculties, and he died, little regretted, in 1722. I cannot notice his diplomatic career; enough to say that he was the master spirit of the Grand Alliance during many years; he kept its ill-connected structure together, and three-fourths of the Princes of Christendom inclined before the genius of an English subject. As a statesman, Marlborough was less successful; he misinterpreted the spirit of the time during the later years of the great war he directed; but his errors and fall were largely due to the faults and the temper of his imperious wife, whom he loved with a fondness not unmixed with terror. A word as to his achievements in the noble art of which he was one of the greatest masters. Marlborough was endowed with the choicest gifts of a warrior; it was his special characteristic that daring, constancy, imagination, and prudence were blended in him in proportions of the happiest kind; and it is a peculiarity of his career that he attained supreme command, for the first time, at a period of life when most great captains have done their work, and that he was never defeated in a pitched battle. It has been said that he had little strategic genius; but a study of his campaigns confutes this error; he was capable of great combinations in war; and if, as a strategist, he accomplished less than other commanders of the first order, this is partly to be ascribed to the contracted theatre which usually was the scene of his exploits, and partly to the interference of the Dutch and their deputies, and to the jealousies and discords of a divided League. Two strategic gifts he certainly possessed in a measure accorded to few commanders; he always perceived the weak point of an enemy on a field of manœuvre as well as of battle, and he was pre-eminent in making the most of success, and in drawing decisive results from victory. In pure strategy, however, he was, I think, inferior in originality to Turenne, and he achieved less than Villars and Eugene, two great names in this sphere of the art; but as a strategist he is second alone to those illustrious chiefs of his era; and he contributed largely to the grand revival of strategy, after a season of decline, which was seen in the War of the Spanish Succession. We must go to the field of battle to behold the genius of Marlborough in its highest perfection. He may have been equalled as a tactician, but he has never been surpassed; his judgment in placing an army on the ground and in detecting the vulnerable points of an enemy; his constancy in pressing an attack home at the spot where success would be most complete, and his wonderful resource and calmness in peril, were unrivalled among the men of his time; and neither Eugene nor Villars can show a Ramillies, a masterpiece of purely tactical skill. For the rest, Marlborough was a great leader of men, like all generals of the first order; and " Corporal John " was as adored by his troops as was the " Little Corporal " of another age. It is melancholy to observe that deep scars of guilt mar the beauty of this magnificent figure; and that we must see in it the dimmed brightness and the ruined glory of the fallen archangel, as well as his majesty and commanding power. Every allowance ought in justice to be made for Marlborough; his crimes were those of a revolutionary age; and few of the leading Englishmen of his day were free from the stain of disloyal, bad faith; but the treason of Brest was a foul deed of wickedness. A singular vein of baseness and meanness ran through, like alloy, this grand nature; and whatever excuses may be made for him, there are " damned spots " upon Marlborough's fame.

CHAPTER III.

FREDERICK THE GREAT.

FREDERICK II. of Prussia, known as the Great, was born in 1712. The associations of his boyhood and early youth were ill fitted to bring out the qualities of a nature which, with many defects, was essentially that of a soldier and statesman. His father, Frederick William, had some parts which entitle him to a place among able rulers ; but, even as a king, he was a harsh tyrant, and in his private life and social relations he was scarcely better than a coarse-minded savage. History has fully dwelt on his strange acts and habits ; how, with ministers mere submissive satellites, he governed his kingdom with a rod of iron ; how he sate, in what was called his Tobacco Parliament, directing the affairs of a growing state according to his despotic fancies ; how he reduced his household to the level of lackeys, caned nobles, ladies, and domestics alike, and was wont to storm against them with oaths and curses ; how, in order to enlarge an overgrown army, he turned Prussia into an immense barrack ; and how he exaggerated in his treatment of his wife and family the barbarities he inflicted on his terrified subjects. That a lad, gifted with fine intelligence, who had a strong will and a genuine sympathy with Letters, Art, and the pursuits of Science, should, as he grew up, regard with disgust this system of cruel and grotesque oppression, and should fiercely resent the inhuman discipline to which he was himself subjected, was only natural and to be expected ; and Frederick and his father seem to have hated each other during several years with a cordial hate. It is unnecessary to dwell on this dreary episode in the life of the great future sovereign; the Crown Prince was beaten, half starved, and drilled into obedience, with a severity that became a byeword; he was forbidden books and liberal studies; and having sought refuge in flight from these unnatural wrongs, he was thrown into prison, condemned to death, and perhaps only escaped a malefactor's fate through the intercession of the Imperial Head of Germany.

In the revulsion of feeling caused by this tyranny, Frederick drew more and more away from the King, his methods of ruling, his ways, and his habits; and when the advent of manhood set him partly free, he surrounded himself with youthful friends of a somewhat wild and licentious turn, indulged freely in the pleasures of his age, and led a life which was a tacit protest against the meanness, the rudeness and the barbarism of the Court. His leisure hours, however, were not wasted; he read a great deal, and to real profit; he attracted several French men of letters to the country house where he passed his time, and, amongst others, made the acquaintance of Voltaire; and though he dabbled in a poetaster's calling, he wrote books which give proof of a keen intellect, not original, but receptive and powerful. He was looked upon, in those days, as a wit and a philosopher of the Parisian type; but this was a superficial judgment, due to the accident of his life of restraints, and the genuine character of the man was completely different. Frederick had far more in common with his half brutish father than, probably, he was himself aware. His instincts were for despotic power; he had, at bottom, the Prussian military taste; and he sympathized with the display of authority in all departments of the State and of Government, and even in the relations of private life, though not exactly after the paternal fashion. As years advanced, too, and his mind developed, he became alive to the real merits, marred as they were by extravagant faults, of the old King's system of administration and rule. Prussia, a weak state in the midst of great monarchies, required a large defensive force, and the Prussian army had been made the best in Europe; Prussia needed an increase of national strength, and during the reign of

Frederick William her population had multiplied and she had grown fast in wealth. The Crown Prince and his father became reconciled; and though, to outward seeming, they were perfect contrasts, they drew towards each other in feeling and thought, and were practically agreed on the national policy. Frederick went to the wars to please his father, and served with some distinction in the last campaign of Eugene, in 1734. Soon after this the King committed a charge to his heir which was, in after years, to become a cause of great events in Europe. The House of Hohenzollern conceived that it had an old claim on the rich lands of Silesia, for centuries a province of the Austrian Monarchy; and Frederick William had often insisted that he had been cheated out of his legitimate rights. Almost in his last days he entreated his son and coming successor to vindicate those rights, in language of passionate wrath and earnestness.

The old King passed away in 1740; and the first act of the Prince, like our Henry V., was to get rid of the Falstaffs and Poinses who had been the former companions of his youth, though he retained his literary friends and tastes, and, indeed, held to them during an eventful life. His second act was to raise the Prussian army, which, in the days of the Great Elector, had never exceeded 40,000 men—and which had seemed of portentous numbers when made 80,000 strong by his late father—to fully 100,000 effective troops, a military force out of all proportion to what was only a third-rate kingdom. Within a few months, he had taken advantage of the bereavement and weakness of Maria Theresa; had laid claim to the whole of Silesia, and had overrun the province with thousands of soldiers before the young Archduchess could even attempt resistance. It was a rapacious and an ignoble act; but, to do him justice, Frederick was no hypocrite; he did not pretend that he was carrying out the injunctions of a revered parent, and he has cynically avowed that his ruling motives were greedy ambition and the desire of fame. It is idle, too, as Macaulay has done, to lay to his charge the whole guilt of the terrible and world-wide contest that followed; the simple truth is that all the Powers of Europe, tired of a long peace and restored in strength, were eager for acquisitions and conquests. France especially sought to regain her influence in Germany, and to weaken her old foe, Austria; and Frederick was not much worse than his crowned fellows.

I must glance at the condition of the military art when Frederick made his first essays in it. There had been little wars and rumours of wars since the great settlement of the Peace of Utrecht, and Austria had overcome the hosts of Islam, but Europe had generally enjoyed repose during the long period of twenty-five years, and there had been nothing resembling the mighty conflicts which had marked the protracted reign of Louis XIV. No occasion, therefore, had presented itself for an exhibition of strategy like that of Turenne, or of tactics like those of Blenheim and Ramillies; and the chiefs of the last great war had died—Marlborough, unlamented, in his rest at Blenheim; Eugene, Villars, and Berwick, covered with honours, and followed to the grave by national mourning. The armies, too, of the great military Powers had been out of joint, and had lost experience and efficiency during prolonged inaction; that of Austria, despite the warnings of Eugene, had been neglected and allowed to decline; the British army had almost gone to' pieces, and that of France, though formidable in numbers and renown, too faithfully represented the feebleness of the State, and the vices of the Regency and of Louis XV. Yet if the art of war seemed thus in eclipse, the theory of war, as usually happens in periods of rest, had had careful students; the elements of military power had grown in Europe, and the facilities to make war on a large scale had been to a certain extent augmented. Saxe, about this time, had done a good deal in simplifying and quickening manœuvres in reviews; Montalembert, struck by the immense advantage secured to the attack by Vauban's methods, had begun to think of transforming fortresses, and experience of the bayonet had caused the numbers of the infantry in every army to be considerably increased, and had made infantry formations more light and flexible. The general growth of population, too, had made the available resources of war greater; the progress of husbandry and the development of roads had enlarged the possible scope of strategy; and the spirit of the age, more humane and civilized, was opposed to the devastation and waste practised in the wars of the seventeenth century, and even to such expedients as great defensive lines, which necessarily injured whole tracts of country. The art, therefore, though it had recently had no grand illustration, was in a state in which progress was at least possible ; and a European struggle, there was reason to believe, might bring into the field armies more numerous and more easily moved than ever had been the case formerly. The most striking military fact of the time remains, however, to be yet noticed. While all other armies had relatively declined, that of Prussia had, I have said, grown to dimensions amazing for so small a State, and her army of 100,000 men was, even in mere numbers, in 1741, considerably greater than that of Austria, and only less, by a third, than that of France. Nor were mere numbers anything like a test of the real military power of the Prussian army. Frederick William's mania for big Grenadiers and for giant Guards may appear ridiculous ; but the King had doubled the strength of the force which he deemed necessary to protect the State ; and his army had become, in his hands, the hardest and best fashioned instrument of war which, hitherto, had been formed in Europe. The subject of his incessant care, it had been drilled, disciplined, and trained in manœuvres by officers of experience and skill, brought up in the great school of Marlborough and Eugene ; and its infantry, in particular, had acquired a precision and celerity of movement, and an efficacy of fire— this last partly due to the iron ramrod, then used by the Prussian soldier alone—which no army in Europe could even nearly equal. An Achilles only was required to prove this mighty weapon of unrivalled temper.

This is not the place to examine the policy of Frederick, in the war of the Succession of Austria. He wrested Silesia from the Empress-Queen, and by alternately taking the side of France and of Austria, and throwing his weighty sword into the scales of Power, the young ruler of a petty monarchy became the arbiter of two-thirds of the Continent. It is indisputable that he had no scruples, and that he often broke faith in this game of ambition ;

but he gave proof of no common statecraft, of precocious dexterity, and of great strength of purpose ; and he has some right to plead at the Bar of History that, with the exception of Maria Theresa, he dealt with Kings and Ministers as false as himself. His kinsman, George II., was not unwilling to see Prussia effaced from the map of Europe, and he was treated by Louis XV. as a mere pawn of France, to be used and sacrificed to promote her objects. Nor shall I dwell at length on the first attempts of Frederick to conduct campaigns and to direct armies. He had not great original genius in war, or in any department of human activity, but his intellect was vivid, penetrating, strong; he was observant, and quick in seizing ideas, and he devoted himself with such steadfast patience to every pursuit undertaken by him that he ultimately became a proficient in it. These faculties made him the first soldier of an age deficient in great commanders ; but his progress as a warrior was slow and uncertain ; and, indeed, his triumphs, even to the last, were rather due, I think, to the force of his character, and the superiority of his disciplined army, than to preeminent excellence in the military art.

The first campaigns of Frederick scarcely require the careful attention of the student of war. He occasionally showed a happy conception, and, as was always his wont, he was prompt and vigorous in taking the initiative and in striking his foe. But he was out-generalled in more than one instance ; and in the campaign of 1744 he narrowly escaped ruin at the hands of Traun, though it is but fair to observe that this was largely caused by the incapacity and tardiness of his French allies. The battles of Frederick during these years—and this is true, indeed, as to his whole career—deserve more notice than his general movements ; and they have this special interest, that they attest the advance he made by degrees in tactics, and the admirable qualities of the army he led. His attack at Mollwitz cannot be justified, for the Austrians held his line of retreat, and defeat, which was probable, would have been destruction. As has often been pointed out, he made no attempt to turn to account the manœuvring power of his troops ; but though he was driven from the field with his horsemen, the terrible fire and the unflinching constancy of his infantry gave him victory at last. At Chotusitz we, perhaps, see the first example of that insight on the ground which became one of his distinctive merits, inferior as he always remained, I think, in this important respect to Marlborough. He charged with his right wing at a critical moment, and the movement possibly assured his success, though the result of the battle was mainly due, beyond question, to his tenacious soldiery. In the operations that led to Hohenfriedberg he displayed no little resource and skill; he lured the Austrians on to make an attack in which the chances were in his favour; and though he committed a mistake in disposing his troops, which the victor of Ramillies would have, perhaps, made fatal—he left a wide gap in an ill-arranged line—still the Austrians did not seize the occasion, and their incoherent and partial efforts were easily defeated by his well-directed movements. It was at Sohr, however, that we see the first instance of the favourite manœuvre employed by Frederick, which, taking advantage as it did of the peculiar excellences of his formidable and highly-trained army, became the means of giving him many a victory, though occasionally he abused it, with disastrous results. By this time it had become evident that his troops infinitely surpassed the sluggish Austrians in rapidity and precision of movement; and like all soldiers, he was, of course, aware that could he attain and turn an enemy's flank without endangering his own position, he would necessarily gain an immense advantage. At Sohr, accordingly, availing himself of the " mobility " and marching power of his army, Frederick turned the Austrian flank with one of his wings, throwing the other back, and only bringing it up when the turning movement had proved successful; and the battle was won by these agile tactics. This manœuvre, repeated on many fields, was the celebrated " attack in oblique order," ever associated with the name of the King, and the theme of a great deal of foolish writing; it has proved successful or unsuccessful as it has been rightly or wrongly adopted; and the first condition of its success, it will be perceived, is the possession of an army more active than its foe, better disciplined, and more exact in its movements.

Prussia was at peace during the ten years that followed the first great defeat of Maria Theresa. Frederick had reached the prime of vigorous manhood, and a word must be said on the character of his rule, and on the tenor and pursuits of his life. His system of government bore a strong resemblance to that of his eccentric father, but with this difference—that mere arbitrary power was tempered by clear-sighted intelligence, and often had enlightened, if ambitious, objects. He was a severe, a meddling, and a pitiless despot; but he checked the abuses of feudal nobles, protected the rights of the middle classes and the poor, enforced toleration in a still bigoted age, as a rule respected justice and law, and, on the whole, had regard to the national interests. The worst features of his *régime* were that he carried the rigid methods of the camp into the free relations of social life, and that he tried to regulate com- merce and agriculture according to crude ideas of his own ; but if he checked the natural expansion of the State, and if his mono- polies and laws of trade did great mischief, and were often failures, still his absolutism was, in the main, beneficent. Prussia was better governed under his stern discipline than any one of the Great Powers of the Continent ; the nation made astonishing pro- gress, and the conquest of Silesia proved a blessing to a people which always detested the Hapsburgs. As for Frederick himself, he was the most industrious and hard-working Head of a State ever seen, and yet he found time for music and art, and for the society of the best men of letters ; and though his quarrel with Voltaire and the jokes and sarcasms he indulged in at the expense of his guests showed that he could be a tyrant even in his hours of ease, he was far the most accomplished Sovereign of his time. As may be supposed, however, the King devoted his chief attention to the care of his army, and everything, in fact, was subordinated to it. He does not appear to have loved war, but he knew that enemies hemmed him round ; he resolved to hold a high place among the leading Powers, and he left nothing undone to bring to perfection the great military instrument he had already proved. The army, growing with the growth of the people, and recruited from the lately-annexed province, was increased from 100,000 to

160,000 men, and it increased in efficiency even more than in numbers. The Prussian cavalry had not been equal to that of Austria in the Silesian war; it was fashioned into a most admirable arm; and it is probable, indeed, that no cavalry has surpassed the squadrons of the renowned Seidlitz. As for artillery, the beginning of horse artillery—a revolution in the arm—may be traced to this time; and while the drill and discipline of the famous Prussian infantry were continued and even largely improved, every effort was made to render its fire more formidable than it had been before, and to cause its evolutions to be more exact and rapid. Frederick's army, in fact, trained to march, to change front, to wheel into line, to gather to a flank, to throw masses of horsemen on a selected point, and, besides, to turn its weapons to the best account, and all this with amazing precision and quickness, was, compared to other continental armies, like a practised athlete to a thick winded clown; and though it was organized still in battalions and squadrons —for corps and divisions came afterwards—its power, "its mobility," its capacity for war, would be deemed wonderful even in our day.

In 1755-6 the occasion came to test again the value of this mighty force. The Empress-Queen had never forgotten Silesia; she thirsted for revenge on one she deemed a robber; and she had succeeded at last in combining a League of the Great Powers against the Prussian upstart, who had exasperated the harlot who reigned at Versailles, and the adulteress supreme in the Muscovite Empire, by his poignant jests on their notorious vices. France, Austria, and Russia agreed to divide the spoils of conquered Prussia among themselves; Sweden and the small German States sought a share of the prey; and it was believed throughout Europe that the Prussian Monarchy, before a year had closed, would be a thing of the past. Frederick saw clearly the extent of his peril, but he saw, too, that he had one chance; the armies of the League were comparatively weak, and, what was more important, were wholly unprepared; he could move his great army at a moment's notice, and he seized the occasion with characteristic energy. Taking the initiative fearlessly, he struck at once, and in the spring of 1756 his trained legions had

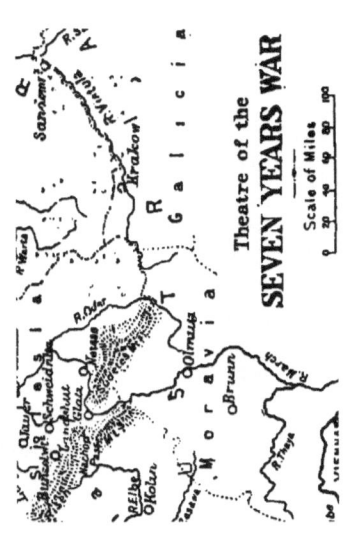

Theatre of the
SEVEN YEARS WAR

Scale of Miles

entered the plains of Saxony, and were pouring through the gaps in the Bohemian hills.

The great War of the Seven Years had begun; and, as regards the military operations of the King, it presents three distinct and well marked phases. France and Russia sent no forces into the field against Prussia in 1756, and Frederick had to cope with Saxony and Austria only, whose united armies were no match for his own. He seized Dresden with an overwhelming force; shut the Saxons up in the entrenched camp of Pirna; and invaded Bohemia in two great masses, the first, under his own command, moving up the Elbe, the second led by Schwerin, a most distinguished veteran, advancing from Silesia, at a great distance, and with the mountains between, by the Pass of Nachod. The Austrian army, inferior in force, on the theatre, probably 60,000 to 90,000 men, was also divided into two parts; Piccolomini, a descendant of a well-known chief of the Thirty Years' War, held Schwerin in check with a comparatively small detachment of troops; Browne, with the principal army, confronted Frederick; and an indecisive battle was fought at Lobositz, on the banks of the Elbe, in which the contending armies seem to have been not far from equal in numbers. The campaign terminated to the advantage of Prussia; Browne failed to disengage the Saxons at Pirna; their army, surrounded, laid down its arms; and Frederick incorporated the men with his own troops, for Germans were usually ready to enter his service. The success was unexpected, and even great; yet, as Napoleon has justly remarked, Frederick might certainly have done more. Schwerin was paralysed by an insignificant force; the King at Lobositz was not stronger than Browne; and in these operations, as often happened, his bold strategy was very far from perfect.

The campaign of 1757, the most memorable of Frederick's career, falls naturally into two parts; and it deserves the close attention of the student of war, for it strikingly illustrates the merits and the defects of this renowned, yet sometimes unsafe, commander. France and Russia, still unprepared, did simply nothing, until the early summer of the year; and Austria, now without Saxon aid, was left isolated for months to sustain the

contest. Frederick was again certainly superior in force; he had
100,000 men at least, the best troops in Europe, against 90,000
Austrians, to a great extent of indifferent quality; and assuming
the offensive he once more invaded Bohemia, by the valley of the
Elbe, Schwerin, as in the preceding year, moving from Silesia,
again separated from the main army, but at a less distance than
in 1756. By the 1st of May the King had sate down before
Prague, having advanced by the western bank of the Moldau; and
Schwerin was still several marches off, with the Elbe and the
Moldau between himself and Frederick. By this time Charles of
Lorraine had taken a position along a series of heights not far
from Prague, and his purpose was not to offer battle until he had
been joined by Daun, moving from Moravia with about 25,000 men.
Frederick, eager to prevent the intended junction, bridged the
Moldau under the eye of the enemy, leaving a detachment upon
the western bank; meanwhile Schwerin had passed the Elbe,
pressing forward to Prague by forced marches; and the two
Prussian armies had come into line by nightfall upon the 5th of
May, the Austrians remaining wholly inactive. The King resolved
to attack before Daun could come up, and by the morning of the
6th his troops were in motion, longing and prepared for a decisive
struggle. The Austrian army, about 60,000 strong, held a defensive
position along a range of hills sinking towards the east into
lowlands and marshes divided by rivers and small lakes; the left
resting on Prague and the Moldau, the centre and right extending
to the hamlet of Kyge, near where the hills fall into the half-
flooded plain. Frederick was probably equal to his foe in numbers,
and judging that the Austrian centre and left could not be forced,
he decided on turning his adversary's right, though the movement
was one of extreme hazard, for it placed his army with its rear
towards Daun, known to be advancing to assist his colleague. The
Prussian army, separated by difficult ground from its enemy,
marched in oblique order, with extraordinary speed and precision;
and it had soon fastened on the Austrian right, making fierce
efforts to outflank and destroy it. Lorraine, however, had thrown
back this wing; it presented a new front to the advancing foes,

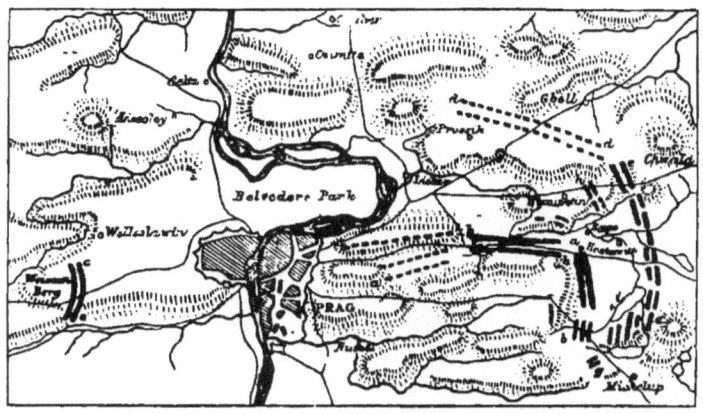

BATTLE OF PRAG
6TH MAY 1757.

a.a.a. First position of Austrian Army.
b.b.b. Second position to meet the Prussian Attack.
c.c. Prussians under Kieth.
d.d. First position of Prussian Army
e.e. Second position of Prussian Army.
f. Schwerin's Prussians.
g. Prussian Horse.
h. Mannstein's Attack.
i. Place of Schwerin's Monument.

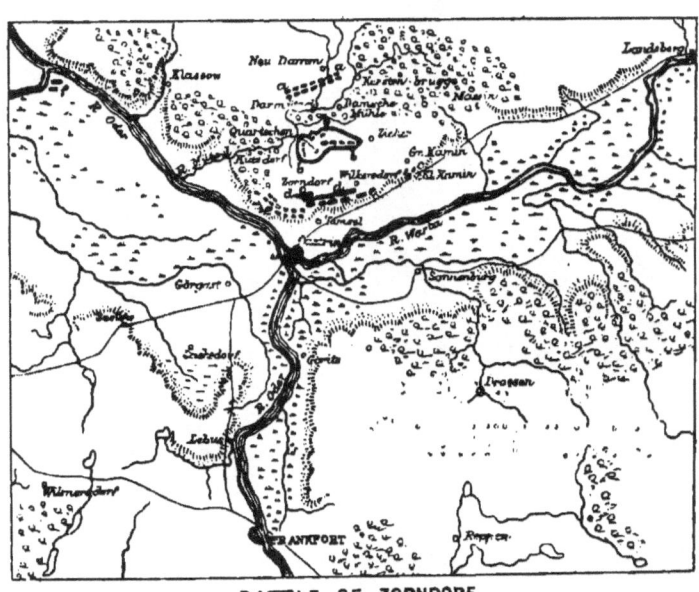

BATTLE OF ZORNDORF
25TH AUGUST, 1758.

a.a. Prussian Army about to cross the Mützel.
b.b.b. Russian Army ranked for Battle.
c. Russian Baggage.
d.d. Prussian Infantry.
e.e. Prussian Cavalry.
f. Prussian Baggage.

and the attack of the Prussians was greatly impeded by the
swamps and ponds covering the Austrian line, which made it
difficult in the extreme to pierce. The battle raged for some hours
with uncertain fortunes ; but the Austrian left and centre continued
motionless, and did not even attempt a counter attack, although
the occasion was most promising. A gap was formed in the angle
where the right of Lorraine had been thrown back from the main
body ; Frederick kept pouring troops against the enemy's flank,
and after prodigious efforts, in which the aged Schwerin, a pupil
of Marlborough, met a soldier's death, the Austrian right was at
last broken, and the whole Austrian army lost the position, 12,000
men having been cut off from Prague and compelled to seek refuge
in the camp of Daun.

Frederick had shown great tactical skill in this battle, and constancy of a high order ; he had detected the vulnerable point in
his enemy's line, and he never relaxed his efforts until he had
gained the day. In this instance, too, his favourite movement
was justifiable in many respects ; the Prussians gathered on the
Austrian flank, protected by difficult ground between, and a
counter attack would have been no easy matter. Nevertheless,
his success was largely due to the immense superiority of the army
he led. Compared to the sluggish Austrians, as has been said, it
was "a panther darting upon an ox." Had Charles of Lorraine
been a great chief, he would have paralyzed the attack by a
movement from his left; and had this succeeded, Frederick, not
improbably, would have been hemmed in between the Prince and
Daun. In this part of the campaign, as in many cases, the strategy
of the King was essentially faulty ; and had he had to deal with
a general like Turenne, he would have been baffled, out-manœuvred,
and forced to retreat without having a chance of fighting a
decisive battle. The invasion of Bohemia on a double line by
the Elbe and Silesia, at far distances, seems to have been justified
by recent events—any other operation is, besides, difficult in the
case of an attack from Prussia—but the principles of the art do not
vary ; and, as Napoleon has said, this strategy gave the Austrian
chiefs an immense advantage. Charles of Lorraine, firmly estab-

lished in Prague, and holding a central position between the King
and Schwerin, ought to have prevented their junction with ease;
and had he been anything like a master of war he would have
marched against each, and beaten both in detail. The King, too,
committed great mistakes—in bridging the Moldau within reach
of his enemy; in leaving a detachment on the western bank, when
he had made up his mind to fight a great battle; and, above all, in
venturing to place his army exposed on its rear to the army of Daun.
Had Charles of Lorraine had the gifts of Condé, the Prussian army,
superior as it was, would have bitterly rued these false movements.

The King, after his victory, besieged Prague; but his sieges
were scarcely ever successful. He drew no lines round the
beleaguered fortress, but contented himself with a mere blockade;
and it was well for him that Charles of Lorraine remained
motionless, and made scarcely a sally, for, as Napoleon has
pointed out, an active enemy would have made Frederick pay
dear for his rash conduct, a remark which proves what would have
been the judgment of the Emperor on Bazaine at Metz. After six
weeks of delay round Prague, the King was obliged to move a
large part of his army to encounter an approaching army of relief.
Daun had fallen back after the defeat of his colleague, having
rallied the 12,000 fugitives of Prague; but ere long he was
reinforced, and by the second week of June he had reached the
Elbe, and was drawing near Prague with 50,000 men. Frederick
marched to oppose him with an army not less probably than
40,000 strong; and on the 18th—a great day in war—Daun was
discovered holding a strong position, extending from near the
Elbe at Kolin, along eminences, with an open country in front,
to the hamlet of Hradschin. The King, elated perhaps by his
recent victory, resolved to repeat the successful manœuvre of
Prague; neglecting the Austrian centre and left, he decided on
falling on Daun's right, and the Prussians once more marched,
in their usual fashion, to storm a village and heights that overlook Kolin. Frederick, however, seems not to have reconnoitred
the ground, and to have held his adversary in complete contempt;
his left, as it gathered on the Austrian flank, had exposed itself

to a counter-attack, for the field allowed this offensive movement ; and, besides, the oblique order was not properly kept, for his right wing and centre were scarcely thrown back, and simply followed the advancing left. The movement, in fact, was a flank march, within reach of an enemy able to strike home ; and the result, as usually happens, was a great disaster. The Prussian left was checked by a body of cavalry ; Daun crushed the centre and right by well-placed batteries ; and though he did not cause his army boldly to engage, he moved it forward so that his enemy was ravaged by a storm of destructive missiles, and ran the gauntlet of deadly musketry. The Prussian left, isolated, was at last routed, though it fought with courage worthy of all praise ; and the whole army was driven from the field with a loss of fully a third of its numbers.

Pedants, who have deemed the attack in oblique order a talisman which assures victory under all conditions of place and position, have tried to explain away this crushing defeat ; but Napoleon's judgment is evidently correct. Frederick made a flank march in open ground, under the beard of Daun, within striking distance, and the result was like what occurred at Austerlitz. Kolin forced the King to raise the siege of Prague, to abandon Bohemia, and to fall back on Silesia ; and had his antagonists been great generals, he might have been overwhelmed before he had passed the ranges which overlook the Silesian lowlands. But Lorraine did not even break up from Prague till July, many days after the battle ; Daun, a stout soldier of the school of Wallenstein, fond of entrenched camps and defensive lines, but in no sense of the word a strategist, lost a week in chanting Te Deums in his camp, to use Napoleon's sarcastic phrase ; and Frederick effected his escape with little further loss, and held positions between Zittau and Bautzen. Nearly two months passed in petty operations, the Austrians plainly shunning a contest, and taking no advantage of their splendid success, when the apparition of new and formidable enemies on the scene compelled the King to retreat towards the Lower Elbe.

We have now reached the second phase of the war, and the second part of the campaign of 1757. Up to this time

6

Frederick had had to cope almost wholly with the Austrians only, and had been superior in force on the theatre of war; the balance was now heavily inclined against him, and it was the conviction of Europe, as it had been from the first, that he would be annihilated by the League of the Continent. France had by this time two armies in Germany; the one 80,000 strong, under the command of D'Estrées, the second not less than 50,000 men, partly composed of contingents of the small German States, led by Soubise, one of the Pompadour's favourites; and Turenne and Villars had overrun Germany, and threatened Vienna with less forces. Meanwhile, Sweden had assailed the Pomeranian seaboard; a Russian army of 60,000 men had crossed the Niemen and attained the Pregel; and though the forces of the Allies were far apart, and D'Estrées was held in check for the time in Hanover by the Duke of Cumberland—the warrior of Fontenoy and Culloden —it seemed impossible that Prussia could withstand the enormous masses arrayed against her. Frederick, always great in the hour of danger, saw what was before him, and made up his mind; though still suffering from the effects of Kolin, he resolved to advance at once against his nearest enemy, Soubise, who had approached the Saale, in the hope of striking a decisive blow; and leaving about 40,000 men to keep the Austrians back, he marched with about 25,000—he had lately been reinforced—to make head against the French commander. Soubise, a degenerate scion of the great House of Rohan, and one of the poorest creatures who ever led an army, though nearly double in numbers, fell back before the King; and several weeks were lost in petty manœuvres, Soubise always seeking to avoid fighting, conduct fatal beyond all others to French soldiers. The news of the success of the Allies elsewhere on the theatre at last, however, compelled the French chief to abandon his timid attitude, and towards the close of October the army of Soubise returned to the Saale, and crossed the river, though it recrossed at the approach of its enemy. On the 5th of November, the Prussian army, which had made a short retrograde movement, was encamped, perhaps 22,000 strong, in a position near the Saale, with its left at Rossbach; and Soubise, who had fully 45,000 men,

SEIDLITZ AT ROSSBACH.

thought that he had caught Frederick, and could cut off his retreat. Full of the theory of the oblique order, but utterly ignorant how to apply it, he defiled in loose and irregular masses, without even an advanced guard, under the eye of his adversary, and well within his reach, in order to fall on his rear, and to turn his right; and the result of this insensate flank march was ruinous and most disgraceful defeat. Frederick, watching like a bird of prey its quarry, allowed Soubise to march to his fate; then changing his front, moving on the chord of an arc, and screening his operations with great skill, he smote the heads of the allied columns, unprotected and surprised, with the fire of well-placed batteries and the charges of the renowned horsemen of Seidlitz; and the whole army of Soubise was literally scattered and half-destroyed by the efforts of a force of only 6,000 or 7,000 men.

Rossbach was one of Frederick's most brilliant victories; Soubise was effaced for the rest of the campaign, and his shattered forces re-crossed the Rhine. The result of the battle was evidently due to the stupid false movement of the allied chiefs; but the King turned this to the best account, and his tactics were in all respects admirable. This triumph greatly strengthened the Prussian cause, and sent a thrill of exultation through German hearts; for Rossbach was the first great fight in which Germans, led by a German, had defeated Frenchmen; and the traditions of the day kept hope alive in the breasts of many a German soldier during the sad years that followed the rout of Jena. The arms of the King, however, had been unsuccessful on other parts of the theatre of war; and, as the close of 1757 approached, his position was one of increasing danger. A contingent of Swedes had, indeed, been driven from Pomerania and forced into Stralsund; but the Russians had gained a great victory at Jägersdorf, near the banks of the Pregel; and though they had re-crossed the Niemen as winter came on, the army opposed to them had been severely treated. The chief peril, however, which threatened Frederick came from Austria and Maria Theresa, his implacable and untiring enemy. Lorraine and Daun had been largely reinforced after Kolin, and ordered to press forward; and at the head of probably 90,000 men, they gradually bore back and

6 *

drove towards the Oder the detachment, not perhaps half in numbers, which the King had given to his lieutenant, Bevern. The Austrian generals seem to have thought that their mission was to reconquer Silesia; they besieged and captured Schweidnitz and Breslau; Austrian horsemen were let loose on the province; and Bevern was defeated under the walls of Breslau with terrible loss, and was ere long a prisoner.

The intelligence reached the King some three weeks after Rossbach; his decision was formed with his wonted promptness, and he hastened to the Oder by forced marches, from the Saale across the lowlands of Saxony. On the 3rd of December he had joined hands with Ziethen, one of his best officers, who had succeeded to the command of Bevern; but the united armies were not more than 35,000 or 36,000 men, for death and desertion had carried off thousands. The Austrians were still probably 75,000 strong—they were certainly in immensely superior numbers—and it seems astonishing that Lorraine and Daun did not try to trample the enemy in the dust who was moving against them from Glogau upon the Oder, and could not have had even half their force. The memory of Rossbach, however, was, perhaps, too recent; and, leaving Breslau, they took a position, defensive as usual, along eminences that look down on the village of Leuthen. The left, under Lorraine, approached the Schweidnitz, a feeder of the Oder, but with a broad space between; the centre held a long line behind Leuthen, with hills and ravines before its front; and the right, with Daun in command, stretched down to a forest and hamlet known by the name of Ny-pern. Frederick, having carefully reconnoitred the ground, put his army in motion early on the 5th of December; an advanced guard was easily driven in; and he pushed forward his right as quickly as possible, to turn and outflank the enemy's left. This time, however, the attack in oblique order was a most skilful and well-planned movement; the Prussian centre and left were thrown back until the effort of the right had told; what was more important, the army marched, screened by the valleys and hills, before the Austrian front; a thick mist, too, hung over the plain, and concealed the advance of the Prussian

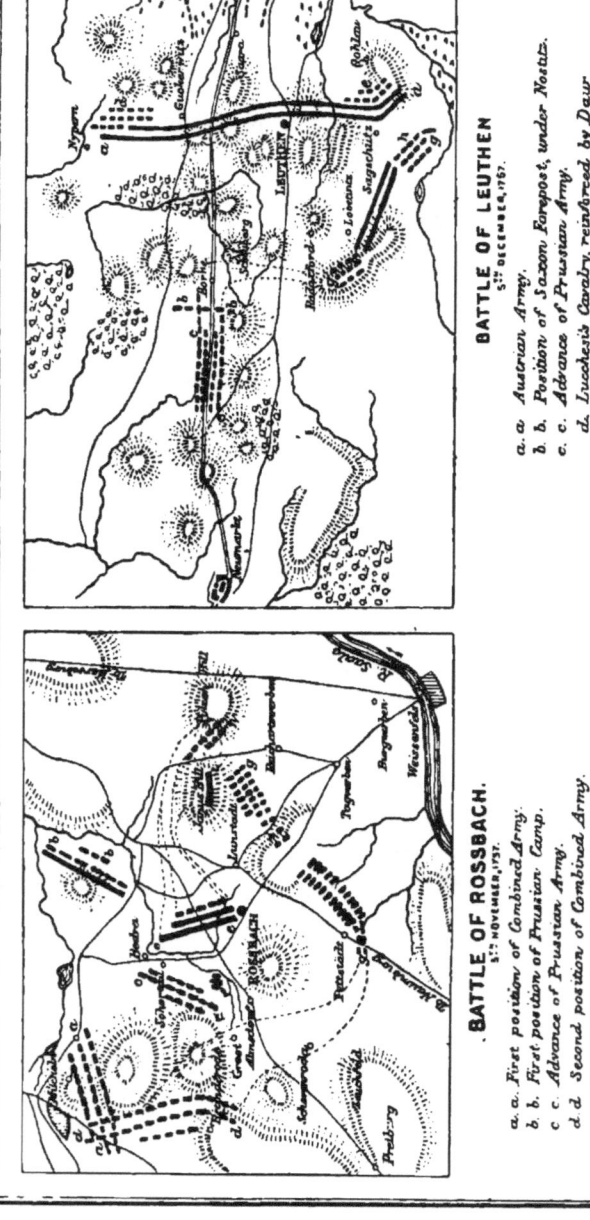

BATTLE OF ROSSBACH.
5ᵀᴴ NOVEMBER, 1757.

a. a. First position of Combined Army.
b. b. First position of Prussian Camp.
c. c. Advance of Prussian Army.
d. d. Second position of Combined Army.
e. e. Prussians retire to Rossbach.
f.   French Cavalry, under St. Germain.
g. g. March of Combined Army, to attack Prussian rear.
h.   Prussian attack led by Seidlitz.
     i. Position of Prussian Guns.

BATTLE OF LEUTHEN
5ᵀᴴ DECEMBER, 1757.

a. a. Austrian Army.
b. b. Position of Saxon Forepost, under Nostiz.
c. c. Advance of Prussian Army.
d.   Lucchesi's Cavalry, reinforced by Daur
e.   Left wing, under Nadasti.
f.   Fredrick's hill of observation.
g. g. Prussian Army about to attack.
h.   Ziether's Cavalry
     i. i. i. Retreat of Austrians

line; and this, therefore, was not a flank march within easy reach of a well-placed enemy. The Prussian right had soon turned and beaten the troops of Lorraine, which happened to be about the worst in the Austrian army; and though the Prince endeavoured to throw back his left, and to form a new front, as he had done at Prague, his efforts proved fruitless, and his whole wing was routed. The centre and left of the King now bore down in irresistible force on the shaken army; and though the Austrian chiefs did all that brave men could do to restore the fortunes of the day, and Daun especially made a bold attempt to advance the Austrian right for a great counter attack, their exertions ultimately were of no avail, and they were driven, utterly defeated, beyond the Schweidnitz. The losses of the victors were not more than 2,000 or 3,000 men; those of the vanquished were fully 15,000, with, it is said, 150 guns; and Breslau, with a very large garrison and all the wounded and sick of the Austrian army, was in a few days in the hands of Frederick. Lorraine and Daun fled from Silesia as best they could, and the situation of affairs, from the Elbe to the Oder, had been completely transformed by a single battle.

"Leuthen," says Napoleon, "is Frederick's masterpiece"; an army, "wholly inferior in force and partly composed of beaten troops," defeated and routed an army two-fold in numbers, and that too with insignificant loss. The victory is the glory of the attack in oblique order, for the Austrian left was turned and destroyed without endangering the assailing army; the Prussian centre and right were engaged at the fitting time; and though a counter attack was tried, it failed, partly owing to the difficulties of the ground, which with the mist had screened the King's offensive movement. But, as Napoleon has rightly observed, the attack in this instance had nothing in common "with a flank march in the face of your enemy"; and it was "in conformity with true principles." The League against Frederick remained unbroken, notwithstanding the reverses of 1757; and in 1758 he had still to confront France, Austria, Russia, and the lesser States of Germany. The odds against him were still enormous; but the armies of the Coalition were widely scattered—Maria Theresa alone had

her heart in the contest—and Frederick had gained one great
ally which has often turned the scale in wars on the Continent.
By this time the first Pitt was supreme in England; he was engaged in a death struggle with the French for empire in India, and
in the Far West; and he turned his eye of genius on the heroic
warrior who had conquered at Rossbach, at Prague, and at
Leuthen. The minister supported Frederick with a small contingent of troops, and lavished on him immense subsidies, which
the King turned to excellent account; and Prince Ferdinand of
Brunswick, a very able man, replaced the Duke of Cumberland,
and opposed the forces of France on the Weser, the Rhine, and the
Main, with an army made up of German auxiliaries. I cannot
dwell on these operations, disgraceful in the very highest degree
to the fribbles and fops who now led the armies of France at the
Pompadour's bidding; suffice it to say that the Prince of Clermont
and poor Soubise were completely beaten, and the French were
driven again beyond the Rhine.

I turn to the theatre of war on the Elbe and the Oder, where
Frederick directed the forces of Prussia. At the beginning of the
campaign of 1758, he had one army on foot in Silesia, threatening
Daun, who had replaced Lorraine, and had fallen behind the Bohemian hills; a second army, under Prince Henry of Prussia, confronted the forces of the small German states in Saxony and along
the Elbe; a third observed the Russians upon the Oder, and the King
had perhaps 140,000 men to oppose to 250,000, not reckoning the
French and Prince Ferdinand's army. The disparity of numbers was,
therefore, immense; but Frederick had all the shorter lines on the
theatre; the Russians could do nothing for months; and the
occasion was one from which Turenne would have probably drawn
no little advantage. Strategy, however, was the weak point of
Frederick; and his first operations in this campaign show small
comprehension of the art of war. Instead of attacking Daun,
inferior in force and isolated, he had recourse to the methods of
the second-rate chiefs of the seventeenth century, now long
exploded; he invaded Moravia, and laid siege to Olmütz, as if the
capture of the fortress, important as it is, could have been attended

with great results. The siege, too, was conducted without regard
to military rules, and the science of the engineer; lines were not
drawn to invest the place; the besieging army was left exposed
in widely divided camps that invited an attack; and, above all,
the supplies required for the siege were drawn from Neisse, at a
great distance, and through the difficult passes of the Silesian
range. It was fortunate that, at this juncture, the recollections of
Leuthen paralysed Daun. Had he fallen on the besieging army, he
might have destroyed it; but though he loitered for weeks, and
remained inactive, he did not wholly throw away the occasion.
With the assistance of Loudon, the most brilliant chief of Austria
in the Seven Years' War, he contrived to intercept and destroy
a convoy directed from Neisse, with munitions for the siege; and
the King recoiled from Olmütz deservedly baffled. Frederick was
now in a situation of grave peril; he was almost surrounded by
Daun and Loudon; his army was in want and distress; and had
Daun been a great commander he would either have forced it
against the Bohemian hills, or made it run the gauntlet of ever-
harassing foes, defeat in either instance involving ruin. The King,
however, was always great in such crises of fortune; out-manœuv-
ring and gaining on his slow adversary, who never knew what
promptness can effect in war, he advanced from Olmütz into
Bohemia, and then, hastening along the verge of the hills, he
emerged successfully into Silesia, making his way through the
passes without loss. The march was one of the most brilliant
and daring of the war.

These operations lasted from the opening of the campaign until
the end of July 1758. Frederick had suffered no defeat like that
of Kolin; but he had missed an opportunity to strike Daun, and
he had only escaped a disaster at Olmütz by his admirable presence of mind and energy. The Russians meanwhile had crossed
the Niemen and the Vistula, and had attained the Oder; and,
about the middle of July, they had attacked Cüstrin, and drawn
near the detachment advanced to hold them in check. The King
marched from Silesia against this fresh enemy; the Russian
chief, Fermor, when informed of his approach raised the siege,

and on the 25th of August had taken a position in a marshy plain in the angle between the Oder and Warta, and overlooking the little hamlet of Zorndorf. His army, about 55,000 strong, was separated from its baggage, left in its camps, and it was drawn up in a huge rectangle, a kind of formation which had proved most formidable to the Turkish hordes, but ill fitted to resist a European army. Frederick, with perhaps 35,000 men, and evidently treating his enemy with contempt, marched right round the vast immovable mass, and attacked it with his left in his wonted manner. His guns wrought frightful havoc in the densely-packed square; but he had once more risked a flank march in open ground, and Fermor flung a ponderous force on the advancing wing, which was nearly crushed by the Muscovite onset. The battle raged for some hours with the most savage fury; the Russians displayed the dogged courage of their race, but Seidlitz and his splendid horsemen turned the scale at last, and Fermor sullenly retired from the field, the victors, however, being unable to seize his baggage or to turn their success to the least advantage.

Having thus disposed of this tenacious foe, Frederick was compelled to retrace his steps towards the Elbe, for his presence in this region had again become necessary. Daun, after his partial success in Moravia, had not advanced, as he ought to have done, and joining the army of the lesser German States, had not overwhelmed Prince Henry of Prussia, an operation which was within his power; but he had not been altogether inactive. He had detached Loudon to fall on the King; he had laid siege to Neisse in Silesia, and he had made a movement which threatened Dresden, timid half measures showing the very poorest strategy. Frederick had reached Dresden by the second week of September, confounding the projects of his hesitating foe; and he set off ere long to relieve Neisse, at the head of about 40,000 men, Daun menacing his flank in his camp at Stolpen. A pause in the operations followed, due probably to the formidable attitude of Daun; but, by the close of September, the King had attained Bautzen in full march for the beleaguered fortress. By this time Daun had been rejoined by Loudon; their united forces must have been from 75,000 to 90,000 strong, and the Austrian chief had taken a position at Hochkirch, amidst woods and hills, barring an advance on Neisse. Frederick was close to Hochkirch by the 11th of October; he did simply nothing for two days, for he was waiting the arrival of supplies from Bautzen; and, confident that Daun would not venture to attack, he felt assured that when his preparations were made, he could easily turn the position of his foe. He paid dearly for his imprudent scorn of an adversary who, though not a great chief, was by no means a contemptible soldier, and who was seconded, besides, by a very able lieutenant. Daun had had ample time to satisfy himself of the numerical weakness of the hostile army; his arrangements were made on the night of the 13th, and on the morning of the 14th, he attacked in full force, and all but hemmed in the astounded Prussians, who, caught and surprised, were completely routed. The King extricated himself with extreme difficulty, and at a loss of fully 10,000 men; but, as usual, Daun made no use of success, and Frederick plucked safety and glory from imminent danger. Always rising superior to adverse fortune, he fell back a short distance only, and perceiving that Daun continued motionless, he actually stole a march on his inactive enemy as soon as his army was fit to march, and made for Neisse with extreme celerity. This was a stroke of extraordinary boldness and skill; and Frederick gained his object, with a defeated army, in the face of a victorious and immensely superior enemy. The siege of Neisse was raised on the 5th of November; Daun, instead of closing on Frederick's rear, having idly turned aside to menace Dresden, a demonstration that altogether failed.

The campaign of 1758, like that of 1757, shows the true qualities of Frederick in war; they were those of an inferior strategist, of a tactician of a very high order, but who sometimes made surprising mistakes, and was specially prone to underrate his enemy, and of a chief who, possessing a noble army, occasionally gave proof of extraordinary resource, and, in particular, was able to subdue dangers which would have overwhelmed a less determined captain. The King ought to have defeated Daun in the first months of the contest, when the Austrian commander stood almost alone ; he should not have attempted the siege of Olmütz ; he should not have risked a flank march at Zorndorf, incapable of manœuvring as the Russians were ; above all, he should not have pitched his camp at Hochkirch, and given Daun a grand opportunity to strike, simply because he thought him a dull commander. On the other hand, Zorndorf was a real victory, no doubt due in a great degree to Seidlitz, but partly also to the energy of the King. Frederick completely baffled his foes at Dresden, and his conduct after Hochkirch in bearding the victors, in eluding them, and in raising the siege of Neisse, was that of a soldier of wonderful powers, though he owed his success mainly to the inactivity of Daun.

There is a sameness in the course of the Seven Years' War, which in some measure detracts from its interest. The contending armies held nearly the same positions in 1759, when the campaign opened, as had been the case in 1758, and their relative strength was nearly in the same proportions. The French, under Contades and De Broglie, invaded Hanover from the Rhine and the Main ; they were opposed as before by Prince Ferdinand, and though De Broglie gained some success at Bergen—the first and last smile of fortune in this war on France—they were ultimately defeated with heavy loss at Minden—a day memorable for the bravery of the British contingent, and for the incapacity of Lord George Sackville—and they fell back discomfited behind the Rhine. In Central Germany, Frederick was again in Silesia and Prince Henry once more in Saxony ; Daun was outside Bohemia and the Silesian frontier, and the forces of the small German States on the Saxon plains ; and the Russians who, after Zorndorf, had returned to their steppes, were still hundreds of miles distant, and had not even drawn near the Vistula. Apart from the French and Prince Ferdinand's armies, Frederick had still perhaps 120,000 men to oppose to 200,000 or 220,000 ; but as had happened in the two preceding campaigns, he was not inferior in force, where he was in supreme command, for the Russians were, for some months, outside the immediate sphere of action. In these circumstances he might once more have at-

tempted to strike a weighty blow at Daun, and Napoleon condemns
him for missing the chance ; but the Prussian army had suffered
immense losses, and was now crowded with ill-trained levies ; and
he deserves less censure for this inaction than in the campaign of
1758. Several weeks were spent in small operations, which show
that the strength of the King had begun to decline ; he attempted
nothing resembling a decisive movement, and the war languished
on the space between the Elbe and the Oder. Meanwhile his
enemies had, for the first time, formed something of a real combination against him. The Empress Elizabeth was savage at the
defeat of Zorndorf ; Maria Theresa had not changed, and a
Russian army, fully 70,000 strong, led by Soltykoff, a true Muscovite, was directed to join hands with the main Austrian army,
and to try to crush Frederick with overwhelming numbers.
Soltykoff having crossed the Vistula about the middle of May, was
upon the Oder in the first days of August, having routed a
Prussian body of troops on his march ; Daun, meanwhile, had
despatched Loudon from Silesia to aid the Russian chief, and their
united armies, about 80,000 strong, had soon effected their
junction near Frankfort. Frederick had advanced, to parry the
blow, to the Oder, with perhaps 40,000 or 45,000 men, and the
hostile forces encountered each other at Kunersdorf, close to
Frankfort, upon the 12th of August. The battle is chiefly remarkable for the characteristic stubbornness and tenacity of the
Muscovite infantry. Frederick's manœuvres gained some success
at first ; indeed, Soltykoff was nearly forced into the Oder, but his
men rallied behind a line of entrenchments, and the Prussians
recoiled, hopelessly beaten, from the bloodstained defences The
King lost a third of his army, and nearly all his guns, and was
with difficulty able to get across the Oder.

The situation of Frederick after Kunersdorf was critical in the
extreme, and might have been made desperate. Daun, obeying
Maria Theresa's orders, had advanced from Silesia towards the
lower Oder ; and, when informed of the results of the battle, he
moved slowly to Triebel on the Neisse, about six marches distant
from the victorious army. Had Soltykoff and Daun now combined

their movements, and cordially acted in real concert, they could have opposed fully 120,000 men, in a central position, to Prince Henry and to Frederick and his beaten army ; and as the Prussian forces were widely divided, and could not have been 80,000 strong, not to speak of the demoralization of defeat, Daun and Soltykoff ought to have crushed their enemy. The discords and jealousies of a Coalition, as has often happened, perhaps, saved the King and his fortunes at this perilous juncture. The Austrian and Russian generals disliked each other ; the policy of their Courts had already begun to diverge on the question of the Turkish Empire ; and Soltykoff was indignant that he had been joined only by the detachment sent forward by Daun under Loudon. The Russians and Austrians did not unite, as was quite possible, about the 25th of August, and Frederick turned this brief respite to the best advantage. His shattered army was reinforced by levies from the north ; the artillery he had lost was replaced from Berlin ; and he was soon at the head of 40,000 men, while Prince Henry had thrown himself, with no ordinary daring, between the two hostile armies. Daun fell back towards Saxony in the first days of September, completely giving up the object of the campaign ; before long Soltykoff was in full retreat, and had recrossed the Vistula by the approach of winter ; and thus Kunersdorf proved an all but barren victory ; Frederick had once more escaped from the toils, and the two Empresses saw their projects frustrated.

The campaign, nevertheless, was a losing one to the King, and it terminated in a very great disaster. During the time when he had been compelled to move to the Oder, in order to face the Russians, the army of the small German states, with some aid from Daun, had taken the offensive upon the Elbe ; and, after capturing Torgau and Wittenberg, it had laid siege to Dresden towards the end of August, the city, it will be recollected, having been in the hands of the Prussians since 1756, and being their main depôt and place of arms. The attack had been unsuccessful until the news of Kunersdorf reached the commandant, with a letter from the King, empowering him to treat and to withdraw the garrison ; the capitulation was signed in the first days of

September, and the portal of Bohemia and the main strategic point of Saxony were thus permanently lost to Frederick, who stormed in vain against his ill-used subordinate. The fall of Dresden was a great reverse, but it was followed by a still greater misfortune. The King, after the failure of the allied armies to join hands, had remained in observation for a time on the Oder; but towards the close of October he fell ill, and for some weeks he was unable to do anything. Prince Henry, meanwhile, had followed the movements of Daun, and had marched into Saxony; and a series of petty operations followed, which are not worthy of special notice. By November, Frederick, himself again, had marched into Saxony and approached Dresden; and, with a want of perception difficult to understand, he committed a mistake, in Napoleon's judgment the most inexcusable of his chequered career. Daun was at the head of his army in Saxony; a large Austrian garrison was in Dresden; and there was no reason to imagine that this resolute soldier was contemplating a retrograde movement. The King, however, took it into his head that his adversary was about to retreat into Bohemia; and always despising Daun, spite of Kolin and Hochkirch, he sent off 12,000 men from the main army to intercept the supposed movement. The officer in command protested in vain; Daun closed on his foe in irresistible force; and the whole Prussian detachment, hemmed in and powerless, was compelled ignominiously to lay down its arms. Napoleon's remarks on the surrender of Maxen possess lasting and peculiar interest for the generation that has witnessed Metz and Sedan.

The third phase of the struggle had now come; Frederick, superior in force until the summer of 1757, was henceforward wholly over-matched by his enemies. The symptoms of decline which had become apparent in the strength of Prussia in 1759 had been greatly aggravated by late events; the losses at Kunersdorf and Maxen had been immense; Frederick had been deprived of some of his best lieutenants, and the magnificent army with which he had begun the war had been reduced to a mere skeleton. On the other hand, his obstinate resistance had exasperated his foes; even the listless and worthless Louis XV., notwithstanding the terrible reverses of France in Canada, in Hindustan, and upon every sea, began to be ashamed of defeats on the Rhine and the Weser ; and Maria Theresa and Elizabeth continued united in their thirst for vengeance. The Coalition made gigantic efforts to bring the unequal contest to a close ; France placed 140,000 men on the Main and the Rhine ; in Silesia Loudon had 50,000 ; Daun was at the head of 80,000 troops of the Empress-Queen and the lesser German States, encamped round Dresden and in the Saxon plains ; and Soltykoff commanded 70,000 Russians directed from the Vistula to attain the Oder. To resist these immense masses, the most numerous that had ever been seen in arms in Europe, Frederick could only oppose Prince Ferdinand and 70,000 men to the French army, twofold in numbers ; and though he was still subsidised by the gold of Pitt, and he had a central position between his foes, he had not more than 100,000 men, composed largely of mere recruits, to contend with the great Russian and Austro-German armies. The eagles seemed to be gathering on their intended prey, but Frederick had resources in himself and in the patriotic nation he ruled which the Coalition had not taken into account. His fierce, determined, and heroic nature exhibited itself in its grandest aspect ; extreme as his peril was, he had no thought of yielding ; his centralized and severe government still drew men and supplies from his half-ruined kingdom, and his people, proud of their renowned Sovereign, strained every nerve to fight to the last.

The opening of the campaign of 1760 seemed to portend the speedy ruin of the King ; Loudon forced a Prussian detachment 10,000 strong to surrender at Landshut, in Silesia, a repetition of the disaster at Maxen ; and Frederick vainly attempted to lay siege to Dresden, an operation as unwise as the siege of Olmütz, which Daun frustrated without difficulty, but which, had he been a great general, he ought to have rendered all but fatal. By this time Loudon had captured Glatz, and was overrunning the Silesian plains ; the King, anxious about the annexed province, which Maria Theresa burned to reconquer, set off from Saxony by forced marches ; but Daun followed on a parallel line, and in the second week of August, he had nearly joined Loudon, and closed round Frederick and his much weaker army. At daybreak on the 15th, Loudon attacked Frederick at Liegnitz, near the stream of the Katzbach, the army of Daun being almost in sight; but the double movement was ill-combined, and the King extricated himself, and even gained a victory. His position, however, was still most critical, and had Soltykoff, who had approached the Oder, co-operated with the Austrian chiefs, the King, humanly speaking, must have succumbed. Prince Henry, however, again interposed— a mere demonstration proved sufficient; the jealousies of the Allies did the rest; and Soltykoff, instead of striking down Frederick, merely marched northwards and plundered Berlin, a diversion that proved of no importance. The King, saved from destruction, re-turned into Saxony; the armies of Loudon and Daun diverged; and while Loudon remained in Silesia, Daun followed his adversary with the main army, and took a position at Torgau, on the Elbe. Frederick attacked Daun on the 3rd of November, assailing him at once in flank and front. The attack he conducted in person com-pletely failed; but Ziethen retrieved the fortunes of the day, and the Austrian army was at last defeated. The "hind doomed to death" was not yet to die, and, after many vicissitudes and a mar-vellous escape, Frederick still held his own between the Elbe and the Oder. Meanwhile, as usual, the great French army had invaded Germany, and had accomplished nothing; Prince Ferdi-nand, as heretofore, had held it in check.

I shall pass rapidly over the last scenes of the internecine and protracted contest. The situation of Frederick in 1761 was much the same as in the year before, save that the process of exhaustion had told more on his resources than on those of his enemies. The French Court made really great efforts to repair the humiliation of four years of reverses; it put on foot a magnificent army of not less than 160,000 men, a force, Napoleon has remarked, sufficient to have conquered Germany if properly led; but its chief was the worthless Soubise; and baffled and out-manœuvred by Prince Ferdinand, it returned to its winter quarters without winning a battle. On the true theatre of war in Germany the King was again immensely inferior in force; he had probably less than 100,000 men against 220,000 or 250,000; but these last, as always, were widely divided. The two Empresses recurred to the project which had all but succeeded in 1759. Daun, who had been severely wounded at Torgau, was left in Saxony to confront Prince Henry, and Loudon, now the real chief of the Austrian armies, advanced from Silesia, to unite with Boutourline, a new commander of the Russian forces. The King, utterly outnumbered, had recourse to the antiquated and barbarous method of wasting whole tracts to keep back Loudon; but the Austrian general made his way to the Oder; and, having left a detachment to besiege Schweidnitz, he effected his juncture with Boutourline's army at Jauer, near Liegnitz, at the close of August. Frederick entrenched himself within defensive lines, after the fashion of the preceding century; he had lost the initiative, and waited on his foes, and he was ere long surrounded in his camps at Bunzelwitz by enemies nearly fourfold in numbers. Loudon, a real general, was eager to storm the lines, and, Napoleon thinks, must have destroyed the King had Boutourline concurred in the attack; but Muscovite jealousy interfered once more, and the Russian commander stiffly refused to support his colleague, and marched northwards. Frederick escaped, as had often happened, by a kind of marvel; meanwhile, Daun had remained inactive in Saxony, and the only results of a campaign which should have overwhelmed Prussia were that the Russians established themselves on the Baltic, ready for speedier operations in the following year, and that Loudon captured the great place of Schweidnitz, the key, as it has been called, of Silesia.

1762 was the last year of the war, and as it opened the prospects of the King had never seemed to be so gloomy and hopeless. The circle of his enemies was narrowing round him; Daun and a powerful army held possession of Saxony and the line of the Elbe; Loudon occupied Silesia in great force; the Russians were preparing to march from Kolberg; and the French had 100,000 men in the heart of Germany. Frederick thought that the end had at last come; yet, unshaken by the approach of the tempest, he confronted it with heroic constancy, and like a lion who marks the advance of the hunters, he moved hither and thither with the wrecks of his armies, watching an opportunity to strike with effect, and determined to challenge fortune to the last. As had always happened in the Seven Years' War, the French operations completely failed, and Frederick contrived to recruit his forces with 20,000 Germans in the Austrian service, unwisely disbanded at this supreme moment. Yet these gleams of success appeared extinguished by an event that portended complete ruin; the fall of Pitt in detaching England from Prussia, and depriving her of her only ally, made the cause of the King apparently hopeless. Nevertheless, his grand strength of character was justly recompensed, and at the eleventh hour a series of strange incidents changed the whole state of affairs in Europe. The Empress Elizabeth suddenly died; her successor, Peter, became an ally of the King; and though Catherine, his murderess, who seized his crown, did not adopt the policy of her late husband, Russia withdrew finally from the Coalition. This became the signal of the dissolution of the League; France, disgraced and defeated all over the globe, made an ignominious peace with England and Prussia; and Maria Theresa, left isolated, and threatened by the Turk, the old foe of Austria, was compelled sullenly to give up the contest. The last event of the war was the recapture of Schweidnitz by the Prussian army; Frederick had successfully withstood the Great Powers of the Continent, and all that Austria, that Russia, that France had done had not even wrested Silesia from his hands.

A few weeks after the Peace of Hubertsburg, the King and his army entered Berlin in triumph. The pageant was very different from that witnessed in 1866 and in 1871, when Prussia had driven Austria from her high place in Germany, and had annihilated the military power of France. The magnificence of war was not to be seen; splendid troops did not line the squares and the streets; there was no procession of superb trophies attesting a series of amazing victories. The army which had begun the contest had well-nigh perished; its ranks were filled by men not of the stock of Brandenburg; its standards in rags, and its war-worn aspect attested the vicissitudes and defeats of a long and

7

uncertain struggle. Yet the spectacle was one of enduring interest, big with great results in a far distant future. That army, made up of many elements from different parts of the great German race, like Wallenstein's army of a century before, embodied, however feebly, the as yet vague idea that Germany was a nation of one blood and language; and it was the precursor of the patriotic league which rose and fought for Germany in 1813-14, and of the gigantic hosts which, in our day, conquered the unity of Germany at Sadowa and Sedan. Frederick had no sympathy with what, in his time, was merely a dream of a few enthusiasts; in taste and thought he was through life a Frenchman, and he never really looked beyond Prussian interests, yet he was the second Arminius of the Teutonic race, and the Seven Years' War was a new era for Germany. For many years, however, his own energy, and those of his people, were engrossed in efforts to repair the appalling ruin which had befallen his kingdom. Prussia was a land of desolation when he sheathed his sword; her population had diminished a tenth; her youth, equal to war, had been reduced one sixth; savage hordes from the East had overrun her provinces; every town was darkened with tokens of mourning; Silesia had more than one silent and deserted village. The Government, too, had become more despotic in the course of the war than it had ever been; the pressure of arbitrary taxation was frightful; a prying Inquisition had entered the homes of all, and, as has been said, "everything that was not military violence was anarchy."

Yet the King was never before so revered by his subjects, and he remained the object of their love and esteem in an age when, in the decay of loyalty, every throne of the Continent was being undermined. This profound national sentiment was partly due to the real merits of the King as a ruler, but mainly, no doubt, to the patriotic pride of the martial and ambitious people of Prussia, which has never ceased to boast that, under its Great Frederick, it defeated the armed strength of three-fourths of Europe. This legend, indeed, is to a great extent a fable; the "miraculous," as Napoleon has said, disappears upon an impartial survey of

Frederick's exploits in the Seven Years' War. For many months he was superior in force on the theatre; Austria, all through, was his only determined enemy; Russia was too distant to act with effect, and had a real interest not to weaken Prussia; and France either did not put forth her force, or—the Bellona of Europe—committed the weapons of Condé and Turenne to Soubise and Clermont, in their hands the darts of an impotent Priam. Even as it was, too, on more than one occasion the King must have been overwhelmed and ruined but for the dissensions of the Coalition; and it was his peculiar good fortune that, if we except Loudon—and this able and brilliant chief held high command for a few months only—he had to cope with generals of the third order. Yet admitting all this, and recollecting besides the many military shortcomings of the King—and his errors were sometimes of the gravest kind—still his achievements are justly held by Prussia as a glorious possession above price; they remain, and will for ever remain, a grand monument of what constancy, decision, and energy can accomplish against odds which appeared impossible to resist.

After the termination of the Seven Years' War, Frederick never fought a battle again. He was threatened, indeed, in 1775, by an Austrian invasion to regain Silesia; and in 1778 the Emperor Joseph arrayed a great army against Prussia, to assert his claims to a part of Bavaria. These hostilities, however, came to nothing, and the King was allowed, during a long space of time, to carry out the policy he had laid down for himself. It was a policy of craft and ambition abroad; and Frederick, in his fixed purpose of enlarging Prussia, was a chief author of the partition of Poland, a crime shared by Catherine, and even by Maria Theresa—the conscience of the last was, however, stung—and the cause of unnumbered woes to Europe. His domestic policy remained one of enlightened despotism, of equal laws and of strong government, of arbitrary, but tolerably just, rule; and his kingdom recovered within a short time from most of the effects of the Seven Years' War, and made rapid strides in wealth and prosperity. The King was justly deemed the first sovereign of his age; but the three accomplices in the destruction of Poland suffered cruelly

7 *

for a great national wrong; but for this, Revolution would have
been quelled in France in 1792 and 1793 ; but for this, Austria
would not have bled at Austerlitz, and Prussia and Russia
mourned for Jena and Friedland.   Though the centralized government of Frederick, too, seemed a masterpiece of wisdom and
power, it proved unable to stand the strain of ill fortune, and it
perished with the renowned Prussian army in the agony of
1806–7. Frederick died peacefully in 1786, having survived
nearly all the sovereigns of his time.   One of his last acts was to
form a league against the pretensions of Imperial Austria; but he
was utterly unconscious that a tempest was at hand which was to
destroy the monarchies of the eighteenth century, and to create a
new Prussia out of the wrecks of the old.

I turn to my immediate subject. What is the place of the King
among great commanders ? Frederick had not supreme original
genius ; he was deficient in imagination, and often in judgment ;
but he had a powerful mind, intensely quick perception, activity
and perseverance beyond praise ; and he was endowed, besides,
with a force of character and a steadfastness seldom bestowed on
man. These qualities made him the greatest captain of an age
wanting in masters of the art; and he accomplished wonders, spite
of his many faults, with an army infinitely the best in Europe.
As a strategist, he stands low in the second order ; his ideas were
occasionally sound and brilliant, but the plans of his campaigns
were, for the most part, bad ; and he had not the faculty of those
great combinations which disclose real strategic genius.   Holding,
as he usually did, a central position between enemies widely apart,
he would repeatedly have defeated them in detail had he possessed
the science and the gifts of Turenne ; and had he had to cope, not
with the Lorraines and the Dauns, but with the general of Castiglione and Rivoli, he would have been struck down over and over
again, as the result of his false and ill-directed movements.   His
place as a tactician is much higher. Frederick had real insight
and skill on the field ; he possessed a great deal of Marlborough's
power of detecting the vulnerable points of an enemy, and of
striking at them until success was attained, and his favourite man-

œuvre, when properly understood, is an illustration of the great principle that you should always so place your troops on the ground as to turn it to the best advantage, and to make the most of their powers upon it. Yet the King had not Marlborough's unerring skill; even as a tactician he made great mistakes. He was deservedly beaten at Kolin and Hochkirch; he had the great fault of sometimes losing his temper. There is a bad mannerism in his conduct of battles, and more than once he completely ignored the conditions under which, and under which alone, the attack in oblique order could be risked or justified. The title of Frederick to rank among the first of warriors depends less, in fact, upon his intellectual faculties than upon his grand and extraordinary moral qualities, tenacity, and marvellous strength of character; no general has surpassed him in the rare gift of overcoming difficulties, and escaping from peril; no general, not even Arthur Wellesley, has confronted a huge superiority of force with more calmness and firmness of purpose; no general, not even his countryman Blücher, a subaltern in the Seven Years' War, has excelled him in rising above defeat, and in mastering an enemy who had seemed secure in victory. If Napoleon says truly—and who can doubt it?—that a strong nature is the greatest gift of a chief, Frederick is eminent among the masters of war.

CHAPTER IV.

NAPOLEON.

THE years that followed the peace of Hubertsburg were a period of repose, if not for mankind, at least for five-sixths of Continental Europe. Russia, indeed, half an Asiatic Power, carrying out the designs of Peter the Great, under the rule of a bad but most able woman, advanced beyond the Tanais to the heads of the Euxine; and Austria, deprived of the genius of Eugene, was more than once engaged in a doubtful contest with Islam, formidable even in decay. But France was scarcely involved in war, apart from a naval struggle with England; hardly a shot was fired in despoiling Poland; save for demonstrations that came to nothing, Germany was at peace from the Rhine to the Oder; and though England founded an Empire in Hindustan, and the Great Republic of the Far West was born, the conflicts that led to these mighty events were outside the pale of the European world. As happened after the peace of Utrecht, few occasions arose during this long season of comparative rest for the illustration of the military art, by examples in the field; the chiefs of the Seven Years' War passed slowly away; and their successors in the direction of armies, for the most part men of the third order, were generally content to adhere stolidly to the traditions and methods of that great contest. The attack in oblique order was assumed to be an infallible method to win a battle by theorists who did not understand the difference between Kolin, Rossbach, and Leuthen; and Napoleon has described, with sarcastic pleasantry, how pedants were wont to flock to Potsdam to behold the manœuvres of the Prussian army engaged in movements to turn a flank at reviews; the great King who still commanded in person, laughing quietly at their shallow conceits. It is remarkable, however, that on the one occasion when Germany was seriously threatened with war, from 1762 to 1791, the strategy and even the tactics of Daun prevailed over those of his renowned antagonist. In 1778 Frederick put two armies in motion to invade Bohemia, by the double line of the operations of 1866; but Loudon and Lacy formed a great entrenched camp. In this position they awaited an attack, interposing between the divided enemy; and the King did not venture even to offer battle.

Meanwhile, changes fraught with momentous results, in the approaching era of world-wide conflict, were gradually making themselves felt in Europe. The armed strength of Russia was immensely increased; and her armies growing with the expanding Empire, though still imperfectly equipped and organized, became instruments of war in the hands of Suvóroff, very different from the half-barbarian hosts which had displayed their savage constancy at Zorndorf and Künersdorf. Simultaneously the military power of Austria, under the rule of the dreamy reformer, Joseph, had relatively declined to a great extent; and the famous Prussian army, though still formidable in numbers, in discipline and in real worth had begun, even in the last years of Frederick, to lose much of its old efficiency; and after his death, it fell distinctly away from the high standard of the Seven Years' War. As for the French army, it had been augmented, and, to outward appearance, had much improved; the Government and the nation had made great efforts to efface the shame of days such as Minden and Rossbach; camps of instruction were formed in parts of the country where the troops were carefully trained and drilled; and the artillery of France, at all times excellent, was remodelled, and became far the best in Europe. Yet the Revolution, already at hand, had impaired the military power of the State; the *noblesse*, still holding all high commands, gave no successors to Condé and Turenne; there were fatal dissensions between the officers and the men; and though the army was very much better than it had been when led by Soubise, it was not the unrivalled army of Louis XIV. It may be said, therefore, that old Europe, from the Niemen to the Tagus, was ill-prepared, at the close of this period, for a great war ; and as for the British army, it was deemed of no account after the disasters of Saratoga and York Town. Concurrently with these changes, the material progress which had been marked in Europe since the seventeenth century, had gone on with increased development, and had continued to affect the conditions of war. While the populations of the different States had multiplied and yielded ample elements of military force, agriculture had made a rapid advance ; and the inventions of the second half of the eighteenth century had given a remarkable impulse to every urban industry. Vast tracts of marsh, of forest, of waste, had been enclosed and brought under cultivation ; new roads and bridges had been largely made ; insignificant hamlets had become towns, and towns had grown into great cities more flourishing and peopled, in some instances, than the older cities they had, in fact, supplanted. As the general result, from a military point of view, the consequences were that armies in the field could obtain far ampler means of supply than ever had been the case before ; on most theatres of war they would possess more roads and facilities of movement than in previous contests ; and the defensive power of fortresses, for a century in decline, had become less than it had ever been, and, indeed, was of little avail on several frontiers.

This period of repose, as has often happened, was marked by speculations of different kinds on the theory and practice of the Art of War. The military writers of the day, however, were, without exception, inferior men ; and this is strange when we bear in mind that the age was about to behold a display of military genius of the highest order. The great increase of roads and of the means of manœuvring did not suggest to these dull theorists that armies could make more rapid movements, and could concentrate more quickly on given points than had been possible in former times ; on the contrary, these facts gave rise to a notion that it had become necessary, in operations in the field, to separate armies into numerous masses, and to cover all avenues that were liable to attack. This false principle was largely confirmed by the growth in the size of European armies, which had been one of the results of the peace. These, it was assumed, in the event of war, would be developed into vast proportions ; and how was it possible to move these large arrays, save by marching on a greatly extended front, and occupying all the roads on the theatre ? Nor did it occur to these writers that the immense increase in the products of hus-bandry, which had been witnessed in most parts of Europe, might enable armies to draw their supplies more fully from resources on the spot, and, therefore, to move with more ease and freedom than had been conceivable a century before ; they emphatically insisted on the necessity of magazines, and of laying in enormous means of subsistence beforehand; and they believed that war would be more methodical as armies grew into larger dimensions. In theory, strategy became much less bold than in the days of Turenne and Marlborough ; the system of advances upon an im-mense front, holding all the roads, and moving very slowly, with huge trains of impedimenta and supplies, replaced the daring manœuvres of these famous chiefs ; and it contributed not a little to the change that Europe was stirred by no great impulse, that the age seemed indisposed to war, and that military energy appeared deadened through the influences of the last half of the century.

Some progress, however, had been made in tactics, and in the mechanism and formation of armies. The method of the attack in oblique order was still considered the best possible; but means to defeat it had been devised, though these had not yet been proved in the field. Frederick's outflanking movement was a rapid advance, made in line, when the enemy's wing was attained; but, admirable as was the training of the Prussian army, this was always attended with difficulty and delay, especially in broken and intricate ground ; and it was proposed to encounter this by attacks in columns, more flexible and easily handled than lines, these being preceded by clouds of skirmishers—an American idea of the War of Independence—which would cover the onset of the larger masses, and, to a considerable extent, would screen their march. In this way the attack in oblique order, it was argued, might be

met and repelled by a simpler and quicker method of tactics; a
new offensive system might replace the old; and, in any event, an
army ought not to remain passive and to allow itself to be turned
on a wing, as had repeatedly happened in the Seven Years' War.
All this, however, as yet was mere theory, unconfirmed by actual
experience in the field; and, for the rest, the current strategic
notions had made their influence felt in tactics, and movements
widely divided upon the theatre, suggested similar movements in
actual battle. In some respects armies had been much improved;
the increase of their numbers had caused battalions and squadrons
to be formed into brigades and divisions, more unity being given
to the collective mass; the value of horse artillery had been fully
recognized; and, as I have said, France had taken the lead in
bringing her artillery to a high point of excellence.

The Art of War seemed thus in a state of decay, and was being
affected by the new theories, when the French Revolution, like a
volcano, burst suddenly upon a terrified world. The invasion of
Champagne in 1792 was followed by Valmy and Jemmapes;
and, in 1793, the hosts of old Europe gathered in arms against the
bloodstained Republic, which had flung the head of a king to its
foes, and had proclaimed the new Evangel of the Rights of Man on
the ruins of a fallen altar and throne. The military operations of
the next few years were marked by the want of strategic insight,
and by the uncertain and unproved tactics which had grown out of
the speculations of the age: and—apart from the tremendous
issues at stake—are not of enduring and special interest. Not,
indeed, that the wretched failures of the Allies where wholly due
to feeble and bad generalship; they were largely caused by events
in the East of Europe, by the discords and selfishness of the
Coalition, and even by its essential weakness. Beside that they
were not prepared for war, the partition of Poland made the
great German Powers comparatively without resources on the
Rhine; it has been said, indeed, that they had no real wish to
effect the restoration of the Bourbon Monarchy, lest it should
avenge a dark international crime. Austria and Prussia, too, and
the lesser German States were at odds with each other, and would

not act in concert; the avowed purpose of the Allies to dismember France threw an enormous weight into the scale against them; and, at the very crisis of the campaign of 1793, when they could without difficulty have advanced to Paris, they separated their forces in order to reduce strong places meant to be permanently retained.

The timidity, however, and the false principles which marked the conduct of these campaigns contributed mainly to their ignominious end. The chiefs of the Coalition divided their armies in fractions, upon an immense front, extending from the Var to the Meuse and the Lys; they occupied all the main approaches to France; and they moved extremely slowly, and with great magazines and incumbrances, through a most fertile country where celerity was of supreme importance, and where their troops could find ample supplies on the spot. As the inevitable result, their forces were weak at every point of their enormous line, and were nowhere able to strike with effect; they were actually unequal to passing fortresses which they sate down to besiege and occupy, though a relieving army was seldom at hand; and their advance was so tardy and beset by hindrances, that they gave France what she most needed—time to organise her strength and to make the war national. The errors, however, of the new strategy were conspicuous also on the French side, though not, perhaps, in such great proportions. The French armies, like those of their foes, were usually disseminated on a vast front, and were, therefore, feeble on the whole theatre; and though Carnot made one or two good movements, and showed that he knew the importance of interior lines along the space between the Rhine and the Lys, the plans of his campaigns as a rule were bad, and displayed the same defects as those of the Allies. On the other hand, the operations of the French were more rapid than those of their enemies; having no magazines and impedimenta of the kind, they flung themselves like a horde on the country, lived on it, and yet appeared in the field; but though this system made their movements more quick, their efforts were usually ill-directed, and had the Coalition shown skill and energy, it must have triumphed in 1793–94. The tactics of the belligerent armies were also influenced by recent theories, and were tentative, unsettled, and in a state of transition. The Prussians attacked, at Valmy, in the oblique order, but they were driven back by the fine French artillery; the Austrians, at Jemmapes, followed the methods of Daun, awaited the enemy in a strong position, and were overwhelmed by superior numbers. In other engagements the Allies adopted the system of attack in ill-combined columns, and were often beaten by their more active foes. More regularity is seen in the tactics of the French, though these as yet were quite immature and imperfect. The practice of advancing in columns, with skirmishers in front, borrowed from speculations already known, fell in well with the existing state of the revolutionary military power of France; the myriads of young levies which filled her armies were formed into masses given cohesion by the disciplined soldiers of the old Monarchy; and these were launched recklessly against the lines of their foes, and, fired as they were with patriotic passion, occasionally gained important success, especially in intricate and wooded country. By degrees these bodies became real soldiers, though their formations were as yet rude; their immense numbers and their enthusiasm told ; though there is little doubt they would not have saved France had they not had the support of her regular army.

Ere long the hour came, and the man appeared who was to educe order out of these chaotic elements, to turn to account, with consummate skill, the new conditions available in war, and to raise the first of arts to the extreme of perfection. Napoleon Bonaparte was born in 1769, a scion of a House of the *noblesse* of Florence— the birthplace of many illustrious men—which had emigrated from Italy in the sixteenth century, and, since that time had found a home in Corsica. The child was cradled, so to speak, in war ; the traditions of Paoli filled his mind in infancy, and it may well be that the heroic figure of the legislator and champion of his little island had an influence on the future author of the Code, and on the chief who raised France to the heights of glory. Napoleon was sent at an early age to the well-known Military School of Brienne, one of the foundations of the Bourbon Kings, and he

passed from thence to a Royal school in Paris, to complete his
education for the profession of arms. Little is known about him
in these boyish years; he was grave, taciturn, and fond of books,
especially of the historical and romantic kind; but except that he
excelled in mathematical science, and that he impressed his
teachers with an undefined sense of power, he was not considered
a lad of extraordinary parts. He entered the army at the age of
sixteen, and the bent of his genius became apparent in his assiduous
attention to the history of war, and especially in his constant
study of military maps, pursuits that gave token of the great
future strategist. Though born a gentleman, and retaining
through life many of the instincts of the ancient *régime*, Napoleon
at this time was a needy youth, with no hope of rising under the
old order of things; and it is not surprising, when the Revolution
broke out, that he eagerly took to the new ideas, and ranged himself
on the side of the soldier, in the divisions that filled the army with
discord. As events progressed, he certainly had relations with Robes-
pierre and some of the Terrorists; but this passage in his career
is still ill-explained. We may accept his statement that he always
stood aloof from Jacobin anarchy and its deeds of blood; and his
well-known exclamation, on the 10th of August, when the Swiss
Guards were slaughtered by a Parisian rabble, shows that, even in
those days, he had that profound contempt of popular movements
of every kind which was one of his most distinctive qualities.

He was a captain of artillery at the memorable siege of
Toulon in 1793; and on this occasion he first gave proof of his
extraordinary capacity in war. Toulon was vainly attacked from
the land side, for its communications with the sea were open; and
the French army, led by incapable men, was too weak to master
its walls and its ramparts. But the Allied fleets were the main
defence of the place; these were crowded within the port and the
roadsteads; and they were liable to be destroyed were they
exposed to the fire of powerful batteries from a small projecting
headland. At a council of war Napoleon declared that this point,
when occupied, would be the key to Toulon; and the truth was so
evident that he convinced his superiors. His admirable prevision

was soon realised. When the promontory was seized, the hostile squadrons, completely commanded, at once put to sea, and Toulon fell in an instant as if by magic. This exploit justly attracted attention. Bonaparte was next employed on the Italian frontier, where his strategic ability manifested itself in turning the positions of the Piedmontese army; and, at the instance of the Government, he quelled the revolt of the Sections on the 13th Vendémiaire, and in this service he showed that he had remarkable presence of mind and firmness. He was now known as a soldier of high promise; and, having married Josephine Beauharnais—partly owing to the influence of her old lover, Barras, but partly, too, because of his acknowledged powers—he was given the command, in the spring of 1796, of some 38,000 or 40,000 men encamped along the Genoese seaboard, with general orders to invade Italy. This operation, however, was to be quite secondary to those of the great armies about to enter Germany, with Jourdan and Moreau at their head; and some of the Directory, it is said, wished to get rid, in this way, of an importunate young man who had pestered them with grand strategic projects pronounced by experienced chiefs to be wild extravagance.

I have now reached the campaigns of Napoleon; I can describe them only in the barest outline; but I must dwell for a moment on that of Italy. The army, in the hands of the young general, had suffered terrible privations, and was in extreme want; but it was composed of trained and enthusiastic soldiers; it had several good subordinate chiefs, and it could be made a most formidable instrument of war under the guidance and inspiration of a great commander. Spread along the coast from Nice to the verge of Genoa, it was confronted by a Sardinian and an Austrian army, perhaps 60,000 strong, if united, led by Colli and Beaulieu, experienced generals, but veterans of the old school; and their forces, based on Turin and Milan, held the hill country, where the French Alps decline and join the extreme western Apennines. Napoleon's first operations strikingly illustrate the intelligence of the theatre and the skill in stratagem in which no military chief can be compared with him. Giving out that he was about to advance by

Genoa, he made a feigned demonstration on his right, causing
Beaulieu largely to detach to his left; and then, counter-marching
with extreme celerity, he poured his troops through the Cadibona
Pass, the lowest eminence in the uniting ranges, and surrounded
and routed part of the Austrian centre. Beaulieu and Colli endeavouring to concentrate, presented their forces, still divided,
to their foe; these were defeated at Dego and Millesimo; and the
baffled chiefs retreated on Acqui and Ceva, diverging towards their
bases at Milan and Turin, and leaving a widening interval between
their shattered armies. Napoleon, standing in strength between
his antagonists, detached a wing to hold Beaulieu in check, and
then drawing together the rest of his forces, he pursued Colli,
struck him down at Mondovi, and compelled the King of Sardinia
to sue for peace. He took care to secure his communications with
France by insisting on the cession of the Piedmontese fortresses;
and having thus gained a new base—he had quietly disregarded
injunctions from Paris to stir up a revolution in Piedmont—he set
off to pursue Beaulieu, in retreat along the northern bank of the Po.

Deceiving again his adversary by a false rumour, Napoleon
next made a forced march to the river, advancing, as he has said,
" with the speed of a torrent," and gathering his supplies on his
way, from the country; and crossing at Piacenza, he forestalled
the Austrians, threatened their rear, and forced them to retire on
the Adda. A fierce engagement at Lodi followed, in which Bonaparte showed remarkable skill in securing every advantage on the
ground; Beaulieu, outmanœuvred, fell back to the Mincio, and
Napoleon entered Milan in triumph, having, like Turenne, conquered by a war of marches. The French army now had some
days of repose; its chief employed them in assuring his base, in
levying requisitions in immense quantities, and in making preparations for fresh exploits; and if he showed no scruple in these
measures, and, in fact, he organized rapine on an enormous scale,
he established himself firmly in the heart of Lombardy. Towards
the close of May Napoleon advanced to the Mincio; Beaulieu,
trying to cover the stream at all points, was easily dislodged by a
daring attack, and the Austrian army, beaten and cowed, was

forced to take refuge in the hills of the Tyrol. By this time Bonaparte had received orders from the Directory to march from the Po to the Tiber, to drive the Pope from Rome, and to rouse Southern Italy; but he refused to follow false strategic plans which, he declared, would involve his army in ruin; and with admirable insight he addressed himself to operations which, if successful, would, he hoped, give France the great prize of Italy. The Austrians were his only formidable foes; the whole peninsula would succumb if their military strength was really broken; and the problem was how to attain this end with a small French army advanced to the Mincio. In the line of the Adige Napoleon perceived the true theatre on which to operate; the river, bounded on the west by the Lake of Garda, hemmed in by mountains as it flowed southward, and ending in tracts of widespreading marshes, afforded an enormously strong barrier, especially if it were held on both banks; and accordingly he took possession of the stream, having, without hesitation, seized the fortresses of the Venetian Republic, on its lower course, and having, meanwhile, sat down to besiege Mantua, the last stronghold still retained by Austria. The conception, original, grand, and simple alike, was an inspiration of true strategic genius, and one of the finest of a marvellous career. Summer had now come, and as the Austrian armies had as yet made no signs of appearing, Napoleon employed this breathing time in pressing forward the attack on Mantua, and in strengthening the power of France in Italy.

The Emperor, meanwhile, had made great efforts to retrieve the late reverses of his troops in Lombardy. The French armies under Moreau and Jourdan, directed on widely distant lines, according to the false strategy of the day, had been held in check by the Archduke Charles, and had achieved no real success in Germany; and Würmser, a veteran of high repute, was despatched from the Upper Rhine with about 30,000 men, to reinforce the defeated army of Beaulieu—that general had been deprived of his command—and with orders to drive the French out of Italy. The Austrian army cannot have been less than from 60,000 to 70,000 strong; Bonaparte had perhaps only 40,000 men besieging Mantua, and along the Adige; and as the value of that barrier, in the hands of a master, was not understood in the Imperial councils, the defeat of the French seemed a foregone conclusion. Believing that Napoleon would retain his hold on Mantua, or, at least, would hesitate until it was too late, Würmser divided his army into three masses, the left and centre under the General-in-Chief moving down the Adige by the valleys and hills that meet the eastern shores of the Lake of Garda, the right, led by Quasdanovich, along the western shore, the object being that the combined forces should close round and stifle the French near Mantua. Napoleon waited until the movement was made plain, and his resolution was at once taken with the strength of character of a great captain. He raised the siege of Mantua on the last night of July, and his enemies being divided by the lake, he turned against Quasdanovich, who was nearest at hand, and drove his advanced guard back for a long distance. Würmser, meanwhile, had forced his way to the Mincio; dividing his army, he detached a part to attack the French supposed to be still round Mantua, and he sent another part to unite with Quasdanovich, assumed by his chief to be close at hand. This gave Bonaparte an opportunity to strike; he had by this time his whole army together; and while he kept Quasdanovich baffled, in check, he encountered the separated forces of Würmser, and routed them in detail, at Lonato first, and then, decisively, at Castiglione. Quasdanovich had already fallen back; Würmser was compelled to recross the Mincio, and his broken army was so demoralised, that he had to ascend the Adige and fly into the Tyrol.

Napoleon now exhibited one of his most striking qualities, his terrible skill in pursuing a defeated enemy. Relying on the moral power of his victories, he marched north of the lake along both shores; and then, concentrating his forces, he beat Davidowich, a lieutenant of Würmser, at Roveredo, just as that tenacious chief had planned another advance on Mantua, moving, on this occasion, from the Tyrol eastwards, to the Lower Adige. Napoleon, leaving a detachment to restrain Davidowich, pressed Würmser with indefatigable energy, came up with him in the defiles of the Brenta, overthrew him completely at Bassano, and drove him, with the mere wreck of an army, into the low country east of the Adige. The situation of the veteran appeared desperate; he was cut off from retreat to the Tyrol; a triumphant enemy was upon his rear; and how was he to get across the Lower Adige, held by French garrisons, where it could be passed, before Bonaparte should reach and destroy him? Napoleon thought he had his foe in his toils; but Würmser was a bold and undaunted soldier, and he managed to force the passage at Legnago, and even to make good his way to Mantua, striking down some small hostile bodies in his path. The old chief, proud of this trifling success, attempted to make a stand near Mantua; but he was driven into the fortress with loss; and Mantua was again invested. In a brief campaign of about six weeks, Napoleon, with a very inferior force, had annihilated a far more powerful enemy; and all that remained of Würmser's army were a few thousand men far away in the Tyrol, and a few thousand more imprisoned in Mantua, a burden rather than a relief to the garrison. Such extraordinary success had never been witnessed before, and it was obviously due to the genius of the French commander.

Austria, nevertheless, with characteristic firmness, did not yet give up the protracted contest. Moreau and Jourdan by this time were in retreat towards the Rhine, the Archduke Charles, who, in this campaign had operated between divided enemies, with a feeble approach to Napoleon's skill, having gained real success in Germany; and considerable reinforcements were sent to the Tyrol, and to the plain country known as Friuli, and were placed under the command of Alvinzi, another old general of some distinction, with directions at any cost to relieve Mantua. Alvinzi had passed the Isonzo by the end of October with from 30,000 to 40,000 men, Davidowich being still in the Tyrol with 15,000 to 18,000; and the plan of the Austrian chief was to make these divided masses converge at Verona upon the Adige; and, having forced the passage, to march to the Mincio. The main French army at this time held the lowlands between the Brenta and the Adige, a considerable detachment under Vaubois being in the Tyrol watching the enemy; and as Napoleon in this instance persisted in continuing the siege of Mantua, and kept a large force around the place, he had not 40,000 men altogether in the field. The first operations of the Austrian leaders were attended with success that might have been made decisive. Masséna, the ablest lieutenant of Bonaparte, held Alvinzi, indeed, in check on the Brenta; but Vaubois was driven, in defeat, from the Tyrol; the important position of Rivoli was lost; and Davidowich had approached Verona by the first week of November. The principal army of the French was now compelled to fall back; Napoleon sent a detachment to support Vaubois; but though Rivoli, the key to Verona, was regained, Alvinzi had advanced and drawn near the city. Napoleon attacked him fiercely at Caldiero, but the French recoiled, baffled, from a very strong position; and had Davidowich at this moment pressed forward boldly, and Alvinzi made good use of his success, they might have effected their junction, seized Verona, and made their way across the Adige. But the spell of defeat was on the Austrian chiefs; and Napoleon, seizing his one chance with marvellous skill, plucked a glorious triumph out of the extreme of peril.

Abandoning Verona, he crossed the Adige; he moved quickly down the stream and recrossed it, and then he suddenly fell on his astounded foe, advancing along the dykes of Arcola, through the morasses of the Lower Adige, where the agility and vehemence of the French soldiery would, he foresaw, give them a great advantage. The battle raged confusedly for several days; Napoleon more than once led his men in person; Davidowich, meanwhile, had reconquered Rivoli; but skill and French valour at last prevailed, and the two Austrian armies were ultimately compelled to fall back behind the Brenta and into the Tyrol discomfited, and with immense losses. Austria, however, would not confess defeat; great efforts were made to restore her armies; and Alvinzi assumed the offensive again, in the first days of January 1797. He had even now probably 60,000 men against 35,000 or 40,000 French; and his plan was to descend the Adige, to occupy Rivoli, and then to seize Verona, and to press on to Mantua, a diversion being at the same time made on the Lower Adige by his lieutenant, Provera. By the 14th of January the Austrian columns had surrounded Rivoli on every side; but in the

8 *

difficult march through the hills, their artillery and cavalry had been attached to one column only, on the best road, and this gave Napoleon, who had his army in hand, though very inferior in force, a decided advantage. The issue of the battle was never doubtful; Masséna displayed conspicuous skill; the Austrians, smitten down by the French guns, and unable to reply, lost heart and were beaten ; and Alvinzi drew off, overthrown and routed. It is unnecessary to dwell on the last scenes of the contest ; Provera contrived to cross the Adige, and even to make his way to Mantua; but he was crushed by Napoleon, who had hurried from Rivoli, and on the 11th of January laid down his arms. The fate of Mantua was now sealed; three efforts to relieve the place had failed; the garrison was reduced to extremities; and Würmser capitulated in a few days. The last Italian fortress of Austria had fallen ; but this was nothing compared to her other losses. Army after army had perished in the attempt to dislodge Bonaparte from the Adige, and the Empire was completely exhausted.

By this time the main seat of the war had been transferred from the Rhine and the Danube to the Adige, the Isonzo, and the hills of the Tyrol; a man of genius had transformed the situation. I shall not refer to the close of the struggle. The Archduke Charles, the last hope of the Hapsburgs, endeavoured in vain to arrest the march of Bonaparte across the Carnic Alps, into the valleys of the Drave and the Mur. In the second week of April the youthful conqueror beheld the steeples of Vienna from the heights of the Simmering, having, with an army never 50,000 strong, subdued Italy and shattered the power of Austria. Nor can I notice Leoben and Campo Formio, or moralize on the Fall of Venice ; nor can I comment on the profound statecraft, very different from the revolutionary cant, shown by Napoleon in the negotiations for peace. Yet a word must be said, by way of comment, on the memorable campaign of 1796–97, by some considered its great author's masterpiece. The dazzling imagination, one of the most striking, and yet a dangerous gift of Napoleon, was not seen in this passage of arms as distinctly as in more than one that followed ; but every other faculty of a master of war was exhibited in the highest perfection. The first accomplishment of a true strategist, skill in so understanding the theatre of war as to make it subserve his ends in view, was displayed in more than one notable instance ; the perception of the importance of the Cadibona Pass, and the grand choice of the Adige as a barrier, are examples that cannot escape the reader. Nor less admirable was the exhibition of another great strategic gift, the combination of force on the decisive points, the usual prelude of real success. Napoleon, always weaker than his foes, if united, was often stronger on the scene of immediate action, and this was largely due to his wonderful powers, if it was also caused by the faults of adversaries who persisted in following a false strategic system. No commander besides, not even Turenne, had approached Napoleon in the great art of manœuvring between divided enemies, of striking them left and right in succession, and of gaining the flank and rear of a hostile army ; the operations against Würmser, and the march to Piacenza, are admirable specimens of this kind of excellence. In the movements, too, and manœuvres of Bonaparte, we see a splendour, and yet a scientific method, and, perhaps most distinctly, a skill in stratagem peculiar to himself, and hitherto scarcely known ; and as for his tactics, the genius with which he chose the ground at Arcola stamps him at once as a master in the highest sphere of this art. Nor less remarkable were his moral qualities ; his energy and resolution, for example, appear conspicuously in the raising of the siege of Mantua ; and no one but Napoleon would have ventured to cross the will of the Directory, as he did more than once, at the risk of his fortune, and perhaps of his life.

Yet in this marvellous display of genius and power we can occasionally see defects and faults. Napoleon risked too much in continuing the siege of Mantua at the approach of Alvinzi. He should not, perhaps, have fought at Caldiero ; and we trace signs of that over-confidence in success, which certainly was his most distinctive error. One general cause of the extreme brilliancy of his movements should be carefully noted. Napoleon, unlike the first revolutionary chiefs, did not merely throw his troops on a country and allow them to plunder to obtain subsistence ; he well knew the fatal results of this system, and he organized magazines and depôts with care; but he perceived, with true insight, that, in Italy at least, it was nearly always possible to find resources on the spot; and his army accordingly moved with much less impediments than that of the heavily-encumbered Austrians, and was often able to assume a bold offensive which generals of the old type would have deemed impossible. This method, however, which he made almost perfect, had a dangerous side as yet unseen, but to be manifested in a still distant future. For the rest, Napoleon, in the campaign of Italy, had good subordinates and an army that became most formidable in his master hand; but the force that really determined events was the great military genius which had suddenly appeared.

I shall pass over Napoleon's career in the East, the Pyramids, and the failure at Acre; these campaigns but slightly illustrate his genius in war. His object in his descent on Egypt was to march through Syria and Persia to the Indus. He always maintained that the design was feasible; but our present knowledge shows that it was quite impossible, and in this, as in other of his military plans, his soaring imagination overcame his judgment. On his return to France in the winter of 1799 he easily supplanted the tottering Government, and, as First Consul, seized supreme power; and though I shall not comment on the 18th Brumaire, it may fairly be said that this *coup d'état* saved France and restored her to her place in Europe. A second Coalition had been formed against her, during Napoleon's absence, after the Battle of the Nile. Prussia, indeed, held aloof, but Russia appeared in formidable strength on the theatre of war; and Austria, aided by the gold and the troops of England, once more placed powerful armies in the field. Notwithstanding the examples of the campaign of 1796, that of 1799 proceeded on the late false principles. The war was conducted on an enormous front, from the Texel, along the Rhine, to the Tiber; and the armies on both sides were split into fractions, comparatively inefficient on a vast field of manœuvre. The Allies, however, gained important success. Masséna, indeed, saved France at Zürich; but Suvóroff drove the French out of Italy, and the Austrians, reversing the events of 1796, advanced from the Mincio, and approached the French Alps. When Napoleon, who, in a few months, had accomplished wonders of administrative skill, in restoring the finances and power of the State, had, in the beginning of 1800, to survey the military affairs of France, her situation was still critical in the extreme. Russia, indeed, had abandoned the Allied cause, but Austria had put her whole strength forth. One great Imperial army, led by Mélas, covered Italy from the Adige to the Tanaro; another, under Kray, was in the Swabian lowlands, holding the southern approaches to the Black Forest; and France, with forces reduced and weakened, was threatened with invasion on the Rhine and the Var.

A man of surpassing powers in war was, however, for the first time at her head; and this proved sufficient to turn the scale of Fortune. Napoleon's project for the campaign was not completely realised; but it was the most striking perhaps of his great career, and it ended in a succession of triumphs. With that wonderful glance which read the whole theatre, and saw how to make the best use of it, the First Consul perceived that the two hostile armies were separated by the vast space of Switzerland, at this time in the possession of the French; and the army of Mélas, about 100,000 strong, and intended ultimately to enter Provence, was the principal army, on what ought to have been the secondary point of attack only; while that of Kray, perhaps 90,000 men, designed, if successful, to attain Alsace, was a subordinate force on the chief scene of action. These being the facts, and as France held Switzerland, projecting like a huge natural bastion between the enemy's widely-divided masses, Napoleon gave Moreau the main French army—it contained perhaps 100,000 troops—with directions to cross the Rhine at Schaffhausen, to fall in full force on the rear of Kray, and to cut him off from his line of retreat; Moreau, at the fitting time, sending a large detachment across the St. Gothard in order to aid the movements of the French chief in Italy. Napoleon selected for 1800 the scene of his exploits in 1796–97; and his design was, avoiding the Piedmontese fortresses, to cross the Alps by the Great St. Bernard range, and then rapidly descending, to seize the lines of the communications of Mélas with the Adige, and supported by the detachment from Moreau, to force the Austrians to fight in a disastrous position. The First Consul calculated that about 40,000 men—France at this juncture could not yield more—would, with the aid from the main army, suffice for his purpose ; but as it was of the first importance to allow the Austrians to advance into the far end of Italy, and to engage themselves on the line of the Var, it was necessary to conceal as much as possible the formation and destination of the new army of Italy, and especially to screen its advance to the Alps. To attain his end Napoleon tasked to the utmost the dexterity in stratagem in which he stands supreme. He assembled a collection of bad troops at Dijon, and ostentatiously announced this was his Italian army ; but in the meantime he quietly drew together his real force from different parts of France, masking the operation with the greatest care and forethought. The main army, I have said, was to cross the St. Bernard ; but a small column was to march by the pass of Mont Cenis—the ordinary military way through the Alps —in order effectually to deceive the enemy.

The campaign only began in earnest in spring, though hostilities had not ceased through the winter. In the first week of May Mélas had part of his army besieging Genoa, under his lieutenant, Ott, Masséna making a stubborn defence ; Elsnitz, another Austrian, was upon the Var, confronted by Suchet, a capable chief well known in the Peninsular War afterwards ; and the rest of the Imperial army held Piedmont, extending thence to the Adige and the Mincio. Meanwhile, Moreau, a general of the second order, had feared to execute Napoleon's design, and to fall on the rear of Kray by Schaffhausen ; he had crossed the Rhine, after his own fashion, by complicated and even hazardous movements, merely threatening, not striking Kray, with effect ; but he had forced the weaker hostile army back ; and he was able to fulfil one great part of his mission, and to send 20,000 men across the St. Gothard, under Moncey, one of the Napoleonic marshals. The First Consul took the field in the second week of May ; his army, secretly moved to the Swiss frontier, its strength still unknown to its enemy, crossed the Great St. Bernard from the 16th to the 19th; and simultaneously the secondary force moved forward through the pass of Mont Cenis. The hill fort of Bard arrested the French for a moment; but the obstacle was overcome skilfully; and by the 23rd the advanced guard of Napoleon was in the valley of the Dora, and in full march for Piedmont. By this time Mélas had heard of the advance of the enemy, but he refused to believe in the force of the French army; he allowed Ott and Elsnitz to remain where they were; and though he moved to Turin in person, it was with not more than a few thousand men, for he felt assured that his divisons in Piedmont would be able to give a good account of Napoleon. The Austrian chief, too, at this critical moment, was deceived by the apparition of the column from Mont Cenis; he thought that it was the chief part of the hostile army; and falling into the snare that had been laid for him, he halted at Turin to draw in his forces.

This gave Napoleon the opportunity he sought; he marched from the Dora across the Sesia and the Ticino with his wonted celerity; and he entered Milan on the 2nd of June, already menacing the communications of his foe. He was soon joined by Moncey's detachment, and being now at the head of 60,000 men, he crossed the Po, holding both its banks, and closed on the rear of the main Austrian army, thrown forward almost to the frontier of France. Mélas, seriously alarmed, gave orders to concentrate his still very superior force; but Ott lingered to receive the keys of Genoa, which yielded only after a most stern resistance, and left a large garrison in the fallen city; Elsnitz was routed by Suchet in his retreat from the Var; and the Austrian army was immensely weakened, when in the second week of June it lay round Alessandria, Ott, who had endeavoured to attain the Po, having been driven back at Montebello with loss. By this time Napoleon had his army divided on either bank of the Po, Moncey watching the course of its Alpine feeders, Napoleon holding the famous Stradella Pass, where the spurs of the Apennines approach the river; and his enemy, even now, was within his toils. But the First Consul gave Mélas credit for more strategic skill than he really possessed; he thought that the Austrian, after the fall of Genoa, might endeavour to make his escape by the coast, or might fall back and overpower Suchet; and he debouched into the great plain of Marengo, in order to observe and close on his foe. His army was not 30,000 strong; that of Mélas was probably 40,000; it was very superior in cavalry and guns, which gave it a marked advantage in open ground; and no doubt can exist that in risking this movement Napoleon made a great strategic error. Mélas, a stout warrior of the school of Daun, attacked the French fiercely on the 14th of June, hoping to defeat his enemy and to escape from the net thrown around him with such forethought and skill; and he nearly attained a decisive victory. Desaix, however, a trusted lieutenant of Bonaparte, arriving from a distance, restored the battle; the horsemen of Kellerman changed the fortunes of the day, and the Austrians at last were completely beaten. The result was then seen of the masterly movements which had brought Napoleon on the rear of Mélas; the defeated army was compelled to make terms, and it evacuated the peninsula even beyond the Mincio. France had regained Italy by a march and a battle.

Austria, always tenacious, resisted for months, and Moreau gained a great victory at Hohenlinden, success in part due to the overboldness of John, a brother of the Archduke Charles, who imagined he had mastered Napoleon's strategy. But Marengo had been the decisive stroke: Austria fought for honour only, after the loss of Italy; and ere long she accepted the Peace of Lunéville, followed by the peace of Amiens between France and England. The campaign of 1800 is the most dazzling of Napoleon's masterpieces, though marred by what might have been a fatal error. Full justice, perhaps, has never been done to the surpassing ability of the First Consul in perceiving the advantage given to France by her hold of Switzerland, and the false position of the Austrian armies; for two Napoleons were required on the scene, to realise completely one grand conception. Had Bonaparte been in the place of Moreau, and debouched from Schaffhausen across the Rhine, Kray would have been cut off, and Vienna laid open; and the ruin of Mélas and the Conquest of Italy was, in fact, half only of what might have been done. Yet, as it was, Switzerland was made a kind of sallyport, to place the French armies on the rear of their foes; Moreau was rightly given the superior force to paralyse Kray, and to keep him off from the Rhine; Napoleon properly distributed the inferior force in Italy, under his own command, for it would suffice to defeat operations in the Var; and though Moreau failed to destroy Kray, Napoleon succeeded in destroying Mélas, thrown forward perilously on the French frontier. Intelligence of the theatre and splendour of design were never, perhaps, more finely displayed; the ordinary reader will dwell on the Alpine march; but the true student of war will rather note the exquisite art with which the army of Italy was collected, formed, and moved to the Alps, all without the enemy's knowledge; the admirable skill by which Mélas was deceived through the demonstration at Mont Cenis; the celerity of the advance on Milan, and the perfect arrangements made to combine with Moncey, and then to encompass the foe. Genius and power of stratagem have never accomplished more; and had Napoleon remained near the Stradella Pass—Turenne certainly would have done this—the execution of his plan would have been perfect. But this wonderful chief was not only too confident throughout his whole career, but often showed* impatience when near his enemy; these faults nearly caused him to lose the compaign; and he certainly ought not to have fought at Marengo, for the chances were in his opponent's favour, though an advance towards Alessandria might have been justified, for Mélas might, perhaps, have escaped by the sea-board, or have crushed Suchet with his weak detachment.

I cannot dwell on the Government of the First Consul, on the Code, the Concordat, the Pacification of La Vendée, the restoration of order and peace in France, the foundation of the only institutions and laws which have lasted during her subsequent history; nor can I comment on his external policy, the settlement of Italy in the interests of France, and the extension of her influence through the Lesser States of Germany. I shall only

---

* This is the sagacious and just judgment of Wellington, a genius of quite a different kind, but a great admirer of Napoleon.

remark that if these achievements reveal the near advent of despotism at home, and the spirit of encroaching ambition abroad, they display administrative excellence of the first order, and profound, if hard and unscrupulous, statecraft; and they bear the marks of ineffaceable greatness. I cannot, moreover, enlarge on the causes which led to the rupture of the Peace of Amiens, and involved England and France in a death struggle. Nor shall I describe the Flotilla and the Camp of Boulogne, the accumulation of a great army destined to cross the Channel, and to invade our coasts, and the energy, the perseverance, and the careful forethought with which this last was prepared to effect the descent. Yet a remark must be made on the fine combinations thought out by Napoleon to carry out his purpose, for they are a notable example of his skill in stratagem. His arrangements to embark his army, and to make the passage, in the flotilla, were but a part of the design; they were largely intended to mask his purpose; his real plan was to conduct the descent under the protection of a fleet which should command the Channel. How indefatigably, and with what consummate art, the First Consul toiled to effect his object, his correspondence abundantly proves; and, it must be added, he well nigh succeeded. The Admiralty was deceived, and Nelson was lured away; and had French seamen been nearly as good as our own, and Villeneuve been a capable chief, Napoleon would have mastered the narrow seas for a time, and his army would have stood on our shores. That he would have found a Moscow, in England, our countrymen believe; he certainly would have been imprisoned within the ground he occupied, for our fleets would have cut him off from France, and his enterprise would probably have been a failure. All this, however, is speculation only; England undoubtedly was in grave danger, and her Government did not understand her enemy; though it deserves notice that Napoleon's idea, that he would subdue England by pulling down the Throne and setting a Republic up in its place, was not only a huge mistake, but tends to show he did not believe that he could succeed only by mere force of arms.

CHAPTER V.

NAPOLEON (*continued*).

THE return of Pitt to power, at the call of the nation; the aggressive foreign policy of the first Consul, and the atrocious execution of the Duc D'Enghien—a crime that may be palliated but not excused—soon led to a new Coalition against France. Prussia, indeed, gorged with spoil after the peace of Basle, stood apart, as she had done in 1799, as if secretly ashamed of an ignoble part; but Russia and Austria joined hands with England. Other petty States took the same side, and by the summer of 1805 the Allies had come to a general agreement to take the offensive. Before this time Napoleon had become Emperor, with the universal acclaim of the French people, and the crowned soldier, who had raised France from the depths of disaster to the head of Europe, and whose strong hand had put anarchy down, now wielded the resources of a mighty State, and made the revolutionary forces which he used and hated the ministers of immense despotic power. The military strength of France, though it was enlarged afterwards, was now really at its extreme height, and Napoleon's army of this period was by far the finest he ever commanded. I must glance at the characteristics of this magnificent force, justly known by the name of the Grand Army, and infinitely the most formidable organization for war which hitherto had been arrayed in Europe. Apart from small Italian and German contingents, the Grand Army at this time was composed of Frenchmen, for the most part troops in the flower of life, but with a large admixture of veteran soldiers; and this vast body was inflamed with a strong spirit of enthusiasm, of patriotism of

its own kind, of thirst for glory, and of intense confidence in
an unrivalled leader. Its physical and moral force was, therefore, enormous; and as five-sixths of it had for many months
been assembled in the great Camp of Boulogne—the general name
of many leaguers—and the troops had been inured to the hard
training of war, its military condition had attained perfection. It
probably numbered at this time about 200,000 men in the first
line, with reserves, perhaps, 200,000 more; and, regiment for
regiment, I certainly think it formed a more efficient instrument
of war than the huge national armies of recent days, composed far
too largely of young conscripts, and never yet subjected to the
strain of ill-fortune.

The general organization of this great force was perfectly
adapted, in Napoleon's hands, to the conditions of war in the
first years of this century. Brigades and divisions had now been
formed into corps, each under the command of able chiefs, too
accustomed, indeed, to look up to Napoleon, and not given
sufficient freedom of action, but all skilful and experienced
soldiers; and the army had more cohesiveness and real power
than ever had been the case formerly. Napoleon, however, apart
from these masses, each an independent army in itself, had large
cavalry and artillery reserves; and he usually kept them under
his immediate control, to wield "his club of Hercules" for
decisive strokes. The Grand Army, too, like that of Louis XIV.,
had its *corps d'élite*—the Imperial Guard—the tenth legion of the
modern Cæsar, and this superb force on many a hard-fought day
turned by its mighty preponderance the scales of fortune. As
for the tactics of the army, they had been perfected in the experience of a long series of wars; columns of infantry, not as yet too
dense, and preceded by skirmishers, were formed for attack; but
they were always supported by cavalry and guns; and Napoleon
invariably took special care that the three arms should act in
concert. These arrangements had given great flexibility and yet
strength to the improved formations; and it was clearly apparent
that the new methods were superior to those of the Seven
Years' War. As for the mechanism of the army, if I may use

the word, the whole system of assuring supplies, of establishing magazines and depôts, and of procuring continual relays of troops, which German science has brought to perfection, had been largely matured by Napoleon; and though he always "made war sustain war," that is, he usually trusted to resources on the spot in order to enable his troops to move freely, he was most attentive to the wants of his soldiers, and provided for them with great administrative skill. Yet, formidable as it was, the Grand Army had marked defects which require notice. It had never lost the habits of the Revolutionary Wars; Napoleon's system, indeed, promoted rapine; it retained some of the instincts of the savage hordes let loose in 1793-94; it was crowded with ignorant and bad officers, the survivors of the huge conventional levies; and the arrangements of the staff were far from good. It still bore the marks of a revolutionary age; and in all these respects it was very inferior to the great army formed by Roon and Moltke.

The Allies had set their armies in motion by the first week of September 1805. They had nearly half a million of men on foot; but, partly owing to divided counsels, and partly to the disastrous mistake of subordinating military to political ends, this gigantic force was injudiciously arranged on the theatre. Four separate attacks had been designed; the first by a small English and Swedish force from Hanover and the North German seaboard; the second by an Austrian and a great Russian army, to be assembled upon the banks of the Danube and ultimately to invade Alsace; the third on northern Italy from the Adige and the Tyrol, conducted by the Archdukes Charles and John; and the fourth by an English and Russian contingent disembarked from a fleet on the coast of Naples. But the first and last attacks were mere weak diversions, which could not alarm a true strategist; as regards the second, the Russian army, still in Galicia and Poland, was at an immense distance from the Austrians upon the Upper Danube; and as for the third, the ambition of the House of Hapsburg, eager to regain its Italian possessions, had repeated the mistake of 1800, its chiefs having placed far too great a force on secondary points, without sufficient regard for those which were of supreme importance, the

space between the Middle Rhine and the Danube. Napoleon seized
the situation with the eye of genius; and the plan of his operations was at once formed. Neglecting Northern Germany and
Southern Italy, and employing only an inferior force to hold the
Austrian Princes in check—they were in command of 100,000 men
—he resolved to fall on the Austrian army on the Danube, which,
not more than 85,000 strong, was thrown forward on the country
round Ulm, to surround and destroy it, under its chief Mack, as
Mélas had been destroyed five years before, and thus to cut it off
completely from the distant Russian army, which could not be on
the spot at the time.

I can only glance at the operations that followed, less dazzling
than those which led to Marengo, but in principle and method
essentially the same, and a notable instance of the great maxim
in war, set at nought in 1798 to 1799, but always observed
by real commanders, that you should find and strike at the
decisive point, and assail an enemy where he is most vulnerable.
The Grand Army marched across France from the camp of
Boulogne with a celerity which confounded its foes; two corps,
under Bernadotte and Marmont, created of late Imperial Marshals, advanced from Hanover and the flats of Holland; a
corp of Bavarians joined the French; and the collected masses,
nearly 200,000 strong, were drawn together to the Rhine and the
Main, ready to attain the Danube, in the last days of September.
These movements led to the great surrender of Ulm, a most remarkable event in the wars of this century. Masking the general
movement by sending detachments of cavalry into and along the
Black Forest—the stratagem again of the column of Mont Cenis
—and spreading his masses over the Franconian plains, the
Emperor moved the converging arrays from the great arc of Stras-
burg, Mayence, and Wurtzburg; and by the second week of October
they were upon the Danube already interposed between Ulm and
Vienna. The net was now rapidly drawn round Mack, who,
stricken with terror, remained almost motionless, changing front
about Ulm, and doing scarcely anything to strike at the enemy
gathering in on all sides. Some mistakes were made in completing

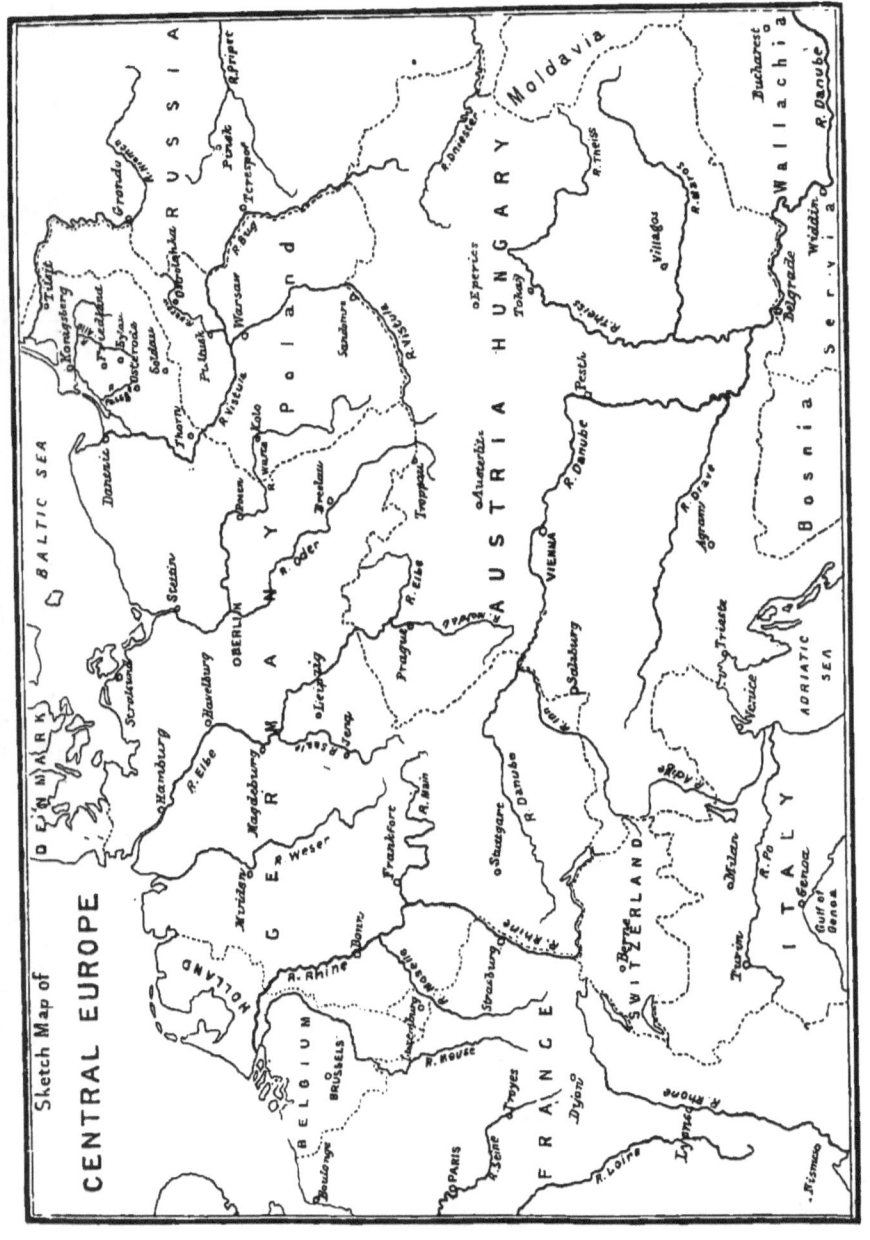

the toils, almost inevitable in manœuvres of the kind, which a capable chief might have turned to account; but these were rectified within a few hours; three bodies of Austrians made their escape; but Mack simply waited on events, unlike Mélas, made no attempt to break through, and capitulated with the mass of his army on the 19th of October. The greater part of the forces which had got off were intercepted and made prisoners; and thus a whole army was literally swept from the theatre by a march without striking one effective blow. Europe never witnessed a scene of the kind again until Metz fell through the treason of Bazaine.

Napoleon, in his rapid advance on Ulm, had spread his army over a vast circumference because no possible foes were at hand; he had made the best use of the good roads which now generally traversed France and Germany; and he had thus turned to the greatest advantage one of the new existing conditions of war. The front of the Allied attack had been broken; and the paralysis, so to speak, of the head, had caused the collapse of the inferior members. The eccentric operations in the North of Germany and in Southern Italy came to nothing; the Archduke Charles and the Archduke John—the first had been defeated at Caldiero, a revenge for the failure of 1796—were compelled to fall back from the Adige and the Tyrol; and the way from Ulm to Vienna lay open. The Emperor, giving effect, in another age, to the great conception of Villars in 1703, marched with the Grand Army down the valley of the Danube, protecting his wings from possible attacks; the Isar, the Inn, the Traun, and the Ens, lines capable of defence, were passed and mastered; and, by the middle of November, the triumphant conqueror had entered the capital of the German Cæsars. By this time the advanced corps of the Russian army, which had marched from Galicia and had attained the Inn, had rallied the fragments of Mack's forces; its chief, Kutusof, a name to become famous, had fallen back, and left Vienna to its fate; and he had come into line with his colleague, Buxhöwden, who had been marching from the Polish frontier, and had made his way into the plains of Moravia. Napoleon broke up from Vienna to pursue his foes, though, notwithstanding his wonderful success, his position

9

was already not free from danger. In the march on Ulm, Bernadotte had crossed a Prussian district; this had incensed the King
and even the nation, for some time chafing at its neutral attitude,
and Prussia had begun to prepare for war, and to assemble troops
on the Elbe and the Oder. The Grand Army, too, had suffered
heavy losses in its forced marches into the heart of Austria; the
system of living upon conquered provinces had not sufficed for
enormous bodies of men; and thousands of stragglers, marauders,
deserters, swarmed along the tracts from the Rhine to the Danube.
The Archdukes, too, in retreat from the south, were straining every
nerve to attain Moravia; and should Prussia march an army
through the Bohemian passes, and throw her sword into the scale
of the Allies, the French, isolated, would, with winter at hand,
and far from their base, be soon compelled to confront an immense
superiority of force.

Napoleon, however, always confident—the modern Cæsar had
faith in his fortunes—did not hesitate to march into Moravia;
and he was at Brünn by the third week of November, with a
considerable part of the Grand Army. At this moment Kutusof and Buxhöwden were near Olmütz about 80,000 strong;
some Austrian contingents had united with them; Prussia had
actually promised to attack Napoleon; the Archdukes were but a
few marches off; and had the Allies only waited a fortnight, they
could have assembled nearly 200,000 men to fight a great battle
with the French Emperor, who could not have assembled 100,000.
But folly and presumption were in the Russian camp, and the
young Czar, Alexander, was persuaded to take the offensive, and
to advance from Olmütz before the available supports of the Allies
were near. A theorist contributed to this fatal resolve, and his
pedantry led to a tremendous disaster. Napoleon at this time was
in position not far from Brünn, on the banks of the Goldbach,
in front of the little town of Austerlitz; and though he had really
about 70,000 men in hand, two of his corps were at some distance.
Weyrother, an Austrian general officer, proposed a grand plan, to
descend from Olmütz, to turn the right wing of the French on the
Goldbach, and to cut Napoleon off from retreat on Vienna, by a

formidable attack in the oblique order. The Allied army, perhaps 80,000 men, was close to the Goldbach on the 1st of December, its columns arranged for the offensive movement ostentatiously talked of and soon made apparent; and Weyrother announced a great coming victory. Napoleon, who had drawn in his two corps, beheld with delight this reckless strategy—a flank march along a wide front, under the beard of the chief of Arcola and Rivoli; that "army is mine," he proudly said, and he made the prediction known in an address to his soldiers. Anticipating what would happen—in part at least—he had assumed a timid defensive attitude, in order to lure his enemies on—another instance of his wonderful powers of stratagem.

The sun of Austerlitz rose on the 2nd, to illuminate one of the great scenes of history. The nature of the ground forbade the manœuvre contemplated by the Allied leaders. Towards their left, in the space in which they proposed to outflank and defeat the French right, spread a region of marsh, around the Goldbach, of wide lakes, and of intricate country, with the hamlets of Sokolnitz and Telnitz hard by; and it formed at once a difficult position to force, and a line favourable in the extreme for defence. Their centre filled the plain round the hill of Pratzen, and was, therefore, dangerously exposed to attack, should it be weakened by a detachment to the left; and their right was almost wholly "in the air," and liable to be turned and destroyed by the low hill of Santon. Napoleon had seized the characteristics of the scene with the insight of the great chief of Ramillies, and his dispositions were made to turn to the best advantage the local peculiarities which he saw before him. He had already secured a second line of retreat, was not bound to his base on Vienna, and was perfectly free to act as he pleased; and his arrangements were the piece of a master of tactics. He placed Davoust, one of the best of the marshals, with only a few thousand men on his right—reinforcements, however, were ready for them—for he wished to draw the enemy on to his ruin, and the position he knew was easy of defence; but Soult, afterwards Duke of Dalmatia, Bernadotte and his corps, with the Imperial Guard, were

massed together in formidable strength, to carry the plain and
heights of Pratzen; and Lannes, with the left and a reserve, held
the hill of Santon and the lowlands around, with every advantage
for an effort against the Allied right. The battlefield, therefore, was
made, so to speak, a theatre by the antagonist chiefs, to assure
defeat and victory alike; and Kutusof, it is said, foretold the issue
with an assurance equal to that of Napoleon.

These operations led to the great fight of Austerlitz, the
masterpiece of war, I think, of this century. By the early
dawn, four big Austrian and Russian masses were in motion
to turn Napoleon's right, advancing slowly in the oblique order;
but they toiled painfully through the difficult ground; and
they were kept at bay by the little force of Davoust, which,
holding Sokolnitz and Telnitz, defied their efforts. Ere long
a tremendous onslaught of war burst suddenly upon the Allied
centre, thinned by the divisions sent to the left; Napoleon, who,
like a crouching tiger, had reserved his strength until it was time
to spring, launched Soult and Bernadotte against Pratzen, and the
enemy's centre was cut through spite of heroic efforts. Meanwhile Lannes had assailed the enemy's right; here, too, a noble
resistance was made; but science and skill, force being nearly
equal, must always prevail over the sternest courage; and victory
soon declared for the French. Early in the afternoon the Allied
centre and right, half ruined, were a dissolving mass; and though
the left had forced Davoust back some distance, it was isolated
and entangled in an intricate region. It was beginning to retreat,
its cumbrous masses demoralised and showing signs of panic,
when Napoleon turned against it with that determined energy
which he nearly always displayed in a successful battle. His
victorious centre was brought to bear in irresistible power on the
flying enemy; a horrible scene of carnage followed; the Austrians
and Russians were slain or captured in thousands without an
attempt at resistance; and multitudes perished in the lakes near
the Goldbach, the French artillery shattering their frozen surface.
The stricken army was well-nigh destroyed; it lost all its guns;
and nearly half its numbers, and its fragments were scattered in

every direction. The coalition succumbed under this mighty stroke; Prussia said "Hail" to the conqueror, and licked his hand; Alexander was too glad to escape beyond the Niemen, with the remains of his army; and Austria, her constancy at last broken, was compelled to accept the Peace of Pressburg, which deprived her of all she had retained in Italy, and contracted the limits of her shrunken empire. In the general dismay of Continental Europe, England alone had consolation and hope; she had lost Nelson, but that greatest of seamen had annihilated the fleets of France and Spain on the ever memorable day of Trafalgar.

It is unnecessary to dwell on the first part of this campaign; for the operations that led to the surrender of Mack were, I have said, akin to those that hemmed in Mélas. The Allies were in a false position on the theatre of war, as the Austrians were in 1800; Napoleon enveloped one of their armies, as before Marengo he had closed round the Austrians. The movements of 1805 were less fascinating, I have remarked, than those of 1800; and the great superiority of Napoleon over Mack in numbers make them less astonishing and strike the mind less; but they were conducted upon a grander scale, were more scientific, and were better prepared. The march on Vienna was a fine operation; but it will always remain questionable if the Emperor ought to have hazarded the advance into Moravia; assuredly had the Allies fallen back and waited, he would have been exposed to the gravest perils.

The grand incident of the contest is, however, Austerlitz, a battle that should be studied by every thinker on war. It is a poor account of this mighty conflict to say that it represents the system of Frederick at odds with that of Napoleon, and exploded by it; the result depends on much deeper causes than tactical orders on a field of battle. No doubt the Allies tried to attack in Frederick's fashion; no doubt the French attacked in columns with skirmishers; no doubt the hostile armies may be compared " to a long bar of iron, inferior in strength and suppleness to a chain of many links," to use the metaphor of an accomplished writer. But Austerlitz was not an affair of mere methods of offence; it was the triumph of marvellous genius in war over pedantry and ignorance of the higher parts of tactics. The Allies placed themselves on the ground as badly as possible; they made a long flank march under the guns of an enemy; their turning movement inevitably failed in the region in which the attempt was made; and had Daun been before them they would have been defeated, though Daun could no more have achieved Austerlitz than he could have written *Othello* and *Hamlet*. On the other hand, Napoleon occupied the ground with perfect judgment, made every feature in it conform to his ends; placed his army upon it in the exact positions in which its attack would be most decisive, and made the very most of the false moves of his enemies. The result was complete; only two-thirds of an army rather weaker than its foe in numbers, and much weaker in guns, simply shattered to atoms a more powerful force, with a loss comparatively very small; and this, though the Austrians and Russians fought extremely well. In all this we see what Napoleon has called the "divine side of war," not its mere evolutions; the difference, he has said, is that between a "book of the *Iliad* and a page of a grammar." Yet masterpiece as this great battle was, I do not think it surpasses Ramillies in the dispositions that were made before it, and in the manner in which the enemy was reached and conquered. We see the same insight in both instances; the same thorough perception of the nature of the ground, and the means of taking the best advantage of it; the same perfect appreciation of the faults of the enemy, the same admirable distribution of the victorious armies. In one respect, however, Marlborough perhaps was inferior to Napoleon in execution; he did not strike down Villeroy with the tremendous force with which the Emperor crushed the Allies, and did not show the same wonderful power in victory. Yet I hesitate here, for we must remember Blenheim, and the absolute destruction of Tallard's army; and in comparing the two battles, we must bear in mind that the three arms in Napoleon's day had acquired a "mobility" and a power in the field unknown in the first part of the eighteenth century, and were, therefore, far more effective against a defeated army.

I cannot notice the Confederation of the Rhine, the creation of vassal kingdoms beyond France, as appendages to the House of Bonaparte, and the enormous extension of the French Empire from the Zuider Zee to the extreme verge of Italy. The dream of setting up again the throne of Charlemagne in the generation of the French Revolution, and of holding down martial States by sheer force of arms, is characteristic of the extravagance sometimes seen in Napoleon; and it indicates also that profound scorn of anything resembling popular rights and movements which is a marked feature of his wonderful nature. War broke out soon again on the Continent, and Prussia, unaided, challenged the French Empire. That Power had been willing to wound, and yet afraid to strike; she had feigned submission after the rout of Austerlitz, but she remained angry and vexed at heart, and the domineering conduct of the Imperial conqueror goaded her at last to proclaim hostilities. The Court and even the nation rushed to arms; the misgivings expressed by veterans of the Seven Years' War, who had followed events from 1794 to 1805, were disregarded with false confidence; and two armies, about 150,000 strong, led by Prince Hohenlohe and the Duke of Brunswick, marched from the Elbe and the Oder to the Thuringian Forest.

The operations of the campaign of 1806 are, perhaps, less marked by Napoleon's genius than that of more than one previous contest; but they achieved success that even now seems marvellous, and they conspicuously illustrate one of his peculiar gifts, power in annihilating a defeated enemy. The Grand Army, about 180,000 strong, was on the Main, not having returned to France when the Prussian chiefs had assumed the offensive, and the Emperor joined it in the first week of October. At this moment Hohenlohe and Brunswick were contemplating an advance to the Rhine. Bold strategy, they boasted, was all that was needed to overcome the Corsican upstart, and the Grand Army was spread from Wurzburg to Bamberg capable of being easily moved on their flank. Napoleon determined to gain this advantage, and, forming his army into three great masses, he began to traverse the defiles that lead from the southern verge of the forest towards the Saale and the Elster. The movement, executed with his wonted promptitude, brought the Grand Army into the plains between the two rivers on the 10th of October, threatening the communications of the enemy with the Elbe; and Hohenlohe and Brunswick, passing from boasting to terror, fell back towards Weimar and Jena, to approach the Elbe. Napoleon, who, at the beginning of the campaign, expressed unfeigned respect for the famous army of Frederick, would not at first believe that generals of a great school would make such a hasty retrograde movement; and he drew part of his forces together, expecting to fight a great battle near Gera and Auma, points in the valleys of the Saale and the Elster. This miscalculation cost him the loss of some time, for his enemy had no intention to stand, and, meanwhile, the retreating armies had fallen back a considerable way towards the Elbe, the main body under Brunswick making for the line of the Unstrutt, a feeder of the Saale, and the defile of Kosen, a smaller force, led by Hohenlohe, halting near Jena in order to call in outlying detachments, and then to follow Brunswick to the Elbe. Napoleon began to pursue when he had ascertained his mistake; he was greatly elated by the results of partial engagements with small hostile bodies, in which the superiority of the French tactics was manifest, and he wished to compel the Prussians to accept battle. But his information was still imperfect; he would not credit so rapid a flight; he believed that by far the greatest part of the enemy's army was concentrating near and around Jena; and his plan was to overwhelm it in front, and to cut off its retreat. With this object in view, he directed Davoust and Bernadotte to seize the defile of Kosen, crossing the Saale at the points of Naumburg and Dornburg; and with the main part of the Grand Army spread out in many columns he drew near the river and advanced on Jena.

These operations led to Jena and Auerstadt, fought on the 14th of October 1806. By the night of the 13th Napoleon had seized, had occupied by an advanced guard, and had crowned with guns brought up with infinite toil—the Emperor followed the train in person—the Landgrafenberg heights, since known by his name, which commanded the approaches to the plains beyond ; and from this point he saw the army of Hohenlohe, the bivouacs marked by miles of fires, extending along the region between Jena and Weimar. He made his dispositions for a great battle, still fixed in the belief that Hohenlohe's army was the principal part of the hostile forces ; and as he knew that, in any event, he would be in preponderating strength on the field, he prepared to attack Hohenlohe in front, and to turn both his flanks, and he directed Davoust to advance even beyond Kosen, to defeat, if he could, the army of Brunswick, and to close on the rear of the two Prussian armies. The battle of Jena began in the early morning ; the first movement of Napoleon was to debouche from the Landgrafenberg into the plains beyond, and this was accomplished with little difficulty, Hohenlohe having altogether failed to perceive the importance of this position. When the French army had fully taken its ground, Napoleon had 100,000 men against 60,000, and the issue of the battle could not be doubtful. Ney, indeed, the ill-fated "bravest of the brave," the warrior of Elchingen and of the Moskwa, engaged his troops prematurely, and met a severe repulse ; and the Prussians displayed the stern devotion, and even the precision and skill in manœuvre characteristic of them in the Seven Years' War. But Hohenlohe's force, weaker as it was, was divided ; the attack of Lannes, the Guard and Murat in front—the chief of the Imperial cavalry is well known to fame—that of Soult and Augereau, another marshal, on either flank, became impossible to resist ; and though the Prussians "fought like tigers," an eye-witness has said, and Napoleon* sincerely praised them in his account of the battle, Hohenlohe's army was before long routed.

Meanwhile a battle of a very different kind had raged at Auerstadt, a few miles off, on the line of the retreat of the defeated Prussians. Davoust had issued, as he had been ordered, from the defile of Kosen ; but as he advanced he became

---

* Bulletin of the Grand Army the day after the battle : " L'armée ennemie etait nombreuse et montrait une belle cavalerie ; ses manœuvres etaient executées avec precision et rapidité."

aware of the great strength of the army of Brunswick, and he entreated Bernadotte to come to his aid. That chief, however, insisted on remaining at Dornburg, relying on the letter of Napoleon's despatches; and it is doubtful whether this unwise resolve is to be attributed to the servile obedience characteristic of the Imperial marshals, or to miserable jealousy and dislike of a colleague. Davoust was now left with about 27,000 men to confront Brunswick, who must have had 70,000 had his force been well in hand; and the Marshal directed one of the finest battles of the whole period of the wars of Napoleon. He tenaciously kept Brunswick at bay for hours, but he must have been overwhelmed had Brunswick displayed the energy of the Austrian chief at Marengo; and in that event the two Prussian armies would have successfully effected their retreat to the Elbe. Brunswick, however, and most of the Prussian leaders, fell, and in a fatal hour the wretched advice was given to retire, and seek the support of Hohenlohe's army, known to be making a stand at Jena. Within two or three hours the wrecks of that perishing force became entangled with the troops of Auerstadt; the contagion of demoralisation and panic spread, and the two armies broke up in headlong flight, ravaged and never let to rest by the French cavalry. Once more Napoleon gave proof of his skill in pursuit, and on this occasion with extraordinary results. The Prussian army had no reserves; the beaten force was completely scattered, and made for the course of the Lower Elbe, and the French Emperor, seizing the chord of the arc, forced it, in masses of shattered fragments, northwards, and cut off five-sixths of it from all possible retreat. Within a few days the conqueror had entered Berlin; some 20,000 fugitives were the sole relics of a fine army of 150,000 men; these were driven into the wastes of the Lower Vistula, and the military power of Prussia was destroyed. Terrible scenes of weakness and despair followed; great fortresses opened their gates to hussars, and the monarchy of the chief of Leuthen toppled down in ruin. One of the last divisions that surrendered was that of Blücher, a rude soldier brought up in the school of Frederick, and destined to win a name in history.

The campaign of Jena, it has been remarked, bears a singular resemblance to that of 1870, in which, however, victory passed from Gaul to Teuton. In both instances there was the same arrogance and precipitate haste on the defeated side ; in both the same hesitation followed by panic ; in both the same superiority of force, general-ship, of all, in short, that secures success in war on the side of the triumphant conquerors ; in both the same utter collapse of a great military State. Prussia, however, unlike France, made no national effort to struggle out from under the heel of the victor. There was no siege of Berlin like that of Paris ; no Prussian Chanzy made his powers manifest ; no Prussian Gambetta refused to despair of his country, or organized a resistance, misdirected no doubt, but not the less heroic and even formidable. In this campaign, I have said, the strategic gifts of the Emperor are not so strikingly seen as in others which I have tried to sketch. The plan of debouch-ing into the valleys of the Saale and the Elster from the edge of the forest, though certainly the best, would have probably occurred to a general of the second rank ; and, as a matter of fact, it occurred to Jomini, then a young officer in the Imperial Service. In the operations, moreover, that led to Jena, Napoleon made more than one real mistake ; he lost time in preparing to fight near Gera and Auma. He was convinced that he was dealing with the main Prussian army at Jena. He ordered Davoust to advance beyond the pass of Kosen, and to close on the enemy, upon the false assump-tion that the force of Brunswick was not very great ; and owing to these misconceptions, he so placed his army on the scene of the two battles that Davoust escaped a complete defeat by a chance only —a result that would have caused the failure of the campaign. Most probably Bernadotte was to blame for not joining his brother Marshal, and averting a blow that might have been disastrous ; but Napoleon's orders to go to Dornbürg seem clear, and, in any case, as General-in-Chief, he is mainly accountable for a decided error. Yet the true student of war will not think the less of the Emperor for mistakes such as these. The greatest commanders must make mistakes, for they must act at once on imperfect know-ledge ; and the aphorism of Turenne is the simple truth, " He is the best general whose mistakes are the fewest."* For the rest, in the campaign of 1806, Napoleon's general conceptions were, as always, masterly. It is not surprising that he could not believe in the precipitate flight of a most renowned army; and his arrangements in the actual contest at Jena were those of a captain of the highest order; though he was so superior in force, they have little interest. What is to be chiefly dwelt on in this campaign is its illustration of the wonderful powers of Napoleon in destroying a retreating enemy. Many a chief would have followed the Prussians to the Elbe; the Emperor completely cut off their retreat, forced them into nooks and corners where they could not escape, and compelled the great body of them to lay down their arms. Napier was, perhaps, thinking of this great achievement when he compares Napoleon's battle to the "wave that effaces the landscape."

Napoleon, after the subjugation of Prussia, came into conflict with a more distant enemy. Alexander, the future head of the Holy Alliance, half French in ideas, but at heart a despot, had undertaken again to defend Old Europe; and notwithstanding the experience of Austerlitz, had solemnly vowed to avenge Prussia. His armies, however, moving slowly through the immense spaces of the Russian Empire, were unable to avert the ruin of Jena, or to prevent the fall of the Prussian Monarchy; it was November before they reached the Niemen, and they had not approached the Vistula for some time afterwards. The conqueror, who, in the intoxication of success, had launched against England the well-known Decree which declared her excluded from commerce with Europe, and established the famous Continental system, resolved to march against the new foe, and to strike down the Russians in the wilds of Poland. He made preparations, in Berlin, for a great winter campaign; and, looking behind and before, he left nothing undone to gain opinion in France, to make his military power irresistible on the theatre of war, and to secure a fresh base for an offensive movement. His arrangements were farsighted and masterly; for there is no

---

* This saying has been ascribed to Napoleon; it belongs to Turenne: "Les plus habiles sont ceux qui font seulement le moins de fautes."—*Memoires*, p. 5. Ed. Hachette, 1877.

wilder mistake than to suppose that Napoleon, though his imagination at times overcame his judgment, was not always the most profound and capable, as well as the boldest, of strategists. Magnificent public works enchanted Paris; rewards were lavished upon the Grand Army; and France, ever liable to be carried away by "glory," was, so to speak, entranced in dreams of Imperial grandeur. Meanwhile thousands of levies were called to join the eagles; the fatal system of anticipating the conscription began; vast bodies of troops were sent from the Confederation of the Rhine, from Italy, from Holland, and even from Spain; and these were stationed at intervals along the space extending from the Rhine to the Elbe and the Oder. Nor did the Emperor omit precautions to provide for these immense masses; the granaries of Germany were made to furnish supplies; the French cavalry were remounted in regiments from the establishments of the troopers of Seidlitz; and enormous magazines were prepared to support the hosts of Western Europe, in their march to the East. Napoleon, too, cast a scrutinizing eye on possible enemies and possible allies; he arrayed an army in Italy to observe Austria; and he tried to cajole the Sultan into attacking the Czar.

Towards the close of November, the Grand Army, extending from the Meuse and the Rhine to beyond the Oder, had reached the great strength of 300,000 men; and Napoleon expected a speedy triumph. Yet that vast host was already different from the soldiers of Austerlitz and of Boulogne, it was a "*colluvies gentium*," in the historian's words; it was crowded with young levies and half false auxiliaries; and the wand of the magician, so to speak, had changed in his hands. As yet, however, these elements of decline were not perceptible to any large extent; the warriors of Jena formed the first line; and the front of the Grand Army was moved to the Vistula, strong detachments being made to protect its flanks, and to subdue the fortresses Prussia still held in Silesia. Napoleon had reached Posen by the end of November; his troops had soon covered the plains of Poland; and when he attained the scenes of the famous Partition, the Poles greeted him as the coming liberator of their race. The Emperor, however, true to a nature to which popular stirrings were simply abhorrent, put off his suppliants with fair speeches; he enrolled the Poles in his ranks by thousands; but he never sought to make them an independent people. Irresistible in strength, as he believed himself to be, he had no wish to exasperate Austria, one of the partners in the destruction of Poland; and hard statecraft concurred with instinct in causing him to adopt a purely selfish policy. As yet, however, all went well; the Grand Army, probably 130,000 strong, held the line of the Vistula, and filled the tract between Thorn and Warsaw by the second week of December; the remains of the Prussian forces, and two Russian armies which had approached the river fell back at all points; and the formidable barrier of the great stream of Poland, held on both banks, was completely mastered.

The position of the enemy on the theatre of war now invited one of Napoleon's strokes. The hostile armies were widely apart, and disseminated upon a vast semi-circle; Lestocq, with the relics of Jena, about 20,000 strong, holding a line from Soldau to the Lower Vistula; Beningsen, a Russian chief, with perhaps 50,000 men, being in the angle where the Narew and the Wkra meet before they merge in the Vistula's waters; Buxhöwden, with probably 40,000, being far in the rear around Ostrolenka, in the country about the Upper Narew. The Grand Army, between Thorn and Warsaw, was in possession, therefore, of all the shorter lines on the field of manœuvre against its foes; and Bernadotte and Ney, on the left, were directed to attack and overwhelm Lestocq, while the corps of Augereau, of Lannes, of Davoust, and the Guard, with Soult in the rear, were to fall on Beningsen, to cut him off from Buxhöwden, and to drive the two armies into the deserts between the Bug and the Narew. The project was worthy of its renowned author; and the Grand Army began the movement from the Vistula in the last days of December. Napoleon, however, for the first time, found the forces of Nature and the state of the theatre arrayed against his rapid offensive strategy; and his conception was not even nearly realised. The region traversed was one of morasses and woods; there were scarcely any supplies to be found on the spot; the French soldiery, living on magazines from the rear, and sinking in expanses of swamp, were hardly able to march; and the cavalry could not ascertain the movements of the enemy behind whole leagues of forest. Comparative failure was the result; the allied armies effected their retreat; Lestocq eluded Ney and Bernadotte; Beningsen, who had encountered Lannes at Pultusk, and Davoust at Golymin, without a defeat—the corps of the Marshals had been misdirected, for it was impossible to reconnoitre the country—contrived to join Buxhöwden, though with great loss; and the converging armies found rest for some days on the vast and lonely plains of Eastern Poland. Napoleon, baffled, returned to the Vistula and placed the Grand Army in winter quarters extending from Warsaw almost to the coast; and his forces were spread on an immense line, for it was difficult in the extreme to find supplies, and there was no apprehension of possible danger.

Beningsen, however—he had been placed in supreme command—elated at what he deemed success, resolved to assume a bold offensive; he defiled between the long screen of forest and lakes, which divides the Narew from the Passarge; and he all but reached the corps of Bernadotte and Ney, a nearly isolated wing of the hostile army. Napoleon prepared a decisive counterstroke; he ordered Bernadotte and Ney to fall back, with the view of luring the enemy on; and he directed the other corps of the Grand Army to close on the rear of the Russian chief, when fully committed to the forward movement. It was a design worthy of the chief of Austerlitz; but Beningsen found it out through an intercepted despatch, and he instantly fell back from the Passarge to the Alle, in the hope of escaping his terrible enemy. Napoleon pursued with his accustomed energy; the vast plains, hardened by the frosts of the North, enabled his troops to move more rapidly; and he came up with his adversary, in position, round Eylau, where Beningsen, urged by his army, had consented to stand. The battle was fought on the 8th of February 1807; it was one of the most sanguinary of the wars of that age, and in the result it was a mere Pyrrhic victory. Each army was about 80,000 strong; but the Russians had many more guns; and this told heavily on the lines of the French, for Napoleon delayed his attack for some hours in order to allow his supports to come up. It is unnecessary to retrace the scenes of a conflict unmarked by peculiar tactical skill and notable chiefly for the stubborn constancy shown by the Muscovite soldier on many a field. The centre of the French, attacked in a tempest of snow, was shattered, and well nigh pierced through: a charge of Murat, and all his horsemen failed against the tenacious Russian infantry; the arrival on the scene of Davoust and Lestocq made the issue at several moments doubtful; but the scale was ultimately turned by Ney, who had hastened to the spot, by a forced march. The Russians, scarcely defeated, only just fell back; and Napoleon had suffered too much to move.

The carnage of Eylau on both sides was terrible; the corps of Augereau was nearly destroyed; and the Russians, packed in dense masses, had suffered frightfully from the continuous fire of the French artillery. But of the two conflicting hosts, the Grand Army was certainly the one most exposed to peril; the Russians were almost on their own ground; it was far from its base, with Germany in its rear, and its position for a time became extremely critical. Napoleon's triumphs, in fact, had been so unbroken, that he was deemed vanquished even in a drawn battle; a thrill of alarm and anxiety ran through France, and the humbled Continent was stirred to its depths. Had Beningsen possessed the gifts of Frederick, he would, at this juncture, have resumed the offensive; in that event, Napoleon must have retreated to the Vistula, at least, perhaps to the Oder; Austria, in all probability, would have taken the field; and the great Teutonic rising of 1813 might have been witnessed in 1807. But the Russian chief, though a capable man, was not a commander of the foremost rank; he had suffered immense loss, and he retired behind the Alle in order to place his army in winter quarters, confessing defeat by this retrograde movement. Indomitable constancy, we shall see hereafter, was not one of Napoleon's distinctive qualities, but he perfectly knew what a prodigious effect an imposing attitude has on mankind, and would necessarily have in the present state of Europe; and his conduct was that of a consummate warrior. In order to convince a doubting world that Eylau had been a French victory, he moved his army forward a little distance, and instead of falling back on the line of the Vistula, he ostentatiously placed every corps at hand in cantonments behind the course of the Passarge, braving a northern winter on the very verge of Russia. Meanwhile, he applied himself, with that amazing energy, that mastery of detail, that administrative power, for which he has perhaps had no equal, to reinforce and secure the Grand Army; to establish it firmly in its present position; and to make his military ascendency supreme. Two fresh levies of conscripts were made; his vassal kings, and still submissive Allies, were compelled to furnish more contingents to the theatre of war, and to comply with enormous demands for supplies; the forces required to hold Austria in check and to keep Prussia down were largely increased; Masséna was summoned with his corps from Italy to strengthen the front of the Grand Army; and Mortier, Duke of Treviso, another marshal, was sent with a considerable detachment to the Pomeranian sea-board, in order to guard against a descent from Stralsund on the communications and flank of the Imperial hosts expected to be made by a British force. Concurrently, a corps under Marshal Lefebvre was moved to undertake the siege of Danzig, a place of capital importance still held by Prussia; the sieges of the Silesian strongholds were pressed, and an alliance at last was made with the Sultan, who even proclaimed war against the Russian Empire. Months were spent in making their last preparations, at Osterode, near the banks of the Passarge; and Napoleon's correspondence alone can give the student of war an adequate notion of the prodigious ability of their great author.

The Emperor's exertions were completely successful; the Nemesis of conquest had not yet drawn near; and by the spring of 1807 his military power was established on broader foundations than ever; and he was ready to take the field with most imposing forces. By this time Eylau was a mere recollection; the Continent

10

had relapsed into bondage; and the Imperial armies, filled with bad elements as they were, reached the enormous number of half a million of men, spread from Champagne to the limits of Eastern Prussia. Meanwhile, no attack had been made from Stralsund; Danzig had fallen with the Silesian fortresses; the Porte had compelled Duckworth to leave the Dardanelles; the Turk was in arms against the Czar; and the cause of old Europe seemed once more desperate. With both his flanks covered, and his base secure, Napoleon had 160,000 men in perfect order upon the Passarge, ready to take the offensive at the first moment when the growth of vegetation would supply the means of subsistence to his thousands of horses. Yet such is the waste and strain of war that, even at this time, 60,000 men were missing from the rolls of the Grand Army, and spread along its rear, living on plunder and straggling; and this, notwithstanding the astonishing efforts of Napoleon throughout the whole winter. In fact, railways being as yet unknown, the means of transport were still imperfect, and the admirable arrangements by which the German armies of the present day are moved and supplied were impossible, especially along an enormous line.

The success of the Czar in reinforcing his armies had been trifling compared with that of Napoleon; and England, as we have seen, had made no diversion. The Russian Guards were despatched from St. Petersburg, and troops were in march from other parts of the Empire; but Beningsen, in the last days of May, had scarcely more than 120,000 men to oppose to the Grand Army of 160,000; and this though the Russians were close to their frontier, and the Emperor was hundreds of miles from the Rhine. In these circumstances, the Russian chief ought to have stood cautiously on the defensive; but he endeavoured to repeat the attempt of the winter; and breaking up from his camps on the 5th of June, he fell on Ney, somewhat widely detached, and on the extreme left of the Grand Army. Ney, however, a tactician of real skill, held the enemy in check, and slowly fell back; Napoleon tried a counter-attack once more; and he marched against Beningsen, from the Passarge, in the hope of gathering on his flank and rear. The

Russian contrived to effect his escape ; a great entrenched camp which, after the fashion of Daun, he had fortified, arrested the onset of the French ; and he reached the Alle and began to retreat along the right or eastern bank of the river, in the hope, apparently, of reaching Königsberg, where immense supplies had been stored for his army. The Emperor followed along the western bank, his object, too, being to attain Königsberg ; and his foremost corps came abreast of the Russians, the rest of the Grand Army being somewhat divided, and a considerable part being in the rear. This state of affairs encouraged Beningsen, in an evil hour, to try to attack his enemy. On the 14th of June 1807, he began to cross to the left bank of the Alle, at daybreak, with more than half his army; and by midday he had assailed the corps of Lannes, for the moment isolated and in advance. The French marshal, however, made a determined stand ; in a short time Mortier, the Guard, the chief part of the cavalry, and Napoleon, had arrived on the scene, and the corps of Bernadotte and Ney soon made their appearance.

Napoleon seized the position of affairs at a glance, and made everything ready to destroy an enemy who had recklessly offered battle with a great stream in his rear. With complete mastery of the grander part of tactics, he commanded Lannes and Mortier to fall back, in order to draw Beningsen some distance forward ; and Ney and Victor, another marshal, in temporary command of Bernadotte's troops, were directed to seize the bridges thrown across the river not far from the little town of Friedland by Beningsen, and to cut off his retreat. This admirable stroke completely succeeded; and apart from the fact that Napoleon's forces were by this time greatly superior in numbers, the defeat of the Russians had been rendered certain. Beningsen fell imprudently into the snare ; Lannes and Mortier seemed to yield to the Russian masses ; and when these had advanced too far to escape, Ney, covering his attack with a tremendous fire, and his colleague made the decisive movement. The bridges were taken and destroyed after a stout resistance ; and the Russians were forced back against a deep river, hemmed in, captured, and drowned in multitudes. A fragment

10 *

only of the army got across the Alle; and Beningsen fled to the line of the Niemen, followed by his indefatigable and pitiless foe. The Grand Army halted on the Muscovite frontier; the Czar had no choice but to seek an armistice; and the French eagles which had flown from the Channel, overshadowing Germany in their ravening flight, closed their Imperial wings on the edge of Old Europe. Troops of Tartars and Kalmucks armed with bows and arrows, and scattered along the banks of the Niemen, in the vain hope of arresting Fate, attested the exhaustion of the Russian Empire.

The twofold campaign of Eylau and Friedland does not exhibit in its highest aspects Napoleon's marvellous genius in the field. His project of attacking the Allied armies on the Wkra and Narew, at the close of 1806, undoubtedly was worthy of a great strategist; and his plan of falling back to draw Beningsen, and of doubling on him when he marched from the Passarge, reveals once more his pre-eminent gift of stratagem. The stroke delivered at Friedland, decisive and splendid, was that, too, of a master of tactics in their highest sense; the vulnerable side of the enemy was at once detected; and his position on the battle-field was made to cause his ruin. Still, the strategy of the Emperor in this contest comparatively failed in more than one instance; the extension of his cantonments—this was due, I repeat to the extreme difficulty of supporting his army—exposed him to attacks of a formidable kind; and he barely escaped defeat at Eylau. The most conspicuous proof this campaign affords of his military capacity is his steadfast attitude amidst a host of enemies, when beyond the Vistula, and his administrative triumph in restoring his army; these are examples of powers of different kinds, but alike indicate supreme ability. The chief lesson of this campaign, however, is that even Napoleon's wonderful gifts could not overcome impassable obstacles; his grand offensive strategy hardly succeeded, because the conditions forbade success; his brilliant manœuvres missed their mark, because his troops could not live in Poland as they had lived in the fertile plains of Italy, and could not move rapidly in wastes of swamp; the Phaeton of war found himself opposed by the forces of Nature and well nigh succumbed.

The end, nevertheless, was as yet distant; and Fortune raised her favourite to a still more dazzling eminence. Napoleon had felt, during recent events, that prodigious as his military power was, he was isolated in a hostile or unfaithful Europe, and he resolved to turn to account his recent victory by endeavouring to make his humbled adversary a permanent ally of the French Empire. To attain this end he had two great advantages, the ascendency of astonishing success, and a power of subjugating men which seemed like magic; and Alexander, indeed, wounded to the quick by the conduct of England in the affair of Stralsund, was ready to yield to England's deadly enemy. In the presence of their armies on either bank, the two Sovereigns met on a raft on the Niemen; the town of Tilsit was chosen as the seat of the conferences which immediately followed; and the fascinations of Napoleon had soon won over the young Czar to alliance, and even to friendship. All that passed in these interviews is still unknown, but the Revolutionary Monarch and the half Oriental despot agreed to re-model the map of Europe, and formed plans of the most far-reaching ambition. Each declared England the common enemy; and Alexander consented, at Napoleon's instance, to adopt the Imperial Continental system, to close the ports of Russia to British commerce, to summon England to make peace at once, and, should she refuse to array against her the navies of every state in Europe, invited or compelled to obey the mandate. Meanwhile, Sweden was to be despoiled of Finland; the never-changing ambition of the Czars was to be gratified by great Turkish provinces; Constantinople was talked of as a prey; and a Russian advance to the Indus, it is believed, was discussed. In return for these immense concessions to a defeated enemy, Napoleon obtained the recognition of the French Empire, and of the order of things he had set up in Europe; the Czar pledged himself to make common cause with his ally in his contest with England; and Alexander perhaps agreed to the conquest of Spain. To complete the new arrangement of the European world, in the interest of the Lords of the

West and the East, Prussia was to lose nearly [half her territory, and to be reduced to a second-rate power. Napoleon announced that he would have gone farther but for his regard for his Imperial friend. Saxony was to be made a counterpoise to her old rival in Germany, as a mere French dependency; and the craving of the Poles for national life was to be appeased by the mock creation of a Grand Duchy of Warsaw for the House of Saxony.

I cannot dwell on the policy of Tilsit, unequivocally condemned by all writers. It was a conspicuous instance of the extravagance sometimes shown by Napoleon, even in war, but often in the less familiar sphere of politics. It was a mistake to challenge England, the ruler of the seas, and the treasurer of Europe, to prolong a contest in which, after Trafalgar, she could not be invaded; and the Continental system was a chimera of force more injurious to French than to British interests. It was a mistake to reverse the policy of France for centuries, to abandon Sweden, and to betray the Turks, especially when these had become her allies; and it was idle to suppose that the fiat of a Czar would add to the stability of the French Empire. It was a mistake, too, of the worst kind to trample on the State and the people of Frederick; and it was an insult to the Poles to put the nation off with the phantom of a Grand Duchy of Warsaw. But the greatest mistake of all was to give a free rein to the ambitious impulses of two despots; to place the Partition of Europe at the will of two men essentially opposed in nature and interests; to suppose that the rulers of France and Russia could ever join in a lasting alliance. General war, the shifting of the boundaries of States, the destruction for a time of the European system, and implacable international passions and hate, were the inevitable results of this scheme of rapine; and beside that it had no element of strength and endurance, it was certain to lead to a rupture between its authors. In this unnatural arrangement we see no trace of the genius of Richelieu, of Cavour, of Bismarck; it was a mere ephemeral product of force, in opposition to the nature of things, and simply impossible to become permanent. This, however, was not perceived by the conqueror, covered with the adulation of France and the Continent; and Napoleon at this moment might, indeed, imagine that his power was beyond the perils of Fortune.

A word on the state of Napoleon's Empire, at this time at the height of its greatness, though its borders were to be still extended. France had long ago reached what the national instinct had pointed to as her natural limits; she was bounded by the Rhine, the Alps, and the Pyrenees; but girdled all round by dependent States, and supreme in Italy and in fully half of Germany, she was really the mistress of Continental Europe. Nor was this immense dominion the mere spoil of conquest; the vigorous and able rule of Napoleon had done wonders for old France, and had conferred the greatest benefits on her new possessions; and the institutions he founded still flourish far beyond the Rhine, and even along the Danube. The prosperity of the Empire was growing and splendid; the continuance of order and the collapse of anarchy had given free play to the energetic interests which the Revolution had called into being; nay, the tributary States had, to a great extent, been renovated by the hand of Napoleon. The creative genius of the Emperor, too, had accomplished marvels in administration and finance, and had completed fine monuments of material grandeur; magnificent roads overcame the Alps, and connected the Atlantic with the Mediterranean shores; and Paris, rich with treasures of art from all lands, and crowded with new and imposing structures, put on the aspect of Imperial Rome, and gathered into her lap the fairest spoils of conquest. Military power, besides, invincible as yet, and the glory of years of triumphs in war, protected this fabric of far-spread dominion; the ruling race still prevailed in the Grand Army; its commanders, lavishly rewarded, were docile instruments of a chief still in the flower of his age; and the flaws and defects in it were not yet conspicuous. Nevertheless, even now, one or two deep thinkers, amidst the terror and submission of three-fourths of Europe, had declared that the Empire could not be lasting. With its vassal Bonapartes, its enormous extent, its sway over subdued but mighty races, its mediæval pomp, its *parvenu noblesse*, its violence, and its despotism of the sword, it was an anachronism in the nineteenth century; its grandeur and even its beneficence could not hide its oppression; it was established among a people prone to change, and demoralized by Revolutionary passions; and, in antagonism to all moral and social forces, it depended on a single life and a conqueror's genius. Greater as it was, too, than the monarchy of Louis XIV., it was shut out from the sea by England, a source of weakness and peril to a maritime State; and it had no foundations in the organic structure, the history, or the traditions of the French people. Most ominous of all, the Empire seemed to destroy intellect and public worth in France: it was barren of great men of letters, and of great citizens; it produced only soldiers and a servile herd of functionaries.

I pass over the immediate results of Tilsit, the oppression of every small neutral Power, Copenhagen, the invasion of Finland, and the dissensions which, following the friendship pledged on the Niemen, were left unappeased by the meeting at Erfurt of the two potentates already distrusting each other. Napoleon soon began to repent of the promises he had made to Alexander respecting the Turks; but he continued to use the Russian alliance, unstable as it was, for his grasping ambition. The Czar, I have said, perhaps consented that his conqueror should work his will on Spain; and before the Grand Army had nearly returned to France, Napoleon had begun to make preparations to annex the whole of the Iberian Peninsula. A quarrel was forced on Portugal, on the pretence that she was evading the Continental system, and would not exclude English trade from her ports; and Junot, Duke of Abrantes in the Napoleonic peerage, was sent with an army of conscripts, at the close of 1807, from the Pyreneean frontier, to occupy Lisbon. The fate of Spain had been already settled; that Monarchy had, for many years, been almost an abject vassal of France; it had given her ships, soldiers, and a noble colony; and it had sacrificed a navy in her cause at Trafalgar. But the fiat had gone forth that the House of Bonaparte should replace the House of Bourbon on the throne of Charles V. Junot was ordered to "observe" the Spanish fortresses; and large bodies of French troops were gradually moved towards the borders of Spain, from the Loire and the Garonne. I cannot dwell on the Machiavellian statecraft which brought about the invasion that followed, on Aranjuez, and the plot of Bayonne. The dotard Charles fell into the arms of the tempter; the rights of Ferdinand his son were set aside with contempt, and Joseph, a brother of Napoleon, put off the Crown of Naples to assume that of Spain and the Indies.

The Emperor, however, might have recollected what the character is of that strange people, which has more than once baffled the greatest warriors, amidst the ranges of its hills and defiles, and has done wonders in the defence of its cities. Spain sprang up to a man, from the coasts of Galicia to Andalusia and the Pillars of Hercules; "Death to the foreigner!" was the fierce national cry; local juntas were formed in every province to direct and sustain the great movement; levies were poured into the army by thousands; and a call to arms, like that of France in 1793, led to an almost universal rising. Napoleon ere long found that it was no easy task to pacify and subdue a country like this; and his contemptuous scorn of popular passions—"the stirrings of the *canaille*" was a common phrase of his—made him neglect obvious precautions of war, and had soon involved his arms in a signal disaster. When the insurrection broke out, in the summer of 1808, he had about 120,000 men in Spain, along the main roads between Bayonne and Burgos; and had he operated after his wonted fashion, he could easily have conquered the northern provinces. But in his disdain of "armed mobs," he tried to overrun the whole country at once; and, simply ignoring every rule of strategy, he divided his armies into small fractions, and sent them, in flying columns, west, east, and south. Thus employed, his forces could not perform their task; Bessières, indeed, a marshal, the Duke of Istria, routed a considerable army at Rio Seco; Moncey penetrated into the heart of Valencia; and Dupont, a soldier of brilliant promise, marched into Andalusia, sacked Cordova, and even approached Cadiz. The insurrection, nevertheless, was everywhere; swarms of guerillas, gathering on all points of vantage, and impossible to destroy, cut off the French by hundreds; and Moncey and other generals found themselves

checked by armed multitudes, formidable behind ramparts. Ere
long, terrible news from the south arrived ; Dupont was caught and
surrounded by the chief part of the regular army of the fallen
Monarchy, in the recesses of the Sierra Morena, and with his
troops was compelled to lay down his arms ; and though possibly
he might have done more than he did, he was hemmed in by immensely superior numbers. Even worse intelligence came from
Portugal, and the French army at the mouth of the Tagus. I shall
afterwards review the career of Wellington ; enough here to say
that he first set foot in Portugal in the early days of August 1808 ;
and he defeated Junot, who by this time, too, was isolated in the
midst of a national rising, with considerable loss to the French, at
Vimeiro. The beaten chief and his army were too glad to effect
their escape from a victorious foe, and an insurgent country, by
accepting terms ; and they were ultimately embarked in British
transports, and landed on the western coast of France. By the
autumn of 1808 the French armies in Spain, humbled and baffled
by a despised enemy, had evacuated almost the whole Peninsula,
and had fallen back behind the course of the Ebro.

The indignation and amazement of the Lord of the Continent at
these untoward events, may be easily conceived. The great master
of war had been found wanting ; " a French general," he exclaimed,
" had justified Mack " ; and, worst of all, his trained and disciplined troops had failed before rude and half-armed masses. He
shut Dupont up in a State prison, and kept him immured through
the rest of his reign ; and how bitterly he felt the disgrace of his
arms is seen in his admirable remarks, made at St. Helena, on the
ruinous effects of capitulations in the field. The Emperor lost no
time in endeavouring to repair the injured renown of the French
army—the Czar and his ministers had secretly rejoiced—and, in
November 1808, he left the capital and invaded Spain with an
enormous force, determined, he wrote, " to put down rebellion."
He had five corps and the Guard in his hands ; the weak Spanish
armies, indulging in foolish boasts, and spread upon an immense line, extending from Biscay to the verge of Aragon, were
pierced through and scattered like sheep ; and Espinosa and

Tudela were two battles that were little better than huge butcheries. Yet these "examples," as they were called by the Emperor, were not attended by decisive success. Napoleon's manœuvres were perfectly designed; but plunged in the depths of a hostile country, and utterly unable to procure intelligence, Soult and Ney failed to cut off the retreat of the Spaniards, and the wrecks of their routed forces were soon restored by insurrectionary levies flocking in by; thousands. The way to the capital was, however, open; Napoleon mastered the Somo Sierra by a magnificent charge of his Polish horsemen, for he scorned to make a regular attack; and he entered Madrid, in the last days of December, at the head of a force that defied resistance. King Joseph was now installed on his throne; but there was no popular voice to say "God bless him"; the city was one of silence and mourning; and though a Constitution was announced for Spain, which abolished all kinds of old abuses and inaugurated many real reforms, the invaders remained as detested as ever. Against the feeble protests of his crowned dependant, Napoleon continued to rule by terror and force; when, as 1808 was closing, his attention was directed to a new enemy.

After Vimeiro, the successful army, placed under the command of Sir John Moore, had held Lisbon and been reinforced; and a fresh body of troops, led by Sir David Baird, had landed at Corunna to assist the Spaniards. Moore had marched northwards and joined Baird; and near the close of December he had approached Valladolid, threatening the communications of the French with Bayonne, and at the head of about 30,000 men. Napoleon had soon broken up from Madrid with an army perhaps 40,000 strong; he crossed the Guadarramas by a forced march in the hope of reaching and crushing his foe; and he directed Soult to combine the movement so as to fall on the rear of the British force. Moore, however, ably changing the line of his operations, made for Corunna; the Emperor pressed his enemy in vain; and he abandoned the pursuit in the first days of January, the attitude of Austria having become menacing and requiring his immediate presence in France. It is unnecessary to dwell on the events that followed; the British army made good its retreat, though with heavy loss, through the mountainous tracts that divide Leon from the Galician seaboard; and Soult proved unable to to bring it to bay.   Moore turned to fight at Corunna when about to embark; he beat Soult off in a well contested action; and though he fell, he knew that he had saved his army.   He had shown great ability in this brief campaign, remarkable for this too, that it was one of the few occasions on which the Imperial Guard beheld British troops, until ruin lowered on it on the field of Waterloo.

CHAPTER VI.

NAPOLEON—(*continued*).

THE Emperor, on his return to Paris, found a rupture with Austria already imminent. That great Power, tenacious but always prudent, had been forced to accept the Peace of Pressburg; but she never intended permanently to submit to an arrangement that perilously weakened the State. Meanwhile, she had been treated by Napoleon as a kind of reluctant vassal; he had armed against her in 1806-7; she had been shut out from the settlement of Tilsit, she had been compelled to accede to the Continental system; and she was alarmed at the announced extension of Russia along the verge of her Eastern provinces. She had gradually been increasing her forces for war; a great national militia—a strange institution in the realms of the Hapsburgs—had been created; her armies had been remodelled on the French system, and had adopted the French tactics; she had accepted large subsidies from the British Government; and Stadion, a patriot, and a deadly enemy of France, had for some time been her First Minister. The diversion of a large part of the Grand Army from the Rhine, and the successive disasters in Spain and Portugal, afforded her the opportunity she sought; and she had made great preparations for a fresh struggle with France, during the events of 1808 in Spain. Napoleon, unwilling to have two wars on his hands, tried to induce the Czar to enforce peace, by intervening in arms in Galicia; but Alexander eluded the demand; and, though he pretended to threaten Austria, and even sent an army to her eastern frontier, intended ultimately, perhaps, to act against the French, he really maintained a strict neutrality. The French Emperor concealed his resentment; and instantly made ready " to punish Austria" for what he called "her perjured and shameless conduct." His administrative faculties were again taxed to the utmost to attain his great ends ; but, as in 1807, they proved adequate.

A considerable part of the Grand Army was recalled from Spain, and moved to the Rhine ; the French garrisons which had occupied the Prussian fortresses were replaced by Poles, and restored to their colours; and Italy and the Confederation of the Rhine were again directed to yield their auxiliaries. Meanwhile conscripts were enrolled in thousands ; a levy was made from past conscriptions which produced numbers of adult men ; ingenious devices were tried to obtain a much needed supply of inferior officers; and though the finances of France were strained, the *matériel* for a great war was rapidly increased, and directed to the Rhine and thence towards the Danube. By the early spring of 1809, Napoleon had more than 400,000 men on foot; but the Grand Army too much resembled that which had been drawn together in 1807 ; though it had a great advantage in two respects, it was not summoned to fight on the verge of the Continent, and its inherent defects were not so apparent; and the Bavarians, who filled a large space in its ranks, had been for centuries foes of the Austrians. Yet Austria had had the start of Napoleon, notwithstanding his genius and his vast resources ; she was ready to strike with effect before him ; and had she struck at the end of March 1809 she might have achieved important success. She had learned a lesson from 1800 and 1805 ; and her forces were now arrayed on the theatre of the war at hand with a due regard to strategy. Her main army, nearly 200,000 strong, and under the command of the Arch- duke Charles, was in Bohemia, approaching the Danube, and obser- ing Bavaria, known to be hostile; a considerable force, under the Archduke John, was in the Tyrol—lost through Austerlitz, but always loyal to the House of Hapsburg—and was ready to make a descent on Italy ; and detachments were on the frontiers to watch the Poles and the Russians—these last were not really feared— and to observe Istria and Dalmatia, now Italian provinces. The

Archduke Charles, therefore, was in formidable strength on what was the principal scene of action ; and the forces of Napoleon were still much weaker, being not more than about 100,000 men, the corps of Davoust, advanced to Ratisbon, and the Bavarians holding the course of the Isar. The rest of the Grand Army was as yet on the Rhine, or only near the extreme heads of the Danube ; and the Archduke had an immense opportunity. For the rest, the Emperor had assembled a large army to defend Italy, and had given it to Eugene, son of the Empress Josephine ; but this was only a secondary force ; the valley of the Danube was the decisive point in the operations about to begin.

Napoleon was fully aware of the danger ; and at this very time he gave positive orders that, should the Austrians take the offensive, Davoust and the Bavarians should fall back on Donauwörth, and wait the arrival of reinforcements. These injunctions, however, were not complied with ; even now the reason is not known—the two exposed corps retained their positions ; and had the Archduke advanced from Bohemia, he must have taken Ratisbon and overwhelmed Davoust. But he hesitated, and lost precious days ; and at last, listening to feeble counsels—at heart he was not convinced by them—he broke up from his camps, made a circuitous march, crossed the Danube at Lintz, and arrived on the Inn, the ordinary line of Austrian attacks on Bavaria. He was on the Isar by the 15th of April, at the head of about 140,000 men ; he had left 40,000 behind in Bohemia ; and he forced the passage in three great masses, the Bavarians falling back, and drawing towards the Danube, midway between Ingoldstadt and Ratisbon. Had the Archduke collected his forces and moved rapidly, he should have still crushed Davoust, as yet, "in the air," and in great peril ; but he kept them apart on distant lines, and he actually detached his right wing towards Ratisbon, in the belief, it would seem, that his Bohemian corps would join him there and cut off Davoust. By this time, the 18th of April, Napoleon, who had left the capital five days before, had reached Ingoldstadt upon the Danube ; and the situation of affairs was such that the ablest commander might have felt alarm. Davoust was still at Ratisbon with 60,000 men; the Bavarians and other German auxiliaries were around Neustadt, perhaps 50,000 strong; and a part of the corps of Lannes, in the temporary command of Oudinot, afterwards Duke of Reggio, was with that of Masséna in march from Augsburg, both numbering perhaps 50,000 soldiers. The hostile armies were thus nearly equal in force; but that of the Archduke, although divided at greater distances than it ought to have been, was far more concentrated than the French army, which had been almost surprised and was still outgeneralled.

In this difficult position the situation was changed in an incredibly short time by Napoleon's skill and, it must be added, by the Archduke's blunders. Davoust was drawn in from Ratisbon towards the German corps; this was a flank march with an enemy at hand, but it led only to slight combats, and was not seriously checked or molested;* and Masséna and Oudinot were pushed forward with extreme velocity to Pfaffen-hoffen, to threaten the Austrian left which, in its march from the Isar, was round Mainburg, not far from the Danube These movements were executed by the 19th; and thus Napoleon's army was well drawn together, its right gathering on the enemy's flank, while that of the Archduke remained still scattered. The operations that followed recalled the exploits of the youthful chief of the army of Italy. On the 20th, the Emperor attacked the Austrian centre, now separated from the right near Ratisbon, with part of the corps of Davoust and the German contingents; he remained with the Germans during the battle—a marked instance of military tact—and he defeated the enemy with heavy loss near Abensberg. Meanwhile Oudinot and Masséna had reached the Austrian left, and had forced it back in retreat towards the Isar; and this, with the success at Abensberg, led to a complete triumph. Napoleon, leaving a large detachment to keep back the Archduke, bore down on the retiring enemy; and, joining Masséna, drove the Austrian left across the Isar, utterly beaten, and pursued to the Isar by a great mass of cavalry. The Emperor next

* The last words of Napoleon's despatch to Masséna are characteristic : " Activité. Activité, vitesse! Je me recommande à vous."

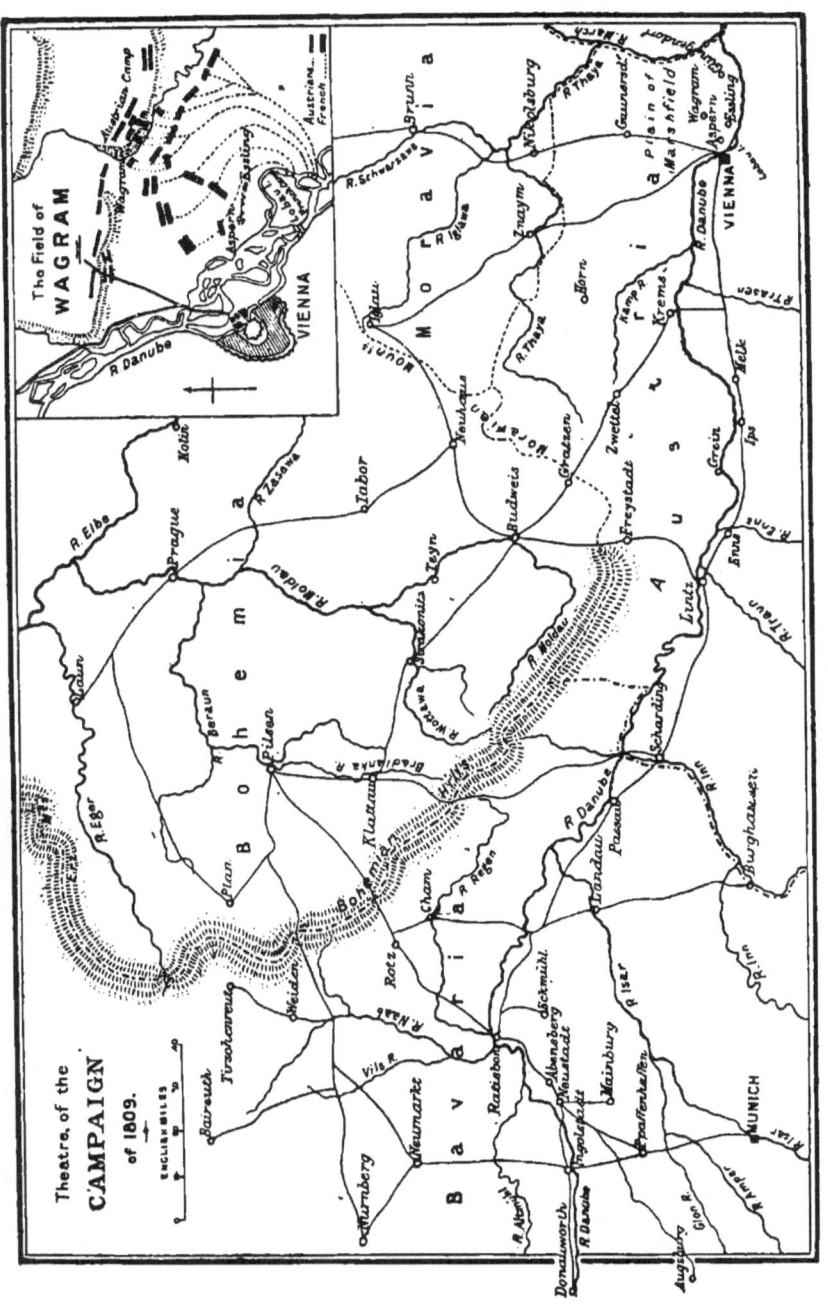

Theatre of the
CAMPAIGN
of 1809.

The Field of
WAGRAM

turned against his remaining foes; the Archduke drew n his right on his centre, and endeavoured to stand on the 22nd; but he was struck down at Eckmühl by superior forces; and with difficulty effected his escape on Ratisbon. By this time his lieutenant, Bellegarde, had reached the place with the Bohemian force, but farther resistance had become impossible; and the Archduke, with the remains of the principal army, was compelled to cross to the northern bank of the Danube. The shattered left wing was on the southern bank; and thus the great army which had crossed the Isar a few days before with every prospect of success had been cut in two, and was in eccentric retreat, divided by a broad and impassable river.

This splendid success on the principal scene effaced the results of French reverses on secondary parts of the theatre of war. Eugene Beauharnais had been defeated at Sacile, and driven behind the line of the Adige; the Tyrolese had broken out in revolt, and an Austrian army had entered Warsaw, and overrun the adjoining region. But Napoleon held the course of the Danube; the way to Vienna was thrown open; and victory at the decisive point made him master of the situation for the time. He was soon joined by the Guard, by fresh German contingents, by Bernadotte, and a great mass of cavalry; and, having detached Lefebvre to subdue the Tyrol, he began his second march to the Austrian capital. The operations were not so easy and rapid as they had been in 1805. Davoust was sent to the northern bank of the Danube, to observe the movements of the Archduke Charles; the defeated left wing, under the Archduke Louis, fought a desperate action against Masséna in pursuit; it crossed the Danube by the last bridge near Krems; and though Napoleon mastered the line of the stream, and covered his communications with large detachments, the two Archdukes effected their junction, and ere long had reached the great plain of the Marchfield, which stretches down to the northern front of Vienna. The Emperor entered the city on the 11th of May, and as he had probably 100,000 men, and the Archdukes had barely 80,000, he resolved to cross to the northern bank of the Danube, to overwhelm his much weaker enemy, and to finish the war in one decisive battle. But how was a river

11

hundreds of yards wide, of great depth, and with a powerful current, to be traversed by a large army under the guns of an enemy still formidable and holding the opposite bank ? Napoleon's extraordinary skill in choosing the ground for every operation of war was not found wanting, and his selection of the spot for the passage was perfect. Just below Vienna, a very large island, that will be known in history by its name of Lobau, breaks for some miles the course of the Danube; the channel between it and the southern bank, held by the French, is profound and broad; but it nearly touches the northern bank, and is only divided from the Marchfeld by a narrow channel. Napoleon, screening the work by all posssible means, threw a strong bridge over the great channel, thus connecting Lobau with the southern bank; and as the island is of ample size, he massed into it a large part of his army, and made preparations to secure the passage across the narrow channel by numerous bridges.

By the 20th of May the corps of Masséna, 30,000 strong, had debouched from the island across these ways into the edge of the Marchfeld; and it entrenched itself in the two villages of Aspern and Essling, its chief assured that the greater part of the army would cross by the morrow. The main bridge, however, over the great arm of the Danube—and it will be borne in mind there was only one—was broken in the night by the force of the current; and on the 21st the Archduke Charles attacked Masséna with greatly superior forces. The villages were defended with great skill and courage; but though the French succeeded in maintaining their ground, thousands were very nearly forced into the river; and had the Archduke struck home he must have been victorious. Great efforts were made on both sides to renew the struggle the following day.; Lannes with his corps, and part of the Guard and the cavalry, effected the passage during the night; and the Archduke called up all the reserves at hand, to make a stroke for a complete triumph. A murderous battle was fought on the 22nd; Lannes— he met a soldier's death on the field—made a formidable attack on the Austrian centre; and Masséna was about to debouch from Essling, when the news arrived that the principal bridge had broken down again, and had become impassable, and that munitions were short for a prolonged contest. The advance of the French was at once checked; their lines fell back behind Aspern and Essling, and though they kept their hold on the bloodstained Marchfeld, they suffered frightfully from the converging fire of the hostile batteries arrayed against them. By the 23rd they had taken a position in Lobau; and the army was so shattered that Napoleon's marshals pronounced an immediate retreat necessary.

Napoleon peremptorily set at nought these counsels; and, maintaining the attitude he had held at Eylau, refused to allow his army to stir from the island. His position, however, had become critical; the long line of his communications with the Rhine was largely guarded by mere auxiliaries; indignant Prussia was struggling in her chains; the secret societies, which were to rouse Germany to arms, spread from the North Sea to the Danube; and the French had escaped a disaster by mere accident. Yet their chief relied on his genius and the terror of his name, as he had relied when upon the Passarge; and the event justified his proud self-confidence. He evidently had perceived that it was a capital mistake to have committed his army to a single bridge across a river of the first order; and he applied himself, with accustomed decision and skill, to make the passage of the Danube assured, and to enable the Grand Army, whatever its size, to issue from Lobau and command the Marchfeld. I cannot describe the admirable works—marvels of engineering, never, perhaps, equalled—constructed under his eye, to carry out his purpose; his *Correspondence* remains to attest these monuments of his gifts as a warrior. The neighbourhood of a great city fortunately supplied the material required for his designs; in twenty days, three great bridges—one of boats, two on piles—spanned the main channel, and formed causeways, completely protected, and strong enough to bear the weight of the largest masses; and the efforts of the enemy to destroy them, by various devices, proved quite abortive. At the same time, Lobau was made a vast entrenched camp, armed with numerous batteries to defy attack; it was occupied by ever-increasing forces, as the strength of the Grand Army was raised;

11 *

and preparations were made so to bridge the small channel that it could become, so to speak, a series of highways. Meanwhile, the Emperor strained to the utmost his faculties to bring every available man and horse to the scene of decisive action. Eugene, who, after the success at Ratisbon, had followed the Archduke John from Italy, and was approaching Hungary, was called to the Danube ; so was Macdonald, another marshal, honourably known in history as Duke of Tarentum ; Marmont, Duke of Ragusa—an unhappy name—was summoned with his corps from the Dalmatian wilds; and while the lines of communications were firmly held, reinforcements were sent to the Grand Army from the divisions placed higher up the Danube. By these means the Emperor had made the passage of the river as certain as that of a plain ; and he calculated on having about 180,000 men concentrated for the grand and final effort.

The Archduke Charles, on the other hand, had failed to see through Napoleon's projects, and had not made nearly such good use of his time, though placed in the centre of the Austrian monarchy. He seems to have convinced himself that a great army could not issue from the camps in Lobau, within two or even three days ; and if he fortified Aspern and Essling, he did not guard the approaches eastward, though the island extends along these to the Marchfeld. His army, therefore, was not prepared for an attack from Lobau, sudden and in immense force, especially to the east of the villages ; and it was spread through the Marchfeld, some miles from the Danube, offering a vantage ground to his terrible enemy. Nor had the Archduke, though a general-in-chief, and having it would seem unlimited powers, strengthened his army as much as ought to have been possible. He left a very large detachment on the Polish frontier, where its presence could be of no avail; and he did not insist that the Archduke John—an insubordinate and conceited theorist—should join him with all his troops on the Danube. The Austrian army, therefore, was certainly weaker than it might have been on the principal point ; and it had not been largely reinforced by reserves or levies. It appears probable that it did not exceed 140,000 or

150,000 men, a force comparatively small if we bear in mind that of the two antagonists one was at home on the Danube, the other, far from the Rhine. In this, as in everything else, the contrast between the commanders opposed is most striking.

All was in readiness by the first week of July, for the grand operation of crossing the Danube. Thousands of troops, with all the impedimenta of war, guns, trains, field hospitals, and a huge *matériel*, had defiled over the great bridge; and on the night of the 4th, 160,000, French, Saxons, Bavarians, Italians, Poles, and auxiliaries from the petty German States—Napoleon's concentration had been made complete—were assembled in the entrenched camp of Lobau. Demonstrations had been made to deceive the enemy, and to conceal the real points of the passage; but the movement, though screened in part by the darkness, was soon heard along the silent shores. In an incredibly short time, not less than six bridges were thrown over the small arm of the river; and the army began to cross to the northern bank, covered by the fire of hundreds of guns in position. The different divisions — the Emperor himself had arranged their march with extraordinary care—were directed towards the expanse of the Marchfeld east of the points of Aspern and Essling; and they scarcely encountered any resistance, as this vast space had escaped the Archduke's notice. By the early morning of the 5th, 70,000 men had taken possession of the far-spreading plain; the rest of the Grand Army followed in order, and by the afternoon its extending masses held a long line from the right at Glinzendorf, to the extreme left on the verge of the Danube, the fortified posts of Aspern and Essling having been turned by this movement and rendered useless. The Austrian army, though completely surprised and outmanœuvred by Napoleon's strategy—a masterpiece from every point of view—had, by this time, advanced towards the enemy; some skirmishes of little importance occurred; but an effort made by Bernadotte against the Austrian centre, not far from Wagram, was sharply repulsed.

The hostile armies made their bivouacs in the plain, and prepared for the great fight of the morrow. The morning of the 6th rose on the great arrays that extended, on either side, for miles; and it witnessed the most far-spreading battle which had yet been fought in the civilized world. I cannot retrace the scenes of the contest; and, indeed, they have no features of peculiar interest. The Archduke, certainly much inferior in numbers, had resolved, with little prudence, to attack; and his general plan was to fall on the French right, so to force it back as to enable his brother, the Archduke John, to arrive on the field, and simultaneously to assail the French left in great strength, and to endeavour to cut it off from the Danube. The effort against the right failed; for Napoleon, aware that the Archduke John was approaching, had placed Davoust and Oudinot, with a great body of troops, on that wing; but the attack on the left proved formidable in the extreme. Masséna and Bernadotte were almost driven from the field; and the young levies and auxiliaries fled in thousands. Panic began to spread through the Grand Army— no longer the army of Jena and Austerlitz—and had the Archduke made the most of his success, he might, perhaps, have achieved victory. The extension, however, of both his wings had left his centre comparatively weak; and Napoleon was not slow to seize the occasion. He massed the whole Italian army, together with other contingents and the Imperial Guard, and struck a terrible blow at the vulnerable point; and the attack was preceded by such a fire of cannon as had never before been seen in the field. The battle, however, continued to rage; the Austrians fought with devoted courage; the ardour of the auxiliaries was not great; and though the pressure was taken off the Emperor's left, and Bernadotte and Masséna regained ground, the Archduke in the main retained his positions. His left, at last, was forced by a well-directed attack; Davoust and Oudinot carried the low uplands of Wagram; and the Austrian army slowly left the field, as the Archduke John showed no signs of appearing. The retreat, however, was not molested. The result of the day might have been different had the Archduke had the support of his brother; the carnage of the battle had, indeed, been terrible; but the victors captured few guns or prisoners; and Wagram did not approach Austerlitz. Still, Austria had made her last effort; she submitted to a humiliating peace ; and Napoleon returned in triumph to France, though he had been made painfully aware that the Grand Army was not the instrument of war he had at one time wielded.

Napoleon's genius in war shone grandly out in the memorable campaign of 1809. The movements around Ratisbon, he has said himself, were the most perfect of his military career ; and it would be impertinence to dispute his opinion. His army, in a position of extreme difficulty, was extricated by a series of marches, scientific, rapid, and daring alike ; and the enemy, who had gained a marked advantage, was outmanœuvred and completely defeated. Decision, energy, consummate skill, and the boldness that runs risk when there is no help for it, are the distinctive marks of these wonderful efforts ; and the operations against the Austrians, when once divided, are equal to those against Beaulieu and Colli. The march on Vienna, though not as rapid and decisive as in 1805, was in complete accordance with true strategy ; it was bold, and yet made thoroughly safe ; and the communications with the Rhine were made quite secure—as regards the numbers of defenders at least—for in this respect the Emperor was never careless. After the failure at Aspern and Essling, too, the resolution of Napoleon to hold his ground, spite of doubting lieutenants, and a plotting Continent, reveals the chief of supreme capacity ; and the administrative powers, the untiring energy, and the masterly art with which he drew together every possible man to the decisive point, deserve the admiration of all students of war. As for his choice of Lobau as the place to cross the Danube, in the face of the enemy, it is characteristic of his all but perfect insight ; the means he employed to protect his army, and to render the passage safe and certain, are models of conspicuous forethought and skill ; and the movement by which he turned the position of the Archduke, caused his defences to fall, and attained the Marchfield, at the head of immense forces, was a most striking exploit. Yet, in these dazzling displays of genius, one grave error was indisputably made ; the relying on a single bridge to conduct a great army across the Danube cannot be justified ; this nearly led to a frightful disaster ; and here we see, once more, that confident arrogance and that too passionate energy which show that the faculties of this marvellous being were not always controlled and balanced by sound judgment.

It should be added that these prodigies of war could not have occurred had Napoleon had an adversary worthy to cope with him. The Archduke Charles was a learned soldier; he had studied war, and proved more than equal to confront men like Moreau and Jourdan; but in his operations at Ratisbon, in his indecision at Essling, in his failure to prevent the French from crossing the Danube, in his remissness in not collecting his forces, in the incapacity with which he allowed his enemy to issue in to the plain of the Marchfeld,* we see a commander quite of the second order; and, in truth, like all the Continental generals,† he was paralyzed by terror when before Napoleon. As for the Emperor at Wagram, his skill in the great moves of tactics was conspicuous in his attack on the Austrian centre when weakened by the extension of the wings; the Archduke, too, did wrong in attacking, though he all but routed the French left; but these are not the most striking features of this well-contested battle. What the student of war should specially observe is that Wagram marks a notable change in the quality of the armies which met in conflict; a change that was to be yet more developed. The Austrians fought with heroic courage; they were animated by a strong national feeling, seen among them, perhaps, for the first time; they were wholly unlike the mere soldiers who had been routed under Beaulieu and Würmser. On the other hand, the Grand Army showed signs of weakness; except the Bavarians, the immense contingents of the auxiliaries were half-hearted and feeble; and the young French levies disbanded in thousands. The Austrian tactics and the formations of the troops, had also been extremely improved, while that of the Grand Army had changed for the worse. Conscious of the in-

---

* The monarchies and aristocracies of old Europe had an immense opinion of the Archduke Charles; but his reputation has steadily declined. He was as inferior to Napoleon as Pompey, the admiration of the Roman patricians, was to Cæsar.

† "Mais, Monseigneur, figurez vous qu'au lieu de Bonaparte, c'est Jourdan que vous avez devant vous," was the exclamation of an aide-de-camp, when the Archduke was in this mood of fear and hesitation.

feriority of the men in their hands, the French commanders had tried to make up for this by rendering their columns of attack more large and solid; and Napoleon had begun to adopt the system of increasing the number of guns to support his infantry. The density of the masses formed in this way—and the skirmishers, too, were not what they had been—made them heavy and inefficient in the shock of battle, and exposed them when engaged to most destructive fire; and the change in the proportion of foot to artillery was followed by evil results to both arms.

I cannot allude to the divorce of Josephine, the sacrifice of the young child of the Cæsars, flung into Napoleon's arms as a hostage of war, and the further extension of the immense Empire which, in its author's eyes, grew in strength as he enlarged its limits. To ordinary observers, the power of the Emperor seemed at its highest in 1810–1811; the Continent had succumbed to his omnipotent will; he had annexed Rome, Holland, and the Hanse Towns without a word of protest from the great German States; the Pope was a captive in gilded chains; the material and moral forces of five-sixths of Europe had yielded to that all controlling dominion. Yet the Empire was distinctly declining; and the truth had been perceived by more than one statesman, and by soldiers as different from each other as Blücher and Wellington. Napoleon at this time had 800,000 men in arms, including all his reserves for war; but the Grand Army had for some years resembled the enfeebled army of Imperial Rome, filled with barbarians who hated her yoke; the dominant race had ceased to be supreme in it; and unwilling or lukewarm allies, nay, the forces of conquered and reluctant nations, sustained the ill-cemented structure of conquest, itself an unnatural and monstrous portent. While central and eastern Europe, too, seemed to submit to bondage, Spain continued the struggle against her oppressor; the ubiquitous insurrection had never ceased, and defied the efforts of the Imperial Marshals; and the arms of Napoleon had received an affront, and had suffered reverses which had amazed Europe. Masséna had recoiled from Torres Vedras; a small British army, under an unknown commander, had baffled the might of the whole

French Empire, and had triumphed upon the Douro and at Talavera; and the jealousies and discords of Napoleon's lieutenants had led to all kinds of untoward events, and had wasted his forces throughout the Peninsula.   There was light at one point amidst the gloom which seemed to enshroud a vanquished world; and though Germany—then a divided land, and wholly unsuited to partisan warfare—had returned to quiescence after Wagram, the growing indignation against the rule of France, which had already made itself felt, was preparing the way for a universal rising.

Yet the signs that the Empire was in decay were not less apparent in France herself, the centre of that domination of the sword. The nation, always prone to change, had begun to get tired of a despotism opposed to " the principles of 1789 "; its appetite for glory had been more than sated; new ideas and forces growing up within it already indicated another coming era.   The power of these tendencies had been greatly increased by the sufferings the people were now enduring, by the severity of the Imperial rule, by the poverty and distress it had for some time entailed on once flourishing cities and districts.   Flattering bodies of State and satellites of power might boast that France was the Queen of Europe; but the devouring waste of the Spanish war brought desolation to thousands of hearths; and peace, under Napoleon, appeared impossible.   The never ceasing demands of the conscription, too, provoked general and bitter discontent; the laws on this "blood-tax" had been made barbarous; and the extent of the burdens imposed by the State had become, year after year, more onerous. The Continental system, besides, the most extravagant of Napoleon's projects, while it led him to aim at universal conquest, enormously lessened the resources of France; Marseilles, Bordeaux, and Havre became half deserted, and seethed with indignation at the Imperial rule; and the Continental war with England destroyed French commerce.   In addition, the finances had begun to decline; the frightful results of 1791–93 became apparent in a great falling off of youths fitted to enter the army; and, in short, despotism had done its work of exhaustion, causing general decay.   The feeling of stability and of assured greatness which had pervaded France at the peace of Amiens had for some time been passing away; and, a most significant fact, though a son was born to Napoleon— heir of world-wide grandeur—this made no change in the general sentiment. Yet the conqueror, from the heights of his splendour, did not see the shadows of night approaching; and though the war in Spain consumed the flower of his armies, and he had seen at Wagram what the Grand Army was, and the condition of France had become ominous, and Europe, he knew, was hostile to him, he committed himself to the most gigantic enterprise which ambition has ever, perhaps, suggested. False to his own genius, which must have shown him that Spain had become the principal scene of action for him, he resolved to invade and subdue Russia.

Peace, in fact, with the great Power of the North, had, for several years, been almost hopeless. The League of Tilsit was an impossible compact, full of seeds of disunion and ultimate strife; and war between France and Russia had become imminent. The Russian nobles detested the French alliance; the trade of Russia perished under the Continental system; the establishment of the Grand Duchy of Warsaw, a kind of pledge that Poland might again be a nation, was a direct menace to Russian ambition; and Russia could not regard with indifference the subjection to France of three-fourths of Germany. Alexander soon escaped from the spell of Napoleon; he secured, indeed, the spoils flung to him; but he bitterly resented Napoleon's conduct in having extended the Grand Duchy, and in refusing to promise that he would not restore Poland; and he was indignant at the recent annexations to France. On the other hand, the Emperor had not forgotten the lukewarmness and, perhaps, the treachery of the Czar in the contest of 1809; he charged him with evading the Continental system; he pretended that he was an ally of England; he treated with scorn his solemn protests against the addition of Holland and the Hanse Towns to the Empire. Preparations were made on both sides for war, as early as the autumn of 1811; Alexander abandoned the Continental system; made overtures to England, which were received; entered into negotiations with his Ottoman foes; and began to draw together two large armies towards the heads of the

Dwina and Dnieper—the river frontiers of old Muscovy—there to be combined with a third army from the South, when peace had been made with the Turks.   The arrangements of Napoleon for his gigantic enterprise were, necessarily, on a much larger scale; they were extraordinary in extent and grandeur; and they exhibit in the very highest degree his characteristic skill in stratagem, and his great capacity for organizing war.   One of his first objects was to gain time to collect his enormous military means, and to advance his huge arrays, when ready for the field, by degrees even to the Russian frontier, without opposition on the part of the enemy; and having attained this position of vantage, and mastered the resources of Eastern Europe, his purpose was to pour across the Niemen such forces that to resist would be useless.   To reach these ends, he kept up a show of diplomatic professions for months, which bewildered the Czar and made him hesitate; and, meanwhile, he secretly and swiftly combined the forces of Western Europe for his prodigious venture.   His experiences of 1806–7 made him perfectly aware of the difficulties of a task which no other man would have dreamed of attempting; but he said, "My means are vast, and I can devour obstacles"; and he addressed himself to the mighty work with wonted perseverance and administrative power.

His first care was to provide for the huge armies which were to march into the wastes of Russia; and for this purpose, as in 1806–7 the resources of Poland, of Prussia, and even of States on the Rhine, were placed in requisition for immense supplies; bases of operation and magazines were formed along the tract from the Elbe to the Vistula; a system of water-carriage, admirably planned, conducted all that was required for armed multitudes to the Vistula and the mouths of the Niemen; and the expedition was delayed until the summer of 1812, in order that myriads of horses should find pasture on the long march to the Russian frontier.   Meanwhile, Napoleon collected the forces he deemed necessary for this colossal effort.   Austria was now his ally, and Prussia a vassal; and both Powers furnished contingents to the Imperial host, which were to join as it approached the Niemen.   Bavaria, Italy, the Confederation of the Rhine, and

Holland, of course, obeyed their master and arrayed troops in immense numbers; and unhappy Poland, deceived yet trusting, sent tens of thousands of her brilliant horsemen to take part in a crusade which might give her freedom. France, the dominant Power, once more saw the Grand Army collected in strength; but Napoleon did not, in 1812, anticipate the conscription as in 1807; he enrolled masses of levies and reserves; but he dreaded an outburst of hostile opinion; and he tried to lessen the strain of the war on Frenchmen. By these various expedients 600,000 men, collected from every part of old Europe, were arrayed in arms in the spring of 1812; and these vast masses were slowly moved to their positions between the Rhine and the Vistula. Napoleon set off from Paris on the 1st of May; he left France, alarmed and discontented, behind; scarcely a cheer greeted the departing conqueror; his very Marshals disliked the enterprise; and even his docile Ministers and mute bodies of State were anxious and feared some great coming danger. Another sight, however, rose before his eyes when he entered Dresden after a rapid journey; a humbled Continent, in the person of the Head of the Hapsburgs, of kings, princes, dominations, and powers, bowed before the Charlemagne of a changed world; Napoleon received such homage as was never seen since Rome hailed her ruler as a god; and the enterprise was deemed so assured of success that it was talked of as a mere passage of arms. The Emperor reached the Niemen in the last week of June; and by this time the first line of the Grand Army, numbering upwards of 420,000 men, with 70,000 cavalry, and 1,200 guns, was extended along the Russian frontier, from the verge of the Baltic to the Galician plains. The sight might have turned the head of a Xerxes; but to the experienced eye of a great master of war, it ought to have been significant of evil omens. In that enormous army there were probably not more than 100,000 really good French troops; the rest was an assemblage of young French levies, of Austrians and Prussians, enemies of France, of auxiliaries who, except the Poles, had no sympathy with her cause or her chief, and who had, for the most part, showed what they were at Wagram.

The centre of the host, led by Napoleon, with Oudinot, Ney, Davoust, and Murat, inferior chiefs, crossed the Niemen on the 24th of June, in the angle, entering at Kovno, the Russian frontier ; the left, composed of the corps of Macdonald and the Prussian contingent, crossed round Tilsit; and the right, an enormous array, comprising the army of Eugene, Poniatowski and the Poles, for the present commanded by Jerome Bonaparte, King of Westphalia, with his auxiliaries, the two corps of St. Cyr and Junot, and far away, Schwartzenburg with the Austrian forces marched along the space between the centre and the heads of the Bug. This movement, which enabled the Grand Army to issue into Lithuania as from a salient, brought it almost within reach of the hostile armies, which, under Barclay de Tolly, by descent a Scotchman, and Bagration, a chief of the Muscovite nobles, had advanced from the Dwina and Dnieper, where their sources meet, and had approached the Niemen with no fixed purpose. The generals of the Czar, all but surprised and outmanœuvred, fell back at all points; and Napoleon was at Vilna, within four days having gained an immense strategic advantage. He made a long halt of about a fortnight; this has been condemned as a capital error, even by the cautious and far-seeing* Wellington, and, as events happened, it would have been better perhaps had he pressed, at all hazards, his offensive movement. But his *Correspondence* shows that, from a military point of view, this delay may be very well justified ; the Grand Army, burdened with impedimenta of all kinds—a necessity in districts with few resources, and filled with weak elements, was in a bad condition; the auxiliaries and conscripts had fallen away in thousands; and time was required to reorganize huge arrays already beginning to dissolve and break up.

The situation, in short, had brought the Emperor to a stand; and yet an opportunity was given him to strike the Czar a blow more decisive than his sword could inflict. He was

---

* See a masterly paper, from Wellington's hand, on the campaign of 1812. The Duke's knowledge of the facts is not complete, for the *Napoleon Correspondence* had not yet been published ; but the criticism is admirable. I have made ample use of it in this sketch. *Despatches, Correspondence, and Memoranda of Field-Marshal the Duke of Wellington, K. G.*, vol. iii., 1866.

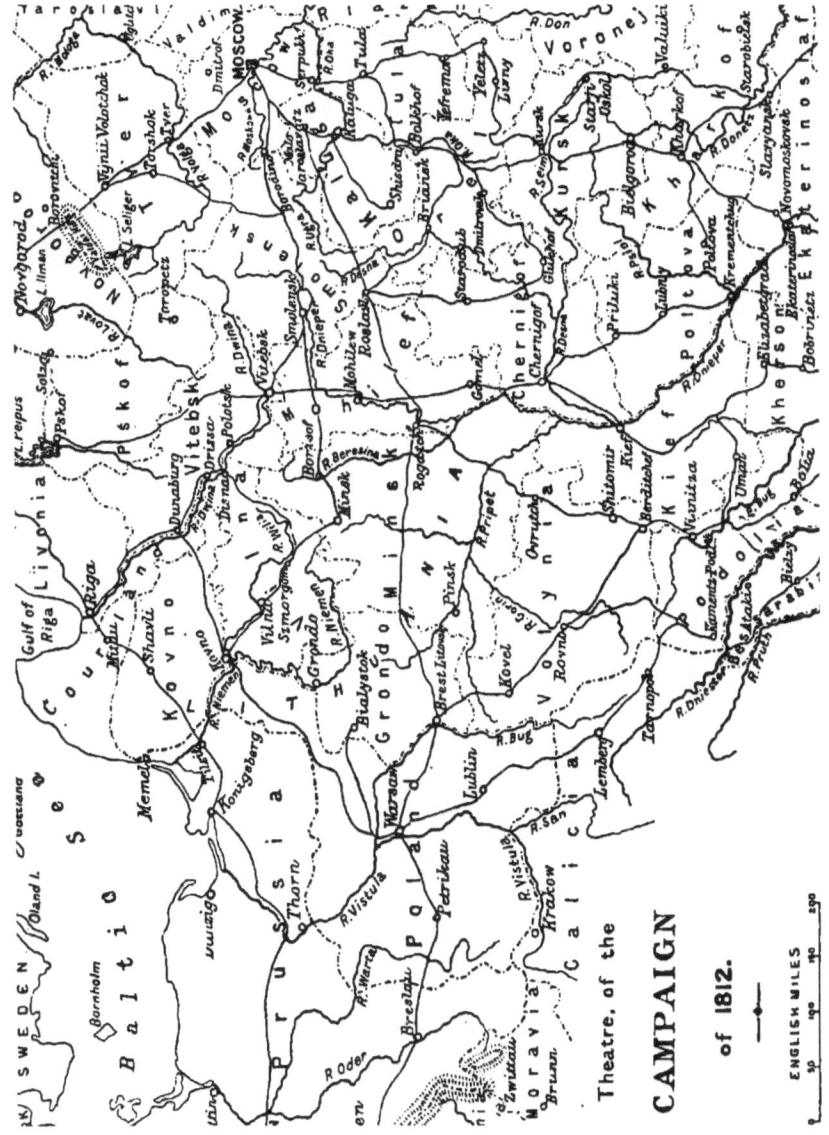

Theatre, of the

CAMPAIGN

of 1812.

ENGLISH MILES

in one of the capitals of ancient Poland ; he was greeted with
enthusiasm once more by the conquered race ; and had he spoken
the words " Poland is to be free," the Russian Empire would have
been thrown back at once to the distant limits of old Muscovy.
But Napoleon adhered to the policy of 1806 ; he caressed the Poles
and enrolled their levies ; but he paltered with their demands to
be made a nation ; and he even intimated that he would not annul
the Partition.   Meanwhile, after a few days of delay, he despatched
Davoust and part of his right wing to pursue Bagration, trying
now to join his colleague by a circuitous march ; but partly owing
to the difficulties of a way through immense woodlands scarcely
traversed by roads, and to the slow movements of heavily-laden
troops, and partly to disputes between Davoust and King Jerome,
the effort failed ; Bagration escaped ; and he ultimately attained
the Dnieper.   By this time the Emperor had formed a great plan to
cut off and annihilate Barclay de Tolly, who had dangerously exposed
himself to his foe ; and the project was worthy of a great master
of war.   A German theorist, possibly struck by the results of
Wellington's defence of Portugal, had persuaded the Czar to con-
struct a huge camp at Drissa upon the Lower Dwina, to concentrate within it his two armies, and to offer battle behind its fortified
lines ; and Barclay had reluctantly obeyed the command ; Bagration, too, drawing near him from the distant Dnieper.   This
strategy, it is needless to say, had nothing in common with that
of Torres Vedras ; it was really the old routine of an obsolete
school ; and Napoleon broke up from Vilna on the 16th of July,
hoping to surround Barclay, to destroy him in his camp, and then
to turn and overwhelm Bagration.   In all human probability he
would have succeeded, had the Russian commander stood in his
lines ; but Barclay saw his peril, and left them in time ; and he
made a very able movement to Vitepsk, across the front of the
approaching enemy, in order to reach and join his colleague.   The
Emperor pursued with his wonted energy ; but nature and the
defects of the army interposed ; and he attained Vitepsk too late
to catch and destroy an enemy still eluding his grasp.   He was
again forced to make a long halt at Vitepsk, from the reasons

which had made him halt at Vilna; the state of the Grand Army had become alarming, and the appalling fact was brought before the eyes of its chief, that, though no real battle had yet been fought, 150,000 men were missing out of the 420,000 who had begun the invasion. Such waste of war had never been seen before; yet Napoleon still had faith in his genius; he made a daring flank march, behind a screen of forests, in order to effect a junction with his right; and this, he hoped, would enable him to reach the enemy between the Dwina and Dnieper, and compel him to fight. The movement had only partial success; a fierce encounter took place at Smolensk; but the French army only gained ruins, and Barclay and Bagration, having joined hands at last, disappeared into the remote interior.

Napoleon's manœuvres up to this time were worthy of his strategic genius; in theory they had been almost faultless; but they had been baffled by obstacles not to be overcome, and by the conditions of the war and the state of the army. The middle of August had now arrived; the Emperor was at the portals of old Russia, hundreds of miles from his nearest base in Germany; was he to advance further into the recesses of the East, and to brave the fate of Crassus in the Parthian deserts? His lieutenants, to a man, entreated him to halt; to establish himself between the Dwina and Dnieper; to call up all available reserves; and, extending his wings on either side, to overrun Volhynia and subdue Courland. This probably would have been done by Turenne or Wellington; but there were military reasons against a delay, which must have led to a winter campaign; and after long reflection, the spoiled child of Fortune resolved to advance to Moscow, and to find peace, after victory, in the old capital of the Czars. Yet he did not take this momentous step inconsiderately, or without ample precautions; he exclaimed: "I will find no Pultowa on my way"; and he left nothing undone to render his communications secure, and to avert every peril from the invading army. His situation, at this moment, appeared safe; for to the left Macdonald occupied Courland, and was besieging the important place of Riga; Oudinot had defeated the

corps of Wittgenstein, left behind by Barclay in the retreat from
Drissa; and Schwartzenberg had repulsed the army of the South,
moving, under Tormazoff, from the Pruth and the Dniester. Yet
the Emperor would "make assurance doubly sure;" he summoned
Victor, with his corps, to Smolensk; he ordered Augereau to
advance towards the Niemen; he moved up his second line to the
tracts round the Oder; he organized Lithuania under a local
government, and directed the formation of immense magazines at
Smolensk, Vilna, and all the way to the Niemen. He broke up
from Smolensk, in the last week of August, at the head of about
160,000 men, the best and most solid part of the Grand Army.
The troops had been provided with large supplies, for the Russians
had wasted the line of the retreat, even in Lithuania, without the
aid of the people, and it had been foreseen that in old Russia the
peasantry would assist in the work; and for some days the invaders
moved without distress along the vast uplands, which divide the
streams that reach the Baltic, the Black Sea, and the Caspian.
As soon, however, as provisions fell short, the army began to
suffer terribly in what had been made a harried wilderness;
30,000 stragglers became missing; and Napoleon declared, that if
nothing new occurred, he would return to Smolensk and find
winter quarters. At this critical time, intelligence arrived which
caused him again to pursue his march. The Russian army,
furious at a retreat of hundreds of miles before the invaders, had
insisted on fighting a great battle; the Czar had dreaded to refuse
the demand; and Barclay had been replaced by Kutusoff, the chief
who had made his mark in 1805, and who, though approving
Barclay's conduct, had promised to encounter the approaching
enemy. On the 5th of September 1812, the horsemen of Murat
came in sight of the Russians, in position along a line extending
from Borodino on their right to the wood and village of Outitza
on their left, their front covered by redoubts and field works.
Both armies spent the following day in preparation for the conflict
at hand, and as light rose on the morning of the 7th, Napoleon exclaimed to his staff of Marshals: "It was time; but there is the Sun
of Austerlitz!" The armies opposed were about equal in numbers,

12

130,000 to 140,000 men; and for some time the course of the battle went rapidly and decidedly on the side of the French. Napoleon, with the eye of a master, had seized the weak point of his adversary, and assailed his left; the redoubts and other defences were stormed and captured, and Kutusoff, who had unskilfully crowded his right with masses of troops that could hardly move, was in extreme peril. Had the Emperor at this crisis sent part of his reserve to complete the defeat of his foe, he must have won the battle, but he refused to believe in such rapid success; he was not as active as was his wont on the field, and a change soon came in the tide of Fortune. The Russians, after a great effort, retook the redoubts; Kutusoff detached troops by degrees from his right, and the battle raged furiously for several hours in which each side fought with heroic courage. At last the Russian left was again broken; once more the French stormed the fortified works, and, though a fine charge was made by the Russian cavalry, the defeated army began to fall back. Napoleon was implored to launch the Guard, at this decisive moment, against the enemy; but he remained inactive, and would not employ it; and the battle closed with a frightful duel of guns, in which the Russians were literally slain in thousands. The struggle was the bloodiest even seen in war; the Russians lost nearly 50,000 men, the French probably 30,000; and though the beaten army drew off from the field, Borodino was only a greater Eylau.

Napoleon was ill on this terrible day; and it has been supposed that his powerful frame showed on this occasion, for the first time, the symptoms of a disease that was to prove mortal. His hesitation, however, to use his reserves and the Guard has been explained by himself: "I will not," he said, "throw away my best protection" at an "immense distance from its nearest supports"; but this fact alone condemns the whole enterprise. On the 14th of September 1812, the Grand Army beheld the temples and domes of Moscow rising from the surrounding plains; it had soon filled an almost deserted city; and the Conqueror, at the summit, as he dreamed, of his unequalled fortunes—his eagles were on the Niemen, the Elbe, and the Tagus—imagined that

NAPOLEON WATCHING THE BURNING OF MOSCOW FROM THE PETROVSKI PALACE.

Alexander would sue for peace, as he had sued for it after the rout
of Friedland. Before many hours the capital, self-destroyed, was
a hurricane of devouring flame—a sinister monument of internecine war—and the victorious army had to establish itself in a
desolate expanse of charred ruins, spreading far into a wasted
country. Yet Napoleon clung to the wreck of Moscow; he
believed that the enemy would be forced to treat; he slaked the
pride of his still exulting soldiers by grand reviews and exhibitions
of their power; and, as supplies were found in abundance in
underground recesses, the army retained its order and discipline.
Weeks, nevertheless, ebbed away and the Czar made no sign.
Meantime Kutusoff had rallied his defeated army, had distributed
it in a series of camps, some distance from Moscow, on the flank
of his foe; and while the French cavalry and artillery became
rapidly feeble—there was no suitable food for the horses—thousands of recruits, and especially a host of Cossacks, the Bedouins
of the deserts of the North, assembled to defend "Holy Russia"
to the death. At this crisis—always in this consistent—the Emperor refused to adopt a course which must have compelled
Alexander to yield. He would not listen to the idea of proclaim-
ing the freedom of the enormous masses of serfs in the Muscovite
Empire; and, rejecting even now the notion of retreat, he formed
vast designs for a march on St. Petersburg, or a descent into
Southern Russia to find winter quarters. His lieutenants, however, condemned schemes strategically grand, but perhaps impossible. He did not silence them with his wonted authority in
the critical position in which they all stood, and at last, in the
middle of October, he consented to retreat, the delays which had
already occurred having no doubt been largely due to the guile of
Kutusoff, who, anticipating the future with sagacious forethought,
feigned negotiations to deceive and detain his enemy. The retrograde movement began on the 19th of October; and the Grand
Army, as it defiled out of Moscow, presented a strange and
ominous aspect. It was still about 100,000 strong; the infantry
were in a tolerable state, but the cavalry and horse artillery were
few and enfeebled; the proportion of guns was far too great, and

the divisions, bearing with them an enormous booty, and dragging a huge *matériel* and *impedimenta*, were incapable of making an energetic movement. Napoleon endeavoured to steal a march on Kutusoff, still on his flank, but at a wide distance, and to retreat towards Kalouga, to the south-west of Moscow, through a fertile region not yet destroyed ; and probably he would have attained his object had he had an efficient and active army. But his enemy forestalled him at Malo-Yaroslavetz ; a murderous and indecisive battle followed ; and Napoleon—it was the first council of war he ever summoned—yielded to his Marshals, and abandoned the attempt to break through and reach Kalouga, a decision fraught with momentous results. The French army was now forced back on the line by which it had advanced to Moscow, but it had sufficient provisions for some days ; the climate as yet was not threatening ; the Russians cautiously kept aloof, and the still hopeful soldiery believed they would reach Smolensk and good quarters in ten or twelve forced marches. Ere long, however, the supplies fell short ; the army, passing through a ruined country, was scarcely able to procure the means of life, however widely it spread to pillage ; men began to disband and straggle in thou-sands, and want hastened the destruction of all that gives power to armed men. Early in November, the icy hand of winter fell suddenly on the host already breaking up ; horses died in multi-tudes in a single night ; guns, trains, carriages were lost and abandoned ; and the army became a shattered horde without re-sources, military strength, or discipline. Kutusoff, who had steadily followed the retreat, saw that the expected time had come ; swarms of his light horsemen hung on the rear of the French, cutting off the wounded, and making numerous prisoners ; and attacks, hesitating at first, but growing formidable, were made on the exposed flanks of the retreating masses, now almost wholly without the help of cavalry. The perishing army reached Smo-lensk by the middle of November ; it had dwindled from 100,000 soldiers to 40,000 worn out fugitives, deprived of the greater part of their guns and *matériel* ; and it was soon discovered that the the long-expected haven could not afford refuge even for some days. The magazines, which Napoleon had commanded to be made, were not furnished with nearly sufficient supplies ; they were not properly secured or guarded, and the famishing soldiery recklessly wasted and plundered the scanty resources they had, for subordination and military obedience had been almost lost.

At Smolensk, Napoleon received intelligence more appalling than ever had reached a commander. Victor and his corps had come up to Smolensk, and had thrown reinforcements into the town, but he had left under the stress of the gravest peril. Wittgenstein, whose army had been largely increased, had eluded Macdonald far away in Courland, and had defeated Oudinot, very inferior in force ; and Victor had marched to assist his colleague. The two Marshals, however, could not shake off their foe ; Wittgenstein was advancing on the Upper Dwina, at the head of about 45,000 men ; and the left wing, therefore, of the Grand Army, once apparently secure, was in daily growing danger. Meantime, Tormazoff had been joined by Tchitchakoff, an admiral, with a fresh army from the south. The Saxon auxiliaries had been defeated ; Schwartzenberg, at a hint given from Vienna, had fallen back before the approaching enemy ; and Napoleon's right wing was left uncovered and threatened by nearly 50,000 men. Kutusoff was already close to Smolensk ; what if he continued his ceaseless attacks, while the hostile forces, converging from the rear, should drive in the already broken wings, and should close on the rear of the army from Moscow ? Mack and Mélas were never in such a woeful plight, and Napoleon at once broke up from Smolensk, to make a great effort to avert destruction. He had not been equal to himself since he had left Moscow ; whether illness had impaired his great faculties, or, more probably, because he had no experience of defeat ; and, under-rating the real force and the skill of Kutusoff, he sent off his army, strengthened in some degree, in separate masses, that scarcely supported each other. The Russian chief seized the occasion, and became more bold. He endeavoured to cut off a large part of the retreating forces, and though the effort failed, the French had to run the gauntlet of enemies ever gathering on their flanks and their rear, and slaying, capturing, and destroying thousands. The horrors of the retreat to Smolensk were surpassed; the dissolving masses, which had been 60,000 strong when they left the place, were but 20,000; and the heroism of Ney, who covered the rear, was the one gleam of light in a long night of darkness. Victor and Oudinot had now drawn close to Napoleon, but Kutusoff, Tchitchakoff, and Wittgenstein were at hand; and the three French armies, 70,000 fugitives in the last days of November, found themselves arrested by the broad and half-frozen Beresina, while the enemy, fully 120,000 strong, was gathering on all sides to prevent the retreat. The situation seemed utterly hopeless, but Napoleon's genius suddenly revived; and he extricated himself from the jaws of destruction by one of the finest efforts he ever made in his career. Deceiving his adversaries by feints of all kinds—he actually drove a huge body of stragglers to the wrong place to conceal his purpose—he threw two bridges over the wintry stream; the soldiers who could move and keep together succeeded in crossing under the Russian batteries; thousands perished, indeed, but the army was saved; though Wellington has observed, with strict truth, that had the Russian commanders struck home, it must have been destroyed as a military force. I shall not dwell on the closing scenes of the retreat: the wrecks of Moscow, and the corps of Victor and Oudinot, were about 50,000 men when the Beresina was passed; the enemy had abandoned the pursuit; and yet these bodies shrunk to about 30,000 in not more than five or six marches. At Smorgoni Napoleon left his army, in order, he told the Marshals, to awaken France; political considerations plead for the act, but it would not have been done by Turenne or Frederick; and, with other instances, it shows, I think, that this supreme military genius, matchless in success, was not equally great in extreme adversity. After the Emperor's departure, the diminishing arrays toiled hopelessly through the Lithuanian wastes; each day very many hundreds dropped off; Murat, placed in command, all but lost his head; reinforcements caught the contagion of despair, and the armed multitude completely broke up. The frightful scenes of demoralization and terror witnessed at Smolensk recurred at Vilna. Great magazines had been collected there, but they were sacked and destroyed by the mobs which attacked them; and the French fled to the Niemen in petty knots and bands, and at last sought refuge behind the Vistula. Such a tragedy of war had never been seen since the immense host of the Assyrian tyrant perished through the inscrutable will of Omnipotence. More than half a million of soldiers, including reserves, had crossed the Niemen a few months before; 50,000 did not recross the stream, and the cavalry and artillery were almost destroyed. The losses of the Russians were also terrible; but bearing in mind that they were at home, and that numbers of the disbanded and wounded rejoined their colours, they were ultimately, perhaps, not more than 120,000 men.

The causes of this immense disaster, the prelude to the fall of the French Empire, have been examined by many writers. We may dismiss the pretence that "it was all the cold." This equally affected both armies, and it weakened the Russians quite as much as the French. The conflagration of Moscow no doubt contributed largely to the events that followed. The Grand Army but for the fire, might have found winter quarters in a rich capital; but we can hardly agree with Napoleon's phrase: "I would have emerged like a ship from the ice in spring"; his cavalry and artillery would have been ruined, for the horses had no hay, and would have had insufficient provender. The chief causes of the catastrophe are, I think, two: the Grand Army was the worst instrument of war, which Napoleon had hitherto had in his hands; it was feeble despite its enormous size; more than half the soldiers were bad or unwilling; and it was incapable of great and rapid efforts, especially in a theatre of war like Russia. The paramount cause, however, beyond dispute, was that the grand offensive strategy of the French Emperor was all but impossible in such a campaign. The army, unable to find resources on the line of march, was obliged either to carry large supplies with it or to scatter over the country to obtain subsistence; in either case, daring and decisive movements were frustrated or had few results;

and, curiously enough, the very expedients Napoleon adopted to support his troops, great magazines at a variety of points, so encumbered them that they baffled his efforts. As for the Emperor, his conduct in the campaign has never yet, perhaps, had an impartial critic. His operations at the beginning of the war bear the ineffaceable stamp of his powers : they were masterly, perfectly conceived, and brilliant; and had he commanded the army of Austerlitz, he might have separated Bagration and Barclay, and perhaps won a Jena, before he reached Smolensk. It is wholly untrue besides, that he plunged into the depths of old Muscovy without forethought ; he spared no pains to make his bases secure, and to protect his communications in every way; and his great. faculties were seen in perfection in his escape on the Beresina from a host of enemies. Undoubtedly, however, he may have been too cautious in husbanding his reserves at Borodino; he certainly delayed too long at Moscow; he ought not to have recoiled at Malo-Yaroslavetz ; he should not have divided his columns when he left Smolensk ; he ought never to have given Murat the command of his army. All these, however, were mere mistakes, and every commander must sometimes go wrong; but what really was most to blame in him was his inactivity during a great part of the retreat, and his abandonment of his troops at Smorgoni. This indicates a defect in this great master ; there were vulnerable points in the Achilles of war, and Napoleon never was in the hour of misfortune the perfect chief he was in the hour of triumph. Still, his capital error in the campaign was that the enterprise, as he conducted it, was beyond his powers : he defied space and Nature when he advanced to Moscow, and he paid the penalty in terrific ruin. The result might have been different had his operations been more methodical and more prudent; and here we see, again, how imagination and pride occasionally mastered his better judgment. As regards the Russian commanders, their first movements were timid, aimless, and yet presumptuous ; they ought not to have approached the frontier ; they should have kept away from the camp of Drissa ; they ought not to have fought at Borodino at all, a battle, besides, which they directly badly; and if they imitated Wellington in the retreat from the Dwina, the imitation was poor and unskilful. Barclay, however, showed resource in the march to Smolensk; and though Kutusoff probably could have done more than he did, his choice of a position on the Emperor's flank, and his unceasing attacks on the retreating enemy, are good illustrations of the military art. Nevertheless, the fame of the Russian chiefs, due to the results of the war of 1812, has diminished with the progress of time; and none of them can rank as truly great captains. The most conspicuous fact on the victorious side is the stern endurance of the Russian soldiery, and the resolution shown by the Czar and the nation; thus patriotism in Spain and in Muscovy baffled Napoleon. Two of the most striking incidents of the war, as a whole, are Napoleon's refusal to set the Poles free, and even at Moscow to emancipate the serfs; in his hatred of all that is national, liberal, popular—of what he called the "ideology of the Rights of Man"—he would not adopt measures that would have disabled his foe, and certainly would have saved the Grand Army.

CHAPTER VII.

NAPOLEON—(*continued*).

NAPOLEON—he had travelled in disguise through Poland and Germany—returned to Paris as 1812 was closing. On his arrival he had proofs, not to be mistaken, of the increase of the adverse opinion of France, and of the real instability of the Imperial throne. An obscure Republican officer had conspired against him; and though the conspiracy had been nipped in the bud, the capital had heard of the crime with indifference; and, most significantly, no one seemed to think that the infant King of Rome—his ill-fated son, the Astyanax of the fallen House of Bonaparte as he was called by the captive of St. Helena—would succeed to the heritage of the French Empire. Napoleon, after reproving his still servile ministers, and the silent and docile Bodies of the State, addressed himself to redeem the pledge he had given his lieutenants when he left Smorgoni; he exerted himself with even more than characteristic energy—" I am now General, not Emperor," is a phrase in his letters—to repair the tremendous disaster which had befallen his arms; and he was seconded with real zeal by a nation which, though the Revolutionary fervour had ceased, and it feared and disliked the Imperial rule, has often done wonders in an effort to retain the military supremacy which is its great ambition. The Emperor, who had called out the Conscription of 1813, ventured to anticipate and call out the Conscription of 1814; immense bodies of National Guards were enrolled, and invited to serve; the depôts of the Empire were emptied, to furnish every trained

soldier who could bear arms; *matériel* of war was found in abundance in the arsenals of France to replace what had been lost; and
veterans of the past and officers from Spain were forthcoming in
hundreds to prepare the new levies. The genius of Napoleon
and the ardour of France were successful, to an extent that appears
astonishing; half a million of armed men were on foot by the early
spring of 1813; gifts of horses, and purchases on an immense scale,
had in some measure replaced the destruction of the cavalry which
had disappeared in the retreat; and though these masses could
scarcely be called an army, they were being skilfully drilled and
organized, and they had the national aptitude to become quickly
soldiers. Napoleon had calculated that, by the coming summer,
he would be able to take the field at the head of 250,000 men, with
armies of reserve on the Rhine and the Elbe; and he had boasted
that with these forces, and the troops that had come back from
Russia, he would conquer the Czar and keep Germany down.
Events, however, had completely changed since he had abandoned
the wreck of the Grand Army. When he set off from Smorgoni,
Macdonald on the left and the Prussian contingent were almost
intact; Schwartzenburg, on the far right, had a considerable force;
though the army from Moscow was almost destroyed, a great part
of the second line of the Grand Army, assembled in 1812, was
cantoned between the Elbe and the Vistula; and Napoleon's previsions, therefore, were not illusory. But since his return to France,
the Prussian corps, and its chief, had ostentatiously revolted and
joined the enemy; Macdonald, hard pressed and deserted, had
escaped with difficulty, through a host of enemies, and attained the
Vistula; Schwartzenburg, with his Austrians, had marched into
Galicia, and evidently was waiting on the policy of his Court; the
army that had left the Beresina had, we have seen, perished; and
down-trodden Prussia had suddenly flamed out in a tremendous explosion of national passion, which was rapidly making itself felt through
Germany, prepared for years for a patriotic outbreak. Murat, left
in command of the French army, proved utterly unable to confront
misfortune; he fled to his treasured kingdom of Naples; and the
conduct of operations was given to Eugene Beauharnais, devoted to

the Emperor, but not a great chief. Eugene, collecting the fragments of Macdonald's corps and the survivors of the troops who
had entered Russia, had endeavoured to make a stand on the
Vistula; but the approach of the Russians and Prussians, and the
rising of Prussia, compelled him ere long to fall back; and he
ultimately retreated to the line of the Elbe, bringing along with
him the greater part of what had been the second line of the army
of 1812. He was in positions on the Elbe, in the first days of
March, at the head of perhaps 45,000 men; about 40,000 were in
march from the Oder; and these, apart from a few thousands
more sent to strengthen the garrisons in the Prussian fortresses,
were the whole forces that could be brought together out of the
enormous mass of 600,000 soldiers arrayed, the year before, to
invade Russia! Yet Eugene had conducted the retreat ably; and
this was admitted, at the time, by the sternest of censors.

These disasters frustrated Napoleon's projects, and accelerated
his appearance in the field. He endeavoured to arrange the dispute with Rome, acquiring influence again in Imperial France;
issued a paper money to sustain the finances, too like the assignats
of 1791–3; the Treasury was in a critical state; and he was at
Mayence in the middle of April, having summoned the Princes of
the Confederation of the Rhine to arm and put down the great
Teutonic rising, described by him as a mere "Jacobin movement."
His troops had been for some time in motion, and were probably
120,000 strong on the Rhine; and he hoped that with these and
the army of Eugene he would surprise and overpower his enemies,
who had incautiously exposed themselves to his terrible strokes.
I shall say a word hereafter on the reorganization of the Prussian
army, after the ruin of Jena, and of the great consequences which
flowed from it; but the suddenness of events had taken the nation
by surprise; it had not had time to put forth its strength; and,
for the present, the Prussian forces in the field were not more
than 50,000 or 60,000 soldiers. The Russians had a much larger
army, but their chiefs were obliged to leave detachments behind;
and when they joined hands with their new allies, in march from

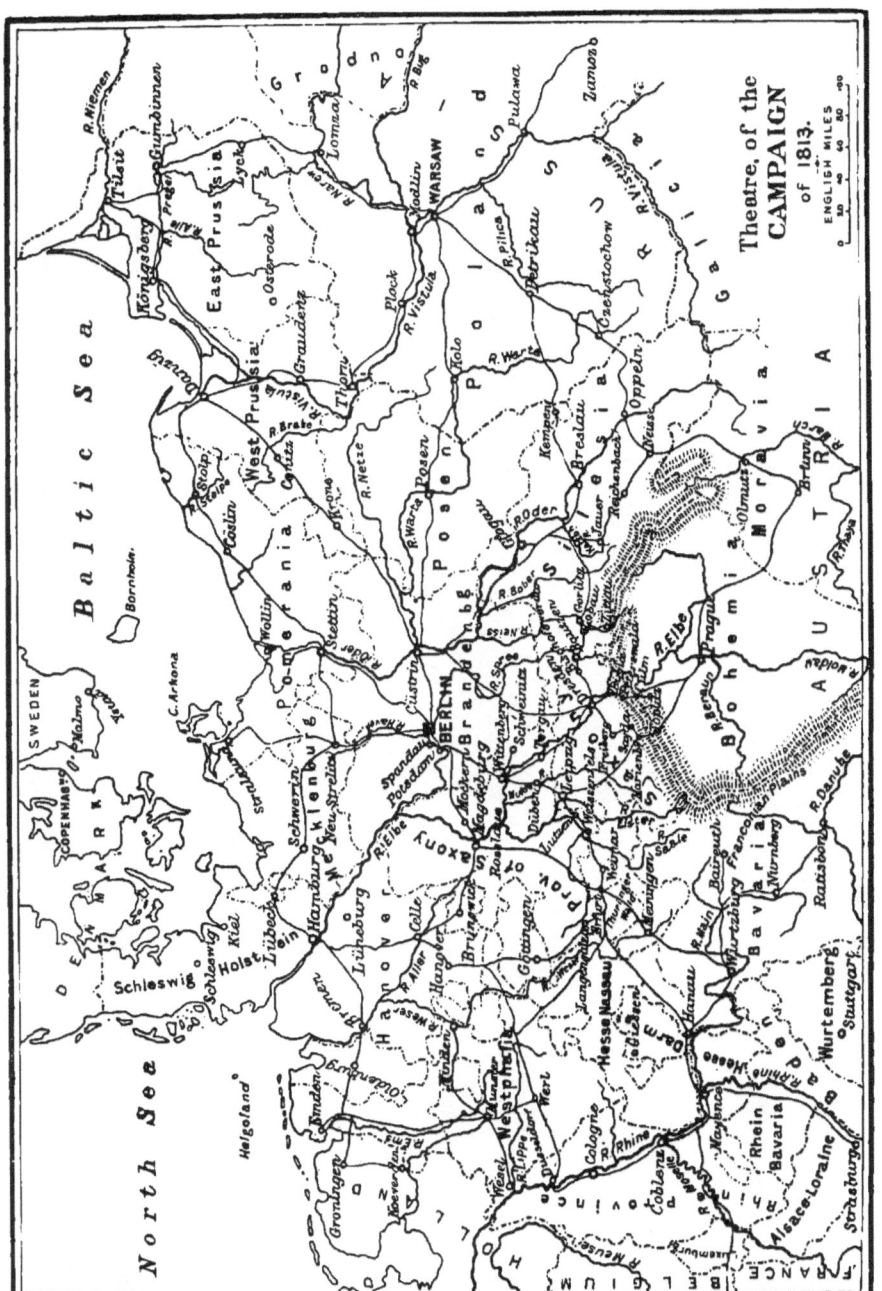

the Vistula to the Oder, the collected forces were probably not more than 130,000 or 140,000 strong.

In this position of affairs, against the advice of Kutusoff—the warrior died a few weeks afterwards—the Czar, dazzled by an immense triumph, and yielding to the prayers of the Prussian commanders—Blücher was the most pressing and bold of these— was persuaded to advance into the heart of Germany, in order to turn to account the national rising, and to sweep into it the Confederation of the Rhine; and the allied armies had approached the Elbe, about 100,000 men in the first line, disseminated, too, in divided masses. This was the repetition of the faulty strategy which had led to Jena and all that followed; and though times had changed, and Napoleon had suffered disasters beyond example in war, the movement was wrong from a military point of view, for it placed the Allies, thrown much too forward, and comparatively weak, in a situation of peril. Soon after the Emperor had reached Mayençe, his enemy had mastered the line of the Elbe: York, the Prussian chief, who had been the first to revolt, and Wittgenstein threatening the great place of Magdeburg, at the head of about 35,000 men, Wintzingerode, a Russian, and fiery Blücher holding the river round Dresden with perhaps 50,000, and Milaradovitch, with about 15,000, advancing along the edge of Bohemia, to encourage Austria in a policy hostile to France. This disposition of the allied forces gave Napoleon an opportunity to strike; he drew Eugene towards him with admirable skill from the Elbe, behind the Saale, as a screen; he broke up from Mayence with about 100,000 men, and made for the Saale, through the scenes of Jena; his purpose being to join Eugene, and at the head of their united forces, 140,000 strong at least, to surprise and assail the divided enemy, to cut him off from the Elbe and Dresden, and to force him against the Bohemian ranges, where it would be difficult to avoid destruction. The Emperor and the Prince effected their junction, between Merseburg and Naumburg, on the 30th of April; the young levies of France and the war-worn troops of 1812 met with sympathetic pride; and the Grand Army, given the name again, marched across the Elster into the great plains of Leipsic, in order to carry out a strategic project as brilliant as any of its renowned author's. The troops of Jena and Austerlitz were, however, gone; the movement of the army was extremely slow; the want of sufficient cavalry was severely felt; and Napoleon was compelled to advance cautiously, for the enemy was known to be at hand, and reconnoitring was difficult. A skirmish, in which Bessières perished, gave the Emperor a warning he did not despise; and he moved into the open tract between Lützen and Leipsic, combining his corps with such skill that each could easily and quickly support the other. Meanwhile, however, the main part of the allied forces had drawn together, and at the suggestion of Diebitch, a real future chief, and at the entreaty of Blücher, passionate to fight, it was resolved to assail the Emperor in the vast and unprotected plain, where the Russian and Prussian cavalry would have an immense advantage, though Milaradovitch was many leagues distant.

On the 2nd of May Eugene had attained Leipsic, and was attacking the town with an advanced guard, when the hostile army, about 70,000 strong, fell furiously on the French centre, holding, under the command of Ney, a cluster of villages, but otherwise exposed in the great tract around them. The young French soldiers, fired by the heroism of their chief, made a gallant resistance for some time; but strength and practised valour gradually prevailed; there was nothing to oppose to the allied squadrons, and the centre of Napoleon was all but broken, when the precautions he had so carefully taken enabled him to restore the uncertain battle. The corps of Marmont, of Oudinot, of Bertrand, so placed as to come into line quickly, reinforced by degrees the divisions of Ney; the Emperor was soon on the scene with the Guard; and a converging line of fire began to envelop the enemy, greatly overmatched in numbers, and carried destruction into his diminishing ranks. A desperate effort, however, made by Blücher, nearly pierced through the French centre once more; and it required the discipline and power of the invincible Guard—still largely composed of trained soldiers—to win for Napoleon a doubtful victory. The Allies left the field in unbroken array; few prisoners or guns were taken by the French; and owing to the feebleness of their levies, and the want of horsemen, anything like effective pursuit was impossible.

Lützen, like Eylau, was a fruitless battle, and must have suggested painful thoughts to Napoleon. His strategy had been after his wonted fashion; the Allies had made a distinct mistake in fighting without Milaradovitch; the French army had been largely superior in numbers, and yet it had narrowly escaped defeat. The young soldiers, no doubt, had shown brilliant courage, but they had recoiled before their veteran foes; the Emperor had been saved only by his wise caution, the enemy had successfully effected his retreat, and from their weaknesss in horse the French had accomplished little. The great object Napoleon had had in view, forcing the Allies into the Bohemian hills in complete ruin, had not been attained; and operations which, with the Old Grand Army, would probably have led to a second Jena, had proved to a great extent abortive. He had, however, restored the glory of his arms, and he entered Dresden in a few days in triumph. He soon compelled the old King of Saxony, wavering in his faith, like all the Allies, to furnish him with a large contingent; and his other vassals among the German princes sent troops at his imperious command, ready to abandon him at the first change of fortune. He set off from Dresden in the middle of May, confident that the enemy had at last fallen into his hands. The Russians and Prussians, after Lützen, had recrossed the Elbe and marched into Saxony, and they had been directed to the verge of Bohemia, in the hope of winning Austria to their cause. That Power, always tenacious, but always wary, was still an ostensible ally of France, and was bound to Napoleon through the young Empress, but it had long been playing a double game; it had dealt with the Czar in 1812; it had winked at Schwartzenburg's evident neglect to cover the Grand Army during the retreat; it was not heedless of German opinion; and, under the direction of the sagacious Metternich, it was seeking to turn the situation to its own advantage. It had offered council to all the belligerents, had gradually taken the attitude of a powerful arbiter, and had quietly begun to prepare armaments; but though sympathy and instinct drew it towards the Allies, it feared the Emperor's power, and it was still neutral.   The Allies, however, thought they could gain Austria, especially as Napoleon had charged her with bad faith, and, sacrificing military ends to politics, they had placed their armies in positions round Bautzen, at a short distance from the Bohemian frontier.   The operations that followed were on a theatre made memorable in the Seven Years' War, not far from the famous field of Hochkirch, where Daun had surprised and and defeated Frederick.

Fancy may picture the shade of the old Austrian chief directing the conduct of the Allies; they had entrenched themselves within two defensive lines, covered by the Spree, and a stream behind; and in these positions, with little power of movement, they had resolved to await the shock of Napoleon.   That great warrior, on the other hand, had imitated Frederick to this extent; he would attack the enemy in front, and reach his flank, but the turning was to be a strategic movement, carried out far off, and perfectly safe, not a tactical stroke on the field and hazardous.   The battles that followed are full of interest, and should be carefully studied by a thinker on war.   The Emperor attacked on the 20th of May; he perceived with his wonted insight that the force of the enemies was too large on their left; so, neglecting the Tronsberg heights, which they held with this wing, he directed his main effort against their centre and right, placed along the marshy ground that surrounded the Spree.   The resistance was prolonged and vigorous; but passive defence had often failed before, and was certain to fail under the strokes of Napoleon, and the first position was at last forced, the French being greatly superior in numbers, perhaps 150,000 to 110,000 men.   The Emperor renewed the attack next day, but meanwhile he had taken care to mature an operation promising decisive success.   Ney had been ordered to march on Würchen and Hochkirch at the head of about 50,000 men, making a long circuit far to the left, and when the enemy had yielded to the attack in front, he was to close in on his line of retreat, and to place him in the position of Mélas.   The second line of defence was also carried, and when the Emperor beheld his foes falling back, he looked eagerly in the direction where his trusted lieutenant was to be on the spot, to make his triumph complete. Ney, however, whether it was because his young troops had been slow in their movement, or, more probably, because he had lost something of the perfect confidence of unbroken success, had hesitated when far from the main army, and never attained the points of Würchen and Hochkirch ; Blücher confronted him with heroic energy, the defeated army found an avenue of escape, and it effected its retreat, though with heavy loss. The indignation of Napoleon may be conceived ; he had a right to find a Marengo at Bautzen, and yet, master as he was, he had once more been baffled. "What a butchery for nothing !" was his angry remark when he found that the enemy had escaped from the toils.

Napoleon was all himself at Bautzen ; his strategy and tactics were alike perfect ; and the manœuvres which ought to have destroyed his enemies, prove his immense superiority to Frederick in the field, when following, partly, Frederick's methods. The Allies were completely defeated, and fell back ; the Grand Army advanced to the Oder ; and once more the Emperor beheld the vision of the Continent prostrate under his eagles. Yet the Prussians and Russians had not been crushed ; Napoleon had learned, by hard experience how inefficient his army was, especially in the essential force of cavalry ; and, confident in himself and the magic of his sword, he accepted the famous armistice of Pleistwitz, with the object, as he avowed afterwards, of organizing and training his immature levies, of increasing them, above all, in horses, and of making them capable of great offensive movements. This truce has been called the greatest mistake of his life ; and history fully confirms the judgment. The Allies, though baffled, had not been broken ; the Czar, eager to become a second lord of the Continent, had engaged the strength of his realms in the war ; and Prussia, placing herself at the head of Germany, was proving what her armed might had become, and gave reliance and weight to the great rising now in full force from the Rhine to the Oder.

13

The military power of that martial State had become transformed since the day of Jena, and was now capable of immense
development. The army had been reorganized in all its parts;
the officers, no longer a mere noble caste, comprised men of all
classes fit to do their duty; and the soldiery, fired with intense
patriotism, were burning to avenge and restore the nation. The
most remarkable change which had taken place, however, was in
the effective force and the character of this fierce array of warriors.
Napoleon had restricted the numbers of the Prussian army; but
his craft and oppression had not attained his ends; the contingent
under arms was not large; but the conscription had been applied
to Prussia; thousands of youths had yearly passed through the
ranks, and had learned the elementary work of soldiers; and the
army was now capable of being enlarged to 200,000 or 250,000
men, especially under a strong popular impulse. Scharnhorst had,
in fact, outwitted the Emperor; the foundations had been laid of
the great system of which we have witnessed the results in war
in this age; and in the summer of 1813 Prussia was able to place
fully 200,000 men in line for the approaching contest. Meanwhile, immense bodies of troops had been marched from the
Niemen to take part in the struggle in Germany; and it was
calculated that, should Austria join the Allies, 900,000 men would
appear in the field to engage with Napoleon in a mortal struggle.
The forces available for the imperilled Emperor were hopelessly
inferior to these enormous masses. France could yield no further
supplies of troops; and even reckoning the contingents of the
Confederation of the Rhine, notoriously disaffected and eager to
desert, 600,000 men formed the extreme limit of the soldiers
capable of joining the Grand Army, and 200,000 of these, at least,
were of scarcely any use. The armistice, therefore, was a capital
error; yet Napoleon maintained his attitude of pride; he employed
the breathing time he had chosen for this end, in drilling and
improving his young levies, in purchasing horses in vast quantities, in making, in a word, the Grand Army an instrument fitting
to answer his purpose; and considering its state and its imperfect
structure, it is astonishing what was accomplished by his untiring

energy, by the practised skill of high and subordinate officers, and by the willingness and intelligence of the French soldiery. His capacity and genius shone out splendidly, though his health showed occasional signs of weakness; and he gradually matured a gigantic design of contending for Empire in the plains of Saxony, to which he trusted for ultimate success.

The theatre of war bore a kind of resemblance to that in which he had triumphed in 1796–7; the Bohemian hills were like those of the Tyrol; the Elbe, like the Adige, was a great river barrier; and the Emperor, in his own words, "took again to the trade" of the warrior who had struck down the Hapsburgs, with a relatively small force, on the verge of Italy. Napoleon took possession of the whole course of the Elbe from the Erzgebirge to its mouths at Hamburg; he secured the passages at every point in order to have full freedom of action; he placed the bulk of his forces around Dresden, with detachments, however, along the stream; he threw secondary armies out to the Oder, while he kept his communications with the Rhine well guarded; and, at the head of from 300,000 to 350,000 men, he made ready to defy his enemies, whatever their strength, on this vast field of manœuvre. His letters breathe nothing but stern confidence; he felt convinced that he could defeat the Allies; and his assurance was such that, playing for his old domination, he left thousands of troops shut up in the fortresses of the Oder and Vistula.

By this time it had become apparent that Austria would be of immense weight should she place her sword into either scale; and the Allies and Napoleon during the truce endeavoured to win her over and to obtain her support. Her inclinations had been never doubtful; she had favoured Russia and Prussia all through. Napoleon, too, had insulted her by bribes and threats, and had almost outraged Metternich in a fit of passion; but she refused for many weeks to make up her mind; and it was only the success of Wellington in Spain, and especially the great day of Vitoria, that at last determined her halting purpose. On the 10th of August 1813 she declared war against France once more; 250,000 men, who had been assembled in Bohemia, joined the allied standards;

13 *

and Napoleon, with ruin impending in Spain, with France even now on the point of exhaustion, and with auxiliaries, for the most part, worse than useless, was left to confront the power of Europe.

The forces on the theatre of war in Saxony were about 500,000 to 300,000 men—50,000 French were between the Rhine and the Lower Elbe—and the disproportion of numbers against the Emperor was less than it had been against the youthful Bonaparte. But the situation, even in pure strategy, was less favourable to Napoleon than it had been in 1796: and other circumstances increased the chances against him. The long line of the Elbe was more difficult to hold than the short and scarcely passable line of the Adige; the secondary armies that reached the Oder were far more exposed, and less easy to call in, than the detachments of Masséna and Vaubois; the retreat of the French army was better assured; in 1796 than in 1813, and all this gave the Allies advantages, and subjected the Emperor to real dangers, which scarcely existed in the earlier contest.

The allied armies, it should be added, were different troops from those of Alvinzi and Würmser; the young levies of 1813 were not the fierce Republicans of 1796; and here again the scale turned against Napoleon. He maintained, however, his unbending attitude; and the plan of operations formed by the Allies, if well designed, proves how he was still dreaded. Their general purpose was to attack and weaken his lieutenants, in their distant positions; to avoid a great battle with their terrible foe, but to wear out his strength in repeated marches; and then, and only then, to risk an encounter, when their superiority of force would make success certain. This strategy, if timid, had real merits; and it shows how, in most respects, the condition of affairs was different from what it had been in the campaign of Italy. As was his wont, Napoleon took the initiative; he set off from Dresden, in the middle of August, to attack Blücher, already seen to be by far his most resolute enemy, and he had soon driven him back to the Katzbach, for the Prussian chief, as had been agreed on, retreated, when made aware of his presence. Meanwhile, Schwartzenburg, with the chief part of the Austrian army, had issued through the Bohemian passes, and, gathering Russians and Prussians on the way, had advanced against Dresden in the Emperor's absence; and St. Cyr, who had been left to defend the city, announced that he had no means to resist an enemy apparently 200,000 strong. Napoleon returned, to make head against the approaching foes; he hesitated whether he would attack Schwartzenburg, and fall on his rear, as he had attacked Würmser in the defiles of the Brenta; but time and distance made the attempt hazardous; and he marched with 100,000 men to the relief of Dresden. A terrible battle was fought on the 26th and 27th of August; the Allies were greatly superior in numbers, perhaps 190,000 to 140,000 men; but Napoleon had his genius, and the advantage of the ground; he rested his weakened centre on the defences of the place, and assailed Schwartzenburg with both his wings in great force; and he gained a complete and splendid victory, remarkable for the death of Moreau in an Austrian camp. The Emperor's fortunes seemed restored, when a sudden disaster befell his arms. Before he reached Dresden he had sent off a lieutenant, Vandamme, to menace Schwartzenburg on his march, near Pirna; and as the allied army had been utterly beaten, and was retreating in disorder through the Bohemian hills, he ordered Vandamme to push forward boldly, and to close in force on the enemy's rear, intending to second the movement himself. The events that followed are still obscure; Vandamme seized Culm and the Austrian slope of the range; but Mortier and St. Cyr perhaps did not support their colleague; Napoleon,* owing to illness, or to some unknown cause, did not advance with the Imperial Guard; and Vandamme was left almost wholly isolated. In this position he was assailed by the defeated army; he was overwhelmed by superior numbers; a Prussian detachment hemmed him in, and, instead of breaking up a routed enemy, he was compelled to surrender and lay down his arms. Thirty thousand men were thus lost to the Emperor; it had become evident that, in the present

---

* Napoleon was certainly unwell; poison has been suspected; but probably ho was again showing signs of disease.

war, the events of Auerstadt would not happen again ; the apparition of a hostile force on the rear of his foes would no longer make them disperse and succumb.

Culm effaced Dresden, and disasters fell in quick succession on the secondary parts of the Grand Army, far away from its centre. Macdonald and Poniatowski were completely defeated, on the verge of Silesia, by fierce old Blücher ; and their shattered levies dissolved in multitudes. A similar reverse befell Oudinot, who had approached Berlin, at the hands of Bernadotte—the Marshal had given up his staff, had been declared heir to the throne of Sweden, and was now an obsequious vassal of the Czar—and this front of the Grand Army was also broken. Napoleon, losing heavily already through long forced marches, hastened from Dresden again to assail Blücher ; but the veteran fell back into the Silesian plains and the Emperor failed to bring his foe to bay. Ney was now directed to march on Berlin with another division of the secondary arrays ; but he was routed, with crushing effect, at Dennewitz ; for Napoleon, who had intended to join hands with him, had been recalled to the Elbe to oppose Schwartzenburg, threatening Dresden from Bohemia again ; and the Marshal had been, like Vandamme, isolated. Through these successive defeats the Grand Army had lost nearly 100,000 men, whole regiments disbanding, disease falling with cruel severity on the young soldiers, and many of the auxiliaries breaking out in mutiny ; and it had become evident that Napoleon's plan for the campaign, as a whole, could not be realised, that his forces on the Oder were far too distant, that his strength was being destroyed by his fruitless efforts to support them, and to strike with effect,* and that his enemies had learned his game, and would not approach him to court defeat. He drew in the remains of his shattered armies, and placed them in collected strength on the Elbe, holding the bridges and passages at all points ; and, still hopeful, he awaited

---

* It has been said—and the fact is probable—that the general scheme of the operations of the Allies was formed by Moreau, a chief of the second order, but a capable, sagacious, and far-sighted soldier. Their strategy was better than that of the Russians in 1812, and than their own in 1814.

the attacks of the Allies in a central position, analogous to that which he had held at Mantua, but not, I have said, so favourable to the French. His enemies paused, still afraid to assail the terrible adversary who had so often proved what genius could achieve in a situation like this. A long series of manœuvres followed, but at last Blücher and Bernadotte made for the Elbe ; Schwartzenburg finally issued from the hills, and the huge converging masses, describing a great arc, were directed towards the central point of Leipsic, in order to fall on the line of Napoleon's retreat, and to cut him off from his communications with the Rhine.

The Emperor thought his opportunity come ; he was operating between widely divided enemies, and he had accomplished wonders when so placed ; and, following exactly his strategy in 1796, he left St. Cyr and Lobau to hold Dresden ; detached Murat with about 50,000 men or more * to restrain Schwartzenburg, and advanced in person against Blücher and Bernadotte, with perhaps 140,000 of the main army. Operations, however, on the long line of the Elbe were more uncertain and likely to fail than on the short and difficult line of the Adige ; and other causes concurred to frustrate a project marked with the accustomed skill of its author. Blücher crossed the Elbe in the second week of October, and, eluding Napoleon, made for Schwartzenburg, though his colleague Bernadotte was still far off ; and it seems certain that this audacious movement, not scientific but bold to rashness, and very characteristic of the Prussian chief, was unknown to the Emperor for some days on a vast and imperfectly observed theatre. Napoleon now resolved to overwhelm Bernadotte, to advance and to occupy Berlin, the centre of the great Teutonic movement—a "focus of insurrection," in Imperial language—and this grand stroke was, I believe, possible,† had the

---

* Owing to the losses of the French by disease, desertion, and defection, it is impossible to determine, even approximately, the numbers of the Grand Army in this part of the campaign. Those of the Allies are better known ; but patriotism and pride have tended to make them smaller than they were.

† Napier insists on this, though he was so enthusiastic an idolator of Napoleon that he is not an impartial judge.

conditions of the war been of the ordinary kind. But intelligence came that the Bavarian troops were dangerous, and that Bavaria herself was to make common cause with the Allies; and Schwartzenburg was moving down the Elbe, on the left or western bank, to approach Blücher. Napoleon was compelled to abandon his project; he directed Murat to come to his aid, though he did not call in his divisions at Dresden; and collecting all his other available forces, he marched towards Leipsic with the view of assuring a retreat to the Rhine, should this be necessary, but ready to fight a decisive battle. His attempt to reach and strike his divided enemies, and to repeat the marvels of 1796, had failed; and he was now exposed, with a greatly weakened army, to be surrounded, beaten, and cut off from France, by enemies immensely superior in numbers, Germany, up to the Rhine, conspiring on his rear, and his German auxiliaries eager to revolt. Strategically, his position resembled that on the Beresina a few months before, though the peril was not yet frightful or imminent.

Apart from general causes affecting the contest—a word must be said on these afterwards—the student of war should note the reasons why the strategy of 1813 had results opposite to those of the strategy of 1796. Napoleon was the same commander on both occasions; and his great faculties had not diminished, though his bodily strength was not what it had been, and his arrogant confidence had certainly increased. But the barrier of the Elbe could not be defended as that of the Adige had been, and Blücher mastered it easily with a large army, effecting his junction with the Austrian forces; the French corps detached to the Oder were far from the main army, and were not in hand, like the small bodies which covered Mantua, so that instead of strengthening they weakened Napoleon, by compelling him to make harassing marches; the Emperor, when threatened by his foes at Leipsic, had no choice but to concentrate his troops, for otherwise his retreat would be barred; and the Grand Army, though improved since the spring, was an imperfect and not trustworthy instrument. Yet the chief reason, perhaps, has yet to be noticed: Würmser and Alvinzi in

1796-7 exposed themselves to Napoleon's strokes, and were struck right and left, and beaten in detail; the Allies took a wholly opposite course; they kept steadily aloof from the enemy they feared; they did not venture to approach him until he was almost crippled, and they gave but few chances to his grand offensive strategy.

History dwells on the famous days of Leipsic, for they set Germany free from the Imperial yoke, and finally broke down the power of Napoleon; but they have few features of interest for the student of war. Schwartzenburg attacked Napoleon, on the 16th of October, in positions a considerable way from Leipsic with probably 200,000 men; and Blücher, though not yet in line with his colleague, simultaneously attacked with about 70,000. The efforts of the assailants were still feeble; the Emperor had perhaps 170,000 men, and stood between enemies still apart; a magnificent charge of the French cavalry, reorganized and admirably led by Murat, was nearly attended with marked success; and though Blücher and his Prussians made some progress, the battle was drawn, and had no result.

Retreat for Napoleon was now easy; the way to the Elster and the Rhine was open, and might have been made completely secure; and Schwartzenburg, at least, would have been too rejoiced to leave a golden bridge for his still dreaded enemy. But Napoleon refused to acknowledge defeat; he insisted on gambling with adverse fortune, and scorning to fall back before foes he despised, he resolved to stand and fight a decisive battle. The 17th was spent in preparations on both sides; Bernadotte and Beningsen came up with their armies, and the combined allied forces probably reached the enormous number of 300,000 men. The Emperor had no reinforcements to expect; the Grand Army was not 150,000 strong, and the issue of the conflict could hardly be doubtful. Yet the attacks of the Allies were partial and timid; they have been compared to the peckings of crows round an expiring eagle; the French fought admirably when brought to bay, and but for the defection of the Saxon contingent, it is questionable if they would have suffered defeat. A retreat, however, had become necessary; it was precipitate, and it led to a frightful disaster. The Elster had not been bridged by the French; the retiring columns were stopped or retarded; an explosion destroyed the one bridge over the stream; a large part of the Grand Army was cut off; Poniatowski perished with thousands of his troops; and the allied commanders could now fairly boast that they had won a great and decisive victory. The remains of the defeated army, strewing its path with wounded, dying, and straggling men, moved feebly across the Franconian lowlands; a ray of light shone on its arms for a moment, for Napoleon crushed a Bavarian force which had endeavoured to cut him off, but it was a mere mass of fugitives when it attained the Rhine. By the flight from Saxony, the corps left at Dresden and the distant garrisons on the Oder and Vistula were completely and irrevocably lost.

Napoleon, it is scarcely necessary to say, ought not to have fought the second battle of Leipsic; he should have retreated after the first battle; and he ought to have bridged the Elster for his still large army. Turenne and Marlborough would not have made such mistakes; but those who have really studied this wonderful being will understand how he made them, despite his genius. Independently of the military causes which made the results of the campaign in Saxony so different from those of the campaign of Italy, there was a general cause for Napoleon's overthrow; he contended for the prize of his whole Empire, for domination over three-fourths of Europe; this is the true reason why he threw forward secondary armies from the Elbe to the Oder, and why he left thousands of men in the Prussian fortresses, operations contrary to sound principle, and wholly opposed to his own wonted strategy. Ambition, arrogance, and the lust of power, in fact, "distorted"—as has been truly said—"the marvellous conceptions of the matchless chief," and he underrated the strength and the resolution of his foes, and vainly trusted to the last to false auxiliaries, for whom treachery to the flag meant faith to their country, rising to a man against wrong and oppression.

On his return to Paris, in the middle of November, the Emperor had soon abundant proofs of the ruin of his power, and of the collapse of his Empire. The relics of the Grand Army, spread along the Rhine, scarcely exceeded 100,000 men ; until reorganized they were of no use ; they were dying in heaps by contagious disease ; they required horses, guns, and all kinds of *matériel* ; and the demoralization of the troops had become frightful. Yet even this was by no means the worst : the huge fabric of conquest formed by the sword was evidently doomed by the sword to perish. Soult had been driven by Wellington beyond the Pyrenees, and was endeavouring to defend the Adour and Gascony ; Suchet had recoiled to the line of the Ebro ; the mock throne of Joseph had been abandoned ; the Confederation of the Rhine had vanished, annihilated by the rising of Germany ; Eugene, beaten by a secondary Austrian force, had been repelled to the Adige and the Mincio ; unfortunate Murat was plotting treason, and trafficking with the enemy to save Naples ; Holland, half beggared by the Continental system, was striving to shake off Imperial bondage ; and stirrings of revolt were feared in Belgium, and in the German provinces west of the Rhine. Even in old France the position of affairs, and the state of the public mind, was portentous of ruin. The nation had lavished most of its youth fit for war in the effort of the year before ; the depots were empty and the arsenals stripped ; supplies of arms of all kinds were short ; and the *matériel* of war which remained to the Empire was now, for the most part, beyond France, stored in fortresses on the Elbe, the Adige, and the Po. The destruction, too, of the material resources of France, was less ominous than the national attitude. The fervour of 1813 had completely disappeared ; the mass of the people had become indifferent to patriotism, and only thought of repose ; and the cries against the Empire heard in 1812, swelled into a vast murmur from ruined cities, from half-starving seaports, from discontented provinces. Even the machinery of government was breaking down ; the conscription was evaded in whole districts ; there was an increasing movement not to pay taxes ; and the Treasury, buoyed up by paper for a time, was scarcely able to avert bankruptcy. The very functionaries of the Empire forgot their servility ; the silent Bodies of the State dared to make complaints ; the military chiefs secretly condemned the war ; and a conspiracy against Napoleon, immature as yet, was slowly formed by disgraced Ministers, by the remains of the Royalists and Republicans, scarcely heard of since the 18th Brumaire, by the men of new ideas, who aspired to give free institutions to a reformed France, and to save her from despotism and ruin at hand.

The Emperor proudly confronted misfortune; and did not abandon his still assured confidence, that he would emerge safe from this vast sea of troubles. One circumstance fed his hopes at this crisis; the Coalition had paused after Leipsic; its armies had halted as they approached the Rhine; and it made overtures of peace to Napoleon, partly because it feared a death struggle with him, and partly because it had begun to be divided in interests, passions and feelings. The Emperor sent an ambiguous reply, to proposals which would have left him ruler of a France enlarged to the " natural boundaries "; but it is questionable if he really wished to treat; and, like the armistice of Pleistwitz, this was a capital error. He was convinced that he would not be assailed for some months; he made preparations for a new campaign; and it is evident his purpose, once more, was to contend for a scarcely diminished Empire. He called out the Conscription of 1815; forced old soldiers into the ranks of the army; made another appeal to the pride of Frenchmen; supplied the failing Treasury from his Privy Purse; endeavoured to restore the *matériel* of war; and tried to arouse the passions of 1793 against " an invasion of the sacred soil," though, as he bitterly said, he had " crushed Revolution and would not rely on his worst enemy." These efforts, however, though his administrative powers and genius for organization were as great as ever, produced comparatively small results; France could not and would not supply the means required to further his ambitious ends; and yet, I have said, his intention was to play again for supreme dominion. If Soult was required to oppose Wellington, Suchet was left in Spain, and Eugene in Italy; the forces which still remained to France were not concentrated within her borders, for Napoleon thought invasion remote, and would not give up his ambitious projects; and this strategy, essentially false, and unlike that of the best days of the Emperor,

largely detracts from the conspicuous merits of the grand campaign
of 1814. The Allies did not give their foe the long breathing time
on which he had unwisely reckoned. Divided as they were, they
had a common enemy. They resented Napoleon's still warlike attitude; and when signs of his real position had become manifest, in the
rising of Holland, the defection of Murat, the victorious progress
of the arms of Wellington, the misery of France, and the growing
hatred of the Imperial rule from the Scheldt to the Po, they resolved to seize the occasion, and to cross the Rhine. By the end of
December and the first days of January, the forces of the Coalition,
spread on a vast front, were set in motion to invade France; and
this bold offensive effort beyond question disconcerted Napoleon,
who would not believe in such resolution and well-sustained
energy.

Schwartzenburg, at the head of about 160,000 men, marched
from Basle, across the plains of Franche Comté; Blücher, with
an army perhaps 60,000 strong, advanced from Maycnce and
Mannheim, and traversed the Vosges; and Bulow and Wintzingerode, far to the north, moved, with probably 70,000 troops,
from the upper Rhine towards the Aisne and the Oise, the object
of the chiefs of these converging masses being to unite in Champagne and to press on to the capital. The invasion was so sudden
that the surprised Emperor had but small forces to oppose to it.
The remains of his armies, not half reorganized and only recruited
to a slight extent, fell back at all points, through Lorraine and
Alsace, not more, probably, than 80,000 strong; and the invaders
for weeks met no resistance. By the close of January Schwartzenburg had crossed the range to the east of the great upland of
Langres, and had arrived at the heads of the Seine; Blücher had
passed Nancy, the old capital of Lorraine, and was in full march
for the Upper Marne; and though the Northern column was far in
the rear, a speedy advance to Paris was deemed imminent. The
only enemies in the way were the shattered corps of Mortier,
Oudinot, and Gérard, round Troyes, of Macdonald, Marmont,
Victor and Ney around Châlons; and though these had been hastily
reinforced, they certainly could not oppose 90,000 men, largely

composed of beaten and despondent soldiers, to victorious enemies at least twofold in numbers.

Having left Paris, and sternly rebuked one of the heretofore servile Bodies of the State, which at this crisis found heart to murmur, Napoleon reached Châlons in the last days of January. Some reinforcements were upon the march ; but, for the moment, he brought nothing but his skill to assist his collected marshals, who with shattered forces had begun to despair. Yet he retained his haughty and serene confidence ; he had formed a general plan of operations for the campaign which once more revealed his unrivalled power of turning the theatre of war to account, and his insight into passing events ; and it was to lead to some of his most splendid exploits. Blücher and Schwartzenburg had advanced from divergent bases ; their supports in the rear were far distant ; they had the old Prussian and Austrian dislike of each other, and they had now reached the valley of the Marne and the Seine, deep rivers traversed at many points by the main roads converging on Paris, the object aimed at by the allied chiefs. They would probably, therefore, march on two lines, Blücher along the Marne, his colleague by the Seine, and would be separated by a wide distance ; and the obstacles which the rivers might be made to present would give a great advantage to a really able enemy. Napoleon had fully perceived this ; he resolved to oppose one front of defence to a double front of divided attack, and, interposing between his foes, to strike them in succession and to beat them in detail ; and for this purpose he had given orders to fortify the passages on the Marne and the Seine, and had formed his base in the intermediate districts. This was one of his most brilliant conceptions, but the Emperor was very nearly crushed in his first operations through his extreme confidence. In an effort to attain Blücher, drawing near his colleague, he fought an indecisive battle at Brienne—the place where he first studied war—and he was defeated with heavy loss at La Rothière, an engagement he certainly should have avoided, for his enemies were nearly threefold in numbers. His situation appeared hopeless ; he had not more 70,000 men to oppose to fully 200,000, when his mastery of his art and the

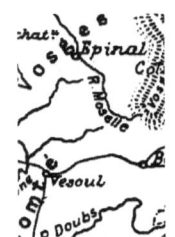

blunders of his foes changed the position of affairs, and caused a last ray of glory to irradiate the ruin of his falling Empire. As he had expected, the allied generals, after La Rothière, fell respectively back to the Marne and the Seine, and moved along the rivers; Schwartzenberg marched slowly along the Seine, throwing out detachments to protect his flanks—for hostile bodies were approaching from the south; Blücher, passionate and impulsive, pushed along the Marne, spreading out his army in disconnected fractions, and burning to run a winning race to the capital.

Napoleon, like an eagle watching his quarry, sent Oudinot and Victor to keep back Schwartzenburg, holding the passages of the Seine in force, and with the rest of his army, perhaps 50,000 strong, he hastened to the Marne to fall on Blücher, whose exposed and divided flank was laid bare to him. The weather was dreadful, and the cross-roads bad; the French army was filled with boyish conscripts, and was encumbered with far too many guns, which retarded the heavy and cumbrous columns—these evils had gone on increasing since Wagram—but Napoleon's genius overcame all hindrances; and the effects of the movement were well-nigh magical. Bursting into the midst of his terrified foes, he overwhelmed Olsuvieff at Champaubert, routed Sacken completely at Montmirail, defeated York at Chateau-Thierry, and finally hurled Blücher back to Châlons, having disabled for a time a whole host of enemies. He now turned against Schwartzenburg, who, pressing Victor and Oudinot back, had gradually advanced along the Seine; and no doubt can exist that, had he been free to act, the Emperor would have descended on the Austrian's flank. But alarm and discontent prevailed in Paris, and in order to produce an immediate effect, Napoleon was obliged to approach the capital, and to attack Schwartzenburg, when reached, in front. These operations could not have the results of the terrible strokes against Blücher's flank; nevertheless, the Austrian chief was beaten; he retreated eastward as far as Troyes; a demonstration by Blücher in his aid proved useless, and by the close of February 1814 the forces of the Coalition, cruelly shattered, were again at the heads of the Marne and the Seine. Genius had triumphed over ill-directed force; and the allied commanders were so despondent that they actually sought and obtained an armistice.

The events that followed strikingly illustrate the character of the antagonist chiefs, and the peculiarities of the struggle for Empire. Napoleon's* arrogance exceeded all bounds; he exclaimed, "We shall soon be again on the Vistula"; and his letters breathe intense scorn of his foes, and absolute reliance on his own military strength. Full of these illusions, he still refused to summon Eugene across the Alps from Italy; and though he drew detachments from the armies of Soult and Suchet, and organized a force under Augereau in the South, he did not bring nearly all his available forces to the decisive point, the theatre in Champagne. Had he conformed to his early and perfect strategy, Schwartzenburg, menaced by Eugene, and with Augereau on his flank—and Suchet might have joined—would have no doubt retreated; Blücher could not have remained isolated; the campaign of 1814 would have had a different close; and this, I repeat, must be borne in mind in judging the Emperor's conduct as a whole.

The operations of the Allies had no resemblance to those of their renowned antagonist; they were timid for the most part, and confessed weakness; but they were prudent, and marked by decision and firmness. At a great council of war held near Troyes, the Czar, the Emperor of Austria, the King of Prussia, and the representatives of the great Powers were present; † the admission was made that Blücher and Schwartzenburg could not hope for success against Napoleon, though he had but about 80,000 men, and their armies, strongly reinforced, were 200,000; the difficulty of operating along the Marne and the Seine, with their enemy

---

* Napoleon's exultation at his feats and those of his army was extravagant. "Ce qu'ils ont fait," he wrote on 12th February, "ne peut se comparer qu'aux romans de chevalerie et aux hommes d'armes de ces temps où, par l'effet de leurs armures et l'adresse de leurs chevaux, un en battait trois ou quatre cents."

† Lord Castlereagh, who was at this council, could not comprehend why Blücher and Schwartzenburg could not defeat Napoleon with their enormous superiority of numbers; and demurred to the expense—England was the paymaster of the Coalition—of bringing up Wintzingerode and Bülow. "Milord," said a bystander, "vous ne connaissez pas cet homme!"

between them, was frankly recognized ; it was resolved to bring up
the greater part of the army of the North, under Wintzingerode
and Bülow, to turn the scale decisively; and whatever may be
thought of these councils of fear, this was certainly wise and true
strategy. Hostilities, which had never really ceased, began again in
the first days of March : and Blücher, with perhaps 60,000 men—he
had reorganized his army with characteristic energy—moved along
the Marne again in the hope of destroying the isolated corps of Marmont and Mortier, for the present covering the main roads to Paris.
The Marshals, however, retreated behind the Ourcq ; and Blücher,
rash to a fault, and not taught by disaster, crossed the Marne,
and endeavoured to bring them to bay. This gave Napoleon his
opportunity again. Quitting his central position, he bore down on
Blücher, now far from his colleague, and crossed the Marne ; and
he was soon on the track of the Prussian chief, who, in extreme
peril, was making for the Aisne, with but a feeble chance of getting
over the river.

A fortunate accident saved Blücher, when perhaps on the verge
of a terrible overthrow. The commandant of Soissons, a weak
man, opened his gates to Bülow and Wintzingerode, advancing
from the North, as had been arranged ; the only passage on the
Aisne fell into their hands, and Blücher joined with delight his
new colleagues, their united forces being about 100,000 men.
Napoleon had not more than 60,000 ; but his passionate ardour
mastered his judgment, as had often happened in his chequered
career ; he attacked the Allies at Craonne and Laon, and, as at
La Rothière he was completely beaten, though he destroyed a
hostile body in his retreat. His second effort against Blücher
had, therefore, had very different results from those of his first ;
he had suffered greatly at Craonne and Laon, battles which he
certainly should not have risked ; and he was now obliged to return
to the Seine, with an army weakened and beginning to lose hope.
IIe had left Oudinot and Macdonald, replacing Victor, to hold
Schwartzenburg in check, as in the first instance ; but the Austrian
chief, in the Emperor's absence, had forced the passage of the
Seine, and approached Paris ; his advanced guard was not far

14

from Melun; and the capital, seething with passion and terror, had not only made no preparations to resist, but was beginning to declare against the tottering Empire, especially since Wellington's victories in the South.   Napoleon left Mortier and Marmont to observe Blücher, and calling up his forces to come into line with him, he endeavoured to operate on the rear of Schwartzenburg; he compelled the cautious Austrian to fall back; but he was surprised on the Aube, near the town of Arcis, was forced to fight a stern but a losing battle, and was ultimately obliged to cross the river.   He had failed against Schwartzenburg as he had failed against Blücher.   How different might the result have been had he called Eugene and Suchet to his aid in Champagne !

The Allies were now in overwhelming force; they thoroughly understood Napoleon's game, and he could no longer continue his late strategy.   He adopted a course almost the counterpart of his projected march on Berlin in 1813—baffled, we have seen, by various accidents—which has been differently judged by disputing critics, but which, as a mere military move, may be pronounced admirable.   His garrisons on the Vistula and Oder were lost; but he had large garrisons in the French fortresses, which, hitherto blockaded by the allied armies, had been nearly set free by the immense demands of Blücher and Schwartzenburg for reinforcements ; and he resolved to make use of what he called those "dead forces," to collect a powerful army, to descend on the rear of his foes, and to cut off their communications with the Rhine.   He always declared that this plan was possible, and when we consider the timid weakness which usually marked the conduct of the Allies, it presented many chances of success, had France been really true to the Empire.   He broke up from the Aube in the third week of March, and summoning Mortier and Marmont to join him, made for Vitry upon the Upper Marne, his object being to attain the Meuse and, rallying the forces released from the fortresses, to attack Schwartzenburg and to seize the line of his retreat at the head of about 120,000 men, the troops from Lyons and the south supporting the movement.

The Emperor's letters still breathe the perfect confidence which distinguished them throughout the whole campaign; and he haughtily spurned proposals for peace, which even now, at the eleventh hour, would have left him the France of Louis XVI. Events, however, were soon to show the vanity of the false dreams of ambition. The conspiracy which had been hatching for months in the capital, against the Empire, had become mature; it was joined by Talleyrand and other dismissed Ministers, by Liberals, Bourbon and Jacobin partisans, and means were found to inform the Allies that should they advance on Paris Napoleon would fall. A second great council of war was held by the leaders of the Coalition on the 24th of March; and it was unanimously decided to march on the capital, leaving a detachment only to observe Napoleon. The allied armies pushed rapidly on by the now abandoned and unguarded lines which, hitherto, they had failed to master, driving before them the feeble corps of Mortier and Marmont, who had been unable to join the Emperor, and could not offer a show of resistance; and on the 29th of March the armies of Continental Europe had come in view of the proud city which, for twenty years, had been the ardent focus of revolution, of war, of glory, of Empire. The marshals fought a battle honourable to both, but it was impossible to withstand the great host of enemies. A capitulation was signed the following day; and Russians, Austrians, Prussians, Swedes, Bavarians, and soldiers from every part of Germany, took possession of the fallen yet not mourning capital. A few hours sufficed to complete the ruin of the despotism of force which had long been supreme. The young Empress and the Imperial Court vanished; the Bodies of the State, for years the instruments of a tyranny they had cringed to but had learned to hate, declared the throne of Napoleon forfeited, and Paris heard, not without rejoicings, that the Monarchy of the Bourbons, which its frenzied citizens had shed oceans of blood to destroy for ever, was to be restored at the will of the conquerors.

Meanwhile, Napoleon, informed of these events, had hastily abandoned his march eastwards; he was at Fontainebleau on the 2nd of April, at the head of nearly 70,000 men, and treating as

14 *

nought all that had been accomplished, he still resolved to strike a blow for Empire. The military situation was not quite hopeless. The generals of the Coalition had most unwisely distributed their armies around Paris, divided by the streams of the Marne and the Seine; and everything was to be dreaded, in a position of this kind, from the terrible enemy placed in their rear. Napoleon made overtures to negotiate, but it is tolerably certain his real object was to gain a few hours to make a desperate effort, and to surprise his foes in their false security; and he has left it on record that he must have won a decisive battle at the very gates of Paris. His marshals, however, refused to follow their chief in a course they believed desperate; Marmont went over, with his corps, to the Allies, and the conqueror saw his invincible sword fall from his grasp through the ill-will and the treachery of the companions in arms he had long led to victory. He abdicated, after the Bodies of the State had pronounced finally; and—a terrible lesson to those who abuse power, and a terrible proof how faith and loyalty are blighted in a revolutionary age—Fontainebleau became quickly a silent desert, abandoned by the functionaries who had grovelled at his feet. His noble words of farewell to the veterans of the Guard in some measure lessen the ignominy of scenes on which the historian dwells with pain; but one incident of shame has yet to be noticed. The fallen Emperor took poison, to end a life of despair. The attempt at self-destruction, perhaps happily, failed, but this is another proof that, when all seemed lost, Napoleon had not the indomitable firmness of very inferior warriors.

Napoleon's operations in 1814, as regards the struggle in Champagne at least, have always been classed with his finest efforts. It was a prodigy of skill that, with a bad army, he should have baffled enemies threefold in numbers, should have all but overwhelmed Blücher, and should have kept the issue of events in suspense; the general of 1796 reappears, in full perfection, in this splendid strategy. Yet even in these noble displays of the art, he fell into serious and plain errors; he ought not to have fought at least four battles, unnecessary, and with the chances against him; and he made two grave mistakes, which proved fatal—the

attempt to contend for his whole Empire, and the omission to concentrate his forces during the armistice. His generalship in 1814,
considered as a whole, was not equal to that of 1796, and his
campaigns of 1812, of 1813, and even of 1814, remind me of
Turner's latest pictures; we see the hand of the master everywhere,
but there is a want of proportion and real harmony, and the
result is sad and general failure.

CHAPTER VIII.

NAPOLEON (continued).

I MUST pass over the attempt to resettle the boundaries, at Vienna, of a changed Continent; nor can I dwell on the pretensions of the Czar to sit in the seat of Napoleon without his genius, on the rapacity of Prussia and the craft of Talleyrand, and on the league between Austria, England, and France, to restrain the ambition of the Northern Powers. Nor can I notice Napoleon's brief rule in Elba, though the administrative powers of the fallen Lord of the Continent were exhibited in this narrow sphere, and have left honourable traditions not yet forgotten. I must also avoid even a short account of the failure of the Restoration in France; how Louis XVIII., well-meaning but feeble, spite of the memories of the old *régime*, fell into the hands of Royalist zealots, and marred the grace of the freedom he claimed to concede; how impossible it became to reconcile the pretensions of returned *émigrés* and a ruined *noblesse* with the interests grown out of the Revolution; how the army, transformed and made the appanage of a Court, chafed in silence, and regretted its unrivalled chief; how the nation after a brief hour of repose, felt humiliated that it had been reduced to the position of a lesser Power of Europe. The discords of the Coalition, and the unsettled state of France, were not lost on the extraordinary man who watched events from his speck in the sea, and who had not forgotten his vanished Empire. Napoleon quitted Elba in February 1815, on the most wonderful enterprise of his whole career. A flotilla bore the few hundred men imprudently left him by the Allies; Fortune smiled treacherously on her audacious favourite, and he had soon landed on the shores of Provence, in order, in the face of embattled Europe, to subvert a Government founded on an European triumph. The very thought seemed akin to folly, and yet it became an accomplished fact in a fortnight. With that insight which was one of his greatest gifts, Napoleon avoided the cities of the coast and the great military stations of his old marshals; he flung himself into the valleys of Dauphiné, a district hostile to the restored Monarchy, and his march seemed like the spread of some mighty influence, which power and authority were unable to withstand. Grasse, Sisteron, and Gap were rapidly passed; a regiment near Grenoble welcomed the sight of its old commander, and fell at his knees; the garrison of the town greeted him with exulting shouts, and wherever a part of the army beheld Napoleon, it followed him, swayed as by an enchanter's spell. Macdonald, with his staff, was expelled from Lyons; Ney, meaning to be loyal, was carried away in the universal military revolt; other chiefs found it impossible to resist; and the discrowned exile was soon on his way to the capital at the head of a great and hourly increasing force.

Napoleon was at the Tuileries once more on the 20th of March; "his eagles," in his expressive language, "had flown from steeple to steeple to the towers of Nôtre Dame," and France, dazzled, surprised, and disliking the Bourbons, accepted a revolution which seemed a kind of portent. The King fled into Belgium with his Court, his nobles, and a few officers of the Empire, who would not break their oaths; the army easily put down two or three risings of Royalists in the Southern Provinces; and Napoleon boasted, with truth, that he regained his throne at the cost of scarcely a drop of blood. After this astonishing return to Empire, Napoleon offered peace, and to remain satisfied with the France of the Treaties of 1814; and probably he was sincere in these overtures. Yet it is not surprising that he was not believed; he had broken faith with Europe in leaving Elba, and, partly through terror and partly from hate, the Allies proscribed him as an enemy of mankind. He addressed himself to the defence of France, but the movement which had set him on the throne was essentially a military revolt; the fierce animosities of French factions embarrassed his Government and weakened the State; the restored Empire was viewed with distrust by Royalists, Liberals, and the old Republicans; the nation treated with indifferent contempt free institutions offered by Imperial hands; and the Chambers, which Napoleon convened to give popular support to his imperilled power, were full of secret or avowed conspirators. Nevertheless, let detractors say what they please, his exertions were mighty and worthy of him; his genius as an administrator shone with fresh brightness, though his health was evidently on the decline, and in a few weeks he had made preparations to resist the Coalition which must be deemed wonderful. One circumstance gave him precious resources; more than 100,000 prisoners of war, trained and excellent soldiers, had been restored to France; and by making use of these and additional veterans, and by employing conscripts and National Guards, he raised the army, which had been reduced to impotence, to a state of formidable strength and efficiency. Meanwhile, he gave its old organization and structure to the instrument of war he had so long wielded; the Guard reappeared, and the loved eagles; corps, divisions, and reserves were again formed; great exertions were made to provide arms, horses, and *impedimenta* of all kinds; and Paris, which had fallen at once in 1814, was to a considerable extent, fortified. By June 1815, half-a-million of men were on foot to take part in the impending conflict; about 250,000 of these were ready; and paper money supplied the Treasury with the means of seconding a great effort which, in existing circumstances, was, I repeat, astonishing.

Two plans of operations presented themselves. Had France been united and loyal as a whole, Napoleon would have, no doubt, followed the grand precedent of the year before, under conditions much more favourable to success; he would have encountered the Coalition in Champagne with forces far more powerful than in 1814, and with Paris a strong entrenched camp in his rear, and recollecting what he achieved on the Marne and the Seine, his triumph would have been not at all improbable. The second plan was much more hazardous ; but it was in harmony with Napoleon's genius, and it followed methods which had often secured him victory. The Coalition had a million of men in arms ; but these masses were spread from the Scheldt to the Po, and easterly, from the Rhine to the Oder ; and the extreme right of the immense line of invasion, the two armies of Blücher and Wellington was isolated and thrown forward in Belgium. It might be practicable then, as it had been at Ulm, to cut off and destroy this detached force ; and many circumstances concurred to give a well-directed attack a real chance of success. The armies of Blücher and Wellington were widely apart ; they rested upon divergent bases ; they were commanded by chiefs of opposite natures ; their centre was weak and greatly exposed ; their line of communication was a single road, at a short distance only from the French frontier, and behind this line lay a difficult country which would make their subsequent concentration no easy matter.

Seizing the situation with the eye of a master, Napoleon saw in this position of affairs an admirable opportunity to strike with effect ; and he resolved to assail and break through the allied centre, and to try to defeat Blücher and Wellington in detail, as he had defeated Beaulieu and Colli in the campaign of Italy. The means he adopted to carry out his project rank among the finest operations of his life, and form a conspicuous instance of his gift of stratagem. Concealing the movement with consummate skill, he drew together four corps from the vast space between Lille and Metz to the edge of the frontier ; the Guard, another corps, and the cavalry marched from the interior ; and the collected masses, perfectly arranged, converged gradually along this immense front, under the eye of the enemy, yet without his knowledge ! No more splendid effort has been made in war ; and had the Emperor had the complete force—150,000 men —which he reckoned on to begin the campaign, in all probability he would have triumphed. A rising in La Vendée deprived him, however, at the last moment, of 20,000 soldiers ; but the die was cast, and he did not hesitate ; and he set off from Paris on the

12th of June to challenge Fortune in a supreme trial. His admirable directions had been admirably fulfilled. On the evening
of the 14th June 1815, 128,000 Frenchmen, comprising 22,000
horse and 350 guns, were assembled from near Maubeuge to near
Philippeville, where the French frontier then entered Belgium ;
and screened by the Sambre, they were a few miles from Charleroi, where the great road to Brussels gave an easy approach to
the comparatively feeble centre of the Allies.

The army was in motion at daybreak on the 15th, the Emperor's object being to cross the Sambre, to occupy Charleroi, and
by a forced march to seize the points of Quatre Bras and Sombreffe, on the great cross road between Nivelles and Namur, the
only line on which his foes could unite without obstacles of no
small difficulty. The operation was not quite successful ; delays
and different accidents occurred. Ziethen, too, one of Blücher's
lieutenants, had checked the advance, not without skill, but
Napoleon's project was nearly realised ; the great mass of the
French was beyond Charleroi, and within easy reach of Quatre
Bras and Sombreffe before night closed on the 15th ; and the
allied centre was threatened if not severed, and could only close
up in effective force, under, so to speak, the guns of the enemy.
The conduct, meanwhile, of the hostile chiefs had perfectly fulfilled Napoleon's previsions, and had given him already an
immense advantage. Blücher had, characteristically, placed three
of his corps in positions around, or not far from, Sombreffe, even
now almost in Napoleon's grasp ; but his fourth corps was many
leagues distant, and could not reach Sombreffe for a battle next
day. On the other hand, Wellington, circumspect and cautious, and
without experience of Napoleon's strategy, had hesitated and delayed at Brussels ; he had not taken a step to join his colleague
until late in the night of the 15th ; and even then, fearing for his
communications and his right, he had not advanced in force
towards Quatre Bras, where his junction with Blücher would be
accomplished. The allied line of communication, therefore, on the
lateral road of Nivelles-Namur was not held by the Allies in force ;
it was all but in the hands of the enemy. The allied centre was

completely exposed, and Napoleon might reasonably expect either
to beat in detail the allied chiefs, should they venture to offer
battle, or to seize the points of Quatre Bras and Sombreffe, and
to interpose between Blücher and Wellington.

This was the situation on the morning of the 16th, and it was
full of great, nay, of splendid, promise. Napoleon was now at
Charleroi, about to start for Fleurus, and to take the command of
his corps near Sombreffe. He has been charged with delay, I
think unjustly, and he was not fully aware of the enemy's movements; but his general position was so good, and his general
directions were so well planned, that accidents only robbed him
of a decisive victory. He ordered Ney on his left to seize Quatre
Bras, driving back any forces of the Duke at hand. The Marshal
was then to descend on the rear of Blücher, who was to be
attacked near Sombreffe, in front, by the Emperor; and had this
grand manœuvre been properly carried out, Blücher must have
been routed and forced away to the Meuse, and Wellington would
have been in the extreme of peril, for both generals were now
trying to join hands at Quatre Bras and Sombreffe, and were
laying themselves open to the whole force of Napoleon. Ney could
have easily fulfilled his mission; but he had lost the confidence
of better days; he waited many hours before he even tried to
move; and he failed to accomplish his main task, falling from
Quatre Bras on the rear of Blücher.

Napoleon, meanwhile, marching from Fleurus, had attacked
Blücher between Sombreffe and Ligny. The battle raged furiously
for a considerable time, to the disadvantage of the Prussians on the
whole, but no decisive success had been won; and the Emperor,
perceiving that no force was closing on Blücher from the direction of Ney, tried to attain his object by another method. One of
Ney's corps had advanced slowly; the Emperor directed this
towards Blücher's flank, while Blücher was to be assailed, as
before, in front; and had this stroke been pressed home, the result
would have been the same as that of the first projected attack.
D'Erlon, however, the unlucky chief of this corps, was, when on
the path of victory, called up by Ney, hard pressed by Wellington

at this moment; and Napoleon, I think, must have concurred in this, for the defeat of Ney would have been disastrous, though this extreme caution was, perhaps, an error. Blücher escaped destruction through these mishaps; but Napoleon's attack in front had partial success, and the Prussian army was driven,. in defeat, from the field. On the other side of the scenes of manœuvre, Ney, we have seen, had not reached Blücher, and had missed his mark; he had most unfortunately recalled D'Erlon, and he had suffered a repulse from the hands of Wellington, who had kept Quatre Bras though with much difficulty. Ney, however, had gained a strategic advantage; he had prevented Wellington from joining Blücher, and as Blücher had been forced away from Sombreffe, the Duke would be compelled to retreat; the line of communication of the allied armies was practically already in Napoleon's hands; and his operations had been largely successful, if they had not led to a second Jena, as he had reason to expect a few hours before. Such had been the result of his fine strategy, although that result had not been complete; and it should be borne in mind that the allied armies were not far from double his own in numbers.

The allied generals, obliged, through the defeat of Ligny, to abandon their proper line of junction—the great road between Nivelles and Namur—were now thrown back into the country behind it, the thick-wooded and marshy valley of the Dyle, very difficult for the passage of armies. The real student of war will not doubt as to what their movements ought to have been; they should either have united their forces at once, a few miles behind Quatre Bras and Sombreffe, or they should have retreated two marches away to Brussels, where, having an overwhelming superiority of strength, they might have derided Napoleon's efforts. They took, however, an intermediate course—a half measure often disastrous in war; Blücher fell back some twenty miles to Wavre, the Duke fell back from Quatre Bras to Waterloo, and holding these positions they meant to join hands and accept, if offered, a great battle.

The idolaters of success, supposed to cover everything, have praised this as scientific strategy, but it was bad strategy, and dangerous in the extreme. Wavre is considerably farther from Waterloo than Sombreffe is from Quatre Bras; what is more important, a most intricate country divides Wavre from Waterloo, and in this operation Blücher and Wellington were playing into the hands of their renowned adversary. Napoleon was given three alternatives, each big with the promise of immense success. He might call on his victorious army to make a forced march, might fall either on Blücher or Wellington, and defeat either within a few hours, before Wavre or Waterloo were reached; or collecting together all his forces, he might attack Blücher at Wavre, or the Duke at Waterloo, before either could join the other; or, in truer accordance with the principles of the art, he might restrain Blücher, with a retarding force, sent quickly from Ligny to hold him in check, and might attack Wellington with the mass of his army—the favourite manœuvre, in which he has had no rival— and in any of these cases he must have triumphed, over-matched as he was by his foes in numbers. The double retreat on Wavre and Waterloo was therefore a thoroughly false movement; and the General of Rivoli would have made it fatal. But the General of Rivoli, full of genius as ever, had lost the iron strength of twenty years before. Napoleon returned after Ligny, to Fleurus, ill; he went to sleep and could not see his staff, and this illness, at a crisis in the campaign, saved the Allies, and had momentous results.

During the night of the 16th and the morning of the 17th, the French army remained motionless. Soult and Ney literally did nothing, no preparations for marching were made; the Emperor sent no orders from Fleurus; and, worst of all, Grouchy given the command of the right on the 16th, made no real effort to reconnoitre the Prussians, and to find out where they had gone. Disease, in fact, had weakened the energy of the chief; his lieutenants, fashioned to servitude, let things drift, and the opportunity of the 16th, given on the 17th once more, was lost never again to return. Napoleon was back at Ligny in the forenoon of the 17th; a letter of Soult, the Chief of the Staff, proves that his first intention was to halt for the day, for he believed that the Prussians, completely routed, were falling back on their base, towards the Meuse, and there would be time, he thought, to turn against and defeat Wellington. On learning, however, from Ney, on the left, that parts of the Duke's forces were still at Quatre Bras, he resolved to advance, and try to destroy them; and he made preparations, now very late, for a combined movement against the Allies. He divided his army into two groups; at the head of the first, about 72,000 men, he meant to attack Wellington and bring him to bay; he gave Grouchy the second, about 34,000 strong, and he informed the Marshal that his mission was to pursue Blücher and to keep him in sight, and to interpose between Blücher and Wellington who, the Emperor added, was to be assailed should he stand near the neighbouring forest of Soignies.

Napoleon broke up from Ligny early in the afternoon; he was soon joined by Ney at Quatre Bras, and he endeavoured to harass the rearguard of the Duke, who by this time had his main force at Waterloo. The pursuit, however, had no results—it was too late, in fact, to be of use—and an extraordinary tempest of rain had broken over the country, and all but stopped marching. Before night fell, the heads of the French army had reached the low hills that overlook Waterloo, and a large army was evidently in position before them. Napoleon halted, hopeful of a great coming battle; but some hours before he sent directions to Grouchy, on his right, which require attention. Before leaving Ligny the Emperor, we have seen, believed that Blücher was making for his base, and had spoken to Grouchy in that sense; but on his way from Ligny to Quatre Bras he was made aware that a large Prussian force had been seen on the Orneau, near Gembloux. He immediately sent new orders to Grouchy, and directed him to advance on Gembloux, and, of course, generally to comply with his first orders. Grouchy, who had broken up from Ligny late, set off for Gembloux in the afternoon; and though Blücher had had a long start, and Gembloux was by no means the best position to be taken for an advance on Wavre, still the Emperor's directions were correct enough to have enabled a bold and capable chief to have fulfilled his all-important mission, to have attained Blücher and kept him off from Wellington. Grouchy reached Gembloux rather late at night—the state of the roads and the weather excuse him—and he can hardly be blamed, though the fact is strange, that even at this time he was not informed with perfect accuracy about the Prussian movements. Within a short time, however, he had ascertained that a great part of Blücher's army had made for Wavre; another part, he was told, was marching on Perwez, towards the Meuse. He communicated this important news to the Emperor, and he expressly added, "that he would advance on Wavre, should the mass of the Prussians go that way, in order to separate Blücher from Wellington," proving that he perfectly understood his mission.

This intelligence—received during the night of the 17th—was calculated to make Napoleon certain, especially as it was his own idea, that he had nothing to fear from the Prussian army; he thought only of fighting Wellington, and he made preparations to attack on the morrow. The Prussian veteran, however, who more than once had baffled the Emperor by his audacious movements, had resolved, whatever the risk, to advance on Waterloo. He had rallied his whole army around Wavre, his first corps, that of Bülow, had come into line, and he had given his word to the Duke, who on the faith of the pledge was in position to fight at Waterloo, that "the whole Prussian army would be on the field by the early forenoon of the 18th of June." Blücher nobly endeavoured to fulfil his promise. Bülow broke up from Wavre at daybreak on the 18th, but the obstacles he met were formidable in the extreme; he was still far from Wellington's lines at noon, and his three colleagues, Ziethen, Pirch and Thielmann, were still close to Wavre, nearly a march distant, and were on a perilous flank march, in long straggling columns.

Meanwhile Grouchy had left Gembloux for Wavre, to follow up the enemy—he had now ascertained that all Blücher's army had gathered round the place the night before—but his operations were simply wretched. He knew that Napoleon meant to fight

Wellington, should Wellington make a stand at Soignies ; he knew that he was detached to hold Blücher in check, and to keep him completely apart from Wellington ; he knew that the Prussians had been round Wavre, and had informed his master, in part, of the fact ; he knew that Wavre was a march from Soignies and Waterloo, and he knew that at Gembloux he was some fourteen miles from Wavre. Knowing all this, he should have left Gembloux at the first peep of dawn on the 18th of June, and have advanced as quickly as possible ; and common sense should have taught him so to make for Wavre as to get across the Dyle, in order to draw near Napoleon and to cut off Blücher on his way to Wellington, for probably Blücher was making the attempt. He took exactly the opposite course ; he left Gembloux many hours too late ; his movement on Wavre was pitiably slow, and he made for Wavre, not over the Dyle, which would have soon placed him on the flank of Blücher, but along the stream, striking Blücher, if reached, in the rear, and pushing him, so to speak, on Wellington. This miserable generalship led to what followed ; and Grouchy was so obstinate, and so blind to fact, that when he heard the far-distant thunder of Waterloo, he refused to follow the sagacious advice of Gérard and to march, at the eleventh hour, towards the flank of the enemy !

While these operations, big with a great future, had been taking place on Napoleon's right, the Emperor had attacked Wellington, who, with faith in his colleague, awaited his foe in a long-studied position.   Napoleon had intended to attack early, but the state of the roads and the weather made an attack hazardous, and he delayed some hours, greatly to the Duke's advantage. The Emperor's general plan—the last exhibition of his genius in the sphere of higher tactics—was to turn Wellington's left and to force his centre, making a demonstration to engage his right ; his adversary's was to hold his ground until the arrival of Blücher would make success certain.   The grand attack on the British left and centre failed, partly owing to the excellence of the British troops, and partly to the density and cumbrousness of the French columns ; and the feint on Wellington's right had no more success, and led to terrible waste of blood.

By this time Napoleon had learned that Bülow was gathering on his flank with 30,000 men, but he hoped this was a stray column which Grouchy might arrest and perhaps destroy, and he turned fiercely against the centre of his foe, abandoning the effort against the British left, which, with Bülow at hand, would have been too hazardous. This attack was successful to some extent; La Haye Sainte, a fortified post, was captured. This made a gap in Wellington's defence, and Napoleon, confident that victory was at hand, launched a great mass of cavalry against the Duke's centre, intending to support the movement with the Imperial Guard. But at this crisis of the battle Blücher was near. Despising wounds, defeat, and days of fatigue, he ordered Bülow to fall on the Emperor's flank. This prevented the attack the Guard was to make, and though the French horsemen made heroic exertions, the British and German infantry "stood rooted in the earth"; and the cavalry, recklessly squandered by Ney but not supported by foot, were at last beaten.

During all this time, Bülow had been striking Napoleon's right; but at about 7 this attack seemed spent. The French still occupied the thin red line of Wellington, the artillery of Grouchy was heard at Wavre—a pledge that he was keeping the Prussians back—and victory for France seemed yet possible. Napoleon formed the Guard into two great columns, but Wellington had admirably strengthened his centre; the first column was fairly beaten, and the second, kept in reserve, could give it no aid. A sudden change now came over the battle; parts of the corps of Ziethen and Pirch appeared on the field; the attack of Bülow was fiercely renewed; British squadrons, let loose, swept over the plain; and the Duke, seeing the day was won, ordered a general advance of his worn-out army. The French, routed and surrounded, had soon no army, and night closed on a scene of carnage and ruin, the presage of Napoleon's second fall.

Napoleon's plan of attack on his last field was perfect, but his tactics at Waterloo show many errors. He was certainly in difficulties after the flank attack of Bülow, but he allowed his troops to be wasted in the feint on our right; he made a premature use

15

of his noble cavalry, and he perhaps missed an opportunity to strike with the Guard before Bülow's diversion had become serious. For these mistakes he must be held responsible, though he was badly seconded by his lieutenants, especially by Ney—desperate, and stung by conscience—but all this was because, as is now well known,[*] he was ill and worn out on the 18th of June. The Duke, on the other hand, was the soul of the defence. He made, indeed, a grave strategic mistake in leaving a large detachment far off on his right, but his conduct of the battle was above praise; and though he must have lost Waterloo had not the Prussians come up, still the defeat would not have been the rout to which Napoleon had looked with confidence.

Nevertheless, the result of Waterloo flowed from combinations outside the field. It was caused by the junction of part of Blücher's army with Wellington; and the question for the student of war is, ought this junction to have been prevented by Grouchy, detached by the Emperor to make it impossible? The answer must largely depend on conjecture; but I, for one, can have few doubts. Had Grouchy left Gembloux at daybreak on the 18th, and, crossing the Dyle, made for Blücher's flank, he would have surprised the Prussian army in divided columns on a flank march of extreme peril; and, giving Blücher credit for his splendid energy, I am convinced he would have paused to confront his enemy, and this must have prevented him reaching Wellington. The same result would have, perhaps, followed, and this is Napoleon's deliberate view[†]— not impartial, perhaps, but not to be dismissed—had Grouchy simply marched on Wavre in time, and fastened upon the rear of Blücher. The Emperor insists that, even in this case, not a Prussian division would have attained Waterloo. The arguments urged against these conclusions disregard the peril of the march from

---

[*] The authorities on the state of Napoleon's health during the campaign of 1815 will be found in Mr. Dorsey Gardener's book on Waterloo, pp. 34, 36.

[†] "Si le maréchal Grouchy eût campé devant Wavre le soir du 17, l'armée prussienne n'eut fait aucun détachment pour secourir l'armée angla'se."—*Correspondence*, vol. xxxi., p. 213. No doubt Grouchy could not have reached Wavre on the night of the 17th, but he might have been there at 11 A.M. on the morning of the 18th; and the result would have been practically the same. Bülow would not have attacked, or perhaps even approached Waterloo, had he been isolated.

NEY AT WATERLOO.

Wavre, and the very events of the day confute them. Grouchy, who should have been near Wavre at 11 A.M., did not reach it until 4 P.M., and yet his apparition stopped the Prussian army; Ziethen and Pirch were delayed, Thielmann was left at Wavre, and Blücher brought only 45,000 men, out of 90,000, to the field of Waterloo, and that too only between 4 A.M. and 8 P.M. In view of this fact, I can draw but one inference, and in this controversy all that has been written by Charras, and authors of his school, seems to me worthless.

A word on this memorable campaign, as a whole, and as to the lessons it really teaches. Napoleon's first operations were a masterpiece of war; and these, and the grave strategic faults of the Allies— Blücher ran into the lion's mouth, the Duke did not know how sudden was his spring—exposed both to alarming danger, and ought to have secured the Emperor a decisive victory. The errors, however, of Ney and D'Erlon saved Blücher at Ligny from utter ruin, and Napoleon's over caution as regards D'Erlon—though this is theory after the event—was certainly unfortunate to the interests of France. The double retreat at Wavre and Waterloo – another palpable strategic fault—gave Napoleon a second great opportunity. No doubt can exist for those who understand his career, that he would have seized it early on the 17th had he been the chief of a few years before,* but he was no longer equal to prolonged fatigue, and the negligence of his lieutenants and his slumber at Fleurus lost him a chance not again afforded by fortune. His prospects were not equally good on the 18th; he calculated on destroying Wellington, but this, I believe, was beyond his powers, and his delays, and the direction given to Grouchy and his wing, made it possible for Blücher to join Wellington, a possibility that might have been wholly

---

* Jomini knew more about Napoleon than any other commentator on the Emperor and is naturally astonished at the delays of the 17th of June. The real cause was not then known, but Jomini's words are significant. *Précis de la Campagne de 1815*, p. 185. "Pour ceux qui se rappellent l'étonnante activité qui présida aux événements de Ratisbonne en 1809, de Dresde en 1813, de Champaubert et de Montmirail en 1814, ce nouveau temps perdu sera toujours une chose inexplicable de la part de Napoléon."

excluded. Nevertheless, he ought to have gained Waterloo. The arrangement of Grouchy's force was sufficiently correct to have enabled Grouchy to stop Blücher, and though the Emperor made more than one mistake—and supreme genius is not omniscience—we still see in this campaign the matchless strategist, great as ever in intellect, but no longer equal, through physical weakness, to work out his conceptions. Yet when this has been said, justice should be done to the allied chiefs; and they deserved their triumph. Both, no doubt, made serious strategic errors; from first to last they proved themselves to be, strategically, unfit to cope with Napoleon, but both exhibited as soldiers the finest qualities. Blücher's conduct in rallying his defeated army, and in attempting the march on Waterloo, shows energy of the highest order. Wellington's constancy and tactical skill at Waterloo are admirable . specimens of his genius in defence. The test of the merits of the two commanders is to compare their conduct with what would have been the conduct of any other chief of the Coalition opposed to Napoleon; Schwartzenburg would not have risked the march from Wavre, the Archduke Charles would have fallen back from Waterloo when he found that the promised support was late, and in either event the Emperor would have won the battle. Two subordinate causes of the issue of the campaign cannot, in addition, be passed over. Napoleon's army was too small; <u>128,000</u> men could, with difficulty, be opposed to <u>224,000,</u> and this led to a distribution of his force—his wings not being well connected with a weak centre—which partly explains his lieutenants' faults, if it does not afford an excuse for them. The Prussian army, besides, was a different army from that which had succumbed at Jena. Napoleon refused to see the distinction; he would not believe—as, in all instances, disregarding national and popular feeling—that it could rally after Ligny, and draw near Wellington, and this had something to do with his overthrow, though, I repeat, Blücher could not have succeeded had Grouchy been a capable chief.

I shall not dwell on the closing scenes of a most strange and eventful history. Napoleon at St. Helena realised the legend of the fabled Prometheus ; Genius, in conflict with Supreme Fact, was chained to a rock, and held down by Force, and humanity turns away from the agony. Yet impartial history will truly say that it was just to deprive the great troubler of the world of liberty, and the animosities and fears of the time account for, if they do not excuse, the indignities suffered by the fallen Emperor. The student of war will turn with gratitude to the rich fruits of Napoleon's exile, his writings on the art, in thought and style superior to all productions of the kind, and those who imagine that German genius has created the latest developments of war will be surprised to learn that if we omit what belongs to purely material inventions, it has been anticipated at every point by Napoleon.

My estimate of this extraordinary man can be easily gathered from what 1 have written. Nature gave her prodigy an imagination such as she gave to Dante and Milton ; she added a power of calculation and thought, such as she bestowed on Newton and Laplace ; she contributed a superabundant and practical energy, embracing alike what was great and small, such as scarcely ever has been seen in man, and she conferred craft, dexterity, readiness, and firmness of character in a most ample measure. Gifts such as these would have made Napoleon one of the greatest of generals in any age ; but he fell on a time when the progress of husbandry and facilities of locomotion, greatly increased, had created new conditions for the military art ; and when, too, Revolution in France had given a powerful impulse to the human mind, and had made it singularly bold and aspiring. Genius and circumstance thus concurred to place Napoleon almost at once at the head of all warriors of modern times ; and for years it seemed, as if Fortune, whatever he did in the field, assured him victory. He was unrivalled, from the first, as a strategist ; the plans of his early campaigns are marvels of genius as distinctive as those of Shakspeare or Raphael ; but though imagination is their most striking feature, this as yet, as a rule, is controlled by judgment, and astonishing as they are, they are thoroughly practical. The peculiar excellence of these prodigies of art is the mastery of the theatre of war, and Napoleon's power in making it answer his ends ; the campaign on the Adige, that which led to Marengo, and that of Austerlitz are perhaps the finest specimens of this supreme merit. Conceptions, however, in war are useless unless skilful execution follows ; and Napoleon's execution of his strategic projects was more wonderful than the projects themselves. In these operations he, of course, adhered to the methods of his great predecessors, for these were in accord with the nature of things, and carried out principles always true ; for example, like every real strategist, his constant object was to bring superior force to the decisive point, and so to baffle and defeat the enemy ; and, with these ends in view, like Turenne, he struck repeatedly at the communications of his foe, and endeavoured to gain his flank or rear ; or, throwing himself between divided enemies, attacked them in detail, and beat them down in succession. But all this he did with an orginality of design, with a force of calculation, and, above all perhaps, with a power of stratagem unequalled by Turenne or by any commander of modern times.

Nothing since the days of Hannibal can be compared to the descent from the Alps, which conquered Italy, and to the march from the Channel to the Danube, which destroyed a whole army by manœuvres, and threw the gates of distant Vienna open. These marvels of war, it must be borne in mind, however, were due not to Napoleon alone ; they were to be attributed, in a great degree, to circumstance and to his perfect appreciation of it. From the new conditions made possible in war, from the growth of agriculture and the multiplication of roads, armies could subsist, in every fertile country, for the most part, on resources on the spot, and could therefore dispense, to a certain extent, with *impedimenta* necessary before ; they could also march on a variety of lines with a rapidity never before possible ; and the art, so to speak, was given wings, and could take a flight into a new sphere. First of the men of his time, Napoleon grasped these facts ; his armies living on the tracts they passed through, and making use of every available road that was compatible with their safety on the march, moved, not without magazines, indeed, nor without a solid base and all kinds of supplies, but with a celerity never before known; and the young chief out-manœuvred and terrified generals accustomed only to the methods of the past. This was one of the secrets of Napoleon's early success; his genius fell in with and made the most of the new conditions of the art of war, and for a long time he came, he saw, and he conquered. Yet what had been a talisman might prove a peril, should these conditions happen to fail; and history was to illustrate this by most striking examples.

Napoleon was thus the first of strategists; he stands supreme, like a Himalayan peak; there is nothing equal to him in this sphere of the art. He has been surpassed in the lesser tactics; he never was a regimental leader; he commanded in chief at too early an age to have had practical experience of the three arms; he perhaps underrated the strength of infantry, and rather exaggerated the force of cavalry, and the only arm he thoroughly understood was artillery. But in the province of the higher tactics, where strategy and tactics blend with each other, his pre-eminence nearly, if not quite, reappears. He detected the decisive point on a field of battle, and the true way to cope with an enemy, almost as surely as on a great field of manœuvre; but faults I shall notice were here sometimes seen, and I do not think he excelled Marlborough, a tactician of the very first order. As a military administrator he was, perhaps, unrivalled. His industry, his grasp of facts in the mass, and his extraordinary mastery of details were marvellous; and though the Grand Army had many defects, for it was the hasty creation of an age of war, still it was the best army that had been seen since the Legions; and, unlike the conscript armies of our age, it was subjected to trials they have never endured. Napoleon's *Correspondence* can alone give us a notion of his administrative powers; and their results are most conspicuous in his immense preparations for the campaign of 1807, for the passage of the Danube in 1809, for the invasion of Russia in 1812; and for the restoration of the military strength of France in 1813 and 1815.

No wonder, then, that this prodigious genius, backed by favour-

ing circumstances, and the French Revolution, should have transformed the art, to a great extent, and have given it an aspect of new
grandeur. Turenne did great things between the Scheldt and the
Inn; Marlborough did great things between the Meuse and the
Danube; Frederick did great things on the Elbe and the Oder;
but what were these achievements, splendid as they are, compared
to Napoleon's march of conquest? He moves from the Var to the
Po and the Adige, strikes down the power of the House of Hapsburg, and dictates peace within sight of Vienna. He issues from
Switzerland across the Alps, envelops his enemy and gains Italy;
and had he had a lieutenant equal to himself, he would have
destroyed the Austrian armies in Swabia in 1800. He imprisons
Mack in 1805, enters Vienna with an army encamped, a few weeks
before, within sight of our coasts, and annihilates for a time the
military power of Austria and Russia on the great day of Austerlitz, the most perfect battle of the nineteenth century. The tale
is the same the following year; the operations are less striking,
but Jena overwhelms the army of Frederick, and a few days of
well-planned manœuvres makes Napoleon master of the Prussian
monarchy.

His unbroken success comes here to an end; but even in his
campaigns of chequered fortunes, nay of disasters, we see the same
grandeur, marred as it often is, of conception and action. He
defies Nature, and receives her warnings in Poland; he narrowly
escapes defeat at Eylau, but his genius and will re-establish his
power, and he strikes the Czar down on the verge of old Europe.
He defies national right and feeling in Spain and Portugal, and
meets reverses justly deserved; but he hastens across the Somo
Sierra to Madrid, and for the time he subdues the Peninsula.
When called back to France by the sound of war on the Danube,
he rectifies errors made in his absence by operations of consummate skill; he once more reaches and conquers Vienna, and
having challenged Fortune at Aspern and Essling, he answers her
rebuff by a prodigious effort of energy and perseverance at Lobau,
and he ultimately triumphs on the field of Wagram.

The Nemesis of power attains him at last; his army is engulfed in the snows of Russia, beyond the confines of the Western World, and yet his movements are admirably designed, and his capacity was, perhaps, never more conspicuous than at the Beresina. He reorganizes his forces in 1813, with a rapidity and completeness that confound the Allies ; and though he loses at last his hold on Germany, he wins four great battles, is able to make the issue of the contest doubtful for months, and succumbs at Leipsic perhaps through defection only.

In the campaign of 1814 he aims at too much, yet his genius shines out with such malignant splendour that his enemies shrink in terror from it ; he is victorious over and over again, and he is only overwhelmed because France and Paris will not support his Empire. In 1815 he sinks at last, through the effects of a crushing military reverse ; yet even in this campaign, spite of the faults of lieutenants and the determination and energy of foes, the presence of the great master is seen everywhere ; and he only just misses splendid success.

Humanity, however, is never perfect, and there were many flaws in this marvellous nature. The intensity of his imagination occasionally mastered the prudence and calculating powers of Napoleon ; we see this even in his early years, in his project to march from the Nile to the Indus, in his scheme of a descent on our coasts in the face of immensely superior fleets ; and we see it more clearly in his later campaigns, in the advance from Smolensk into the depths of Muscovy, in the attempt to reconquer the continent in 1813, in the resolution to strike for the whole Empire, and not to recall all his forces to the decisive point on the theatre in 1814. This dangerous quality sometimes marred the strategy of Napoleon, and marked it with extravagance. He was not so safe a strategist as Turenne, and his strategic reverses were as great as his triumphs. Over confidence, too, and extreme arrogance, combined with this excess of imaginative force, form distinctive faults of Napoleon in war. We see them, even from the first, in the campaigns of Italy ; they appear plainly in his march on Marengo, and nearly caused him to lose the battle ; they are visible in his advance on Austerlitz ; they are conspicuous in his campaigns in Poland; they largely contributed to the ruin of 1812; they prevented him from saving his army at Leipsic; they lured him on to his fall in 1814; they are exhibited in 1815, in the false conviction that Blücher, after Ligny, was utterly routed, and could not rally his shattered army.

To this fault must be added another, a kind of passionate desire to crush an enemy, whatever the risk, on the field of battle. Napoleon showed this at Caldiero in 1796; perhaps at Eylau in 1807, distinctly in 1809 at Aspern and Essling; and most remarkably, and with the worst results, at La Rothière, Craonne, Laon, and Arcis in 1814. This even lessens his excellence as a tactician. With his marvellous insight, in comprehending the ground and the weak points of a foe, he sometimes attacked imprudently, and deserved defeat. He had not the calm intelligence of Marlborough on the field, and here he is certainly less great than Marlborough. Napoleon, too, had another defect, of a moral kind, not to be overlooked; no one could hold a prouder or a more daring attitude, no one knew better the power of the renown of arms, but he did not confront misfortune, when hope seemed lost, with the indomitable constancy of some warriors. He was unequal to himself during the retreat from Russia—he ought not, I think, to have quitted his army; he tried to kill himself in 1814; and in this respect he falls below Frederick, who, in all others, is not to be compared to him.

Yet the most marked of his failures and shortcomings as a leader in war have yet to be noticed. He thoroughly understood the material conditions which made his grand offensive strategy possible. Yet he disregarded the fact when these largely failed; he endeavoured to make the same daring movements in barren Poland as in fertile Italy, in the swamps and forests of Russia as in the plains of Germany; and though he laboured to avert the resulting dangers, he could do so only in a slight degree, and he failed when nature began to fail him.

Napoleon, too, had this special fault; he had many of the instincts of the old *régime*; he simply abhorred Jacobinism, and all its doings; he believed in force only as the means of ruling; and throughout his career he had a rooted dislike and contempt of all popular movements and feelings. This tendency led him into capital errors, even from a purely military point of view; he believed that he could conquer England by a descent; he scorned the national rising in Spain, though it destroyed the flower of his best armies; he would not lift a hand to liberate Poland, though this must have disabled the Czar; he would not even at Moscow set the serfs free; he laughed at German and Russian patriotism, and found the results of his scoffs at Leipsic; he called the liberal movement of France at the close of his reign, "metaphysical nonsense and visionary stuff," and this contributed to his fall in 1814.

In politics in the highest sense, and even in the larger affairs of State, Napoleon did not attain supreme greatness. In this noble province of wisdom and conduct, his genius was not in its true sphere, the force of his intellect was out of its place; he followed false lights, and fell into the gravest errors. His ideas of politics were derived from the ambitious traditions of the old Monarchy, and from the frightful scenes of the French Revolution, and his conception of ruling was to extend the domination of France over a subject Continent, and to keep down anarchy at home by despotic power, magnificent, even national, but sternly repressive. His capacity, his craft, his untiring energy were tasked to the utmost to compass these ends. The Empire bestrode three-fourths of Europe; it extinguished Jacobinism for some years in France, it nursed her in dreams of warlike glory, it established order, prosperity, and material grandeur. Yet this vast fabric of conquest and force, which, like the Satanic temple of the poet's vision, "rose like an exhalation," as quickly vanished. The Empire, founded on international wrong, and depending for its existence on the enforced submission of great races conquered, but spurning the yoke, was a defiance to Law divine and human; it was a contradiction to the nature of things; and the methods by which its author upheld it, harsh tyranny, statecraft, and the Continental system, were assurances of his speedy overthrow.

As for Napoleon's system of domestic government, splendid as it seemed, and as it was for a time, it had no stability and could not endure; it rested on the mere rule of the sword; it had no solid support in old institutions, in settled traditions, in powerful orders of men; it was a despotism controlling a demoralised people, in which revolution had destroyed faith and loyalty. The character, too, of this rule was bad; the execution of the Duc D'Enghien, and many similar deeds of blood, were crimes that shocked the conscience of mankind. Napoleon's Bodies of State, his spy system, his organized informers, his repression of thought, remind us of the Rome of the later Cæsars; and, curiously enough, he hated Tacitus, the immortal censor of Imperial tyranny. Yet the Empire was not a mere scheme of oppression. It had a grand and beneficent side; it bears the marks of the administrative gifts and capacity of its great creator; it largely civilized while it subdued; it saved France from the vile rule of demagogues; it gave her all that is solid in her social fabric, and the Codes will outlive Marengo and Jena.

A word on Napoleon in his tent and his camp, the natural home of this mighty spirit. The great captain was, in the main, a kind master to submissive lieutenants; he lavished wealth and honours on his generals and marshals; he was usually good-natured to these docile servitors. But his personality was so overpowering that he made his subordinates mere pawns on the board; he deprived them of self-reliance and freedom, and as his nature was not magnanimous, he repeatedly blamed them for his own errors. The results were injurious to him as a chief. Few of his marshals were fit for independent command; they had little power of initiative or true capacity, and they indemnified themselves for his rebukes and gibes by squabbling, and often thwarting each other, as was notably seen in Spain and Portugal. It was otherwise with the mass of the army; here Napoleon's influence was immense for good. He obtained efforts from French soldiers, which no other chief has ever obtained; his presence among them it has been said, was equal to 40,000 men; he was prodigal of their blood, and set at nought their sufferings, if any object was to be attained ; but he was careful of their wants, knew how to win their hearts, and was adored with a truly idolatrous passion.

As has been seen in the case of other great men, the inner life of Napoleon had repulsive features ; the figure loses majesty, when undraped of its trappings. He had been brought up in an age of wickedness, and Napoleon could lie, cheat, and forge with complete indifference, if anything was to be gained by it. His manner and voice could charm and fascinate, but his imperious nature made him rude and brusque ; he could scold and fly into fits of temper ; " his very caresses," it has been said, " were feline " ; he could be coarsely familiar and suddenly savage. In his general bearing there was a want of repose, of true self-respect, of natural dignity. In all these respects, as in the weightier matters which pertain to the master art of Empire, Napoleon falls far behind Cæsar through unquestionably the superior of Cæsar in war.

CHAPTER IX.

WELLINGTON.

ARTHUR WELLESLEY was born in 1769, a few weeks before the birth of Napoleon. His family belonged to "the English in Ireland"—a happy expression of Mr. Froude; and the future soldier and statesman in his great career displayed many of the distinctive qualities of a ruling caste which, though of late decried by traders in faction for selfish purposes, has nevertheless given more than a due proportion of eminent men to the service of England. The ancient seat of the Wellesleys has been long a ruin; the traditions of Meath yield few records concerning a House which produced two of the most illustrious names in our eventful history, and all that is really known about the first years of Arthur is that he was a sickly child, overlooked by his parents. At Eton the boy showed none of the brilliancy of his elder brother Richard, a precocious genius; he was unnoticed at the military school of Angers, and no one who saw the two youths in these years would have thought that the fame of "the Wellesley of Assaye" would eclipse that of "the Wellesley of Mysore."

Arthur obtained his first commission in 1787; passed rapidly through the intermediate grades, after the bad fashion of that age of privilege, and was placed, through interest, at the head of the Thirty-third, just as the Great War with France had begun. During the intervening period he had held a seat for the borough of Trim in the Irish Parliament, and had been on the staff of the

WELLINGTON.

Lord Lieutenant Camden ; and some faint memories of his life in those days have survived down to the present time. Passing by idle gossip, the young member spoke on the Catholic Relief Bill of 1793 ; the speech, though dry and blunt, goes straight to the point, and is characteristic in many ways ; and an old house on the quays of Dublin which commands the Liffey and the adjoining streets, and which, it is said, he urged the Government to buy, remains to this day to prove that Wellington had in early youth a true military eye. It is impossible to doubt that, even in these years, Arthur had studied and read a great deal, and was well-versed in his professional work. He had acquired a command of the English and French tongues which made him the master of a vigorous style, not brilliant or striking, but clear and solid ; his writings nearly of this date give proof of thorough information on many subjects, and of singularly ripe and disciplined thought ; and from the first moment that he obtained a regiment, he made his mark as a most promising officer. Like Turenne, Wellesley addressed himself with untiring industry to the care of his men ; he enforced discipline with a steady hand, and showed that he had the faculty of command ; and, like Turenne, he was soon able to boast that his corps was well-ordered and very efficient. The occasion quickly came when the young colonel was to show that he possessed qualities above those of the common herd of men.

In the unfortunate campaign of 1794 the Thirty-third formed part of the British army, which, under the command of the Duke of York, had been separated from the main allied force retreating on a divergent line to the Meuse, and which, hardly pressed by the Republican levies, advancing upon the flood-tide of victory, was endeavouring to make its way into Holland. Wellesley distinguished himself in several rearguard actions, displaying from the first the skill in defence, the resource in danger, and the perfect self-reliance, which were peculiar gifts of the future chief ; and it is significant that he was chosen to cover the retreat, a task he performed with marked ability. These experiences made a profound impression on a remarkably penetrating and sagacious mind ; they seem to have led him to observe carefully, and to form an admirably just estimate of what he called "the new methods" of French warfare, and of what was good and defective in them ; they enabled him to realise the immense abuses then prevalent in the Continental armies, and to a considerable extent in our own ; and, unquestionably, they were of the greatest use as a preparation for the Peninsular War. It is remarkable that, after this first essay in arms, most honourable as it had been to him, Wellesley tried to give up a military career, and actually applied for a post in the Civil Service ; the reason he assigned was that he saw little chance of advancement through merit in the British army, to the short-comings of which he had become fully alive.

Fate happily disregarded Wellesley's prayers; and having escaped exile to the West Indies, he was sent off to Calcutta in 1797. A short time afterwards, his brother Richard, the Marquis Wellesley of a later day, arrived in India as Governor-General, and the real career of Arthur may be said to have opened. Much of his correspondence of this period remains, and it bears the marks of the prudent forethought, of the clear insight into men and things, and, above all, of the moderation of view, which distinguished Wellington when at the summit of fame. He was often consulted by the Governor-General, and it is interesting to note how the ambitious statesman,* a more brilliant but a less scrupulous man, was more than once restrained by the calm-minded soldier. Arthur Wellesley's judgments on Indian affairs were such as Marcus Aurelius might have made had he been a Pro-consul in a province of Rome; he was the constant advocate of peace with honour, of keeping the strictest faith with the Princes of Hindustan, of no undue extension of our growing Empire; and yet he thoroughly understood the true nature of that wonderful domination which, in spite of itself, was winning its way to supremacy in the East, in virtue partly of its own force, and in part of the decay of all powers around it, and of the jealousies and discords of its numerous foes. Another characteristic of these papers is this: they show that the writer had admirable views on military and civil administration alike ; and the remarks

---

* Lord Wellesley's epitaph, chosen by himself, is strikingly characteristic :—" Super et Garamantas et Indos protulit imperium."

on the whole system of our Indian Government, which repeatedly occur, are profound and striking. Peace in India at this time had become impossible; the inglorious satrapy of Sir John Shore had only encouraged the hopes of our enemies; and the news of Napoleon's descent on Egypt, and of his avowed project to march to the Indus, had animated Tippoo Sahib to endeavour to break the settlement made by Cornwallis in 1793. I shall not repeat the often-told tale of the dealings of "citizen Tippoo" with the Directory of France; of the assistance he received from French soldiers of fortune; of the siege of Seringapatam, and his death; this scarcely belongs to Wellesley's career, who was a subordinate only in the attack on the fortress, and who, in these operations, happened to meet one of the few reverses he met through life. He was made Governor of Seringapatam, and afterwards of Mysore; and in this position he first gave proof not only of great administrative powers, but of that capacity for ruling alien races—for reconciling the ascendency of the English name with the obedience of people completely different—a gift partly due, perhaps,* to his Irish experience, and partly to firmness, patience, and a strict regard to justice, which stood him in good stead in Spain and Portugal. Ere long Wellesley, now raised to the rank of General, had an opportunity to show what he was in command.

He had distinguished himself, when at Mysore, in putting down a Mahratta partisan who had ravaged the country with part of Tippoo's forces; and when Scindiah and Holkar in 1803 made a determined effort to destroy our Empire, Wellesley was placed at the head of an independent army, and advanced from Madras into the Central Provinces. I pass over his forced march to Poona, considered in those days a remarkable feat, and his rapid operations in the Deccan; and I proceed at once to the really grand exploit which gave him, for the first time, a great name in India. Wellesley and Stevenson, in September 1803, were near the Kaitna,

---

* It is most remarkable how many of the Irish Protestant aristocracy have distinguished themselves in India. Besides the two Wellesleys, the names of Eyre Coote, of Gough, of the Lawrences, of Canning, of Dufferin, will at once occur to the reader This, no doubt, may in part be traced to their hereditary ascendency over the Celtic Irish.

one of the Godavery's streams, at the head of about 16,000 men; Scindiah's army, 50,000 strong, commanded and organized by French officers, was in camp at no great distance; and the two Englishmen agreed to attack it, on lines divided by a wide range of hills, strategy which, even in the case of Indian warfare, was too hazardous, and cannot be justified. Wellesley came up with the enemy at Assaye, his colleague being still far away; and, as more than once was seen in his career, his boldness on the ground and his quickness in action made more than amends for a strategic error.   Disregarding all odds, like Clive at Plassey, he instantly fell on the masses before him; and though the issue of the battle was doubtful for a time, nothing could stand against his British foot and horsemen, and in a few hours he gained a complete victory.   Stevenson arrived before long, and the campaign ended in the easy triumph of Wellesley's arms, and in a large increase of our Indian dominions.   Yet Assaye had, perhaps, other results; the strategy of Wellesley was, no doubt, faulty; and the battle probably gave Napoleon, who let nothing escape him in war, that first false impression of the "Sepoy general," which caused him greatly to undervalue Wellington, with fatal consequences to France in the Peninsular contest.

Wellington always looked back on India with pride; and nearly two generations after Assaye, when he had been for many years the first of living Englishmen, he actually proposed to set off for the East, when danger threatened our power on the Indus.   An atten-tive observer will, indeed, perceive that his career in Hindustan foreshadows, in part, his more renowned career in Portugal and Spain; we see in both the same sober wisdom, the same admini-strative gifts, the same intrepid conduct, if Wellesley had no opportunity to display his skill in defence in Asiatic warfare.   He was back in England a few weeks before the memorable events of Ulm and Trafalgar; but he was relegated at first to a civil post, and he became Chief Secretary for Ireland under the Duke of Richmond.

The state of the island was very critical; the fires of 1798 were still smouldering, and the unpopularity of the Union strengthened the hands of the remains of the rebel Irish faction, which continually looked to France for aid, though, characteristically, scorned by Napoleon. Wellesley ruled after the fashion of those days: that is, he kept Celtic discontent down and threw bribes and places to greedy seekers of both, in order to extend ministerial influence; but he was perfectly aware of the many abuses then prevalent in the social condition of Ireland, and his warnings on the subject now appear prophetic. He was at the the bombardment of Copenhagen in 1807; was chosen by Lord Cathcart to arrange the terms of the surrender of the fleet with the Danish commander; and won golden opinions in this delicate task from brave enemies, whom he seems to have pitied. At last, in the summer of 1808, fortune found for him a place on the theatre of the great events which were stirring the Continent especially adapted to his peculiar genius, and launched him on the career which has made him famous. By this time Napoleon's first invasion of Spain was ending in calamitous failure; the French armies were falling back at all points, and the British Government resolved to strike a blow at Junot and his corps, isolated in the midst of Portugal. Wellesley set off from Cork in the middle of July, at the head of about 10,000 men; and a remark he made to his friend Croker, when leaving, shows the character of the man and his strong nature. "The French armies," he said, "have beaten all the Continent. They have, it seems, adopted a new system; they have outmanœuvred every enemy they have met, but I do not think they will outmanœuvre me, though, as a matter of course, I may be outnumbered."

Wellesley had landed at Mondego Bay in the first week of August; he was soon joined by about 5,000 men under General Spencer, from the south of Spain, and he ultimately had nearly 20,000 troops, by the addition of a British division and some Portuguese auxiliaries. The effect of the descent was to throw a superior hostile force on the communications of Junot's army, and to place it in grave peril, for it was split in fractions; and Wellesley hoped to cut it off from Lisbon, and, should a detachment under Sir John Moore co-operate, even to intercept its retreat on Elvas, and so to cause its complete ruin. This able plan was frustrated by a series of accidents, though it led to a brilliant if not a decisive victory. Wellesley attacked and defeated a French division at Roliça on the 17th of August; and he was in turn assailed when on the march to Lisbon, at Vimeiro, not far from the coast, by Junot, who had assumed the offensive with from 14,000 to 16,000 men. The efforts of the French completely failed; and as their defeated columns drew off, Wellesley eagerly tried to follow up his success, and to force Junot against the Tagus, where, even without the aid of Moore, he might destroy the Marshal. This bold and brilliant stroke was, however, prevented by the interference of Sir Harry Burrard, a veteran of the old school, who had come from England, unluckily, to take the chief command, and the French army escaped unmolested. The Convention of Cintra soon followed; and though a storm of indignation arose at the time, because Junot and his troops were landed in France, it is but fair to remark that as Moore did not complete the operation laid out for him, the French would probably have made good their retreat. The one real opportunity was lost at Vimeiro, owing to a change of leaders at a critical moment.

This short campaign brought out one of the gifts of Wellesley, capacity for bold offensive movements, not on a grand scale but within limits where readiness and vigour are of special value. His ability was recognized at the inquiry held in England, after the affair of Cintra; and he returned to Portugal in the spring of 1809 in supreme command of a mixed force of British and of Portuguese troops, perhaps altogether 40,000 strong, which had been assembled for the defence of Lisbon, and had been organized by Generals Cradock and Beresford. Affairs in the Peninsula had, by this time, completely changed since the year before; and it was universally believed in Europe that the whole country would in a few months become a vassal province of the French Empire. Napoleon had invaded Spain for the second time, at the head of forces that nothing could resist; he had swept aside the rude levies

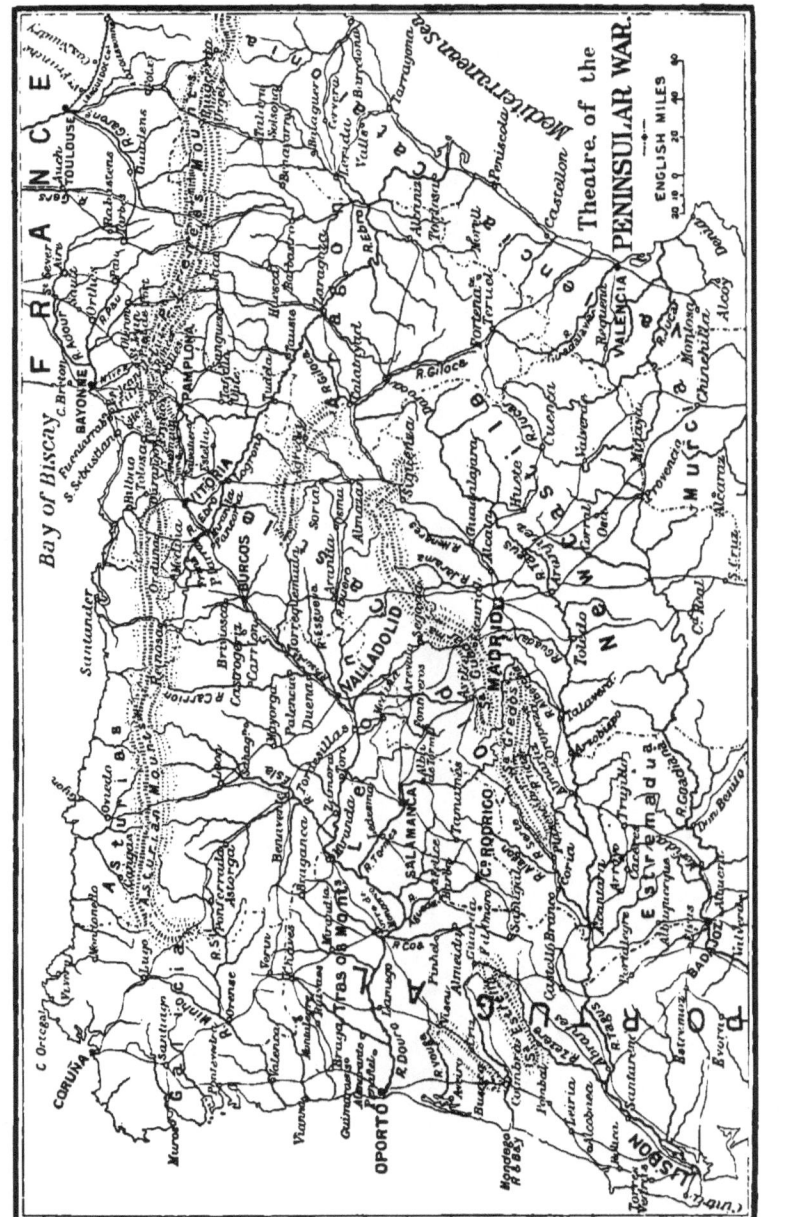

Theatre of the PENINSULAR WAR.

ENGLISH MILES

that crossed his path. Saragossa had fallen ; a British army, led by Moore, had narrowly escaped destruction ; the national insurrection seemed, for the moment, crushed ; and fully 300,000 veteran soldiers, commanded by skilful and successful chiefs, were gathered round the eagles for a march of conquest from the Ebro to the mouth of the Tagus. Yet Wellesley, with deep sagacity and grand strength of character, refused, in this state of things, to despair ; and he drew elements of hope from the peculiar nature of a theatre of operations he had carefully scanned, and from the conditions of French invasion in Spain and Portugal. Portugal, open to England through the command of the sea, and scarcely accessible from the Spanish frontier, the only avenue open to the French armies, could, he insisted, be defended with success, by a small British force if well supported by the national militia and the Portuguese Government ; and he relied greatly on the immense impediments which would necessarily beset the French in Spain, owing partly to the ubiquitous guerrilla risings, partly to the intricacies of a region of mountains and defiles, partly to the exposed state of the communications with France, assailable along a vast line, and partly to the extreme difficulty of concentrating and supporting large forces which, upon Napoleon's principles of war, would be compelled to subsist in a poor and barren country on resources principally drawn from the spot. These admirable views, set out in detail before Wellesley reached Portugal in 1809, anticipate the course of the Peninsular war, and in a great measure foreshadow its event ; and if they do not equal Napoleon's conceptions in splendour, science, and imaginative force, they indicate real genius for defence and military wisdom of the highest order. Wellesley's first operations were of happy augury, and realised his predictions with full completeness. Napoleon, before he set off for Wagram, had made preparations to invade Portugal on what he considered a sufficient scale, while he continued to extend his power in Spain ; and for this purpose he had directed Soult to march on Lisbon with an army supposed to be at least 40,000 strong, while Victor was to second the movement by the valley of the Tagus with about an equal force.

Soult, however, pursued by swarms of guerrillas and making his way with extreme difficulty, reached Oporto with less than 25,000 men ; though Victor routed a Spanish army, he never approached the Portuguese frontier ; and when Wellesley arrived in Lisbon the two Marshals were far from each other, unable to co-operate, nay, perhaps, unwilling, and not in sufficient force to subdue Portugal. Wellesley, rightly aiming at his nearest foe, marched against Soult with about 30,000 men ; and the operations that followed were very brilliant.

Soult, dreaming of a throne for himself in Portugal, and a somewhat indolent though a very able man, was surprised and assailed by his bold adversary ; the Douro was crossed by the British army, under the eyes of a powerful hostile force, by a movement of singular daring and skill ; and a detachment ably sent off by Wellesley all but cut off the Marshal's retreat, and nearly involved him in utter ruin. In fact, Soult only contrived to escape by abandoning his *impedimenta*, and crossing the ranges that lead into Spain with the wreck of an army, and the invasion of Portugal ignominiously failed.

The passage of the Douro in the face of Soult is another instance of the skill of Wellesley in offensive movements upon a contracted theatre. He now turned his attention towards Victor, far off, yet in the lowlands of the Tagus ; but a long pause in the operations took place, due, partly, to the maladministration of the British army, partly to disputes with the dullard Cuesta, in command of the Spanish army of the west, and partly, too, perhaps, because the English general had not the fierce energy, in a situation like this, of the warrior of the campaign of Italy. Wellesley had defeated Soult by the middle of May ; he did not even attempt to advance against Victor until the last days of June, and it was the third week of July before his army, having effected its junction with that of Cuesta, was in the valley of the Upper Tagus, marching in pursuit of the French Marshal. The allied chiefs were now at the head of about 20,000 British troops and 40,000 Spaniards, mostly new levies ; their purpose was to attack Victor, falling back leisurely towards Talavera ; and they moved up the

Tagus, not without hope that they might ultimately reach the Spanish capital, for they expected aid from a Spanish army in the south.

The long delay which had occurred, however, had enabled the French armies in the Peninsula to draw towards each other in formidable strength; the corps of Soult, re-organized and re-cruited, that of Ney, and that of Mortier were but a few marches off, behind the screen of the Avila range. King Joseph at Madrid had a considerable force, which might easily join hands with Victor; and Wellesley and Cuesta were in fact moving into the midst of immensely superior foes, strategy difficult to understand and not to be justified. In the operations that followed, the French lost one of the best opportunities they ever had to destroy our power in Portugal and Spain; and the glitter of success ought not to blind us to the perils incurred by the British commander, from which he only escaped by accident. In the last days of July Joseph had come into line with Victor, who had been well-nigh caught. Their united armies were near Talavera, at least 45,000 strong; and pressing orders had been given to Soult, to fall on the flank of the allied army, with the corps of Ney, of Mortier, and his own, 60,000 excellent troops at least; a movement not in any way difficult, for it only required a short march, and the passes from the hills were but weakly guarded. These dispositions were by no means perfect, but they promised brilliant and decisive success; and they failed only through a series of mishaps and errors. On the 27th of July Victor attacked the Allies, in position at Talavera, between the Tagus on their right and a set of knolls and low hills on the left; and his first effort altogether failed, though he concentrated his main strength against the British troops.

The attack was premature and imprudent, for obviously it was the true course of the French to wait until the advance of Soult would enable them to assail the Allies, in front and flank, in overwhelming strength; but Victor, jealous perhaps of his colleague, and eager to win on his own account, insisted on renewing the fight on the 28th. The battle raged furiously for several hours; all the attacks on the British left were baffled; but the intrepidity and skill of Wellesley were taxed to the utmost to save the centre, and though he undoubtedly gained the day, the French army drew off unbroken.   Ere long, however, the advanced guard of Soult made its appearance in the plains of the Tagus; the defeated army resumed the offensive, and in the first days of August a great French host, from 85,000 to 100,000 strong, was menacing the Allies in front and rear, and seemed as if on the verge of a splendid triumph.   Had the counsels of Soult, to press on and attack, prevailed at this juncture, it is difficult to see how Wellesley and Cuesta could have escaped; and in that event the combined French armies would not improbably have over-run Portugal, and, perhaps, have even attained Lisbon.   The danger, however, passed away; the French chiefs separated, and did nothing; and Wellesley, placing the Tagus between himself and his foes, made good his retreat across the frontier, though unsupported by his worthless ally, whose conduct, it has been thought, was not free from treachery.

Wellesley received a peerage for Talavera, and the battle is honourable to the British army and its chief.   The attacks of Victor were ill conducted, but fully 35,000 French soldiers were opposed to less than 20,000 Englishmen; and yet they retired from the field, defeated.   Talavera, indeed, like Vimeiro before, had proved that the modern French tactics were not calculated to achieve success against those long in use in the British service, as regards defensive battles at least; columns and skirmishers failed to make an impression on the formidable line of the British infantry, a result which was seen two thousand years ago in the inferiority of the Greek phalanx to the Roman legion.   Wellesley's first dispositions were not very good; he did not occupy the ground in force on his left; but he displayed great resource and skill on the 28th, and he deserved the victory he fairly won. His strategy, however, in this campaign was ill conceived, and, indeed, bad; and it can be explained, perhaps, on the supposition only that he had no idea what a great hostile force was ready to descend through the hills on his flank, as he marched in fancied

WELLINGTON AT TALAVERA.

security up the Tagus. As for the French operations, the plan of the double movement of Victor and Soult was not ill designed; but it was frustrated by the inconsiderate haste of Victor, who attacked before the approach of his colleague; and Napoleon truly observed that combinations like these are ever liable to mischance and failure, and that Wellesley ought to have been allowed to advance until the net was made certain to close around him. Wellesley, however, as it was, only just escaped. The wrath of Napoleon* knew no bounds, for a great opportunity had no doubt been lost; and the mistake of the English commander confirmed the Emperor in the low estimate he had formed of an enemy, who was anything but " the presumptuous, rash sciolist " he held up to ridicule after this campaign.

By this time Wagram had been fought. After the defeat of Austria, the whole Continent was more than ever under the yoke of Napoleon; Spain and Portugal were the only points where there was even a show of resistance to that colossal force; and as the Emperor poured fresh masses of troops into Spain, and announced that he would march on Lisbon in person, even the British Government, injured at home by the calamitous issue of the descent on Walcheren, began to quail and to wish to give up the contest. Yet Wellington—we now use the revered name—retained his calm and unbroken confidence; and though the subjugation of Spain seemed imminent—for three Spanish armies had been completely routed, and Andalusia was being over-run—he still contended that the defence of Portugal could be successfully maintained even in existing circumstances. After his retreat from the Tagus, he had returned to Lisbon; and, in the autumn of 1809, despite of the fears of ministers at home, and of the reluctant aid afforded by the Portuguese Regency—a corrupt and incapable body of men—he made preparations for the memorable stand in Portugal which has gained him enduring

---

* Napoleon wrote thus to Clarke 18th August 1809: " Quelle belle occasion on a manquée! 30,000 Anglais et 150 lieues des côtes devant 100,000 hommes des meilleures troupes du monde! Mon Dieu! qu'est ce qu'une armée sans chef! "— *Correspondence*, vol. xix., p. 362.

renown. His own army was now about 80,000 strong; the Portuguese army, drilled and led by Englishmen, had become a trustworthy force of about equal strength; and the addition of other Peninsular levies had placed him in command of more than 100,000 men. Such arrays, however, Wellington clearly saw could not hope to contend, even in Portugal, against the masses of which Napoleon disposed, unless means were taken to place a barrier in the way of the invaders, behind which the forces of the defence could be securely rallied. For this purpose he chose a position between the Atlantic and the mouths of the Tagus, covered in front by a succession of heights, and most difficult to turn on either flank; and thousands of labourers were quietly employed, with a secrecy which appears surprising, in constructing the famous Lines which will make the name of Torres Vedras long live in history. These great works formed a triple range of entrenchments, thirty miles in length on their exterior face and about eight in their second extension; the third was a vast fortified camp, from which the army, if forced, could embark; and the whole were protected by all the means available to the art of the engineer, redoubts, inundations, stockades, escarpments, and formidable batteries commanding vulnerable points. In this "impregnable citadel," as has well been said, Wellington "deposited the independence " of Portugal at first, and ultimately, as it turned out, of Spain; and clinging to a rock on the verge of the ocean, while all was fear and mistrust around, he steadily confronted the might of Napoleon, the undisputed lord of a vanquished Continent. History has no grander instance of heroic constancy, and of self-reliance justified by the event.

By the early summer of 1810, the French armies in Spain had reached the enormous number of 850,000 fighting men, and Napoleon believed the whole Peninsula to be within his grasp. Engrossed, however, with his over-grown Empire, and meditating already the invasion of Russia, he had renounced the idea of crossing the Pyrenees, and conducting the approaching campaign himself; and this was one of the greatest mistakes of his life. The Emperor, shut out from the sea by England, and unable to procure intelligence in Spain, had not the least notion, strange as it may appear, of the real force in the hands of Wellington, still less of the Lines of Torres Vedras, and his plan for the contest, formed without knowledge, was misconceived and false to his own strategy. He believed that the British army was not 25,000 strong; he took no account of the Portuguese forces; he thought that the way to Lisbon was open, or barred only by natural obstacles; and instead of concentrating 200,000 men, in order to overpower Wellington and to turn the Lines on the landward side, at the verge of the mouth of the Tagus—a difficult but a possible enterprise—he disposed his armies in such a fashion that, as the event proved, they were largely wasted and were not strong enough on the decisive point on the theatre. Reasoning on his false data, he left Macdonald and Suchet to reduce the east of Spain; he allowed Soult to remain in the south with a great army, to no useful purpose, and calculating that this force would be more than sufficient, he placed 70,000 men in the hands of Masséna, by far the first of the imperial marshals, with orders to besiege the north-eastern frontier fortresses, and to "drive the English into their ships from Lisbon." This dissemination of his military strength, so contrary to the principles of war, was due not to wilfulness or over-confidence, but simply to ignorance of the real facts; the Emperor knew that the British army was the one enemy he should first dispose of, and he conceived that he had made this result certain; but his reckonings and previsions were wholly wrong, and his projects were based on disastrous errors. The remarkable campaign of 1810 was to illustrate this in a most striking way, and forms Wellington's true title to glory in war. Masséna began operations in the first days of June by investing Ciudad Rodrigo, a famous stronghold and the key of Portugal from the west of Spain, and as he was not to advance until after the summer heats, he conducted the siege in a leisurely manner, though disease and want had begun to prey on his army. Wellington, who had approached the beleaguered fortress at the head of about 30,000 men, when made aware of the strength of the French merely observed the enemy from secure positions; and all the devices of Masséna to tempt him to fight were fruitless against his steadfast prudence. Ciudad had fallen by the middle of July; Almeida, a neighbouring stronghold, met the same fate, and Masséna had set his army in motion—it numbered about 60,000 men—to invade Portugal in the third week of September, the Marshal advancing along the Mondego, and the British commander falling back before him. By the 27th the French had entered a region of mountains and defiles between the great ranges of the Sierra Alcoba and the Sierra Estrella, and they found Wellington and his troops in position on the ridge of Busaco, awaiting their enemy. Masséna did not hesitate to attack, for he had a great superiority of force; but once more the column was repulsed by the line, and the assailants only reached the well-defended heights to be smitten down by the steady British footmen. The Marshal, bold and persevering, now discovered a track which enabled him to move his army and turn Wellington's left. This was not the fault of the English chief, for he had given directions to secure the pass; but his position had become no longer tenable, and the French entered Coimbra in high heart, and confident that they would soon attain Lisbon.

Masséna, utterly ignorant of what was before him, shared this hope with Ney and Junot, his chief lieutenants; and leaving his wounded and sick men at Coimbra, spite of a guerrilla warfare gathering on his path, "the spoiled child of victory" pressed boldly forward, making for the Lower Tagus and the Portuguese capital. To his great astonishment, the hostile army, which had retreated slowly and made scarcely a sign, seemed suddenly to disappear from his view; and Masséna only discovered the cause when, in the middle of October, he saw the Lines of Torres Vedras rising in formidable strength, and his enemy, he knew, was entrenched behind them.

Masséna's army had, by this time, been reduced to about 50,000 men, and his adversary had fully 100,000, within lines not to be attacked in front. Ney and Junot were for an immediate retreat, but the warrior of Zürich, of Genoa, of Essling, whose great merit was tenacious boldness, refused to listen to these desponding counsels. He searched the barrier before him at every point, and only fell back when the state of his troops had warned him that a further stay was impossible. In his march from Busaco, Wellington had given orders to ravage the country, and to destroy its harvests; and though we may, perhaps, regret that he had recourse to a barbarous and obsolete mode of warfare, it was very efficacious against invaders who had no magazines when they left the frontier, and relied for supplies on organized plunder. Within a few weeks after it had reached the Lines, Masséna's army, practised as it was in extortion and rapine, was half-famished; and the Marshal recoiled from Torres Vedras baffled and indignant, but not disheartened. Concealing the movement with great skill, he established his troops in strong positions round Santarem, on the Lower Tagus, where he was almost inaccessible to attack, and where, at the same time, he had several lines of retreat, and he might receive aid from the French army in the South should it advance to the opposite bank of the river. Here the Marshal made a determined stand, disregarding the murmurs of inferior men; he sent flying columns through the surrounding region to obtain means of subsistence by force or terror; he constructed bridges to cross the Tagus, and he despatched Foy, a very able man, to Paris, to ask for reinforcements and to inform the Emperor of the critical state of affairs in Portugal.

Napoleon saw his messenger before the end of November, and it might have been supposed that the first of strategists would have sent every available man, as quickly as possible, to Masséna's aid, for everything, it had become manifest, depended on the course of events on the Tagus. But the Emperor was not pleased with the Marshal, on account of Busaco and the march from Coimbra. He persisted in holding Wellington cheap; he refused to believe in the strength of the Lines; he would see no foes but the British army, and the measures he adopted were quite inadequate to meet a situation already of peril. He ordered a detachment to be sent from the North of Spain, and to join hands with Masséna's army; and he directed Soult to the Tagus from Andalusia, a distance requiring a long and arduous march, giving his lieutenant, besides, a dangerous latitude. The results, due partly to want of knowledge, but principally to obstinacy and unwise arrogance, proved most disastrous to the Imperial arms.

The detachment from the north reached Masséna's camp, but instead of being 20,000 strong, as had been promised, it was not 10,000, a reinforcement of little worth; and Soult never approached the Marshal, either because the difficulties in his way were immense or because, as has often happened with French commanders, and was conspicuously seen in the Peninsular War, he was selfishly jealous of a superior colleague. Yet Masséna clung to his positions to the last. In this unfortunate campaign he showed the great qualities which have deservedly given him renown in history; and it was not until the whole adjoining country had been turned into a desolate waste that he reluctantly yielded to dire necessity He broke up from Santarem in March 1811, having, to Wellington's amazement, contrived to live for nearly four months on the tracts around him; and his retreat was one of extreme difficulty, for the British army was soon pressing on his rear; Coimbra had been taken, and swarms of partisans were gathering around on every side. The Marshal, however, proved equal to himself; he conducted the movement with the greatest skill; Ney distinguished himself in more than one action; and the French army ultimately recrossed the frontier, having saved its honour, it may be truly said, but having injured its fair fame by atrocious excesses. It had been reduced to 40,000 men, in miserable plight and greatly demoralized; a quarrel between Masséna and Ney increased disorder and destroyed discipline; and Portugal had been set free, and, as time was to show, was not to be invaded by Frenchmen again.

Torres Vedras is Wellington's crown of fame, and gives him his true place among great commanders. The Lines might have, perhaps, been turned, had Napoleon put forth his whole strength; but they baffled the force believed by the Emperor to be sufficient to conquer Portugal and to drive Wellington out of the entire Peninsula. The conception of the defence was very fine, for Torres Vedras was all but impregnable; but the conception was nothing to the moral grandeur of the attitude of the heroic soldier, who

from this rocky nook defied the mighty hosts which certainly
might have been arrayed against him. It adds, too, to the just
renown of Wellington that he met a foeman worthy of his steel.
Masséna possibly made mistakes; he ought not to have fought at
Busaco; it is astonishing that he was not informed of the Lines
when he reached Coimbra, a few marches distant; and he ought
not, perhaps, to have quitted that place, leaving thousands of
enemies gathering on his rear. But the Marshal gave proof of
powers of a very high order; he stood before Torres Vedras to the
last moment, surrounded by, but overcoming danger; his choice of
his positions at Santarem may almost be called a stroke of genius;
and he conducted the retreat with consummate judgment. Apart,
indeed, from the decisive effects caused by Wellington's masterly
defence, the failure of the campaign should be ascribed, not to
Masséna, but to the French Emperor. Napoleon, ignorant of the
real state of affairs, did not give his lieutenant a sufficient army;
when made aware of the existence of the Lines, and of the strength
of his enemy's forces, he took half measures, which proved abortive; and the condemnation he passed on his greatest Marshal
was simply a device to screen his own errors, want of real knowledge, contempt of his foes, and directing war at a distance from
the scene. The results of Torres Vedras were immense; the glory
of the French arms was deeply tarnished; a great general had
suddenly appeared, who had baffled completely the Imperial legions.
Continental soldiers began to study the methods of Wellington
with eager hope; the fears of the Government at home vanished,
and it resolved to prosecute the war with vigour; the complaints
of the Junta at Lisbon were silenced; and, above all, Wellington
had been confirmed in the accuracy of his views respecting the contest, and became the master of largely increased resources. Secure
for the present from attack in Portugal, he began to make preparations to resist the French along the western frontier of Spain;
and he already hoped that the day was at hand when he might
carry the war into Castile and Leon.

The campaign of 1811 was a prelude to operations he had
already planned; but it was one of many vicissitudes, and

of doubtful fortune. Wellington commanding the resources of England from the sea, really wielding the power of the Portuguese Government, and turning to account the great advantage afforded him by a central position between enemies divided and scattered, besieged Almeida, Ciudad Rodrigo, and Badajoz, which, with Napoleon, he correctly judged should be mastered to make Portugal secure, and to open an avenue to enter Spain. He failed, however, against the two last strongholds; and though Barrosa and Albuera shed splendid lustre on the British arms, the campaign had no marked results, and Wellington was, more than once, in the gravest peril. The power of Napoleon, though diminished by drafts from Spain for the invasion of Russia, was, in fact, still prodigiously strong; and had the Emperor directed it, he would, humanly speaking, have even now subjugated Spain and Portugal. Masséna, having reinforced his army, attacked Wellington at Fuentes de Onoro; the English only just escaped defeat, owing to a dispute between two French chiefs; and Wellington, indeed, has fairly acknowledged that " had Boney been in command " he would have lost the battle. On two occasions, moreover, the British commander might have been overwhelmed if ably assailed. Marmont—who replaced Masséna, unjustly disgraced—and Soult assembled a great army to relieve Badajoz, and ought to have won a real victory had they fallen on Wellington; and Marmont might soon afterwards have attacked his enemy at Fuentes Guinaldos with fourfold numbers. But the tide in the affairs of men was setting against Napoleon, and was leading his sagacious foe to fortune. The conditions of the war, which he had clearly foreseen, made the dangers of Wellington less than they seemed; the French Marshals, far apart from each other, and unable to feed their troops in a wasted country, could not draw together their divided forces for anything like a well-combined movement; and their increasing discords, the neglect of their master to examine thoroughly the situation in Spain, and, above all, the ascendency of success already gained by the British army and its chief, told with powerful effect on the course of events.

During the last months of 1811, the British chief made great preparations to renew his efforts against Ciudad Rodrigo and Badajoz. He had secretly brought up a powerful siege train to the frontier without the enemy's knowledge; he had made his communications with the sea easy, by opening the navigation of the Upper Douro; and the position of the French armies on the theatre of war remarkably favoured his audacious enterprize. The forces of Napoleon in Spain still numbered at least 250,000 men; but part of Marmont's army had been detached to the East; Soult was in cantonments around Seville; no other French army was near Portugal; and the fortresses had been left almost uncovered, for the Emperor had not the least idea that Wellington had the means to besiege and take them. The English commander first pounced on Ciudad, and captured it, after a furious assault, in the first days of January of 1812; and in a few weeks he had triumphed at Badajoz, the heroism of the attack and the skill of the defence forming a grand episode of the Peninsular War. His troops suffered enormous losses, and the British engineers were not, perhaps, as experienced as the French, in this part of the craft; but Wellington's only chance was to hurry on the attack; two relieving armies were not distant; and he properly made sacrifices for a great object. The fall of the two strongholds incensed Napoleon; but here again he had himself to blame; Marmont had fairly warned him of the danger at hand; and this is another striking instance of his ignorance of what was going on in Spain, and of the mischief of regulating its affairs from Paris. The success of the British chief at Ciudad and Badajoz laid open the Spanish frontier from Portugal, and he resolved to carry out his project of entering Spain; for though his army was very inferior in force to those of Marmont and Soult combined, the conditions of the war remained in his favour.

The marshals, as in 1811, were widely apart; they could hardly unite their armies in a ruined country; and their enemy held a position between them with an army whose wants were well supplied, and with little apprehension that the hostile forces in his front could be largely increased. The first care of Wellington was to seize the passages on the Tagus which enabled Soult and

Marmont to communicate with each other by a short line; and then, leaving a detachment to observe Soult, he crossed the frontier in the second week of June and marched against Marmont with about 40,000 men. The marshal fell back behind the Douro, in order to collect his scattered forces, abandoning works which he had constructed as a centre of defence, in the place of Ciudad; but he was a brilliant, if not a great chief; and he quickly showed that he had no notion of abandoning the initiative to the British general. Marmont recrossed the Douro on the 16th of July, about equal in force to Wellington, but the passage was only a feint; he crossed the river once more, and made for Tordesillas, an able movement which brought him near to reinforcements coming from Madrid, and threatened his adversary's right and communications with Portugal. A series of fine manœuvres followed, the French chief ever trying to outflank his enemy, and the English seeking to cover his line of retreat; and there can be no doubt that in this game of marches, the French army was the more agile of the two, and Marmont gained a distinct advantage. By the 22nd, the marshal had nearly reached the road from Salamanca to Ciudad Rodrigo, the main communication of his foe with the frontier; and Wellington was about to decamp as he best could, when a single false movement gave him a chance and enabled him to win a glorious victory. Marmont, eager and impetuous, and perhaps jealous that Jourdan, the leader of the succours at hand, would claim a share in the hoped-for triumph, incautiously extended his left too far, in order to cut off the retreat of his enemy. A gap was thus made in the French line; Wellington seized the occasion with his accustomed promptness, and he instantly directed a fierce attack against his antagonist's left and exposed centre. The marshal at this moment fell wounded, but his fall could not have changed the event; his able lieutenant, Clausel, made a fine effort to reform the French on a new position, and even assumed an offensive attitude, but the error had been made, and been turned to account; and though the French made a really gallant stand, their weakened line was pierced through and through, and they were forced to abandon the fatal field, where

Marmont had hoped to avenge his countrymen for a long succession of repeated defeats.

Salamanca and the operations before it are characteristic of Wellington as a chief. He was certainly out-generalled in the first movements, mainly because the French marched better than the British army; but probably he would have escaped unscathed, though Marmont had gained a position on his flank, had he been allowed to retreat unmolested. He was, however, unwisely attacked and in a reckless fashion; he instantly fell on the enemy's centre, with the quickness and daring which marked his offensive movements on the ground, and he made the French general pay dearly for venturing on a flank march within reach of his enemy. Salamanca, in fact, has a strong resemblance to Austerlitz up to a certain point, but it wants the grandeur and effect of Austerlitz; and in this, as in all instances, Wellington showed that he could not follow up a victory with the energy and wonderful art of Napoleon.

As for Marmont, he was at first dexterous, but he made an immense mistake in extending his left. Like Victor at Talavera, he should have waited until his reinforcements had come into line; and this, no doubt, is another example how* the characteristic envy of French commanders had the worst effects in the Peninsular War. The results of Salamanca were very great, though Clausel rallied the beaten army with an ability deserving of high praise, and was soon out of the reach of pursuit; the battle exposed the long line of the communications of the French with Madrid, and the prospect of a formidable attack on this vital point, as Wellington had foreseen from the first—and this, too, was Napoleon's judgment—placed the entire fabric of the Emperor's power in the Peninsula in no small danger.

Napoleon was now far away in the wilds of Russia; and in his absence the conduct of the French chiefs was marked by precipitate fear and haste, which, critical as the situation was, was unwarranted, and does them no small discredit. Joseph fled in

---

* Napoleon received the news of Salamanca on the eve of Borodino. His criticism of Marmont is striking and just.

17 *

inglorious haste from Madrid; the forces of Clausel and those in the north were drawn together to hold and guard the communications between Bayonne and Castile; Suchet in the far east was directed to move; and Soult, in the south, received positive orders to evacuate Andalusia and to join the King, though the Marshal was pressing the siege of Cadiz and had matured projects, not ill-designed, for invading Portugal while Wellington was away. A single well-aimed stroke had, in short, imperilled the whole position of the French in Spain, and their operations were so faulty that their domination seemed about to collapse.

In this state of affairs a single incident caused, for a time, a turn in the tide of fortune, and even placed Wellington in such straits that he would have been, not improbably, crushed had Napoleon commanded the French armies. He had entered Madrid in triumph in the middle of August, but he was soon on the track of the retreating enemy; and having driven Clausel's army before him, he sate down before Burgos towards the close of September, hoping to master the great avenue from France into Spain. The fortress was small, but had an able commandant; the British chief had scarcely a heavy gun; the garrison made a stern resistance, and after fierce efforts and very great losses, the assailants were compelled to raise the siege and to fall back before a host of enemies.

The annals of war present few such examples of the value of a well-defended stronghold at a critical juncture. Burgos had held out for a whole month. The time thus gained enabled Soult to come into line with the other French armies being collected in Castile and the north, and Wellington had no choice but to retreat at once before the huge masses directed against him. He conducted the movement with real ability, but his troops were to a great extent demoralized, and on one occasion the English commander was saved by a mere chance from the gravest danger. His army had reached Salamanca by the middle of November; it was within easy reach of the united French armies, twofold probably, at least, in strength, and had the French generals fallen boldly on they ought to have gained a decisive victory. Jourdan eagerly counselled the true course, but Soult, by nature rather a thoughtful strategist than an energetic and determined soldier, and borne down by the ascendency of the British arms, insisted on merely pressing the retreat, and Wellington was soon across the Spanish frontier. The Marshals had lost another of the great occasions afforded them in the Peninsular War.

The campaign of 1812, notwithstanding the disastrous retreat from Burgos, was nevertheless ruinous in its effects to the French. Salamanca had been a decisive defeat; the Imperial commanders had not attacked Wellington, falling back with a much weaker force; the invaders had permanently quitted the south; above all, the precarious nature of Napoleon's power in the Peninsula had been clearly established. In this position of affairs, the tremendous tale of the destruction of the Grand Army in Russia fell with immense effect on the minds of men; it raised the hopes of Wellington to the highest pitch—he had always foretold that some catastrophe would befall Napoleon in his career of conquest—it animated his troops with fresh confidence; it sent a thrill of exultation through Spain and Portugal; it awed and paralyzed the leaders of the French armies. By this time Wellington had all England at his back; he was supreme in Portugal, and swayed the Regency by the glory of success, by his administrative power, by his impartial justice to the Portuguese race; and he was made Commander-in-Chief of the Spanish armies, and disposed for the first time of the military strength of Spain, in spite of the clamour of factions in the distracted Cortes against a "heretic and domineering foreigner." He was now able to place in the field forces nearly equal in numbers to his foes, and in the spring of 1813 he had his preparations made for a great effort to set the Peninsula free. The Imperial armies, however, were still formidably strong, from 190,000 to 200,000 men; they were superior to the Spanish and Portuguese levies, and as we look back at the course of events, we see that even now, had they been ably led, they possibly might have achieved success, and certainly might have avoided disaster. But they were ill-distributed on the theatre of war; Suchet, in the east, had by far too large a force; Soult had left Spain, deprived of his command; Jourdan and Joseph were very inferior men;

the strength of the army confronting Wellington on the frontier was by no means sufficient ; the guerrilla rising was more fierce than ever ; and the French commanders had lost hope and confidence. The general plan of Wellington was to assail the enemy from many points, in order to distract and detain his forces, and at the same time to fall in great strength on the exposed line of the communications of the French ; and though faults may, perhaps, be found in his strategy, the conception was fine, and was admirably carried out. Suchet was held in check by Murray with a small body of men ; Joseph, who had returned to Madrid, was menaced from the south ; a large Spanish army was assembled in the north ; and, meanwhile, Wellington prepared the master stroke on which he relied for final success. His army, now about 90,000 strong, advanced from the frontier in the last days of May, divided into three great masses on a wide front, with hill ranges between ; its chief gave an opportunity, perhaps, but there was no great warrior to cross his path. It had soon mastered the line of the Douro, driving before it foes much weaker in numbers ; it gradually united, joined hands with the levies of the north, and found a new base on the Biscayan seaboard in the English fleet ; and then it seized the main avenues between France and Spain, and sped in full force to the Upper Ebro. This formidable movement compelled Joseph to evacuate Madrid, and to draw together all available troops to attempt a defence ; and the French armies in Castile were ere long concentrated around Vitoria upon the Zadorra—confused masses, already disheartened, and burdened by *impedimenta* such as never before weighed down unlucky troops in retreat. The battle that followed, fought on the 21st of June, was of enormous importance in its results, but has little interest for the student of war. The French were, perhaps, 70,000 strong ; but 15,000 men had been detached to guard convoys, and to secure a retreat ; the English commander had about 80,000, and the event was never for a moment doubtful. Nothing could stand against the onset of the British troops, superior in numbers, and flushed with success ; their foes fought well, as they always did, and Reille, the descendant of an Irish exile, distinguished himself by skill and valour ; but the main road to

Bayonne was lost, and the French were gradually thrown back on the mountain roads that extend to the frontier. The beaten army, however, was not hardly pressed; it effected its retreat in fair order, but it lost nearly all its guns and *matériel*, and it left behind the spoils of a ravaged country, accumulated through years of unscrupulous plunder, and strewn over the field in immense profusion.

Vitoria, fitly called the Leipsic of the south, drove all the French armies out of Spain, with the exception of Suchet's force in the east, and the garrisons of Pampeluna and San Sebastian, reinforced by Joseph before he crossed the Pyrenees. Napoleon, by this time, had made a prodigious effort to retrieve the disasters of the campaign in Russia; France had answered his summons to the field with energy; and he had won great victories at Lützen and Bautzen, followed by the suspension of arms at Pleistwitz. Austria now held the balance between the belligerent Powers; she had long inclined to the allied cause, but she dreaded Napoleon, and held aloof until Vitoria determined her purpose and she threw in her lot with the Coalition which, in a few months, overthrew the Emperor. The campaign of 1813 in Spain, therefore, was really of supreme importance, and a word of comment should be pronounced upon it. The general plan of Wellington was, perhaps, to be justified, as affairs stood; it was his only offensive combination on a grand scale; it was perfectly executed, and it was completely successful. Yet it was no masterpiece of science or genius. The movements by which the old base of Portugal was thrown off, and a new base acquired, and by which the French armies were ever outflanked and their communications threatened and seized, and the march on Vitoria, have been justly admired; but the wide dislocation of Wellington's forces as they left the frontier was, in theory, a fault, and it would have given Turenne or Napoleon an immense chance, which they would have turned to such advantage that the course of events might have been changed at the outset. The splendour of the result cannot conceal the fact that the issue of the campaign was rather due to the incapacity and the demoralization of the French commanders than to conspicuous excellence in the strategy of their foe. Could they have defended the line of the Douro, as Bonaparte had defended the line of the Adige, nay, had they fallen back on the Ebro in time, and concentrated their still fine armies for a decisive battle on equal terms, they might even yet have repulsed Wellington, and assuredly they would not have lost Spain. This was Napoleon's judgment, and, in this instance, I think it certainly was correct ; his views on the military situation in Spain in 1813 are worthy of him ; and here, again, had he been in command, events would probably have taken a different turn. He was naturally indignant at the rout of Vitoria ; and having summarily got rid of Joseph and Jourdan, he sent Soult, with extensive powers, to the Pyrenees, to take the command of his shattered forces, and to endeavour at least to defend the frontier. The next phase of the contest is of extreme interest, and deserves careful and impartial study. Soult found the French army—a confused wreck of armies—in a pitiable state of want and despondency ; and his first care was to secure a base at Bayonne, and to reorganize and restore his defeated forces. He effected a great deal in a few weeks, for he was an administrator of no ordinary powers ; and by the close of July he had his preparations made to assume the offensive with happy promise.

At this time the forces of Wellington—altogether about 70,000 strong—were before Pampeluna and San Sebastian, and along the range of the western Pyrenees ; and this gave Soult—he was about equal in force—an extremely favourable opportunity to attack, for he commanded the passes which led from the plains. He concentrated a very superior force against his adversary's right, concealing the movement with great skill ; and his first operations had real success ; he fairly bore back the weak hostile wing, and he nearly reached Pampeluna and relieved the garrison. But Wellington, always ready on the ground, was too quick for an enemy able in thought but in execution rather dull and weak ; he raised the siege of San Sebastian and reinforced his right ; Soult attacked at Sauroren, and was repulsed, one of his lieutenants, D'Erlon, being not up in time, on this as on a far greater occasion ; the ascendency of unbroken success did the rest, and in a subsequent effort the French Marshal was nearly surrounded at the head of his troops. He recrossed the frontier, a well-designed plan having ended in heavy loss and discomfiture.

The English commander, free from attack for a time, now resolved to take Pampeluna and San Sebastian before attempting to invade France. This conduct has been described as timid, and it enabled Soult to prepare large means of defence, but obviously it was judicious and right; the issue of the war in Saxony was still uncertain, and should Soult be joined by Suchet they would be in great strength. San Sebastian made a protracted resistance, but the place was stormed in the second week of September, Soult having tried in vain to relieve it, and Pampeluna fell at the close of October. Wellington had invaded France a short time previously, and it should be observed that he crossed the frontier before Leipsic, and months before the Allies were on the Rhine. The time spent in the sieges had, nevertheless, given Soult opportunities which he had made the most of; he had constructed lines on the Bidassoa and Nivelle, the last almost as strong as those of Torres Vedras, and he awaited his enemy in a situation like that of Villars in 1710-11. His army, however, had lost heart, and was crowded with rude levies and mutinous Germans; he had not the inspiration of the renowned Villars, and nothing could stand against the overpowering force of the British soldiery in the full pride of victory. Wellington carried the lines in the second week of November, displaying great skill in his dispositions for the attack, and before long he had approached Bayonne, on the confluence of the Nive and the Adour, where Soult had entrenched himself in very strong positions. The British commander, perhaps over confident, perhaps from the want of strategic genius—this undoubtedly was characteristic of him—escaped narrowly a severe reverse; he had divided his army upon the Nive, and Soult, availing himself of his command of the rivers, and of the interior line he possessed, fell on his adversary with skill in design, and tried to overwhelm his separated foes. The peril of Wellington was great for a time, but Soult had the manner of Napoleon, not his masterly power; he did not press the attack home, and his troops were beaten by the tenacity of the British footmen. A pause in the operations followed, and had the Emperor, even at this supreme crisis, ordered Suchet to come into line with Soult, abandoning Spain, now really lost, the French would have been superior in force to Wellington, and affairs might have taken a different aspect. But Napoleon would strike for his whole Empire, a false conception which mars the splendour of the memorable campaign of 1814; he left Suchet in Catalonia, holding the fortresses; the two marshals, besides, did not agree, with the usual tendencies of French commanders; the organized plunder of the French army, in marked contrast with that of the Allies, exasperated the populations of the south against it; the Royalist party began to lift its head after the first defeats of Napoleon in Champagne, and Soult was left isolated to resist Wellington amidst the ruin and crash of a perishing Empire. The British general resumed the offensive in the early spring of 1814; he had won golden opinions, even from the invaded Gascons, for the strict discipline he made his troops observe, for the exactness with which he paid for supplies, for his humane government of the country he held, and though he was not without real difficulties of his own—he was condemned in the Cortes and denounced in Portugal, and he actually sent back a large Spanish detachment because he could not control their excesses—still he was greatly superior in strength to his foe, and his arms were obviously on the verge of triumph. Nevertheless, Soult made an admirable stand; his army was being constantly weakened by drafts for the army on the Marne and Seine; it was oppressed by the prospect of coming defeat, and yet the Marshal proved that he was a real chief, and this is the best part of his chequered career. He disputed stubbornly every inch of the country between the lines of the Adour and the Garonne; he kept Wellington many weeks in check, and though ultimately repulsed with loss, he very nearly won a battle at Orthez, and at last he took a formidable position at Toulouse, still doggedly contending against adverse fortune. The battle was fought on the 10th of April, unhappily after peace had been made; superiority in numbers and the moral power of success explain, and partly justify, Wellington's tactics; but he risked a flank march of peculiar danger, under the eye of an enemy watching to strike, and had Soult struck home at the decisive moment he probably would have won a victory. The Marshal, however, as was his wont, was remiss in action; the French army was unequal to itself, and Wellington forced his adversary to leave Toulouse, though the battle was really nearly drawn. Toulouse, indeed, adds nothing to his renown as a warrior; his true titles to fame in this campaign are his administrative virtues, and the most significant fact that he detained forces in the south which might have turned the scales of fortune in the struggle in Champagne.

Wellington was back in England in 1814, justly greeted by the acclaim of the nation, raised to the highest honour the Peerage can give, and ever since known as "the Duke" to his countrymen. His exploits, indeed, had been truly great; with an army, swelled no doubt by auxiliaries, but seldom numbering more than 30,000 British troops, he had destroyed the power of Napoleon in Spain and Portugal, backed by 300,000 French veterans, had defeated the best Marshals of France one after the other, had fought his way from the Tagus to the Garonne, had thrown his sword, with effect, into the balance of events trembling in the east of France, had ruled the Peninsula with a far-sighted wisdom, spite of the passions of faction, admired everywhere. The fame of Wellington as a commander depends, beyond question, on his direction of the Peninsular war; and an impartial judgment should be pronounced upon it. We may pass by enthusiasts who ascribe his success to genius never approached in his day, and the notion current seventy years ago that an English soldier can beat three Frenchmen; and we may equally reject the French delusion that Wellington owed everything to the freaks of Fortune. It must be recognized that in the war, small as his force was compared to his foes, he had certain advantages of peculiar value; he had the command of the sea, and of the resources of England; his position in Portugal was formidably strong; he was supported by a vast national rising; he stood in the centre of divided enemies; whereas the French armies, large as they were, had most vulnerable communications to guard, were exposed to swarms of destructive guerrillas, were necessarily separated by vast hill ranges, and, owing mainly to the Napoleonic system of warfare, were unable to muster for any time in strength because they could not subsist in a barren country.   These conditions of the strife were all in favour of the British chief, and told powerfully; but this does not in the least detract from his merits; he anticipated them with prophetic insight, and they simply made his defence possible; just as Napoleon's choice of the Adige enabled him to baffle the whole power of Austria.   It should be admitted, too, that throughout the contest he was greatly seconded by the shortcomings of his foes; more than once he ought to have been overwhelmed or crushed, but for the miserable discords of the French marshals; and Napoleon himself played into his hands by his ignorance of events, by his lust of conquest, by the false system of directing war from an immense distance; above all, by his contemptuous disregard of an adversary most unwisely scorned.   Yet this, the only meaning of what has been called the "good fortune that attended Wellington," does not lessen his title to fame; I certainly think, had he had to encounter Napoleon with all the Peninsular armies he would have been forced out of Spain and Portugal, nay, he might have been beaten in 1811, 1812, and 1813; but, tried by this test, we might just as well deny Napoleon genius in war; he would not have won Rivoli, Jena, Austerlitz, had he been opposed to really great captains.   Undoubtedly, moreover, in these campaigns the generalship of Wellington was not of as high an order as some eulogists have made it out to be; he committed grave strategic mistakes; his plan for the offensive on a great scale, and at a distance, is not very striking—I refer especially to 1813; his tactics were sometimes far from perfect; he was not masterly in following up success; there is something narrow and contracted in some of his movements.   But when this has been said, he gave proof of genius in defence of the rarest kind; his campaign of Torres Vedras reaches the sublime, in conception and execution alike; he was admirable in rapid and bold attack; he was almost always great on the field; his tenacity and judgment are above praise. Add his most remarkable administrative powers, his capacity for ruling foreign races, and his moderation in the hour of success, resembling in this the great warriors of Rome, and we shall understand how he will live in history. A word, too, should be said on his British troops; that army—largely his own creation —which he said—and Wellington was no boaster—"could go anywhere and do anything." From the first moment his soldiery showed the high qualities of their race, endurance, vigour, fierceness in attack, perseverance in defence, and the skill in the use of their arms of the archers of Crecy. The army, however, was for a time ill-organized ; its movements were slow, and it was overburdened with camp-followers and *impedimenta*; its officers, heroes in the fight, were seldom skilful; in short, it was an imperfect instrument of war. It is one of Wellington's distinctive merits that he made that army, always superior to the French in discipline, fortitude, and steadiness in the field—and this, indeed, is the true reason why its line was able to defeat their columns—equal to the best of Napoleon's armies—the Emperor has made the admission himself—in readiness, in training, in skill in manœuvring ; though Salamanca tends to show that in the power of movement it was not the equal of its most agile foes.

Great as a soldier, but certainly greater as a man, it was the destiny of Wellington in 1815 to meet the most perfect master of modern war. The campaign of Waterloo belongs to the career of Napoleon, and in a sketch of his extraordinary deeds I have endeavoured to retrace its main features. Idle flatterers and the idolaters of success have given Wellington the palm in this mighty conflict, but he knew that he was outmanœuvred, and he did not claim it; and he disliked the subject, when all the facts were known, though he wrote on it in extreme old age. The simple truth is that Blücher and Wellington, considering the enormous hosts being arrayed against him, did not think that Napoleon would spring on Belgium ; even their own forces, they well knew, were nearly double those of their foe ; and though they made dispositions on the supposition of an attack, these were ill-conceived and essentially faulty. Their armies, in the first place, were spread along an immense line, with divergent bases ; in the second, they were scattered up and down Belgium ; in the third, they were far too near the frontier, at the points of concentration marked out for them ; and in the fourth, the two chiefs were too far from each other, and could not communicate without perilous delays.

Availing himself of these palpable mistakes, Napoleon broke in on the exposed centre of his adversaries with a grandeur of design and a skill in execution never surpassed ; he was close to their weak line on the 15th of June, and a single march had placed them in extreme danger. Then came the confusion and the divided counsels common with allied chiefs, and foreseen by their foe. Blücher rushed hastily to confront the Emperor before his army had been drawn together ; Wellington, misconceiving the real state of affairs, stopped, hesitated, and left a wide gap open ; and an opportunity was afforded to the General of 1796, as favourable as ever was won by genius. But for a series of misadventures I have noticed elsewhere, he ought to have overwhelmed Blücher with ease on the 16th ; and, in that event, nothing could have saved Wellington, though the French were only 128,000 against 224,000* men. Strategy had only just missed one of its grandest triumphs ; in fact, the allied chiefs were all but checkmated, though Wellington made an able stand at Quatre Bras, and this went some way to baffle the Emperor. Napoleon was given another chance on the 17th, by the double retreat on Wavre and Waterloo, which might have proved fatal to both his adversaries ; but he was not well, and his lieutenants failed him. Soult, always indolent, was greatly to blame ; the retreat of the Prussians was not followed up ; Grouchy was detached late to hold Blücher in check ; and when Napoleon, true to the principles of the art, turned against Wellington and attained Waterloo, he was not aware that the Prussians were near and were ready to unite with the Duke, mainly owing to the faults of the incapable Grouchy.

* I refer to the combined forces of the Allies. The Duke's army was from 100,000 to 106,000 strong, counting all the troops in Belgium.

The morning of the 18th saw Napoleon and Wellington confronting each other for the first time ; the state of the weather, no doubt, gave the British chief an unforeseen advantage. The Emperor's plan of attack was perfect ; but Wellington's dispositions were also excellent, except that he made the strategic error of leaving a large detachment behind at Hal. In the great battle that followed Napoleon was ill, and the tactics of the French were incoherent and bad ; the genius of Wellington in defence reappeared, and shone out with conspicuous lustre ; and this great quality largely redeemed his shortcomings in this memorable campaign. He fought Waterloo on the assumption that Blücher would join him early with the whole Prussian army ; no aid reached him until nearly 5 P.M. ; Ziethen and Pirch, who decided the result of the day, were not on the field until after 8 P.M. ; and yet Wellington, with a very inferior army, contrived, during seven long hours, to resist successfully the Imperial host, and he had fairly repulsed the attack of the Guard before Ziethen and Pirch dealt the final stroke. His intrepidity, his tenacity, his tactical power on that memorable day were worthy of him ; no other general on the allied side, it may confidently be said, would have made such a stand ; and though he would almost certainly have lost the battle but for the arrival of Bülow in the early afternoon, still the defeat would not, I think, have been crushing, and Napoleon must have at last succumbed. Nevertheless, Waterloo, as I have endeavoured to prove, was decided by operations outside the field. Had Grouchy been equal to his appointed task, Blücher ought not to have been able to reach his colleague ; the strategy of Napoleon throughout the campaign, spite of mistakes and failures, well-nigh triumphed ; and the one merit of Wellington—and it was immense—was the masterly defence he made at Waterloo.

The Duke commanded the Army of Occupation in France, after the second fall of Napoleon and the return of the Bourbons, and he admirably fulfilled a most arduous mission. He has been condemned for not saving Ney ; but he had no right to interfere with the Government of France, and he showed characteristic tact and clemency in his relations with the French army, the Court, and the nation. His grand civil career begins at this point; but I must pass from it with scarcely a word of comment. He was a representative of England at the great Congress which met at Vienna to resettle Europe; and he was engaged in other important missions of the kind. In these diplomatic duties he was, no doubt, inferior to Marlborough in suavity and delicate art; he was sometimes, indeed, outspoken and blunt, but his simplicity, his candour, his ripe judgment, made him a negotiator of a very high order. His position as a statesman was noble and striking. His nature and profession drew him to the Tory Party, and he was for years its acknowledged head; his ideal was a strong aristocratic government; he detested modern Radical cant and theory; and though he was a Constitutional politician in the broadest sense, he did not understand the play and tendency of popular forces. But he had no sympathy with extreme Toryism; he ridiculed the Holy Alliance and its dreams; he knew how to make concessions in time; no reformer more sternly put down abuses; he was always Conservative, but wise and moderate. He commanded the army for some years; in this high office, unlike Turenne, with whom he had certain points in common, he was not in advance of the ideas of his time; he was rather obstinate and narrow in his views; but one great work he at least prepared; he urged the necessity for assuring the defence of England, and this generation at last has accepted his teaching. He spoke very often in the House of Lords; as an orator he had no accomplishments, but it was said he always "hit the nail on the head," and his sagacity was, perhaps, the more noted because it was not set off by eloquence. As he grew old, he became the national mentor; his counsels were felt to be words of wisdom, and his place in the State was one of commanding dignity.

He passed quietly away in 1852; England mourned him as her foremost citizen, and she justly regards him as the most illustrious of her worthies of the nineteenth century. It ought to be possible to pronounce a sound judgment on his military career, after all these years, and yet impartiality is still difficult. Wellington was endowed by nature with real wisdom, with strength of character seldom equalled, with singular moderation and calmness of thought, and yet with a rapid intelligence and clear insight. She denied him imagination, passion, and, in some measure, sympathy; and we see these excellences and defects in his life as a warrior. As a strategist, on the offensive, he stands low; for strategy, in this aspect, must see into the unknown, and requires a fiery energy he did not possess; and he was incapable of such exploits as the campaign of Marengo. In defensive strategy, however, he has been never excelled; for here the elements of the problem are easier to ascertain, and sagacity and firmness are most effective; and his campaign of Torres Vedras is, beyond comparison, the finest specimen of defence, in the strict sense of the word, that was seen in the Great War with France. As a tactician he was admirable in attack and defence, for when the field was before him, his promptness, his coolness, his constancy, stood him in good stead; but he was, on the whole, better in defence than attack; his Salamanca falls short of his Waterloo; and he was inferior to some tacticians in his arrangements on the ground, and, conspicuously, in following up a victory. Though there was something contracted in his exhibitions of the art, he has no doubtful place among great captains; and yet Wellington was greatest, perhaps, as a citizen, by reason of his profound wisdom, his administrative powers, his statesmanlike views, and, above all, his capacity for ruling alien races. In one quality of a chief he was, no doubt, deficient. He was respected, but not beloved, by his officers and men; he could not command their hearts like Napoleon or Condé, and this was largely due to the Spartan turn of character which distinguishes the aristocratic caste of Ireland. Taken altogether, he was one of the most illustrious men who have ever appeared on the stage of History; his grand life justified the poet's epitaph: " O Tower full square to all the winds that blew ! "

18

CHAPTER X.

MOLTKE.

I FEEL it difficult to attempt a sketch which must be inadequate, and perhaps partial. Moltke is a living man, though in extreme old age; flattery and envy have obscured his real image; and his place among great commanders is still a problem. Yet the General who triumphed in 1866-70, and whose name history links with Sadowa and Sedan, is assuredly a master of modern war; and I shall try to disengage his personality from the facts accumulated around it and still imperfectly known. Helmuth Charles von Moltke was born in 1800, a scion of a noble Danish house, of ancient descent but shattered fortunes. The family had produced more than one good soldier. It appears in the Thirty Years' War; the father of Moltke attained the rank of General in his country's service, and was, perhaps, an officer in the Prussian army; and one of his uncles perished amidst the wreck of the Grand Army in the retreat from Moscow. Little is known about him in early boyhood, except that he grew up under the cold shade of poverty; his first recollection was of the sack of Lübeck, where Blücher succumbed after the ruin of Jena; in his case, the strong impressions of youth were formed by the events of the gigantic strife which marked the beginning of the present century; he saw the Continent at the feet of Napoleon; he was a witness of the great rising of Germany; he may be said to have watched Leipsic, Montmirail, and Waterloo. The image of war, therefore, in its grandest aspects, and with consequences akin to a world-wide earthquake, was stamped on his mind when it was most ductile;

MOLTKE AND HIS MASTER.

and these associations, doubtless, had much to do with the distrust of France as the disturber of Europe, and the blended scorn and dislike of all that is French which were to be characteristic of the future warrior. Moltke became a cadet at the Military School of Copenhagen at an early age; and some years afterwards, having meanwhile obtained a commission in the Prussian service, he was a pupil at the Staff College of Berlin, an institution which may be traced to Frederick, and which has always been of very high repute. The youth made his mark at both these seminaries; privation had steeled his strong nature; his intelligence was superior, and his industry intense; he had a special faculty for mastering facts, and a fine taste in Letters and Science, resembling Frederick in all these respects; and it is no mere tradition that his promise was great, when he received his first appointment on the Prussian staff. Moltke passed some years at a desk in Berlin, doing the routine duties of the War Office; and as he had fallen on the days of the Long Peace, which followed the Revolutionary and Napoleonic wars, the prospect was faint that the accomplished soldier would ever become an illustrious warrior.

When he was past thirty, however, he found an opening for the display of some of his eminent parts; when travelling through the East, he attracted the notice of Sultan Mahmoud, lately engaged in the task of transforming the Turkish army; and Moltke gave him valuable advice, especially on the defence of the Dardanelles and the Bosphorus. Like Eugene of Savoy, it was his fortune also to see war for the first time, as it was carried on by the arms of Islam. In company with a small party of Prussian officers, he was present at the decisive fight of Nisib, which made Mehemet Ali an independent ruler; and it has been said that he recommended a movement which might have made the result of the battle different. Moltke has left a record of these experiences in a series of letters, still of value; but a history from his pen of the Russian invasion of the Ottoman Empire in 1828–29 is the most important monument of this part of his career. The book reveals the nature of the man; it wants imagination and the charm of genius; but it is thoroughly well-informed and full of good

18 *

criticism; and while it does justice to the powers of Diebitsch, its peculiar characteristic is the minute attention bestowed by the writer on all that relates to the mechanism and organization of the contending armies, and to the geography of the theatre of war. The reputation of Moltke grew by degrees; in the fine words of the Roman poet, it was like the silent growth of a tree; he rose slowly to the rank of general, and he was for some time the first aide-de-camp of the Crown Prince of Prussia, the late Emperor Frederick of no inglorious memory. He made several visits of state with his chief, and has left an interesting account of all that he saw; but his mind was engrossed by what belongs to war; and it is curious to observe that he has far more praise for the steadiness and obedience of the Russian infantry than for the agility and intelligence of the French soldiery, associated in his mind with carelessness and want of discipline.

In 1857 Moltke received the office of Chief of the Staff of the Prussian army. The position was one of the highest eminence; it had been filled by distinguished men; but the names of these are of no significance compared to that of the renowned soldier who has made it famous in all lands. Moltke was in his fifty-eighth year when he was raised to the post; he had never commanded troops in the field, nay, had taken no part in European warfare; and yet he possessed qualities which made his selection for the place a great day in Prussian history, for scarcely a living man so thoroughly understood what were to be the true conditions of war in our time, what its characteristics, and its coming development. We shall perceive this better if we glance at the state of the art during the long period of almost unbroken peace which succeeded Waterloo. For more than thirty years after 1815, every Power in Europe felt the exhaustion caused by the gigantic strife at the first part of the century; and though "the war drum was not hushed," in the poet's language, their energies were mainly directed to the great problems, political and social, which had come into question. In this state of affairs they generally reduced their armies; what was more important, they took little heed of all that concerns the military art, and their war offices were, without exception, directed

by men whose minds had been formed on the battle-fields of the
preceding age. When the Revolution of 1848 passed over the
Continent, the Russian army was far the most powerful in Europe;
the armies of France, of Austria, of Prussia, of England, had largely
declined from their old standards; and the great names of Wellington, of Soult, of Paskiévitch, were typical of the system of unchanging routine, which, in every service, prevailed in high places.

This strong conservatism was not much shaken by the memorable events of the next few years. The military operations
of 1848–49 resembled those of 1805–14, except that they displayed
less genius; and even the experience of the Crimean War did not
produce a wide-spread conviction that a new era in the art was
about to open. Nevertheless, throughout those long years since
the Peace, forces of all kinds had been steadily at work, which
were to affect greatly the phenomena of war, and if not to change
the essential truths it teaches, to modify it profoundly in some of
its aspects. The population of every State had continued to increase, especially in Central and Eastern Europe; and the rude
material, therefore, of military power had been augmented, and
was still growing. The resources of most nations had been doubled
and trebled; agriculture had made enormous strides; roads and
communications had become more numerous; and while this progress, dating from centuries before, had been going on with accelerated speed, a new element of mighty force had appeared in the
railway system, which, spreading over Europe, had made the
means of transport and of locomotion infinitely more easy, more
vast, and more rapid than ever had been known before in history.
Though the truth had not dawned on ordinary minds, it had become certain, thirty years ago, that in any great European contest armies would be larger than they had ever been; and the
facilities of moving huge bodies of troops, and of munitions and
supplies on a prodigious scale, it is now perceived, were to have
these results; that the efficacy of fortresses was still further to
decline, and that military operations might be more ample, have
more celerity, and be more decisive than had been the case even in
the age of Napoleon. Other influences, too, had made themselves

felt, to be attended with great results in war. The age was one of material inventions; the weapons of destruction used by armies had been almost transformed within a brief period; and appliances of a different kind had, to a certain extent, been turned to account. Rifled cannon and the breech-loading musket had been manufactured and partly employed; these mechanical improvements, it is now apparent, have necessarily led to changed formations and tactics; and the discovery of the field telegraph has, in some measure perhaps, affected strategy. Education, moreover, after the Peace had been generally diffused through Europe, especially in Prussia and Northern Germany; this had greatly increased the self-reliance and the intelligence of the individual soldier; and the result, we can now see, has had a potent influence in the conduct of armies and the arrangements of war.

It was the distinctive merit, I have said, of Moltke, that he appreciated these facts, and all that resulted from them, with perfect judgment and the most sagacious insight. He was deeply versed in the history of war; like every true student of it, he had seen that Napoleon was, by many degrees, the first of captains, and he had the capacity to perceive that the new conditions, especially the development of the railway system, favoured the grand and daring Napoleonic strategy. He grasped the truth, too, that the immense size of the armies in coming European conflicts would lead to more independence in separate commands, and would require a larger number of able chiefs than ever had been the case before; and he saw that preparation was more than ever necessary, the operations of modern war being so quick and decisive. The superiority of a rapid and bold offensive, the advantage of the diffusion of skill in the high ranks of an army, and the value of careful organization and well-planned arrangement, formed, so to speak, his military faith; and, coming to other details, he distinctly declared that the new arms would make the efficacy of fire the greatest element of success, that the importance of mere charges would largely decline, that formations in the field would become more flexible, and less dense than they had been formerly, and that real culture and mental training made a man an infinitely better soldier.

Moltke impressed these principles, which thirty years ago were not generally accepted or understood, on the Prussian army from the first moment, and with what results is now well known. The first great event in this part of his life was the reorganization of the military strength of Prussia, a reform completed in 1860. This vast work was probably due more to the king and Roon than to anyone else; but Moltke, we may be sure, approved of the measures by which the numbers of the army were largely increased and its real efficiency was, perhaps, quadrupled. The new arrangements did not change the bases on which the military power of Prussia rested, the general duty of the subject to serve, and the organization of the army on the local system ; but the yearly contingent of recruits was augmented a third, the time for service in the reserve was doubled, and the army, which had become too like a militia by a large admixture of landwehr, was made a completely distinct force, the landwehr forming only its last reserve. The hand of Moltke may be distinctly seen in almost every improvement thenceforward made in this great force, composed, after 1860, of fully half a million of trained fighting-men. Holding fast to the principle that offensive strategy would more than ever succeed in modern war, he directed his efforts to have the Prussian army ready to take the field as quickly as possible, and to be prepared to attack at once ; with this object in view, the local arrangement of the national forces was steadily retained, for it assured the rapid assembly of masses of troops ; but it was subjected to minute and careful central direction ; and elaborate preparations of all kinds were made to secure speedy " mobilization," and the regular transport of whatever is required for the conduct of a campaign by turning railways and other communications to account. Another great object of Moltke was to provide for general efficiency through all commands, from the highest down to the lowest grades. He had excellent materials for this at hand, in the practised officers who abound in Prussia ; and steadily applying himself to his task, he succeeded by degrees in placing the army under the control of capable men, from top to bottom, producing in this way that hierarchy of good leaders which Thucydides declared, two thousand years ago, was one of the secrets of Spartan success; and creating that division of skilful labour which has become a necessity in modern war. Moltke addressed himself, also, to the reforms in tactics which he had foreseen were to be essential; but here his exertions were less successful; he was steadily obstructed by routine and tradition; his own views, probably, were not fully formed, and years were to elapse before the Prussian army was to attain its present excellence in this sphere of the art. The greatest reform, however, effected by Moltke remains to be stated, and had immense results. The Prussian Staff stood high since the days of Frederick; but under the care of its greatest chief, it gradually reached a state of extreme perfection. Divided mainly into two branches, it supplied the commanders of corps with able advisers, trained in strategy, in tactics, in the direction of troops, and in providing for their needs in the field; and it has accumulated stores of knowledge in all that relates to military history, to the geography of war, to the resources and armies of civilized states, which have proved to be of the greatest practical value. Moltke, it should be added, like all true leaders, inspired the army generally with his high aims and spirit; he encouraged the mental training of soldiers and officers, but he paid special attention to order, discipline, and to everything that secures obedience to command.

Moltke could never have accomplished these tasks had he not had the all-powerful support of the King, a really able and far-sighted ruler, and a soldier of no ordinary gifts. Within seven years from the time when he was raised to his post, the Prussian army, which since 1848 had fallen low in universal repute, had, under Moltke's care, become, we know now, unquestionably the first of European armies, as superior to those of every other State as the army of Frederick was to the armies of his day. The time was at hand when the strength and worth of this mighty instrument was to be proved in the field. I pass over the petty Danish war, and proceed to the great conflict of 1866, fought with memorable and lasting results for the Continent. Prussia instantly took a bold offensive attitude, and the celerity with which her main forces were

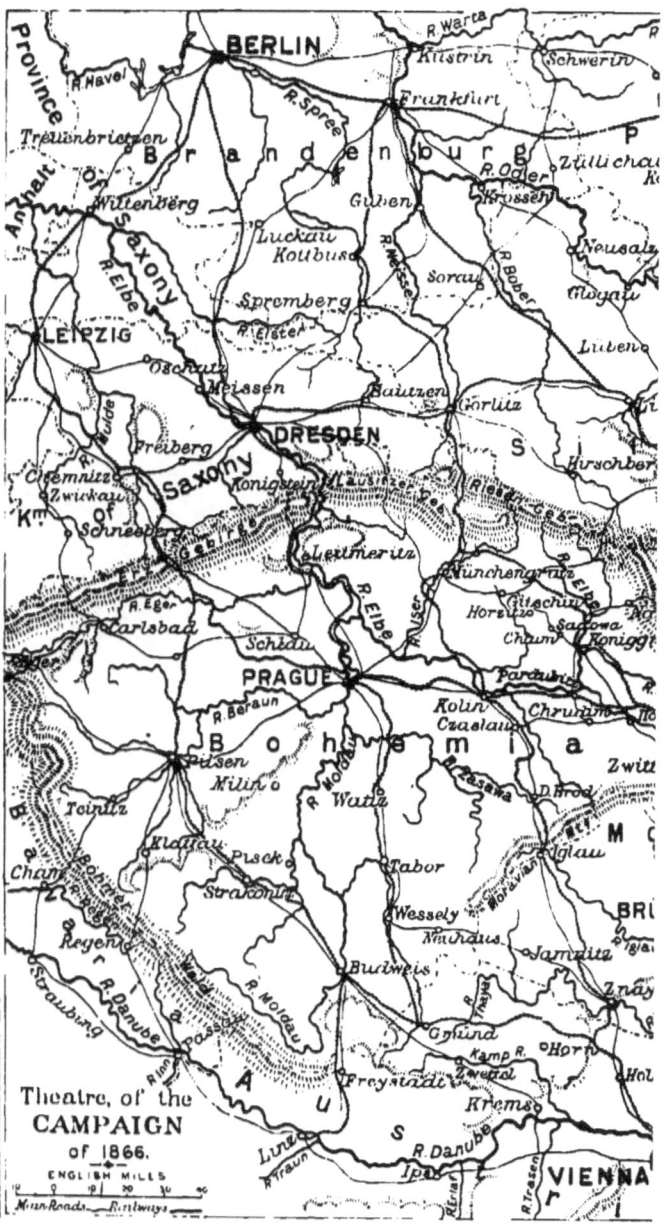

Theatre of the
CAMPAIGN
of 1866.

ENGLISH MILES

Main Roads ———— Railways ————

" mobilized " and directed towards the Bohemian frontier, with every requirement to begin a campaign, surprised all who understood the subject. The invasion, too, of the Northern German States was admirably planned and well carried out; and the ability with which a small Prussian army held in check and baffled the whole of South Germany remains a specimen of fine generalship. The distribution, however, of the principal army on the theatre of war to oppose Austria can be praised by the courtiers of fortune only, and is certainly open to grave objections.

On the 15th of June 1866 this huge array, about 250,000 strong, and divided into three great masses, was disseminated along an immense front, extending from the Elbe almost to the Oder, and not far from the main Bohemian range ; the right, the Army of the Elbe, being near Torgau, the centre, or First Army, being around Sorau, the Second Army, the left, holding the tract round Neisse. At this moment the chief Austrian army, nearly equal in numbers, reckoning its Saxon allies, was in Moravia, spreading about Olmütz ; it held a central position between scattered foes, and it is now acknowledged that it was ready to advance, and could have assumed a decided offensive. It is vain to deny that in this state of affairs it already possessed an immense advantage ; and, whatever the cause, the Prussian strategy which gave it this grand chance must be deemed faulty. All the apologies that have been made on this subject will not mislead the true student of war. It has been urged that the dislocation of the Prussian armies was necessary " to cover Berlin and Breslau " ; but this argument is of no avail. You should never risk a whole army for such objects, and if you try to defend everything, you run all hazards. It has been said, again, that it was not possible to assemble the Prussian forces in any other way, regard being had to the lines of railways ; but that is no reason why the three armies should have been distant from each other near the Bohemian frontier. Lastly, it has been alleged that the superior quality of the Prussian troops, if considered, excuses their chiefs ; but this superiority had yet to be proved ; and any operation, however defective, may be justified by this kind of reasoning. The examples set by really great captains show what Benedek—a good soldier, but unfit to command a large army—might have accomplished at this conjuncture. Napoleon, in the place of the Austrian chief, would have made for the salient of the Bohemian hills—would have debouched through the passes into the Saxon plains, and holding the army of the Elbe by a detachment in check, would have fallen in superior force on the First Army, and then would have turned victoriously against the Second Army, which, thrown forward into Upper Silesia, might have been cut off from its base and destroyed. Turenne, less daring but more safe, would have advanced to the southern verge of the Bohemian range, and, occupying the position he always sought to gain, would have invited the attack of his divided enemies, and interposing between them would have beaten them in detail. In either case, the Prussians should have been defeated; and, indeed, why they were placed in this way on the theatre has never yet been really explained.

On the 16th of June the Army of the Elbe entered Saxony, and had soon seized Dresden; and about the 20th it had nearly joined hands with the First Army which, under Prince Frederick Charles, had been moved close to the Bohemian frontier. The Prussian right and centre were thus almost united; but the left, commanded by the Crown Prince, which had advanced from Neisse towards the passes near Glatz, was isolated from its supports, and at a great distance; and if the invaders were not in immediate danger—for Benedek had only begun to move—their strategic position remained critical. In this situation the Prussian armies, now practically two, not three masses, were directed to pass through the range, and, approaching each other, to effect their junction around Gitschin, a point considerably to the south of the hills, not far from where Benedek had some troops, and where he might have had five-sixths of his army. This strategy was exactly the same in kind as that which had proved fatal in 1796, when attempted against the chief of Rivoli; and the excuses that have been made for it are weak and baseless. Two large armies, such as those of Prussia were, though far from each other, are no doubt in less peril if they invite the attack of a single army equal to both in strength, than two small armies would be under like conditions, and this would specially be the case where, as in the present instance, the field of manœuvre was somewhat contracted. All this, however, proves no more than that the converging movement of 1866 was less to be blamed than that of Würmser; it does not show that it can be justified, and the experience of ages clearly condemns it. Benedek, who broke up from Olmütz on the 17th of June, might have reached Gitschin with the mass of his forces before the Prussian armies could have come into line; and in that event he would have had at least an opportunity to fall on his divided enemies, and to achieve success, more or less important. Unfortunately for himself, however, the Austrian chief was unable to seize the occasion before him; instead of turning his central position to account, and advancing northward with all his corps in hand, he adopted half-measures of extreme feebleness. He sent a detachment only, comparatively small, to hold the Prussian right and centre in check. He struck at the Prussian left with inferior forces, and he hung back himself with the mass of his army, irresolute, hesitating, and, at best, inactive.

The result was what might have been expected. Clam Gallas and the Saxon contingent were overpowered by Prince Frederick Charles, who attacked with largely superior forces; the Crown Prince, as he emerged from the defiles, defeated with ease the three hostile corps opposed to his much more powerful army, and though the issue was partly due to the excellence of the Prussian infantry, and to the efficacy of the arms they wielded, it is chiefly to be ascribed to the grave faults and the shortcomings of the Austrian leader. The victorious armies, though still far apart, now advanced along the heads of the Iser and the Elbe. The Austrians, beaten and demoralized, slowly fell back; and yet such was the inherent advantage of the central position still held by Benedek, that had he known how to make a true use of it he might even yet have turned the tide of ill-fortune. By the 29th of June he had his army nearly united; the two Prussian armies were leagues from each other, and part of the First Army was dangerously exposed; and it has been justly remarked that had Benedek boldly attacked Prince Frederick Charles on this day, he ought to have won a real victory, and, in that event, he would still have had a chance to strike and defeat the Crown Prince of Prussia. As is well known, however, the ill-fated chief did not attempt an offensive return, and continued his retreat until he had passed the Bistritz ; here, like Daun, he took a position of defence, and he passively awaited the onset of his foes, anticipating already impending ruin. Yet even at this moment, had he been a general of a high order, he might perhaps have triumphed. I have no space to describe the great of day Sadowa; it was, no doubt, a splendid and decisive victory ; but the operations of the Prussians once more gave their enemy an advantage which he might have seized, and turned to account with immense results. The First and Second Armies remained still divided; for many hours on that eventful forenoon, an almost insignificant force was opposed to the mass of the Austrian army ; and it was only when the Crown Prince reached the field, at about 2 P.M., and was able to attack, that the chances of the battle became equal, and that success was made even possible. Had Benedek at any previous moment fallen in full force on Prince Frederick Charles, it is difficult to suppose that the Austrian chief might not have, at least, averted defeat.

The campaign of Sadowa is a striking instance how generals who steadily carry out ably a plan essentially faulty in itself may defeat a commander who waits on his foe, and cannot take the initiative or seize the occasion. In justice, however, to a departed veteran, let us say that the Prussian army was, in most respects, very superior to that arrayed against it ; the Austrian army was crowded with discontented levies ; the Prussians, too, possessed a breech-loading rifle, the fire of which had great effect, though it is idle to contend that it decided the war; and these facts told in the final issue. As for the Prussian strategy, it was not good. We can imagine the shades of Turenne and Napoleon indignant that a violation of their art should have been followed by ill-deserved success ; and if Moltke really directed these operations of 1866, his first essays in war are not admirable. The movements, however, which led to Sadowa are almost identical with those of

Frederick in Bohemia in 1756–57 ; and I cannot help conjecturing that King William—his reverence for his ancestor was a kind of worship—was in a great measure their true author, though those of Frederick have been condemned by Napoleon with no uncertain censure.

After the events of 1866, it became apparent that Prussia and France would ere long quarrel ; and I must say a word on the preparations made by the two Powers before the impending conflict, and on their military resources when it at last broke out. Northern Germany was practically added to Prussia ; treaties were made with the Southern German States ; the unity of Germany for war was well-nigh accomplished ; and the German armies which could be brought into the field, more or less organized on the Prussian model, reached the enormous number of a million of men, 500,000 forming the first fighting line. Extraordinary attention, moreover, was given to the improvement of the instrument of war which had crushed the power of Austria in three weeks, and to the removal of every defect which had been discovered in it. The "mobilization" was made more effective ; the experience of 1866 was turned to account to make the evolutions of foot more quick and exact, and to adapt infantry tactics to modern arms. Great pains were taken to reform the cavalry, which had been scarcely equal to the fine squadrons of Austria, led by the brilliant Edelsheim, and to give it celerity and strength in the field ; and the artillery, it may be said, was transformed, old smooth-bore guns being finally condemned, and artillery tactics being greatly changed by abandoning the system of huge reserves of guns—a tradition of the Napoleonic era, but obsolete under the new conditions of war—and by directing every battery that could be made available as quickly as possible to the front of battle. By these means the Prussian army of 1866 was expanded into the vast German army which overran France from the Rhine to the Loire ; and the hosts which triumphed at Metz and Sedan were infinitely more formidable in all respects than that which had overwhelmed Benedek.

Let us now turn to the attitude of France, in view of the contest known to be imminent.   Napoleon III. and one or two French chiefs had not failed to observe the immense increase of the military power of Prussia and Germany ; and they perceived how enormous was the importance of the great trained reserve of the German system, which had nothing corresponding to it in their own.   The Emperor and Marshal Niel accordingly proposed that the nominal reserves of the French army—masses of men on paper —should be in some degree disciplined, and that the Garde Mobile, a new force, should be formed ; and had this been effected the military power of France would have been largely augmented, though it would have been still very inferior to that of Germany. Tradition and faction, however, prevailed ; a reform, of which Napoleon had laid down the lines at St. Helena fifty years before, was disregarded and not carried out ; and the strength of France for war was left as it was, that is, miserably weak compared to that of Germany.   This difference was in itself immense, but there were other differences of perhaps equal moment.   France was not prepared for a great modern war ; her military organization was out of joint ; she had not had a good Minister of War since Soult ; her chiefs, formed for the most part in Africa, had little strategic or scientific knowledge ; she had nothing resembling the Prussian Staff, the brain of the army, as it has well been called ; she had not in her service the perfect gradation of united commands which was one secret of the success of Prussia in 1866.   Her whole military hierarchy, and all that depends on it was, therefore, in far from a good state ; her chiefs had no settled convictions in war, and were divided upon the great question whether the offensive or defensive was the better strategy ; and, besides that it was weak and without a real reserve, the condition of her army was very defective.   It was, no doubt, a fine professional army ; but it had been injured by the system of commuting service ; it had many bad and worn-out soldiers ; it had not been practised in manœuvres in the field ; it had not anything like fixed rules of tactics ; and though its infantry possessed an excellent rifle, much better than the needle-gun of Prussia, and its cavalry was a noble arm, its artillery was very inferior to that of the Germans. The most marked distinction, however, between the two nations in their capacity for a campaign has yet to be noted. The railway system of Germany was designed for war; that of France was formed on no such principle; the local system of Prussia made it quite certain that the German army would be placed in the field more quickly than that of France could be under her centralized and ill-arranged system; and these two circumstances, little perceived at the time, were of extreme if not of decisive importance.

The general result of this state of things was that Germany could "mobilize" and send into the field half a million of men, backed by enormous reserves, well organized, disciplined, trained, and commanded, within three weeks after a declaration of war; that France could hardly assemble three hundred thousand soldiers, unsupported by any solid reserve, ill-prepared, and under inefficient chiefs; and that, in point of time, she would be far behind her enemy. There was no comparison, therefore, between the two powers, and France had scarcely a chance of success, though if her military strength had been well directed, she need never have signed the Treaty of Frankfort. The conflict began in July 1870. Napoleon III., the mere shadow of a mighty name, assumed the command of the French armies, and his plan was to advance from behind Metz and Strasbourg, to cross the Rhine between Spires and Landau, and to interpose between the South and North German forces, which, it was assumed, would not be ready in time, and divided. The project, the Emperor has told us himself, was founded on that of his uncle in 1815; but Moltke had foreseen and provided against it, and it is useless to examine a mere scheme on paper, which was no sooner conceived than it proved abortive. Napoleon III. calculated that he would have 250,000 men round Metz and Strasbourg ready to march, with 50,000 in immediate reserve; but he had little administrative power or resource; the existing system of France proved inefficient; her organization for war broke down, the "mobilization" of her troops was slow and partial, and when the Emperor reached Metz in the third week of July, he had not assembled 200,000 soldiers, and these were hardly in a state to take the field. This was very different from that prodigy of skill, the concentration on the Sambre before Waterloo ; and in these circumstances, the unhappy sovereign ought to have renounced a hopeless offensive, and to have placed his army on the line of the Moselle, in order to defend the Vosges and Alsace, a course which Moltke believed he would take. But the Emperor thought he had no choice. He was goaded on by opinion in France ; the folly of allowing politics to master strategy, one main cause of the disasters that followed, had already begun to produce its results ; and he advanced to the frontier with forces, compared to those of the Germans, pitiably weak, and but ill-provided with all kinds of requirements. When he had attained Alsace and the Sarre he paused, afraid to strike, but he felt that he was not in nearly suffi- cient strength, and, waiting on his enemy, he allowed his army to be disseminated upon a vast arc, extending from Thionville to the gap of Belfort, and dangerously exposed along its front.

The conduct of Germany and of the German chiefs contrasted most strikingly with this exhibition of maladministration, feebleness, and incapacity for war. The contest, Frenchmen thought, was a mere affair of "glory"; in Germany it caused a great national rising for unity and independence, and to avenge Jena. The Teutonic race sprang fiercely to arms ; the feuds between North and South Germany ceased ; the orders for the "mobilization" of the German armies were carried out with wonderful skill and pre- cision, and more than 800,000 men, with great reserves behind, were in a few days arrayed on the frontier, an astonishing result of patriotism and organization for war, partly due to a well- planned railway system. Three great armies were now quickly formed. This time Moltke certainly had the general direction of operations in the field, and he instantly assumed a determined offensive. The situation dictated his plan ; there was nothing original in it, as has been said by flatterers. In fact, it was that of Marlborough in 1705, and it had been actually laid down by Gneisenau ; it consisted, simply, in invading France from the Palatinate, along her most exposed frontier, but it was executed in the main ably, and with conspicuous forethought and vigour.

The First Army, led by the veteran Steinmetz, advanced from Treves towards the Lower Sarre; the Second, under Prince Frederick Charles, moved from Mayence through the German Vosges; and the Third, commanded by the Crown Prince of Prussia, marched across the Rhine and attained the Lauter, the three masses acting well in concert. The poor affair of Sarrebruck only quickened the movement; and, in the first week of August, a great tempest of war burst over the verge of Lorraine and Alsace. The first efforts of the Germans were, no doubt, premature; Frossard might have gained some success at Spicheren had he been seconded by the corps in his rear, and the impatience of the invaders, and of one or two of their chiefs, precipitated the well-fought battle of Wörth. Moltke, however, is not to be blamed for this; he was far away from those scenes of action, and his strategy completely attained his object, though his subordinates made more than one mistake. As for Wörth, it does honour to the arms of France; on that day 45,000 Frenchmen held double their number, for hours, at bay; and the issue might have been very different had De Failly come into line, as was possible. Macmahon, however, a soldier but no chief, cannot escape blame for not having drawn off his troops while retreat was still open and safe, especially when the great superiority of the enemy in force and in artillery had become clearly manifest.

Spicheren shattered the front of the French army—it had been named the Army of the Rhine; and Wörth forced its right wing in confusion and rout far to the south, in eccentric retreat, laying bare the defeated centre and left. Napoleon III. fell back with his beaten forces; and the next few days, big with the fate of France, witnessed a wretched succession of divided counsels. It was proposed to attempt a stand on the Nied, in Lorraine, to join Macmahon, or to call him up to Metz; but all that was done was to retreat on the fortress, to cause a weak reserve to advance from Châlons, and to impair the moral worth of the French soldiery, when ill-led, never great in misfortune. Meanwhile, the hosts of the invaders, largely reinforced, were moving slowly through the passes of the Vosges; the First and Second Armies filling the

19

tracts between the Sarre, the Nied, and the Seille, the Third Army far to the south, round Nancy; and, whatever may be said, ample time was given to their enemy to make good a retreat westward. This movement was not arranged until the 12th of August, a precious week having been thrown away; and the Emperor handed over his command to Bazaine, a chief, whose antecedents had, at best, been doubtful, with a general direction to fall back on the Meuse. Moltke's plan of operations became now developed; the First Army was moved towards Metz, in order to detain the retreating enemy; part of the Second Army was pushed across the Moselle, its march screened with remarkable skill; and the Third Army made a step westward, the object being to force the Army of the Rhine into the north of France, and to cut it off from Paris.

Steinmetz attacked Bazaine on the 14th of August. The battle was stern and well contested; but it kept the French back for a whole day, and it facilitated, as was intended, the forward movement of the Second and Third Armies, which was Moltke's object. A great mistake, however, was here made; the German chief believed that the Army of the Rhine was already far to the north of Metz; but Bazaine was moving directly westward, and on the evening of the 15th he had his whole army, at least 140,000 strong, concentrated along the roads that lead from Metz to Verdun, by Mars La Tour and Etain. One German corps only was on the spot; Prince Frederick Charles, no doubt unaware of the immense superiority of his enemy in force, attacked on the morning of the 16th; and had Bazaine had any skill in war, he ought to have swept his assailant from his path. The Marshal, however, could not handle an army; he kept the Imperial Guard inactive near Metz, he made little use of two of his corps; the hard pressed Germans were reinforced by degrees; a magnificent effort of the German cavalry had a marked effect on the fortunes of the day; and evening fell on a scene of carnage, in which neither side could lay a claim to victory. The result proved the ascendency won by the Germans, and was for them a splendid passage of arms; but the effects of Moltke's error were not yet got over—it was like that of Napoleon before Auerstadt—for, as I have remarked, the campaign of 1870 resembles that of Jena in many respects; he had not 80,000 men in hand, and Bazaine had still a strategic advantage, from which a real chief would have at least plucked safety. As Prince Frederick Charles has said, he should have attacked on the 17th; and in that event he ought to have won a battle, or, at all events, have made good his way to Verdun, a result which would have given a new turn to the war. A much grander game, however, was open to him; and a German commentator—Moltke, I suspect—has remarked that Napoleon would have played it, and have perhaps gained important success. On this day, a decisive moment in the campaign, the First Army was still east of Metz; the Second Army was partly west of the Moselle; the Third Army was leagues away to the south; and the communications of the invaders would be dangerously exposed, could an enemy descend from Metz on Nancy. Had Bazaine, therefore, fallen back on the fortress, and issued from it in force on the 18th, advancing between the Moselle and the Seille, he ought to have been able to seize and hold the line of operations of the hostile armies, and the consequences must have been very great. He might have stopped the invasion, perhaps for weeks; he would have certainly saved himself and his army, and the situation would have been wholly changed.

Unhappily for France, she had not a captain who could seize the one great occasion given by Fortune in the first part of the war of 1870-71. Bazaine, a soldier fit to command a division, but utterly unable to direct large masses, had experience of the power of modern arms, and he had a fixed belief that mere defensive tactics were the means to assure success in battle. He resolved, therefore, to stand and to fight; and he arranged his forces, still 120,000 strong, along a range of uplands, from near Metz on the left to St. Privat and Roncourt on the right, which formed a fine position for a passive defence, the system on which the Marshal relied. Moltke, on the 17th, drew together the greater part of the First and Second Armies across the Moselle; the huge masses, probably 210,000 men, were west of Metz on the

19 *

morning of the 18th, intercepting, a retreat to the Meuse and Verdun; but, strange as it may appear, the German commander was still ill-informed of his enemy's movements; he believed that Bazaine was falling back northwards, and when he discovered where the French were, he was convinced, for some hours, that the positions they held did not extend nearly as far as Roncourt. This and other mistakes dispose of the theory that Moltke is a kind of Providence on the field, gravely asserted by certain worshippers of success, and tend to show that German reconnoitring may be less perfect than has been said; but fools only can claim omniscience for chiefs; and, in fact, under the new conditions of war, with its vast operations and its immense battles, the ablest captains will fall into error more frequently than has been the case formerly.

Partly owing to the miscalculations of the German leader, and partly to tactics essentially false, the tremendous battle of the 18th of August—known to history by the name of Gravelotte—was undecided up to the last moment, large as was the superiority of Moltke's forces. The assailants, thinking they were turning the French right, fell in front on the centre strongly entrenched, and failed to make the slightest impression on it; Steinmetz, on the German right, made repeated charges, in the close columns of the days of his youth, and the First Army suffered enormous losses. The Prussian Guard, too, were cruelly stricken in an attempt to carry St. Privat by storm; indeed, until near nightfall, the Army of the Rhine had a marked advantage along the whole line of battle; and had it been able to make a grand counter-attack, especially when the right of its foe was shattered, it not improbably would have achieved success. At last, however, the inherent vices of a passive defence became manifest; the German chiefs, given the offensive all through, and allowed to search the positions of the French everywhere, brought their masses to bear against the extreme French right; Roncourt was carried by a great turning movement; the whole position became untenable, and the French army gradually fell back on Metz. Yet no doubt can now exist that had Bazaine been a capable chief on that terrible day, the battle would have been at least drawn, inferior as were his troops in numbers, and, in some degree, disheartened by defeat. Had the Imperial Guard, as was quite possible, been moved to the aid of the French right, the last effort of the Germans must have failed; and in that event the contending armies would have retained their places on the field unchanged. The Marshal, however, unequal to his task, and thinking only of merely holding his ground, kept this noble reserve near Metz unengaged; and 20,000 men were left out of the struggle who could have turned the balance in the scales of Fortune. Gravelotte, in truth, is a notable instance how a resolute offensive, even though ill-conducted, may, notwithstanding the arms of the age, prevail over passive tactics of defence; the attack on the French right, made at the last moment, after many mistakes, gained decisive success; and all the efforts of an army which had not the means to attempt at any time a counter-attack, and simply waited in position on its foes, proved ultimately fruitless, though for hours hopeful. The battle, the student of war will note, has a strong resemblance to that of Malplaquet; but the operations of the Germans are not to be compared in skill to those of Marlborough and Eugene; and the tricolour was defended by a very different chief from the illustrious warrior who upheld the lilies.

Within two or three days after Gravelotte, the German armies had closed around Metz and the army of Bazaine, which had clung to the fortress. The left wing and centre of the whole French army were thus, so to speak, removed from the theatre, at least for active operations in the field; and, notwithstanding mistakes and shortcomings, the plan of Moltke, if not realised, had been attended with more than expected success. The right wing, half destroyed at Wörth, remained, and we turn to the movements of this force, on which the fortune of France for the time depended. Macmahon had been joined by De Failly and his troops, by the corps which had been placed at Belfort, and by a new corps despatched from the capital; and by the 20th of August the collected array, numbering from 120,000 to 130,000 men, was assembled around the great camp of Châlons. The Marshal was in supreme command; he properly resolved to keep the only army now left to

France to defend Paris; but as Bazaine conceivably might be not distant, he marched on the 21st to Rheims, holding a position on the flank of the German invasion, and in the hope that his brother chief might approach, but with the determination to fall back on the capital. This was in conformity with the principles of war; and had Macmahon kept firm to his purpose, the catastrophe that followed would not have happened, and France would not have mourned for the extreme of disaster. Unfortunately, however, the Duke of Magenta, a hero in the field but a weak man—the character is by no means uncommon—was led astray by pernicious counsels; Palikao, a new Minister of War, whose chief thought was for the tottering Empire, and to satisfy the desires of Paris, insisted that Metz must be relieved; and he urged Macmahon to advance to the Meuse, to slip outside the flank of the hostile armies, and descending from Montmédy on the beleaguered fortresses, to join hands with and to extricate Bazaine, and to strike a bold stroke for a decisive victory. In an evil hour for France and himself, the marshal gave ear to a fatal project, as reckless as ever was made in war; for the march to the Meuse, and thence as far as Metz, would be a flank march of the most hazardous kind, the enemy holding the chord of the arc; it would be a march perilously near the Belgian frontier, where a lost battle would mean ruin; it was a march to be made by an enfeebled army in the midst of the victorious Germans, threefold in numbers; above all, it was a march which would draw away from Paris, the centre and vital point of the national defence, the only organized force that remained to protect it. Macmahon, it is said, was still doubting—he knew that the course proposed was insensate, not strategy, but the throw of a gambler—when an ambiguous message sent by Bazaine, and implying that he was on his way from Metz northwards, at last caused the luckless commander to yield. Once more the plainest military rules were sacrificed to political ends; and once more Bellona, who brooks no rival, was, so to speak, challenged and wildly provoked. The army of Châlons broke up from Rheims on the 23rd, and it was on the Upper Aisne on the 25th, approaching the region of defiles and forests, which extends from

the Ardennes to the Meuse. Macmahon spared no effort to make
the movement rapid, for celerity he knew was his only chance;
but the march of his army became slow, and by the 27th it was
still far from the Meuse, in the tract between Tourteron, Le Chêne,
and Buzancy. It had already begun to shows signs of weakness;
it was ill-provided and badly organized; the soldiers were discontented and ill-disciplined, and the mind of its chief was full of
misgivings.

I proceed to the operations of the German armies, very different
from those of their ill-directed enemies. The main body of the
First and Second Armies was required for the investment of Metz;
but three corps, called the Army of the Meuse, were detached to
co-operate with the Third Army, by this time west of the Moselle,
in the borderlands of Lorraine and Champagne; and the converging masses, 230,000 strong, advanced steadily upon a broad
front towards the heads of the Marne and the great roads to Paris.
By the 24th of August, the cavalry outposts which preceded the
movement had ascertained that the Army of Châlons had left
Rheims, and was on its way to the Aisne eastward; but Moltke
refused for some time to credit the rumour that it was making for
Metz, for this, he rightly thought, would be the height of folly.
He learned the truth, however, positively on the 25th, and his
resolution was formed with that prompt decision which is a characteristic of real chiefs, and has been exhibited by him at grave
crises. The measures he took to baffle Palikao's scheme were not
wonders of genius, as has been said by flatterers, but they show
true insight, and most comprehensive judgment; and they were
carried out with consummate skill. The Army of the Meuse was
directed to recross the river; two corps were detached from Metz
to join it, and to stop Macmahon should he get near the fortress;
and the Third Army was ordered to advance northwards through
the district of the Argonnes and the Ardennes—the scene of the
campaign of Valmy—and to gather on the flank and rear of the
Army of Châlons, which would thus be placed in a difficult strait at
least. The execution of this fine strategic movement was admirable
in the highest degree; the great invading hosts, ruled by one

master's will, well-led, supplied, and trained for the field, marched with speed and precision through an intricate country, and the careful preparation, the organization for war, the perfect unity and gradation of command, and the intelligence of the individual soldier, which are distinctive marks of the army of Prussia, were made fully and grandly manifest.

By the 27th of August the German squadrons were gathering rapidly upon their foes ; Macmahon, though without the least notion of the enormous force that was closing round him, perceived that his army was in grave peril, and he gave orders for a retreat on Mézières, hoping to attain Paris by a march from the frontier. For the second time, however, the incapable chief succumbed to the temptation he should have spurned. A message, that " revolution would break out should Bazaine be abandoned at Metz," induced him to continue the advance to the Meuse, and to court the ruin which he knew was probable ; and it is but just to observe that Napoleon III.—he accompanied the Marshal since he had left Châlons—protested against conduct which was almost criminal.* Macmahon now tried to make a forced march ; his army was divided into two great columns, in order to make its movements rapid, and the first column reached the river safely, and had crossed it by the 29th of August. The second column, however, was far to the south, and separated by a full march from the first ; it was largely composed of beaten troops, already desponding, nay, half-mutinous ; it was charged with *impedimenta* of all kinds, and it toiled slowly through the passes and thickets it had to traverse on its way to the Meuse. This gave Moltke the opportunity to strike ; the Army of the Meuse was recalled to the (west of the stream, the two corps from Metz having been sent back ; a part of the Third Army was pushed forward, and the Germans fell with terrible effect on their enemies, caught in flank and surprised, at Beaumont and other places in their march. The second column was routed with immense loss ; it reached the Meuse a mere

---

* This is the expression of Napoleon in a somewhat analogous case. The orders of a Government, if not precise, obviously should not excuse a general-in-chief on the spot.

shattered wreck, pursued by the indefatigable Prussian horsemen ; and its ruin involved a part of the first column, which crossed the river to give it support. By the evening of the 30th the Army of Châlons, one corps of it as far as Carignan, was on the eastern bank of the Meuse, but half of the French troops were a demoralized mass ; and the German advanced guards were already at hand, in close communication with the hosts in their rear.

Macmahon, at this time, was at Carignan ; he confidently expected that he would reach Metz ; he boasted, it is said, that victory was at hand. The news of the events of the 30th dispelled these dreams ; he hurriedly fell back with his one intact corps, and by the morning of the 31st he had assembled the still large, but beaten, Army of Châlons in the tract that surrounds the fortress and town of Sedan. The state of the French troops was of the worst omen ; but an occasion was still open to a great chief, to extricate them from impending ruin. Mézières was not distant, and a French corps had reached the place to support the Marshal ; the Meuse spread between his army and the foe, and had he left his *impedimenta* behind, and made a rapid march, without the loss of an hour, he would certainly have escaped with the great mass of his forces. It is this circumstance which makes the strategy of Moltke inferior, fine as it was, to that which shut up Mack in Ulm ; and the Grand Army, it will be borne in mind, had been saved on the Beresina when in far worse straits. Macmahon, however, would not stir from Sedan ; there is reason to believe he never knew the immense strength of the hostile force, and he arrayed his army, " ready," he said, " to fight," along the uplands, encircled by streams and villages, which overlook Sedan and the valley below. The evening of the 31st had come ; the German horsemen made the situation known ; and Moltke, who up to this time had only hoped that he might succeed in forcing his enemy across the frontier, saw that he could reckon on a decisive triumph. Orders were issued for an immediate night march ; the great German divisions, perfectly led, and the men scenting approaching victory, moved rapidly over the space between, and preparations were made to assail and surround the feeble and shattered Army of Châlons.

It is unnecessary to retrace the scenes of Sedan, the just retribution of foolishness in command, a battle decreed by Fate, in its irony, to be fought around the birthplace of Turenne. The French were first attacked, on that fatal morning, on their southern and eastern front towards the Chiers; and they made for a time a gallant resistance, though the fall of Macmahon and a squabble between two of his lieutenants had a bad effect on the troops. By degrees, however, the overwhelming pressure of forces immensely superior told; the line of defence on the Givonne was carried; and the French were driven back, on Sedan, routed, and huddled around the walls of the fortress. Meanwhile a tremendous attack had been made on the northern and western fronts of the defence; the Germans advancing to the heights of Illy, and moving from the opposite side round the bend of the Meuse, which half encircles the outskirts of Sedan, closed gradually round their doomed foes; and though the French cavalry made heroic efforts, and one corps nobly struggled to the last, it was impossible to withstand overpowering numbers. The last remains of the Army of Châlons were forced, like the first, against the fortress; the German artillery—throughout the campaign it had proved an arm of enormous strength—was brought to bear in masses on the perishing wreck; the fire of 500 pieces searched the scene of carnage; and a white flag soon announced that resistance, no longer possible, had completely ceased. Within a few hours 85,000 men, the survivors of more than 120,000, the victims of worse than insensate leading, were a collection of helpless prisoners of war; and their cries of impotent fury and despair —this was the attitude of by far the greater part—only provoked the pitying scorn of the victors.

This immense disaster, added to that of Metz, all but destroyed the military power of Imperial France on the theatre of war. Moltke had acted harshly at the capitulation of Sedan; he had no respect for the French character; like Hannibal and Napoleon, he treated the force of patriotic passion with contempt; and, leaving a considerable detachment behind, he directed an immediate advance on Paris. The German armies rolled steadily onward, through the valleys of the Aisne, the Oise, and the Marne, masking fortresses and occupying points on their way ; and they appeared before the capital on the 19th of September, the chiefs convinced they would meet no resistance. Their expectations seemed about to be realised ; an attempt to assail the invaders in flank, as they gathered upon the uplands south of the Seine, was easily defeated, and had bad results ; and the Germans were permitted, without a further effort, to surround and invest the beleaguered city. Their lines, constructed with skill and forethought, spread on a circumference of great extent, from the confluence of the Seine and the Marne, by St. Denis, round through Versailles to Bonneuil ; and though the besieging forces were at this moment not 150,000 strong, no doubt existed in the German camp—it was, indeed, the general belief of Europe—that a few days would see the surrender of Paris.

Weeks, however, passed, and it became apparent that this calculation was a complete error. The Empire had fallen on the 4th of September ; a Government of national defence had been formed ; and this Revolution, in the main caused by the passionate wrath of the great mass of the citizens, quickened the general resolve that the capital should hold out, and confront the power of the German armies. Preparations had been made to stand a siege ; immense supplies of provisions had been stored ; the *enceinte* and the forts which protect the city had been hastily manned and armed ; enormous bodies of men had been assembled to take part in the defence of the place ; these were supported by a corps of trained soldiers, and by the corps which had appeared at Mézières, and had been brought back after a skilful retreat ; and though these arrangements were rude and imperfect, the strength of the city to resist attack was infinitely greater than Moltke had supposed. Sorties began to be made by degrees ; these, though always repulsed, were not contemptible ; the armament of the forts was completed ; redoubts and entrenchments rose at many points to strengthen and to perfect the zone of defence ; the citizens, warlike in all ages, though in peace addicted to pleasure and ease, acquired gradually something like discipline ; the materials at least of armies were formed, and Paris assumed the aspect of a huge fortified camp, with a garrison certainly immense in numbers. Moltke took pains to secure his position; he tacitly admitted that he had made a mistake in marching on the capital without having his communications or his base assured, and with forces comparatively small; but he held his ground with determined constancy; he summoned reinforcements to head-quarters, and several corps were employed in besieging Strasbourg and other strongholds on the way from the frontier, and in overrunning Burgundy and Franche Comté. The front and lines of the invasion were thus strengthened; and, though time had passed, the submission of France was held to be a fact of the immediate future. The German chief was to be again deceived, as many warriors had been before, in his estimate of a people, great and heroic, despite of many national faults and failings. It is all very well for the Prussian Staff to sneer at Gambetta, as it has done in its book; but he was a man of great powers, if of real shortcomings; and he was but the most striking figure of millions of Frenchmen. A great and sudden national rising took place; it was more spontaneous than that of 1793; in an incredibly short time 250,000 men were in arms to resist the German hosts; and by making use of the resources of France for war—old soldiers, troops in depôts, and reserves—vast arrays were mustered, which at least contained the elements of real military power. These levies, of course, were bad soldiers, but they were formidable in numbers and in aptitude for war; and, whatever may be said, the position of Moltke had become critical as October was closing; the German armies were, for the most part, engaged on the investment of Paris and to the east of Metz; they were conquerers, and had all the power of success; but they were exposed to attack from within and without at the centres to which they were, as it were, bound; and they were in the midst of an immense insurrection spreading all round.

At this conjuncture, a great disaster showed that Fortune was still most adverse to France. Bazaine had been shut up since Gravelotte at Metz; he had kept his army almost inactive, and he had made no real effort to break the investment. I cannot examine the crooked intrigues in which he played an ignoble part;

but he surrendered the great fortress on the 28th of October, and the world beheld the most disgraceful capitulation ever known in war. Even on his pitiful system of passive defence, the Marshal did not nearly do his duty; the place could have held out a fortnight longer, and the respite would have been of extreme importance. The First and Second Armies were now set free to take part in the great invasion; several corps were sent to the north, to crush levies formed in Normandy and other provinces. One was despatched to support the siege; and the remainder, under Prince Frederick Charles, held the tract between the heads of the Seine and Burgundy. The grasp of the Germans on France was thus greatly strengthened; yet the position of Moltke was so unsafe that it was endangered by a single trifling reverse. An army, partly composed of good troops, but in the main of improvised levies, had been assembled south of the Loire; it had been placed in the hands of D'Aurelle, a veteran of real organizing skill, and in a few weeks it numbered 60,000 men, and had acquired something like military worth and power. A Bavarian detachment, perhaps 20,000 strong, and a division under the Grand-Duke of Mecklenburg, sent off to put down insurrection in the west, were the only hostile forces between this large mass of Frenchmen and the lines round Paris; and D'Aurelle, aided by a young chief, Chanzy, who was to prove that France had yet real captains, resolved to attack the Bavarians and to retake Orleans, which had fallen into the enemy's hands. The Army of the Loire broke up from its camps, and crossed the river in the first days in November; it fell on the Bavarians near the little town of Coulmiers. Had the orders of Chanzy been well carried out, and a turning movement been completed in time, the invaders must have been utterly routed; but, as it was, they were beaten with loss; and they were compelled to fall back on the roads to Paris, abandoning Orleans and the adjoining region.

When this intelligence arrived, unfeigned alarm prevailed at the German head-quarters at Versailles; the besiegers were threatened by an army of relief, and by the unknown multitudes of armed men in Paris; and disseminated as they were on an immense circumference, they were in a situation of no common peril. Moltke made up his mind, as became a true chief; he despatched pressing orders to Prince Frederick Charles to hasten to the capital by forced marches; and, like Bonaparte before Mantua—a Journal, said to be his, alludes to this —he resolved, whatever the result, to raise the siege should the Army of the Loire appear from the south. This single circumstance shows how precarious the position of the Germans had become; and had D'Aurelle boldly followed up his success the consequences to France might have been momentous. Chanzy, it is known, was for the more daring course; Napoleon would have taken it, I cannot doubt; and though it is idle to speculate now, the siege would certainly have been given up and the war would have taken a different turn. D'Aurelle, however, refused to advance; he constructed a great entrenched camp near Orleans; and here he increased and trained his levies, hoping before long to resume the offensive. This, probably, was too great caution; but there were reasons for the step of real weight. Prince Frederick Charles was but a few marches off, and should he reach the flank of the Army of the Loire, on its way to the capital, he would perhaps destroy the best organized force possessed by France. This clearly shows that had Metz resisted, and detained the Prince only a few days longer, the French chief would have had, and perhaps would have seized, an admirable occasion offered by Fortune; and, indeed, a German writer has drily remarked that "the capitulation came in the very nick of time."

The victory of Coulmiers sent a thrill through France, enormously increased the power of Gambetta, and caused levies to flock to the war in thousands. Notwithstanding the fall of Metz, and all that followed from it, the situation of the Germans was still critical; and owing to the undoubted strategic mistake of marching on Paris with too weak a force, their movements had been incoherent, and far from masterly. By the close of November the Great City had formed three armies out of her armed multitudes; and two of them, probably 150,000 strong, had acquired a certain degree of efficiency; the third, perhaps 200,000

men, being only fit to defend the ramparts. I cannot describe the
great sortie which followed ; Ducrot crossed the Marne and carried
two villages, which had been made part of the besiegers' lines ;
but ultimately he was compelled to retreat ; and, in fact, the
effort was doomed to failure, for the zone of investment and the
zone of defence had by this time become all but impregnable, or
could be mastered only by the art of the engineer. The sortie
from Paris was contemporaneous with an advance of the army of
D'Aurelle's northwards ; but here Gambetta unhappily intervened,
and his meddling and presumption did enormous mischief. The
young civilian had done, no doubt, great things, but since Coulmiers, he had become a kind of Dictator—the history of France
has too many examples how foolish hero-worship has such results
—he insisted that the Army of the Loire should make for the
capital, whatever the risk, though Prince Frederick Charles was
near at hand ; and, as he had made that army 150,000 strong, he
refused to believe that there was serious danger. D'Aurelle and
Chanzy protested in vain ; two detached corps of the Army of the
Loire were directed against Prince Frederick Charles, and were
easily defeated by an inferior force ; and the Prince, a chief of a
very high order, made immediate preparations for a great counterstroke. The Grand Duke and the Bavarians had been approaching ; he quickly united these forces to his own, and he bore down
in irresistible strength on the army, mainly of recruits, opposed to
him. The centre of the Army of the Loire was broken ; its wings
fell off in eccentric retreat ; one part was driven across the river,
and the triumphant invaders re-entered Orleans, having gained
rapid and complete success. By the first days of December it had
become apparent that Paris could not burst the chain cast around
her ; and the army had been shattered which had been employed,
unwisely at the moment, as an army of relief.

The prospect for France was dark and mournful ; but light shone
at one point on the gloomy scene. D'Aurelle had been unjustly dismissed by Gambetta ; and the part of his defeated army which had
crossed the Loire had been placed in the hands of Bourbaki, the
chief of the late Imperial Guard. Chanzy, however, commanded the

remaining part; and a series of operations followed which show that he had real genius in war. He was attacked by the Grand Duke in all the flush of victory; but he had been reinforced by Gambetta's orders; he took a strong position, covering both his flanks; and then with true insight he assumed the offensive, essential in the case of French soldiers; and, on the whole, he obtained some success. Prince Frederick Charles now fiercely turned against him; he concentrated all his available forces; but Chanzy made a magnificent stand; and his conduct deserves the very highest praise. Perceiving that the relief of Paris should be the true object of the French armies in the field, he fell back from the Loire to the Sarthe, drawing toward the capital with great skill; and in this he showed that he was a real strategist. Nor was he less admirable as a tactician; he continually, in retreat, took an offensive attitude; he turned defensive positions to the best account, and he contrived that the superiority of the French rifle should tell with full effect on the advancing enemy. Prince Frederick Charles pursued in vain; Chanzy made good his way to Le Mans; he was nearer to Paris than when he had left the Loire; his army had not been once beaten; and the Germans were not only worn out, but showed signs of demoralization and fear, for thousands had perished to no purpose; the hardships of the winter campaign had been frightful; and it seemed impossible to overcome the enemy.*

A pause in the conflict now occurred, to the astonishment of Europe, still doubtful—a war of races, in which colossal force was confronted by a national rising. The Germans were still, for the most part, victorious; their armies surrounded imprisoned Paris; they had mastered most of the fortresses of France, proved to be of little use in the struggle; and they had made their lines of

---

* Chanzy, a singularly modest and truthful man, gives this account of the state of the Germans after the retreat to Le Mans: "L'ennemi, contenu partout, était devenu de moins en moins entreprenant; il était facile de voir que pas plus que les nôtres, ses troupes n'avaient pas résisté à la fatigue; ses hommes étaient, eux aussi, grandement démoralisés par cette resistance d'une lutte qui se reproduisait constamment, alors qu'ils la croyaient terminée; le désordre se mettait parfois dans ses colonnes malgré sa solide organisation et sa discipline."

operations secure, and had overrun a full third of the country. But Chanzy was in the field unconquered; Faidherbe, a commander of real gifts, had admirably conducted a campaign in the north, attacking the invaders when he saw a chance, and falling back on the strongholds of the Somme; Bourbaki was at the head of a great force, continually increasing, on the Middle Loire; and France had realised her proud boast that she had but "to stamp her foot, and legions would spring from the earth at her bidding." Grave* anxiety was felt at head-quarters at Versailles, spite of noisy boasting of German triumphs; and Moltke, reading the facts with a true general's eye, insisted on having large reinforcements to strengthen the wearied and thinned invaders. Troops in tens of thousands from the trained reserves of Germany were called into the field; shrunken regiments and corps were restored in numbers; new corps entered the east of France, and preparations were made on an immense scale to quicken, by a bombardment, the fall of Paris. The organization of the German armies, though strained to the utmost, bore the test; and if the trials of the war had told heavily on the young soldiers who crowded the ranks, a fierce national passion still upheld the invasion. Moltke made excellent use of these new forces. Up to this time, his movements had suffered from the effects of the premature advance on Paris; but the error was now completely rectified, and his dispositions were able in the extreme. Keeping his grasp on the capital with stern tenacity, he so distributed his corps on the theatre of war that a far-spreading external zone of resistance protected the inner zone of investment; and should an attempt, therefore, be made to relieve Paris, he would have a double set of armies to oppose the French and interior lines on the whole circumference. Secure within this circle, he defied the enemy, but he was ready at all points to take a bold offensive, and he eschewed the whole system of mere passive defence. The exertions of France were also prodigious. Independently of the

---

* This message from Berlin, at this juncture, is very significant:—"La position militaire est regardée comme critique dans les cercles bien informés. On a des inquietudes sur l'issue finale de la lutte."

Parisian forces, she had placed 500,000 men in the field, with from
1,800 to 1,400 guns, and history, despite the Prussian staff, will
pronounce this a gigantic effort. These levies, however, were
most inferior troops. They were no match for their trained adversaries; they were not equal to long marches, and at this
supreme moment they were wrongly directed. Chanzy, the
master-spirit of the national defence, saw what the situation was,
and what it required; he appreciated the ability of Moltke's
strategy; but even now he did not despair of success, and in a
despatch, marked with true insight in war, he urged that all the
provincial armies should endeavour to combine and march on the
capital, which, in turn, should fiercely attack the besiegers. This
last effort would, I believe, have failed; but it was the true course
and perfectly conceived; and it was that which Moltke expected
and feared. Unhappily for France, Gambetta rejected the
counsels of her most distinguished soldier, and, giving ear to a
silly theorist, he adopted a plan for the operations at hand, false
in principle and, as facts stood, ruinous. At this moment Werder,
in the east of France, was engaged with his corps in the siege of Belfort; the garrison was making a firm stand; Bourbaki, in command
of his large army, was in the Nivernais, on the verge of Burgundy;
Garibaldi had a motley array near Dijon, and a large army was
ready to march from the south. In this state of affairs, instead of
directing all the forces of France in a march on Paris, Gambetta
resolved to make a great effect to relieve Belfort and to enter
Alsace. For this purpose the collective forces of Bourbaki, Garibaldi, and the south were to join, and the result, it was hoped,
would place the French armies on the communications of the invaders from the Rhine, and would have great and glorious results.
This plan, strikingly resembling those of Carnot in 1793–1794, was,
even in the abstract, misconceived; the detachment to the east of
the French armies would expose and isolate Chanzy on the west,
and even were the communications of the Germans reached, this
would be at a point too remote to relieve Paris, or seriously to
affect the issue of the campaign. But, in the actual state of
affairs, the project was little less than foolishness; the armies in-

tended to relieve Belfort and to attain Alsace were not equal to a great operation of real danger, and the scheme in truth was of much the same kind as that which had led to the catastrophe of Sedan.

In the last days of December, Bourbaki's army set off from the Nivernais to reach Franche Comté. The march of the columns was pitiably slow; the troops suffered terribly from cold and disease; and signs of evil omen had become manifest long before Belfort had been approached. This eccentric movement set the Grand Duke and Prince Frederick Charles completely free to attack Chanzy upon the Sarthe; and the German chiefs, who had had their forces recruited to a very large extent, broke up from Chartres, Nogent le Rotrou, and Orleans, and bore down on the French commander, advancing on an ever narrowing front. Chanzy had detached flying columns to observe the enemy; these fell back as the assailants drew near; and the French army, by the 10th of January, was concentrated within its lines at Le Mans, which had been fortified with skill and care. A fierce and protracted struggle followed; Chanzy, very different from the incapable Bazaine, really did wonders with his raw young troops; but, at nightfall on the 11th, his extreme right was turned by a desperate effort of Prince Frederick Charles. He evacuated Le Mans, and lost thousands of prisoners; but he made good his way to the Mayenne; and here he still kept his foes at bay, having in his retreat drawn nearer Paris. He was still full of hope, and wrote in that sense; but before long a tremendous disaster befell the ill-fated forces of France in the east. Bourbaki was joined by a part of Garibaldi's troops, and by the army moving from the south; and with this force, fully 130,000 strong, he crossed the Ognon, and almost reached Belfort. He was, however, defeated with ease by Werder, with a force very inferior in numbers; and, after one or two fruitless efforts to outmanœuvre his victorious enemy, he fell back baffled, and made for Besançon. Here he gave up his command, and tried to commit suicide; his ruined army continued to retreat, but Moltke saw that his opportunity had come and he turned it to account, with great skill and decision. Three corps were detached from the external zone; Manteuffel, at the head of them, bore down on the enemy; Werder, with part of his corps, pressed forward from Belfort; and Bourbaki's whole army, under its new chief, Clinchant, was surrounded and driven across the Swiss frontier. This was the end of Gambetta's ambitious enterprise, which alike had caused the defeat of Chanzy and had ruined the last hope of success for the provincial armies.

It fared almost as ill with France in the north, on the theatre where Faidherbe conducted the war. That skilful officer had continued the game of harassing the enemy, and falling back; and he had even fought a battle at Bapaume, which he had some right to describe as a victory. But about the middle of January he advanced towards St. Quentin, in the hope, it is supposed, of either relieving Paris, or of making eastward towards Bourbaki's army. Moltke sent off a corps from the zone of investment, and defeated him with considerable loss; and, though he effected his retreat to Lille, his forces were for the time paralyzed. The military strength of France outside Paris was thus rendered almost powerless; Moltke had made the best use of his interior lines, on a great and complex field of manœuvre; and the false direction given to Bourbaki's army had practically decided the contest in the field. The proud capital alone remained; and invincible famine was already at hand. In the first days of January the bombardment began; for fully three weeks shot and shell crashed through all parts of the beleaguered city; but no impression was made on the *enceinte* or the forts, and still less on the great mass of the citizens. The attack, in fact, altogether failed; it does no credit to the German Engineers, and it attests Moltke's dislike of Frenchmen; and it must be condemned as barbarous warfare, for it was known that Paris must ere long surrender. Towards the end of the month the end came; a last sortie for the honour of arms was easily repulsed with great slaughter; and on the 28th of January 1871 the capitulation was signed. German horsemen defiled under the Arch of the Star, a monument to the Grand Army, as the Guards of Napoleon had passed through Berlin; the tricolour has been plucked down from Metz and Strasbourg;

and France mourns the calamitous Peace of Frankfort. Yet the
defence of Paris, and the efforts made by the improvised armies of
Chanzy and Faidherbe, were exploits worthy of a great nation ; in
the hour of misfortune France may say, like her king, that she
has not lost honour ; the resistance she made, all things considered,
was grander than that of 1798, and it has redeemed the ignominy
of Metz and Sedan.

The success of the conquerors in this gigantic war is the
greatest, perhaps, recorded in history. The Imperial Army of
France was carried away captive; her improvised armies were
nearly half destroyed ; her fortresses yielded one after another ;
her capital held out, but succumbed to famine. The theme is a
fine idol for the worshippers of success ; and Moltke has been held
up to the admiration of mankind as the greatest military genius
in the annals of war. Yet, if we calmly examine the course of the
contest, we perceive that the operations of the German chief do
not reveal one grand strategic conception, and are characterized by
several grave errors ; they exhibit science, decision, and strength of
character, and perfect execution of the thoughts of others, not
originality, or "the faultlessness" claimed for them. Moltke—
and this does not detract from his fame—owed much to his foes,
and much to fortune ; Bazaine and MacMahon, in different ways,
sink to the level of the Soubises and Clermonts ; the fall of Metz was
a godsend to Germany ; but Chanzy was a warrior of real powers ;
he kept the issue of the struggle long doubtful, and had he had the
supreme control of the forces of France, it is impossible to say
what might not have happened. Some of the lessons taught by
the war are commonplace ; well-organized armies, of overwhelming
strength, defeat armies inferior in every respect; trained and
disciplined troops beat raw levies ; disaster is all but certain to
follow when the simplest rules of the military art are disregarded
for supposed reasons of State. Two great facts, however, require
special notice ; the German armies are the most formidable which
have ever appeared in the modern world ; there is an element of
weakness in their young soldiers, but they represent a mighty race
in arms, ready at any moment to march on to conquest ; and this

has been the result of years of training. On the other hand, the national rising of France, after Metz and Sedan, was a noble movement; it was marked by heroic courage and self-sacrifice; and yet it failed, and probably was doomed to fail, though the resources of France for war are enormous, and the French are a people of born soldiers.

I have come to the last of my Great Commanders; what is Moltke's place in that august succession? It is difficult to catch a true likeness of a figure not in the perspective of Time, and whose career belongs to the history of the day. Moltke has many, I think, of the gifts of Frederick; he is a thoroughly accomplished and educated man; he has extraordinary force of application and thought; his perseverance deserves the highest praise; and though he has not been tried by the test of ill-fortune, he has evidently the tenacity and firmness of the Prussian king. Like Frederick, however, he wants supreme genius and the imaginative power of the greatest chiefs; but he is far superior to Frederick in all that relates to the large combinations and movements of war, though probably his inferior on the field of battle. It is his special characteristic that he was one of the first to see what are the new conditions of war in this age, and that he turned them to the very best account; the Prussian Army and that of the lesser German States have been, in a great measure, created by him; and Moltke, I conceive, has "organized victory" more thoroughly than has ever before been seen. His place as a strategist is more doubtful; his countrymen have called him "the great strategist," but this is the exaggeration of national sympathy; and in this sphere of the art, I certainly think he holds an inferior rank to Turenne, and he has not even approached the height of Napoleon. We miss originality in his conceptions of war. If he really directed the converging movement into Bohemia, in 1866, whatever have been the modifications of the art, this was inconsistent with its true principles; his advance on Paris was a distinct mistake; and in his operations at Metz we see many errors which Bazaine possibly might have made disastrous. His peculiar strategic merit is that he can work out to perfection accepted

views, and improve upon the ideas of others ; but in this there is
not the masterly power seen in the campaigns of 1674 and 1675,
of 1796 and of 1800. Still Moltke is a real chief of the grand
school of Napoleon ; he can move large armies on a wide theatre
with remarkable forethought and scientific skill ; his marches
against the army of Châlons, and the army of Bourbaki, are very
fine, and he made the best use of his interior lines in the final
operations around Paris. His merits as a tactician are less easy
to estimate ; in the case of the immense battles of the present day,
the real head of an army can do no more than make arrangements
of a general kind ; but if he directed Gravelotte, it was ill-directed,
though it is well known he condemned Steinmetz; and in theory
he is a master of modern tactics. Moltke seems to have a cold
and passionless nature ; like Wellington, he has commanded the
respect of officers and men but not their devotion ; Prince
Frederick Charles was the real hero, in the eyes of the German
soldiery in 1870--71 ; and this remarkable chief possessed in a high
degree the peculiar gifts of his greatest ancestor. It is astonishing,
however, if we bear in mind that Moltke was in his sixty-seventh
year when he first commanded an army in the field, that he should
have achieved what he has achieved. He is a great commander,
beyond dispute, and as an administrator in war he has never been
excelled.

THE CAMPAIGN OF 1815.

THE CAMPAIGN OF 1815.

CHAPTER I.

I PURPOSE, in this and a subsequent chapter, to describe the main
features of the Campaign of 1815, and to endeavour to pronounce
a fair judgment upon it. Of the interest of the subject it is
needless to speak; this grand passage of arms will attract the
attention of history to it in the same degree as the contest decided
on the field of Zama, or the last struggle between Pompey and
Cæsar. Yet this is not my chief reason for attempting this
sketch; I venture to think, though a large literature has grown
up round the theme of Waterloo, that there is still room for an
impartial study, brief though it be, of the leading incidents of this
ever-memorable and most decisive conflict. Many causes, in
fact, have concurred to obscure the truth respecting the Campaign of 1815, and to prevent a just estimate being formed of
it. On some points our knowledge is still imperfect; passion
and prejudice have distorted the facts, on several others of the
first importance; and commentators on Waterloo, even including
the chief actors in the drama, have, in most instances, either
made palpable and grave mistakes, or have applied a kind of
criticism to the course of events, essentially, and from the
nature of the case, fallacious. The narratives of Napoleon,
in some of their parts, bear the ineffaceable marks of his genius,
but they abound in serious errors of detail, and in places they are
far from just or honest. The apology of Wellington, though the

most truthful of men, written as it was in far advanced age, is not trustworthy in many respects; and all that has emanated from the Prussian staff is by no means accurate, or even always candid. As for historians, Thiers has composed a romance confuted by the evidence in most important points; and the same may be said of the host of Frenchmen who, like him, have slavishly followed Napoleon. We have had a like class of writers in England; from Siborne to Hooper it has been the fashion to describe the Duke as faultless in 1815, in plain defiance of unquestionable facts; and Dutch, Belgian, and German authors have equally erred in claiming praise for chiefs of their races beyond their merits. Then we have commentators, of whom Charras is by far the ablest and most perfect specimen, partisans who test operations of war by an impossible standard of mere theory, and who, in this way, have succeeded in making the greatest chiefs seem inferior men; and Chesney's *Essay*, though in parts excellent, is by no means free from this most unsound criticism. Passing by General Hamley's valuable sketch, I believe Jomini's account of Waterloo to be, even now, the best extant narrative; but it is necessarily wanting in many respects, in the information obtained since his day. I shall try to follow, in these chapters, the method which, in an inquiry of this kind, will most probably lead to just conclusions; that is, I shall rely* only on contemporaneous documents, the genuineness of which is not doubtful; and I shall endeavour to judge of events as they happened, from the point of view of those who took part in them, and not by the mere abstract rules of strategy.

I have no space to discuss the arrangements made beforehand by Napoleon to meet the League of Europe in 1815; but they were most able and even wonderful, and the detraction of Charras is false and unjust. The memories of an immortal campaign would have caused the Emperor to defend France on the Marne and the Seine, with fortified Paris a pivot for his operations and a vast entrenched camp; but the state of opinion made this plan impossible,

---

* My limits preclude me from citing extracts from these authorities. But I shall, when it is required, indicate them; and I hope I shall accurately express their meaning and purport.

and he resolved to assume a daring offensive. His design, resembling in its main features the strategy which led to Ulm and Austerlitz, may be left with confidence to judges of the art, and bears the clear stamp of his transcendent genius. A million of armed men were advancing on France from the Scheldt, the Rhine, the Oder, and the Po; but the hosts of the Allies were widely apart, and at unequal distances from the points of attack; and the extreme right of the vast front of invasion, composed of the armies of Blücher and Wellington, was isolated, and close to the French frontier. It was possible, therefore, to make a sudden spring on this detached part of the Coalition's forces, to surprise and to overthrow it in detail; and if decisive success were achieved, there were reasons to believe that Napoleon's triumph might bring the war at once to a close. The situation, besides, of the menaced armies in Belgium invited a daring attack, even though made with an inferiority of force. They were disseminated along a wide front, from Ghent to Liège, a hundred miles in length, and from thirty-five to fifty miles in depth, from Brussels to the edge of French territory; they were scattered in divisions, covering the roads that led, in many lines, from the frontier of France; and two days, at least, were required before they could even nearly concentrate on a given field of battle. They were thus vulnerable at all points, and the strategy which placed them in such positions has long ago been condemned as false; but many and decisive reasons concurred to induce Napoleon to select their centre, and the space where their inner flanks met, as the first spot on which to direct his efforts.

Were he to assail the Allies on either wing, he would press their armies against each other, and favour rather than retard their junction, the very event to be most avoided; and, besides, they were in greater strength on these lines than at those points of their centre at which their separate forces came in contact. Again, Wellington was based on the sea, from Brussels and Ghent to Ostend and Antwerp; the base of Blücher was the Rhine and Cologne. Were their centre, therefore, fiercely attacked, and their armies compelled to diverge from each other, the probability was

that each chief would fall back on his proper base, as happened in
the campaign of 1794, and that the Emperor would be able to
interpose and, perhaps, to overwhelm their recoiling forces.
Other considerations combined to determine the purpose of the
most profound of generals. Blücher was known to be hasty and
bold to a fault; the genius of Wellington was circumspect and
cautious; and Napoleon calculated—rightly, as the event proved—
that should he fall suddenly on the allied centre, Blücher would
hurry forward to repel the attack, and that Wellington would be
slow to advance; and this single circumstance, it was not unlikely,
would give the Imperial chief an admirable chance to beat in detail
his divided enemies. The peculiarities of the theatre, too,
encouraged an attempt against the allied centre. At each side of
this point the French frontier at this time ran into Belgian
territory, especially from Valenciennes to Rocroy; a great main
road by Charleroi to Brussels nearly traversed the space where the
Allies met, and led into the heart of the Belgic provinces; the
communication between the Allies depended chiefly on one lateral
road, extending from Nivelles to Namur eastwards, and behind
this lay a difficult region of hills and marshes watered by the
Dyle, and unfavourable to the junction of divided armies. Should
Napoleon, therefore, advance on this path, he would have the
shortest line of attack from France; he would have an avenue into
the midst of the camps of his foes, and conducting him to the
Belgian capital; and should he once be able to force his adversaries from their main point of contact, the Nivelles and Namur
road, they would find it no easy task to reunite, and they would
probably be placed in serious peril.

The Allies were thus to be struck at their centre, and their
separated hosts to be rent asunder as Beaulieu and Colli, twenty
years before, when Bonaparte was first revealed to Fortune, were
assailed from the Genoese seaboard and driven in eccentric
retreat from Piedmont. An untoward event at the outset increased
the difficulties of carrying out a plan, which may be pronounced
one of the most brilliant even of Napoleon's marvellous career.
The united armies of Blücher and Wellington were about 224,000

strong; the Emperor reckoned that 150,000 men were required to assure his operations success; and it may confidently be said that, had he had this force, he would, humanly speaking, have been victorious, spite of the misadventures and faults of the Campaign. A sudden rising in La Vendée, however, deprived him of 20,000 good troops; but, though this added largely to his adverse chances, his position was such that he still resolved to persevere in his audacious project. The execution of his profound design was admirable, and, indeed, all but perfect. The divisions intended to make the movement were encamped along the northern frontier of France, or thrown back southward almost to the capital; and the problem was how to draw together these widely separated bodies of men, and to concentrate them at the appointed spot, without interference on the part of the enemy, and without even his knowledge, if this were possible. The operation was accomplished with success, largely through that remarkable skill in stratagem which was one of Napoleon's distinctive gifts. While the corps on the frontier, their march concealed by different expedients with consummate art, were collected together from the vast distance which extends from Lille and Valenciennes to Metz, the corps in the interior were moved forward by degrees, and the united masses were brought into contact, at the points indicated by their great head and leader. On the evening of the 14th June 1815, nearly 128,000 Frenchmen, including 22,000 cavalry, and with 350 guns, had effected their junction, on a narrow front, on the very verge of the plains of Belgium, a few miles from the banks of the Sambre, and converging towards the great main road, running, we have seen, from Charleroi to Brussels; and the concentration, if not quite complete, was, in the circumstances in which it was made, one of the finest known in the annals of war. The Emperor's left wing, about 45,000 strong, composed of the 2nd and 1st Corps, in the experienced hands of Reille and D'Erlon, was near the Sambre at Leez and Solre; the centre, nearly 68,000 men, comprising the Imperial Guard, the 3rd Corps of Vandamme, the 6th Corps, with Lobau as its chief, and the cavalry reserves, under the command of Grouchy, lay in the country around Beaumont; and the right wing, the 4th Corps, led by the brilliant Gérard, and numbering perhaps 15,000 soldiers, was, in part, at Philippeville, its appointed station, a part, however, being half a march distant, the single detachment that had not fulfilled its mission. The purpose of Napoleon was to conduct these forces, assembled at his bidding as if by magic, at daybreak against the enemy in his camps; to cross the Sambre, to enter Charleroi, holding the main road to Brussels before referred to; and having taken possession of the adjoining country, and overpowered, if possible, any foes in his path, to press on to the road from Nivelles to Namur, to occupy on it Quatre Bras and Sombreffe, the two points where the allied commanders would probably attempt to effect their junction, and having attained this position of vantage, to interpose between their divided armies, completing the first act in the drama of the Campaign.

Having made a spirit-stirring address to his troops, Napoleon set his army in motion at about 3 A.M. on the 15th of June. The left wing was not long in crossing the Sambre; soon after mid-day the corps of Reille, that of D'Erlon being some miles behind, had passed the bridge which spans the stream near the town of Marchiennes—it had been left intact by the enemy—and the great French columns had easily pressed back a detachment of the Prussian corps of Ziethen, in observation along the frontier. The march of the centre was greatly delayed; an advance-guard of cavalry, with a weak support of foot, entered Charleroi, indeed, and was over the Sambre a short time after the left wing—the bridge at Charleroi, too, was not broken—but an accident had kept back Vandamme; and it was past three in the afternoon before a part of the Guard, the 3rd Corps, and part of the reserve of cavalry had made their way out of the narrow streets of Charleroi, Lobau and much of the cavalry being still in the rear. The progress of the right wing was even more retarded; it did not move until a part at least of its backward detachment had come into line; the march of the troops was, in some measure, checked by the villainous treason of Bourmont; the country to be traversed was close and difficult; and it was about five before it had passed the Sambre,

—J. Marshman.

"THE IDOL OF THE SOLDIER'S SOUL."—Byron.

even in part, across the bridge at Châtelet—unbroken like those of Marchiennes and Charleroi—more than half the corps being on the southern bank of the river. These delays enabled the bulk of Ziethen's forces—their head-quarters had been at Charleroi—to effect their retreat before the advancing French, and frequently to arrest the heads of their columns. The Prussian commander had manœuvred ably, though he had greatly erred in not destroying the bridges; Ziethen made good his way to Fleurus, with a loss of not more than 2,000 men, any hope which Napoleon may have entertained of surprising and crushing his isolated corps having been at an early hour frustrated. Mainly, too, from this cause, the Emperor failed to seize the two points of Quatre Bras and Sombreffe, on the cross road from Nivelles to Namur, which had been the object of his march on the 15th; and the day, as Charras has said, was, in part, incomplete.

Nevertheless, Napoleon had already attained considerable and most promising success; and he might even now reckon on approaching victory. As evening closed one division of the left wing, supported by a large body of horsemen, was at Frasnes, quite near Quatre Bras; and, in fact, it had been prevented from gaining that point only by a demonstration made by the young Prince of Saxe Weimar, anticipating his orders by several hours. The remainder of the left wing, now under the command of Ney— the Marshal had reached Charleroi some time in the afternoon—was extended from Gosselies to Jumet, holding the great road from Charleroi to Brussels, and from ten to thirteen miles from Quatre Bras, a single division approaching the centre; and a march of a few hours could place it in force on one of the chief points of the allied line of junction. As for the centre, Lobau, and part of the Guard and of the heavy cavalry were still near Charleroi; but Vandamme and the great body of the Guard and of the cavalry reserve were not far from Fleurus, a few miles only from the point of Sombreffe, by which Blücher would unite with Wellington, and filling the country back to Charleroi; while the right wing of Gérard was at a half march's distance. The main body of the French army, about 100,000 strong, had thus attained positions

21

near the allied centre, which already made it difficult in the
extreme for Blücher and Wellington to combine their forces along
the road from Nivelles to Namur ; if the Emperor had not cut
his foes in two, he threatened their communication in a most
dangerous way; he was master of the main road from Charleroi
to Brussels almost up to the point of Quatre Bras ; and notwithstanding several mishaps, he had not 30,000 men in his rear. He
had every reason to assert, as he did, that if not wholly, he was,
in the main, satisfied with the results of the operations of the day.

What had been the dispositions of the allied chiefs, while
Napoleon had gained this immense advantage ? Neither Blücher
nor Wellington seriously thought that their adversary would
venture to invade Belgium, for his inferiority of force was well
known to them ; and Wellington was convinced that the Emperor
would await the attack of the Coalition, as he had awaited it the
year before. This partly explains, though it does not justify, the
dissemination of their scattered forces ; and, as has been said, it
is now conceded that this strategy was essentially faulty. They
admitted, however, that an attack was possible, and everything
tends to show that Blücher conceived that an attack on his centre
and left was the most probable ; while the Duke certainly believed
that the blow would be most likely directed against his right. As
an attempt, however, against their centre might be made, they had
made provision for this contingency ; and it had been arranged
between them that should Napoleon advance by Charleroi on the
great road to Brussels, striking at the point of contact of their
inner flanks, each should concentrate in force on the road from
Nivelles to Namur, holding the two positions of Quatre Bras and
Sombreffe, which they felt assured they could occupy in time,
though the mass of their armies was far distant, and Quatre Bras
and Sombreffe were but a march from the frontier. These calcu-
lations might have proved correct in the case of a foe of ordinary
powers ; but in that of a consummate master of his art they were
pregnant, as Charras has said, with danger. The Duke, however,
and Blücher were not surprised, as has been alleged, in the true
sense of the word, though they were out-generalled by Napoleon's

movement. As early as the afternoon of the 14th of June,
Ziethen had learned that the French had approached the frontier,
and he immediately despatched the news to Blücher at his head-
quarters, miles off at Namur. The Prussian army was about
118,000 strong, including 12,000 horsemen and 312 guns; but
its four corps were widely apart: the first, that of Ziethen, being
around Charleroi; the second, that of Pirch, in camp at Namur;
the third, under Thielmann, to the south-east at Ciney; the fourth
led by Bülow far away at Liège; and it was all but impossible
that the collective mass could be united on the road from Nivelles
to Namur before nightfall on the 16th of June. The ardent
veteran, however, eager for the fray, at about midnight on the 14th,
when Napoleon's advance might be presumed, ordered a general
concentration of his army on Sombreffe, as had been agreed between
himself and Wellington; the Prussian chiefs gave proof of extreme
activity; and while Ziethen, who, as we have seen, had skilfully
retarded the march of the French, fell back to Fleurus, and thence
to Sombreffe, Pirch, by the night of the 15th of June, had got near
Mazy, four miles from Sombreffe, with three of the four divisions
of his corps, the fourth being a short way in the rear; while
Thielmann had attained Namur, half a march from the intended
point of junction. Three corps, therefore, of Blücher's army
could be at Sombreffe on the 16th by noon, ready to encounter
the shock of Napoleon, and doubtless expecting support from
Wellington. The corps of Bülow, however, could not be up in
time; notwithstanding his energy, Blücher had assembled only
three-fourths of his army; and, in the actual position of affairs,
could he confidently rely on the aid of his colleague?

At this moment, indeed, the French outposts were close to the
allied line of junction, and Wellington had made scarcely a sign of
moving. The army of the Duke was about 106,000 men—of these
14,000, or nearly so, were cavalry—with 196 guns; and it was
spread over even a larger space than that of the veteran Prussian
warrior. A motley array of many races, it had been hastily formed
into three masses; the first corps, under the Prince of Orange,
scattered over an arc from Genappe to Mons, and covering two of

21 *

the main roads from the frontier; the second, in the skilful hands of Hill, extending westward as far as the Scheldt, from near Braine le Comte to Ath, Leuze, and Oudenarde, observing, too, the approaches from France; and the third, or the reserve, at Brussels, a long distance off, round the head-quarters of Wellington. A fraction only of the first corps was thus near the road from Nivelles to Namur; the dispositions of the Duke were, in truth, made to protect his right and his communications with the sea, and time was required before he could send anything like a strong force to the support of Blücher. By nightfall on the 15th, when the heads of the French column were but a few miles from Quatre Bras and Sombreffe, the army of Wellington had scarcely stirred, and it was some hours afterwards before the British chief set it in motion in the direction of Blücher, and that, too, slowly, and as if with reluctance. The Duke had heard from Ziethen in the afternoon of the day, that the French were crossing the Sambre, and near Charleroi, and the intelligence was subsequently confirmed by Blücher; but thinking that Napoleon was making a feint, and believing that his own right was menaced, he waited upon his enemy's movements, and merely ordered his lieutenants to be in readiness. As is well known, indeed, he went to the historical ball given at Brussels by the Duchess of Richmond; and it was after ten at night, when he had been made aware that Napoleon had mastered and passed Charleroi, that he took anything like a decisive step. Hill and the Prince of Orange were now directed to concentrate their troops, and to move to their left; but they were to hold a line from Enghien to Nivelles; the reserve at Brussels was still kept back, and nothing like a considerable force was to be drawn towards the allied points of junction, or to be so placed as to approach Blücher. The wide interval, in fact, from Nivelles to Quatre Bras, and thence by the main road to Sombreffe—the communication with the Prussians—was to be left uncovered, and whatever mere partisans may urge, there is not a word to be said for this strategy. Happily for the Allies, subordinates of the Duke interpreted the situation better than their chief. Saxe-Weimar, we have seen, had advanced to Quatre Bras, and checked Ney in his forward march, and

ENGLAND'S HOPE, 1815.

Perponcher, a general in the Dutch service, ere long had occupied that most important point, though he held it with a single division only, which could scarcely offer a prolonged resistance. By midnight Wellington gave further orders for a general concentration to his left, and the reserve from Brussels was directed towards Nivelles; but these orders were extremely late, and it had become most improbable that the British commander would be able to master the road from Nivelles to Namur, even now almost in the grasp of his enemy, to advance along it by Quatre Bras, and approaching Sombreffe, to unite with Blücher. It was, indeed, far more likely that the divided armies would be attacked, and beaten in detail.

The previsions on which Napoleon had formed the plan of his campaign had thus been realised, up to this point, in their main particulars. The divergence of the bases of the allied chiefs had left their centre weak and ill-joined. It was now, after the retreat of Ziethen, connected only by a thread of vedettes; it was within easy distance of the French army; and should it be attacked, and cut in two, Blücher and Wellington would fall back, and probably separate, happy if they escaped a disastrous reverse. Blücher, again, had rushed forward to confront his enemy, leaving 30,000 of his troops far off; Wellington had paused, hesitated, and not approached his colleague, and an admirable chance had been thus afforded to the General of Arcola and Rivoli. The allied commanders, in fact, whatever may be said by apologists, and by worshippers of success, had laid themselves open to a terrible stroke, and though Napoleon is a most exacting critic, I can see no answer to his profound remark, that, out-manœuvred as they had been on the 15th, Blücher ought not to have made for Sombreffe "already under the guns of his enemy," and Wellington ought not to have tried to join him, but that both chiefs should have endeavoured to unite on a line, in the rear, between Wavre and Waterloo. Their strategy, in short, was bad, and they only escaped defeat owing to a set of accidents in which fortune baffled their mighty adversary.

We have reached the morning of the 16th of June, and we turn to the operations of the French army, and to the direction given it by its Imperial leader. Napoleon had returned to Charleroi on the night of the 15th, to "take repose for his wearied frame"; his physical strength had been long declining; and possibly even on the first day of the campaign, he began to give proof of those failing bodily powers which was certainly exhibited before the contest closed.* Yet, though murmurs were heard in the French camp, both Jomini and Charras seem to me to reason too much on mere theory, and to fall into the error of judging only by the event, when they charge the Emperor with sluggishness and delay in his conduct on the morning of the 16th. A large part of the French army was still in the rear; Napoleon did not and could not certainly know the exact positions of the allied armies; he was about to thrust himself between two hostile masses, each nearly equal to his own force in numbers; and though he could have done more had he been omniscient, the circumstances required caution in any forward movement. Be this as it may, his orders were given, at Charleroi, at about 8 A.M.; and if they were founded on wrong assumptions, they proved his perfect knowledge of his art, and were admirably adapted to the events that happened. These orders, contained in four despatches, two from the Emperor to Ney and Grouchy, and two from Soult, the Chief of the Staff, to the same generals, prove that Napoleon did not believe he would be seriously opposed on that day; he thought that his left wing would easily pass Quatre Bras, and that his centre and right wing would easily pass Sombreffe; and he conceived that it was not improbable that he would enter Brussels on the morning of the 17th. This calculation was, no doubt, false; but it was founded on the true strategic view that Wellington and Blücher would not now endeavour to make a stand at Quatre Bras and Sombreffe, on the threatened road from Nivelles to Namur; and what Charras and others fail to point out, but what the real student of war will dwell on, is that, ignorant as he was of the actual facts, the

---

* Napoleon had shown signs of illness in the campaigns of 1812, 1813, and 1814, and was in bad health in 1815. Mr. Dorsey Gardener in his useful work on Waterloo, pp. 34–36, has adduced ample evidence to prove that Napoleon was unwell and out of sorts on the 16th, 17th, and 18th June; and this, I know, was remarked by Soult on the morning of Waterloo.

dispositions made by Napoleon were in accordance with sound principles, and fitted to meet the situation of affairs. Ney, in command of the left wing, was ordered to advance, and go beyond Quatre Bras, concentrating the 2nd and 1st Corps, supported by Kellerman's heavy cavalry, and holding the great road from Charleroi to Brussels; while Grouchy, entrusted in the Emperor's brief absence, with the centre, the right wing, and the cavalry reserves, was to pass Sombreffe, and to attain Gembloux, attacking any enemy in his path, and to stand on a parallel line with Ney. As the army, however, should be well united, Ney was enjoined to detach a division to Marbais, a village near Sombreffe and Gembloux, to give support if required to the centre and right wing; and the Emperor added that, at about noon, he would be on the spot to assume the supreme command.*

Napoleon's orders despatched from Charleroi reached the chiefs of the 2nd and 1st corps, spread, we have seen, from Gosselies to Jumet, on the great road from Charleroi to Brussels, at about 10 A.M. or a little before; they reached Ney at Frasnes at about 11 A.M.; and as† Reille and D'Erlon had been directed to

---

* After the publication of these despatches, and of other documents, especially those collected by the son of Ney, we must reject Napoleon's statement that Ney received " positive orders," to occupy Quatre Bras on the evening of the 15th, and to advance from that place, " at daybreak," on the 16th. Still, I think Napoleon indicated a movement of the kind to his lieutenant on the 15th; the *Moniteur* of the 18th contains a despatch of the 15th, which announces that " Ney had his head-quarters at Quatre Bras." The point, however, is not of very great importance; had the Emperor's orders of 8 A.M. on the 16th been intelligently and rapidly carried out, Ney would have done all that was required, and Napoleon would have gained decisive success.

† The failure of Ney to attain Quatre Bras, and to send a division to Marbais, before the arrival of a sufficient part of Wellington's army to arrest the Marshal's progress, saved Blücher from destruction on the 16th of June, and was fraught with the most momentous consequences, and the truth on this subject has been studiously concealed. Charras and the detractors of Napoleon, eager to condemn the Emperor, and English writers, desirous of hiding what might have happened through Wellington's tardiness, concur in insinuating that Reille and D'Erlon were not to begin their movement until they had received their orders from Ney, who would have to send despatches from Frasnes back to them, and contend, therefore, that Ney could not have been in great force at Quatre Bras before 3.30 or 4.30 P.M., at which time he was fully engaged with Wellington, and could not even master Quatre Bras. This, however, is a complete mistake : Reille and D'Erlon have acknowledged that they received the order for their movement from the aide-de-camp at about 10 A.M.; and, in fact, Ney could have swept all before him at Quarte Bras soon after 1 P.M., and have made the detachment to Marbais, had the order been properly carried out. See the letters of D'Erlon, of Reille, and of

advance by the aide-de-camp who carried the Imperial message; Ney might have been in possession of Quatre Bras at about 1 or 1.30 P.M.; at the head of 45,000 men, and might have crushed Perponcher's feeble division, at the time standing alone at that place. In that event Ney could have seized Quatre Bras, in conformity with the Imperial orders, and have made the required detachment on Marbais; and had this been done, the 16th of June would certainly have witnessed a second Jena. We pass from the French left wing to the centre and right wing, directed, we have seen, at the time, on Sombreffe, and intended to prolong their march to Gembloux. Napoleon had reached Fleurus by 11 A.M.; the Guard, the 3rd and 4th Corps, with most of the cavalry reserves, for a moment under the command of Grouchy, had passed, at about 1 P.M., into the Emperor's hands; the division detached from the left wing on the 15th had come into line, and Lobau, with the 6th corps, was marching from the rear. By this time Blücher stood in the path of the French in an advance on Gembloux; he was in force on the road from Nivelles to Namur, and his three corps held a formidable line, extending from Sombreffe almost to Marbais, and fronted by the villages of Ligny, St. Amand, and La Haye. Napoleon seems to have disbelieved at first that his adversary could be in strength on the field; but at 2 P.M. he sent a message to Ney enjoining him to complete the movement on Marbais, and to fall on the flank and rear of Blücher, and at the same moment the Emperor marched his army from Fleurus against his enemy.

The armies opposed were about equal in force, if we reckon the approaching corps of Lobau; the French being inferior in numbers— 78,000 to 87,000 men—but having more guns and more numerous horsemen; but the superiority of Napoleon's tactics gave him the advantage almost from the first moment. The villages, indeed, before the Prussian front proved defences of remarkable strength, and were taken and re-taken with little results; but Napoleon occupied a full third of Blücher's forces by merely threatening his communications to his left. The French batteries caused frightful

Durutte, quoted by the Prince La Tour D'Auvergne in his book on Waterloo, p. 149, p. 170, and p. 171.

destruction in the Prussian reserves, which had been recklessly exposed ; and while Blücher brought most of his troops into action, the Emperor husbanded his men for a final stroke. The battle, however, was raging furiously and wholly undecided at 4 P.M. ; and as Blücher's rear was not assailed from Marbais, and the roar of cannon announced a battle at Quatre Bras, Napoleon formed a fresh combination to surprise and to overwhelm his enemy. By this time he had no doubt learned that D'Erlon, who ought to have been in line with Ney three hours previously, was still in the rear ; so he sent* an order to D'Erlon to turn aside from Quatre Bras, and, moving towards Ligny, to fall in full force at St. Amand on the right and the rear of Blücher, accomplishing thus, in a different way, the results of an attack from Marbais. D'Erlon had approached Ligny within an hour, but he had so marched that Vandamme pronounced the apparition to be that of an enemy—a part, probably, of Wellington's force—and the Emperor despatched† a general officer to ascertain how the fact stood, retarding meanwhile the course of the battle. Ere long the advancing columns were seen to draw off, and to disappear from the field ; Ney, in fact, now assailed by superior numbers, had angrily ordered D'Erlon to Quatre Bras, and D'Erlon, Napoleon at least consenting—the Emperor would have been in extreme peril had his left wing been defeated and forced—abandoned a movement which, if pushed

---

* A host of witnesses, Soult is the most conspicuous—his well-known testimony of the 17th of June, the day after Ligny, has been shamefully garbled by Charras—have proved that Napoleon sent this order to D'Erlon ; and the fact, I conceive, is indisputable. It is denied, in the face of the evidence, by those only who, seeking to censure Napoleon and to excuse Wellington, pretend that the Emperor had not the means of gaining a decisive victory over Blücher after 1 P.M. on the 16th of June. Even after the failure of the projected movement from Marbais the means were ample ; D'Erlon would have annihilated Blücher had he struck the Prussian right and rear at St. Amand.

† This was Dejean, a favourite aide-de-camp of Napoleon. As the evidence shows that the Emperor ordered D'Erlon to Ligny, so it indicates that he must have permitted D'Erlon to abandon his march, and to retrace his steps towards Quatre Bras when peremptorily ordered to do so by Ney. This, in the events which happened, was over-caution, for D'Erlon would have destroyed Blücher had he carried out Napoleon's order, and Ney, hard pressed as he was at Quatre Bras, could have held his ground against Wellington without the aid of D'Erlon ; and this, I conceive, is the reason that Napoleon's commentaries on this most important subject are vague and unsatisfactory.

home, would have given his master a splendid triumph.* It was now 6.30 P.M., and it was time for Napoleon to endeavour to strike a decisive blow, the march of D'Erlon having not only ended in a disastrous false movement, but caused unfortunate delays at Ligny. During all this time the Prussians and French had been engaged in mortal encounter, but Napoleon's skill had borne its natural fruits. Blücher's left had been held in check and paralysed; the Prussian losses had been enormous; the veteran's reserves had been thrown away, and in an effort to outflank Napoleon's left, Blücher had weakened and almost laid bare his centre. The Emperor, who had his reserves in hand, launched the Guard and a mass of cavalry against the endangered point; the Prussian centre was broken after a fierce contest, and Blücher's whole army was driven from the field, the corps of Lobau, which had come up from Charleroi, hanging on the retreat of the defeated enemy. The losses of the French were about 11,000 men, those of the Prussians not far from 30,000, including 10,000 disbanded fugitives; but how different would the result have been had Ney or D'Erlon fallen on the rear of Blücher!

While the star of Napoleon still shone at Ligny, it had begun to wane hard by at Quatre Bras; and the faulty disposition of his left wing had saved Blücher from a complete overthrow. We left Ney at Frasnes, having received the order of 8 A.M. at about 11 A.M.; and the Emperor's aide-de-camp, we may be quite certain, informed the Marshal that he had communicated the order to Reille and D'Erlon, the chiefs of the 2nd and 1st Corps, at this moment at Gosselies and Jumet, about ten miles off, along the broad highway from Charleroi to Brussels. That order directed Ney to advance beyond Quatre Bras, collecting his 45,000 men, but making a detachment to the right at Marbais; and Ney might have begun at once to execute a movement which, if well carried out, would perhaps have changed the fortunes of Europe. Ney, at 11 A.M., had 9,000 good troops, of whom 4,000 were

---

* D'Erlon detached a division to observe St. Amand before he counter-marched to Quatre Bras. This division, however, merely reconnoitred, and took no part in the battle; it was simply useless.

fine cavalry, at Frasnes, actually in his hands: his only foe was
Perponcher's weak division, 7,000 infantry, with but a few guns, and
almost wholly unsupported by horse ; and the Marshal knew that
within three hours he might expect the aid of more than 30,000
soldiers, including a magnificent body of cavalry.   Had Ney,
therefore, been the chief of Elchingen, he could easily have
overwhelmed Perponcher ; and directing Reille and D'Erlon to
expedite their march, he could have passed Quatre Bras, and
detached to Marbais, at from 1.30 to 2.30 P.M., without encountering any enemy in force.   But, as the whole course of the Campaign
proves, Ney had become demoralized, like most of his colleagues,
by the events of 1812–14, and that even in a greater degree; he
fought with a halter round his neck, and was by turns timid and
unwisely bold ; and he not only did not make a step forward, but
seems to have made no effort to induce Reille and D'Erlon to
accelerate their movements and to come into line.   This delay
saved Blücher, and gave Wellington just sufficient time to repair,
in part, the tardiness and hesitation of the 15th, to check Ney, and
to baffle Napoleon in the manœuvre he had planned, which would
have crushed the Prussians.   The Duke reached Quatre Bras—but
with an escort only, his advancing divisions were still distant—at
about 11 A.M. on the 16th ; and he rode off to near Ligny to confer
with Blücher, whose faulty arrangements to meet Napoleon he
condemned in a characteristic phrase—"they will be damnably
beaten," he said to his Staff—but to whom he promised support,
" if possible."   Meanwhile, Ney showed no sign of moving :
Reille advanced slowly, and the march of D'Erlon from the rear
was a succession of delays ; and it was 2 P.M. before the French
Marshal—one division of Reille had come to his aid—made even
an attempt to attack Quatre Bras.   It is unnecessary to retrace the
scenes of a combat, in itself not of supreme importance, though it
had much to do with the issue of the Campaign.   Perponcher's
division and other supports were nearly overwhelmed at 4 P.M. ;
but reinforcements came up by degrees, moving in haste from
Nivelles and other points, which ultimately turned the scale
against Ney.   The Duke, returning from Ligny, displayed on

the field the intrepidity and the genius in defence which were his distinctive gifts in war; and Ney, as night closed, retreated on Frasnes, having failed to fulfil his appointed mission, which, I repeat, might have been accomplished, having, however, prevented Wellington from sending a man to Blücher. The Marshal had been supported by Reille's corps only, and by Kellerman's corps of horsemen; D'Erlon, loitering in the rear, had been directed, we have seen, to another field at Ligny, and when recalled by Ney came into line too late to be of any use, or even to fire a shot; and Ney had conducted the battle ably, and even performed an important service, though he had thrown away a part of his superb heavy cavalry. He had, however, proved unequal to his task; he had not carried out Napoleon's designs, which ought to have led to Blücher's ruin, as, beyond question, he might have done; and though Reille and D'Erlon, especially the last, who contrived on the 16th to do simply nothing, are in a greater degree to blame, he cannot escape a share of censure.

The first part of the Campaign of 1815 ends with the battles of Ligny and Quatre Bras. Napoleon's operations, up to the evening of the 16th, had been attended with marked success, which might easily have been complete and decisive. Selecting, with perfect insight, the true point of attack, he had conducted his army with admirable skill and secrecy to the Belgian frontier; and aiming at the centre of the Allies, the weakest and most vulnerable part of their line, he had drawn close to it on the 15th June. His enemies had been unable to arrest his progress, disseminated on a broad and deep front; and the impetuosity of Blücher, and the caution of Wellington, gave him, as he had foreseen, a favourable chance to divide his adversaries, and to beat them in detail. Blücher had hurried to Sombreffe to confront the Emperor, leaving a fourth part of his army behind; the Duke had paused, hesitated, and delayed in moving, and it was hours after Napoleon had passed Charleroi that Wellington even made an attempt to draw near his endangered colleague, even then directing his troops to points distant from the selected place of junction. This was the situation on the morning of the 16th, and it gave Napoleon a great advantage, which almost led to a crowning triumph. He may, perhaps, have delayed at this moment, though in this judgment I cannot concur, and his projects were founded on imperfect knowledge ; but his general dispositions were so excellent that he ought to have overwhelmed the Prussian army. Having directed Ney, with his left wing, to pass Quatre Bras and to detach to Marbais, he marched to Fleurus and attacked Blücher ; and had the attack in front at Ligny been combined with an attack in the rear from Marbais, Ligny must have terminated in another Jena. Exactly the same result would have followed had D'Erlon, who had lagged in the rear, continued his movement upon St. Amand ; and a series of misadventures alone saved Blücher from a crushing disaster. Ney was not equal to his appointed mission ; he lost the occasion to reach Quatre Bras, to advance, and to occupy Marbais. Reille and D'Erlon did not second their chief ; and D'Erlon, when launched on the path of victory, was turned aside by an order of Ney, Napoleon, I certainly think, consenting. The blame of these failures must be divided between Ney, Reille, and D'Erlon, who deserves the most ; Napoleon, too, may not have been bold enough, though this is mere theory after the event; but the fact remains that, but for unlucky accidents, Napoleon would have annihilated his foe. As it was, Ligny was a real victory. The Prussian army lost a third of its numbers, and Blücher was driven from the only road by which he could readily join Wellington into a difficult and intricate country. Meanwhile, though Ney had not accomplished all that his master had a right to expect from him, he had, at the opposite side of the line, attacked Wellington and held him in check. The Duke, his forces coming up late and in fragments, was unable to send assistance to his imperilled colleague ; and though he had compelled Ney to fall back a little, Ligny made it necessary that he should quickly retreat, happy if he could effect his escape. Napoleon had thus succeeded on the 16th, though his triumph had been incomplete and partial. He had defeated Blücher, and kept Wellington at bay ; and, above all, he had forced the Allies to abandon the road from Nivelles to Namur, their natural and their only easy line of junction. Would they diverge as Beaulieu and

Colli had done, and give the General of the Campaign of Italy an opportunity to ruin them in detail ? To Napoleon the prospect seemed full of promise, and yet all was not light on the scene before him. He had not gained a decisive victory. Blücher and Wellington were no ordinary foes ; their armies nearly doubled his own ; might they not yet close on the Imperial Eagle, which, terrible and swift as had been its swoop, had not thoroughly grasped and destroyed its quarry ?

CHAPTER II.

IN one of the last and fiercest struggles at Ligny, Blücher had been unhorsed and severely hurt, and the command of the Prussian army devolved on Gneisenau, a capable and scientific officer. It was near nightfall when Ligny had been won—the delay occasioned by the affair of D'Erlon had been injurious in the extreme to the French—and, perceiving that no enemy pressed on his rear, Gneisenau halted, and made preparations to retreat. But whither was the defeated army to move ? Was it to fall back on its communications with the Rhine, opening to Napoleon the path to Brussels, and separating itself completely from Wellington; or was it to endeavour to join its allies, abandoning its line of operations for the time, but appealing to Fortune in another battle ? Gneisenau, urged, it is said, by his heroic chief, who gave the order at night from his litter, resolved to adopt the second course; and the Prussian army was directed on Wavre, a town about twenty miles from Sombreffe, and divided from it by the difficult country—a region of hills and lowlands watered by the Dyle—which lay behind the road from Nivelles to Namur. Wavre is about nine or ten miles from Waterloo, a village in front of the Forest of Soignies, and north of a position marked out by Wellington as an admirable field for a great defensive battle; and it was this circumstance, well known to Blücher, which doubtless led him to fall back on Wavre, in spite of the many impediments in the way, impediments which had caused Napoleon to expect that, if forced from the road from Nivelles to Namur, Blücher would most probably recoil on his base, and not attempt to join Wellington through a mass of obstacles. By daybreak on the 17th, the first corps of Ziethen, and the second of Pirch were on their way to Wavre, by Tilly and Gentinnes, villages some miles to the north-west of Sombreffe; and the third corps of Thielmann, charged to cover the movement, broke up some hours later, and made for Gembloux, one of the points, we have seen, which Napoleon hoped to have reached in the advance of the day before, and to the east of Tilly and Gentinnes. The Prussian army was still greatly shaken, and especially was short of food and munitions; but no enemy harassed or observed the retreat; and before long it was joined by Bülow, who had hastened to march by Hannut to Gembloux, and brought 30,000 fresh soldiers to Blücher.

Meanwhile, Wellington, who, as night closed on the 16th, had had at Quatre Bras a mass of about 37,000 men, was joined ere long by some 8,000 more, marched from Brussels and points on his right, and he was thus now equal in numbers with Ney, who had by this time his two corps in hand*; though he was dangerously exposed should Ney and Napoleon be able to reach him with their united forces. Owing to an accident which befell a Prussian officer, the Duke was not informed of the defeat of Blücher until the early morning of the 17th; he thereupon resolved at once to retreat, but having been apprised that the Prussian army was in full march from Sombreffe to Wavre, and would soon be ready to fight again, he decided on stopping the retreat at Waterloo, and on awaiting there the attack of the French, if he could rely on the support of his veteran colleague. The retrograde movement of the Duke from Quatre Bras, screened by a considerable body of horsemen, began at about 10 A.M., and continued for hours; and, in addition to his 45,000 men, he summoned about 21,000 at Nivelles, and perhaps 4,000 more from outlying points, to Waterloo, the scene of the intended conflict. Fearful and jealous for his right, however, all through, he left a large force near Braine le Comte and Hal; and his whole army, in fact, was never concentrated.

* With Kellerman's heavy cavalry.

The Allies, falling back from their true line of junction, the main road from Nivelles to Namur, were thus trying to unite on a second line, by the bad roads from Wavre to Waterloo. This strategy has been praised by the worshippers of success, even by soldiers like Charras and Chesney, and, in the event, it was more than justified; it was, nevertheless, essentially faulty. It is impossible to refute Napoleon's logic; either Blücher, after his defeat at Ligny, ought to have moved directly on Wellington's army, joining it either at Genappe or at least at Waterloo, or both the Allied chiefs ought to have fallen farther back, to have placed the Forest of Soignies between themselves and their foe, and concentrating their forces around Brussels, to have opposed 200,000 men or more to the 100,000 of the French Emperor, who, in that case, would have been out-generalled and could scarcely have ventured to offer battle. The double retreat on Wavre and Waterloo was, in fact, an imperfect half measure, so often fatal in the operations of war; Wavre was more distant from Waterloo than Sombreffe was from Quatre Bras, by certainly two or three miles, and, what was infinitely more important, was divided from Waterloo by a most intricate country; and, in making this movement, Blücher and Wellington were exposing themselves to crushing defeat, and were rendering their junction extremely difficult. It was to be assumed that a man like Napoleon would be exactly informed of the line of their march, and would do what was the best for his interests; and had Napoleon, on the morning of the 17th, called on his victorious army to make a great effort, he would probably have reached either Blücher or Wellington, still widely apart, and beaten either in detail. Nay, had he, collecting his whole forces, and moving more slowly, either attacked Blücher at Wavre or the Duke at Waterloo, on the 18th, he would almost certainly have won a great battle before the Allies could succeed in uniting. Exactly the same result would have followed had he, acting on more correct principles—and supposing, of course, as was to be expected, that he was thoroughly apprised of the allied movements—detached a part of his army to hold Blücher in check, and assailed Wellington with the mass of his forces; in that case all the chances were that he

22

would be able to overpower Wellington, and to prevent Blücher at Wavre from sending a man to Waterloo. Considering the situation, time, and distance, the boasted retreat of the Allies, therefore, cannot be vindicated, whatever may be said; it exposed them once more to be defeated in detail; and unquestionably their best strategic course was to have effected their junction in the rear, on Brussels, thus completely baffling their great antagonist and not exposing themselves to danger.

The state of affairs, however, in the camp of the French had singularly favoured the plan of the Allies, and had already saved them from impending peril. Over confident in success, his distinctive fault, Napoleon was convinced that the Prussian army had been* completely routed at Ligny, and could not reappear on the scene for some time; and he returned to Fleurus, utterly worn out by the anxieties and fatigues of the two preceding days. He appears to have given no explicit orders, but he left Soult and Grouchy in temporary command; and these lieutenants, experienced as they were, did nothing to repair the gross want of vigilance due, probably, to the state of Napoleon's health. Soult seems not to have even sent a message to Ney, a few miles off, to the left; no attempt during the night was made to discover the line of the Prussian retreat, still less to molest the defeated foe; and Grouchy especially, a cavalry chief, instead of reconnoitring in every direction to ascertain where the enemy was, despatched only one body of horsemen along the road from Sombreffe to Namur, that is, far away from the Prussian line of march. In this negligence and slackness we see no sign of the marvellous activity of Jena and Ratisbon; and Charras, I believe, is perfectly right when he says that Napoleon's "long sleep" at Fleurus made the success of Ligny of no use to him, though Charras, always unjust to the Emperor, makes no allowance for his physical weakness, and refuses to blame either Soult or Grouchy. It was about 9 A.M. on the morning of the 17th when Napoleon drove from Fleurus to

---

* "L'armée Prussienne a été mise en déroute" is the expression of Soult, in the well known letter of the 17th, written under the eye perhaps of Napoleon, certainly according to his ideas.

"TAMBOUR, FAITES-MOI CADEAU D'UNE PRISE!"

Ligny—he had been extremely unwell for hours *—and everything tends to prove he had no doubt but that the strength of the Prussian army was broken, and his first idea was that his own army should take rest† on the spot for the day. He ordered a grand review of his troops, and spent two hours at least on the field of Ligny, distributing rewards and attending the wounded ; and it was not until near noon—having learned from Ney that part of the British army was still at Quatre Bras—that he seems to have resolved on a forward movement. By this time Blücher had completely escaped, and, in fact, was not many miles from Wavre ; the Duke was in full retreat on Waterloo ; and the chance which Napoleon‡ certainly had, and which the youthful warrior of 1796 would most probably have turned to account, that of falling either on Blücher or Wellington in the early morning of the 17th, had been lost never again to return.

The delay, too, in the operations of the French, coupled with the neglect of Soult and Grouchy, had caused the Emperor to remain in ignorance of the true direction of Blücher's march, and had confirmed him in a false impression, which, though not the main cause of his subsequent ruin, undoubtedly in part contributed to it. Clinging to the conception which he had formed from the first, he was now absolutely convinced that, after Ligny, Blücher was falling back on his base to the Rhine ; and the unlucky reconnaissance made in the morning, which pointed to a Prussian retreat by Namur—some prisoners and guns had been taken by the French—only went to strengthen his erroneous judgment. He resolved, therefore, following the grand precedent of 1796, against Beaulieu and Colli—his cardinal idea in the campaign of 1815—to direct the mass of his army against Wellington, and to keep Blücher

---

* Dorsey Gardener (p. 34) cites conclusive testimony to show " that Napoleon went to bed immediately after the close of the battle of Ligny, and was in such a condition that none of his staff dared enter his chamber to procure his sanction for vitally important orders, and that on the morning of the 17th there was the same impossibility of getting access to him."

† See, again, Soult's letter of 17th, " La journée d'aujourd'hui est nécessaire pour terminer cette opération, et pour compléter les munitions, rallier les militaires isolés et fair rentrer les détachements.

‡ What Napoleon might have accomplished on the morning of the 17th is very ably shown by Charras (p. 203, vol. i.), but with too much regard to mere theory.

away with a force sufficient to hold the defeated Prussians in check while he should endeavour to overpower the Duke. This strategy was perfectly correct in principle, but the delay of the morning had been most unfortunate, and the project was founded on a false assumption of the direction taken by Blücher's forces.

The whole French army—except one division left in reserve, it had suffered so much—was now divided into two groups; the first composed of the Guard, a part of the 6th Corps, and some 8,000 horsemen, marching on Quatre Bras, to unite with Ney, with the 2nd and 1st Corps, and about 7,000 cavalry; the second comprising the 3rd and 4th Corps, one division of the 6th, and about 5,000 horsemen. The first group, about 72,000 strong, with not less than 240 guns, was to be under the Emperor's command, and was intended to reach and attack Wellington; the second, some 34,000 men, with from 96 to 100 guns, was the wing that was destined to restrain Blücher. Napoleon broke up from Ligny soon after noon, and gave the command of this wing to Grouchy, enjoining him to "pursue and attack the Prussians, and to keep Blücher continually in sight," and indicating Namur as, most probably, the direction of the retreat of the enemy. The Emperor, too, I can have no doubt, informed his lieutenant that his mission was* to interpose between Blücher and Wellington; and, in fact, an experienced chief like Grouchy must have understood that this was the object of his being detached from the main French army. The direction, however, of the restraining wing was late; Blücher had gained fourteen hours on the foe sent against him; his retreat was on Wavre, not on Namur; and it had already become no easy task to come up with him, and to hold him in check. Grouchy, alarmed at what had been devolved on him, expostulated with his Imperial master; but Napoleon curtly told him "to find out the enemy," and set off to join Ney at Quatre Bras. He met the Marshal at about 2 P.M.; their united forces

---

* This has been denied by Grouchy, but is distinctly to be inferred from his own letters; and, as Jomini observes, the situation dictated the order. Gérard, who however, is unjust to Grouchy, declares that Napoleon gave the most precise instructions nearly to this effect.

were massed together, and they were directed against the army of Wellington, for some hours, we have seen, in retreat. Ney had continued stationary at Quatre Bras, until the Emperor came on to him, and for this inaction he has been severely blamed; but the reproach is* too exacting, and by no means just; the army of Wellington had been placed in safety; and even had Ney advanced from Quatre Bras as soon as he saw Napoleon moving from Ligny, and pressed on the rear of the British force, he could not have gained any marked success. Napoleon began the pursuit at about 3 P.M., following Wellington along the great road to Brussels, leading by Genappe to the Forest of Soignies; but great results were no longer possible; the French merely harassed the retiring cavalry; and, in fact, an extraordinary tempest of rain made military operations practically useless. At about 7 P.M. the advanced guard of the French reached the low hills above La Belle Alliance, in front of the position of Waterloo; and in reply to a challenge made by Napoleon, the fire of many batteries informed the Emperor that a large army was collected at a short distance from him.

We turn to the operations of Grouchy's wing, detached, we have seen, late to follow up Blücher. Grouchy had not set his 34,000 men in motion from Ligny until about 3 P.M., and for this he has been harshly condemned; but, considering that his troops were widely scattered, and that Napoleon did not advance from Quatre Bras until the same hour, or nearly so, I am satisfied the censure is not deserved. The Marshal, a brave but irresolute man— he had shown what he was at Bantry in 1796—was hesitating what direction to take, when a positive order from Napoleon came to determine his still uncertain purpose. The Emperor, when on his way to Quatre Bras, had received the intelligence that a large Prussian force had been seen on the Orneau, not far from Gembloux; and he instantly sent off a messenger to Grouchy—through

---

* Napoleon, conscious of the evil results of the delays of the 17th, condemns Ney for not having fallen on Wellington, at least when the Imperial army was on the march. This criticism, however, is not well founded, or even honest. Napoleon had a right to complain of Ney on the 16th and 18th, not on the 17th.

Bertrand, and not through the Chief of the Staff—every sentence of which should be carefully studied. In this important despatch Napoleon, we see,* believed that Blücher was still falling back, with at least the mass of his army, eastwards; but the proximity of the Prussians at Gembloux surprised him; and he distinctly pointed out that "Blücher and Wellington might endeavour to unite, and to offer battle, in order to cover Liège or Brussels." Suspecting part of the truth, but still uninformed, he now ordered Grouchy to occupy Gembloux—he evidently thought that from this point the line of Blücher's retreat would be ascertained, and that Grouchy would hold a position between the Prussians and the main French army—and he desired Grouchy "to communicate with head-quarters," by "cavalry detachments," along "the road from Namur," showing thus he believed that the Prussian chief was probably retiring in force towards Liège, that is, towards his base on the Rhine.

This order was still founded on the false impression of the direction really taken by Blücher, for Gembloux is to the east of Wavre, and thirteen or fourteen miles from that place; but in spite of all that the Emperor's censors have said, it was sufficiently correct to have enabled Grouchy, had he been a capable and active chief, to have, in the main, fulfilled his mission, and to have interposed between Blücher and Wellington. Grouchy set off without further delay—responsibility was a heavy load on him; the storm of rain which had kept back Napoleon retarded also the Marshal's columns; the roads, too, to Gembloux were exceedingly bad; and it was not until 9 P.M. that the whole force of Grouchy was collected near and around Gembloux, part east of the town and part still in the rear. Grouchy had pushed on to

---

* The operations of Grouchy on the 17th and 18th of June had a decisive effect on the issue of the campaign, and have been the subject of volumes of controversy. I have relied mainly on the papers written at the time, but in part guided by Jomini's sagacious direction. Napoleon, writing at St. Helena, was largely ignorant of the details of these movements, and is unjust to his luckless subordinate. Thiers, and authors of the Napoleonic school, exaggerate the unfairness of the Emperor; on the other hand, Charras, Chesney, and others are not trustworthy authorities, and are thoroughly prejudiced against Napoleon. This part of Charras' book is the theoretic reasoning, after the event, of a malignant partisan critic.

Gembloux some hours before, with an advanced guard, to endeavour to find out the true direction of Blücher's retreat; but though it is certainly strange that this was not discovered beyond the possibility of doubt by this time, and the march to Gembloux had been slow, I believe the Marshal cannot fairly be blamed. In this position of affairs Grouchy sent a despatch to the Emperor, now in front of Waterloo, at 10 P.M. on the night of the 17th, and another at 2 A.M. on the morning of the 18th; and these, too, require close attention. In the first of these letters Grouchy announced that the Prussian army was still falling back, almost certainly formed* "into two great columns," the one moving on Wavre by Sart les Walhain, a place a few miles to the north-east of Gembloux, the other retiring on Perwez towards Liège; and the Marshal added that if "the mass of the enemy had made its way to Wavre" he would "follow it up in that direction," "in order to separate Blücher from Wellington." The second letter has been lost, but its contents are known; the Marshal wrote that he was about to march on Wavre by Sart les Walhain on the track of Blücher; and this is confirmed by a third message,† sent to Pajol, one of his light cavalry chiefs, which directed a speedy advance on Wavre.

The information thus conveyed by Grouchy was only a partial approach to the truth, and it was calculated to mislead Napoleon, and to inspire him with disastrous false confidence. Blücher was not retreating in two divergent columns; he had never thought of drawing towards Liège; and, at this moment, the night of the 17th, the four corps of his army, now well supplied and rested, and still numbering about 90,000 men, with from 270 to 280 guns, had been concentrated around Wavre, on either bank of the stream of the Dyle, and ready in the morning to march on Waterloo. The knowledge even now acquired by Grouchy was 'amply sufficient to urge that chief to advance on

---

* Grouchy also incidentally refers to a third column retreating by Namur.

† This despatch was discovered by the Prince La Tour D'Auvergne (see his book on *Waterloo*, p. 318), and is of extreme importance. It was written "at daybreak, on the 18th, and ordered Pajol to hasten to Tourinnes, "*afin que nous poussions en avant de Wavre, le plus promptement possible.*"

Wavre as quickly as possible, for it was by that line only that, from his point of view, even one hostile column could join Wellington ; and his letters prove that he understood his mission. But his messages to Napoleon were of such a nature as to cause the Emperor to feel assured—especially as this was his own idea—that a large part at least of the Prussian army was leagues away in retreat eastward, and could not possibly assist the Duke ; and, in any case, he had a right to infer that if part of Blücher's forces was at Wavre, Grouchy would be fully able to hold it in check. Buoyed up by these hopes, the Emperor spent half the night of the 17th in watching the lines of fire which marked the British bivouacs, and he had but one fear, that the state of the weather—the rain had continued to descend in torrents—would prevent him from bringing Wellington to bay, and would enable the English chief to decamp ere the morrow. It is, however, a complete mistake to suppose, as Charras and other detractors have urged, that the Emperor at this critical moment altogether neglected to watch his right, or to keep in communication with Grouchy at Gembloux. I cannot, indeed, accept his statement,* for it can hardly be reconciled with the published documents, that he directed Grouchy, on the night of the 17th, to send a detachment to the main French army, in order to fall on the flank of Wellington—the counterpart of the march from Quatre Bras to Marbais—though this incident of the campaign has been ill explored ; and there are reasons to think the order was made, apparently opposed to the known evidence. But he sent horsemen to scour the country towards Gembloux, and even within some miles of Wavre. He certainly ascertained,

---

* This is one of the most obscure and disputed passages of the campaign. Napoleon positively declares that he ordered Grouchy to detach 7,000 men from Gembloux to attack Wellington, and he is followed by Thiers and a number of writers. But, as Charras and others have fairly pointed out, no copy of the order can be found in the register of the Chief of the Staff; the name of the bearer has never been given, and the order seems inconsistent with a subsequent message sent to Grouchy in the morning of the 18th. Still there are indications that the order was given; Napoleon would hardly utter an audacious falsehood on such a subject. Thiers narrates an anecdote which confirms his conclusion; and, as we have already seen, the Emperor did not always convey his directions through Soult. The matter, however, is scarcely of the capital importance ascribed to it by some writers.

before daybreak on the 18th, that a Prussian column was near Wavre, and he communicated, we shall see, the news to Grouchy, Relying, however, on the Marshal's account, he assumed that Grouchy would be in sufficient force to paralyze and perhaps destroy this foe, and he was justified, from what he had been told, in a supposition of the kind.

It was now the morning of the 18th of June, and Napoleon perceived, with exulting pride, that Wellington had not attempted to retreat, and that the Duke's army retained its positions. The Emperor felt assured of a decisive victory ; he was certain that Grouchy could easily master any forces that might threaten his right, if such forces were at hand at all ; and he exclaimed to Ney, as they sate at breakfast, that the "chances were ten to one in their favour." Napoleon had intended to have his army in line, and to begin the battle at 9 A.M.,* but the severity of the weather had made the ground very difficult for the manœuvring of guns. He believed that a grand demonstration would shake the nerves of the Belgian and Dutch troops, who had been lately in the Imperial service, but who now formed a large part of Wellington's force ; and, at the instance, it is said, of Drouot, one of his most skilful and trusted officers, he put off the attack for nearly three hours, the state of his frame, which needed repose, very probably, too, affecting his purpose. This delay was immensely in the Duke's favour. Waterloo, but for it, could hardly have been won, and it may truly be said that, on this day, the sun in its courses fought against Napoleon. Meanwhile Wellington had drawn together his army, about 70,000 strong, comprising 13,000 cavalry, and 160 guns ; and relying on the pledge of the word of Blücher, who, conquering pain and superior to defeat, had promised to come up in line at Waterloo, "with his whole army," by the "forenoon at latest," he calmly awaited the attack of his renowned antagonist. He might, even at this moment, have had a much larger force on the ground, for, apprehensive for his right to the last, he had left 17,000 men far away at Hal, a strategic

---

* This is placed beyond doubt by Prince La Tour D'Auvergne, *Waterloo*, p. 251, and disposes of the able but ill-founded remarks of Charras.

mistake which cannot be justified, and which placed him in grave
peril during the ensuing battle.

While Waterloo was being thus prepared, Blücher had broken
up from his camps round Wavre, intent on carrying the support
to his English colleague which he felt would secure the Allies a
triumph. The veteran did not suspect that Grouchy was not far
off with 34,000 men; the Duke and Blücher, in fact, believed that
Napoleon had all his army in hand, with the exception of the
one corps of Vandamme; and this single calculation condemns the
generalship of the double movement on Wavre and Waterloo; for
had Napoleon had 90,000 men to oppose to the 70,000 of Wellington, and been able to attack early on the 18th, Blücher never
could have been up in time to avert a defeat that must have
been certain. No hostile column, however, appeared from Gembloux, to threaten the Prussians on their flank march, and yet
the difficulties and obstacles in the way—imperfectly understood
by the Prussian staff—were so great that the advance from Wavre
was exceedingly slow, and perilously delayed. Bülow, starting
from beyond the Dyle at break of day, was not at Chapelle St.
Lambert, with even a few men, until noon, still far from Napoleon's
right; Pirch and Ziethen were not in march for Waterloo until
11.30 A.M., and even then lingered; and Thielmann, with a considerable part of his corps, was left behind to defend Wavre.
Nothing but the heroic ardour of Blücher and the energy of his
fierce soldiery enabled the movement to be made at all, and but
for accidents and bad generalship I think it could not have been
accomplished with results leading to success at Waterloo.

While Blücher was thus toiling to attain Waterloo, Grouchy was
on his way from Gembloux to Wavre. To appreciate thoroughly
this passage of the campaign, I must ask the reader to retrace his
steps, and to turn back to part of the preceding narrative. Grouchy,
sent to Gembloux with 34,000 men, to pursue and to attack
Blücher, and, doubtless, to keep him aloof from Wellington, had not
ascertained, even at the close of the 17th, the exact positions of the
whole Prussian army; but he had been informed that part of it
was falling back on Liège, and that another part was retreating on

Wavre; and he had, in the two letters cited, apprised Napoleon that "should the mass of the Prussians go that way," he would take care to advance on Wavre, and thus "separate Blücher from Wellington." This information was not wholly correct, but it was so to a certain extent; and it ought to have at once suggested to Grouchy—a general-in-chief in command of an army, and he perfectly understood his mission—the necessity of marching quickly on Wavre by the earliest dawn of the 18th; for any Prussian column retiring on Liège was abandoning altogether the theatre, and might, therefore, be left alone; whereas a Prussian column directed to Wavre would be approaching Wellington, and might molest Napoleon. This was the more essential, because the Emperor, upon leaving for Quatre Bras, had told Grouchy that his intention was to attack the Duke should he make a stand "in front of the Forest of Soignies," the very spot where the Duke now was; and also, notably, because the Marshal's despatches were such as would lead Napoleon to think that no Prussians could even approach Waterloo. The duty of Grouchy to keep Blücher and the Duke apart ought to have induced him likewise, in his march from Gembloux, to draw towards Wavre along roads tending towards the Emperor's position and Blücher's flank, should the Prussians attempt to make for Waterloo; for thus only could he accomplish his task, of which he was well aware, as his own messages show. These roads existed, and were even open; they led across the Dyle by two stone bridges at Mousty and Ottignies, left intact as those on the Sambre had been on the 15th; and they could have borne Grouchy's army in seven hours at latest—the distance, we have said, is thirteen or fourteen miles—either to Wavre, or to intermediate points between Wavre and the Duke's lines at Waterloo.

Common sense, therefore, should have inspired Grouchy to leave Gembloux as early as possible on the 18th, to divide his troops into two columns at least, in order to expedite the march, and to make for Wavre by Mousty and Ottignies; and had this been done, I agree with Jomini, Blücher would not have made his way to Waterloo. Unfortunately, Grouchy, we have seen, had resolved to advance from Gembloux on Wavre—and he was hesitating even in this purpose—not by the roads that would bring him on Blücher's flank, but by Sart les Walhain, and a circuitous road that would place him only on Blücher's rear, and therefore in a much worse position to intercept a Prussian flank march on Waterloo; but though this was a grave strategic error, it was perhaps not an irreparable mistake. Where Grouchy's conduct cannot be excused, and what condemns him at the bar of history, is that, in opposition to his obvious duty and to the rules of mere common prudence, he left Gembloux at* so late an hour that it became difficult to attain Wavre in time to be of much use to Napoleon; and that he so disposed his army as to render its march unnecessarily and even extraordinarily slow. Instead of breaking up at 3 or 4 A.M., he did not break up until 8 or 9 A.M.; instead of forming his men into two columns at least, he allowed them to march in one huge column; and thus hours of inestimable worth were lost, and a movement which ought to have been as quick as possible was retarded in every conceivable way.

Napoleon, meantime, had been preparing a grand and decisive attack on Wellington. His army had been some time in motion to take the positions assigned to it, when he sent off by Soult a message to Grouchy, at this moment on his way from Gembloux. In this letter, written at 10 A.M., the Chief of the Staff informed Grouchy that, besides the two columns the Marshal had mentioned, intelligence had been received of a third Prussian column falling back on Wavre by Gentinnes; and he approved of Grouchy's intended march on Wavre—inferred from the despatch of 2 A.M.—but he enjoined him to approach the Emperor, and to enter into communication with the main French army, which, he added, was about to engage in battle " near Waterloo," before " the Forest of Soignies." By 11 A.M., Napoleon's legions had taken their ground on their last field, and the annals of war have seldom presented so magnificent and imposing a spectacle, described by the Emperor himself in most striking language. The French army, spread out

---

* Detractors of Napoleon and encomiasts of the Allies have concurred in endeavouring to excuse Grouchy. They begin by referring to the state of the weather on the morning of the 18th as accounting for Grouchy's delay in leaving Gembloux. It is enough to reply that Bülow started for Waterloo at daybreak through a most difficult country.

like a gigantic fan, resplendent in all the pomp of battle, was formed into three great masses; the first, composed of the 2nd and 1st Corps, deployed in lines from Mon Plaisir on the left to near Frischermont on the extreme right; the second, a superb array of cavalry, in line, to the rear of Reille and D'Erlon; and the third, in close columns, made up of cavalry, of Lobau's 6th corps, and of the Imperial Guard, intended to deal the decisive stroke. Napoleon's position crossed two roads, one the great highway from Charleroi to Brussels, the other a good cross road from Nivelles running into the first at Mont St. Jean; and the three arms could concur in the attack, though his adversary's front was protected by obstacles, and the rain of fifteen hours had made an attack difficult through dense fields of rye and miry enclosures. The Emperor rode in front of his line, accompanied by his gorgeous staff; exulting cheers burst from the martial host, proud of the renown of a hundred victories; and the sight, as Napoleon calculated, made a profound impression on the thousands of men in the hostile array who had but recently served under the Imperial eagles.

The Duke, however, had his arrangements made; they fully revealed his defensive skill; and if some of the auxiliaries had faint hearts, he knew that he could thoroughly rely on his British and most of his German soldiery. His lines, running from his right to his left, extended from beyond Hougoumont, in front of Mon Plaisir, to Papelotte and La Haye, in front of Frischermont; but he had some thousands of men on his extreme right, holding Merbe Braine and Braine L'Alleud, and communicating by vedettes with Hal, where, we have seen, he had left 17,000 men; and his extreme left had outposts reaching to Ohain, on the road to Wavre, whench he expected Blücher. Hill commanded the right wing, Picton held the left, the Prince of Orange was at the centre; and though the Duke's army presented a less compact front than that of his Imperial foe, it was admirably arranged for a defensive battle. Before the position stood the château of Hougoumont, covering the right and the right centre of the Duke; beyond was the farm of La Haye Sainte and the hamlets of Papelotte and La

Haye, advanced posts on his centre and left; and these points of vantage had been carefully fortified and held by considerable bodies of men, to break the first fury of the French attack. Behind these obstacles the main army held a formidable position, guarding the two roads from Charleroi to Brussels and that from Nivelles; and it had this special characteristic, that its possessors could sweep the assailant's columns at all points with fire, and that it afforded cover in the rear to screen the reserves, exactly the opposite of the case of the Prussians at Ligny. The Duke, however, like all true generals, did not rely only on a passive defence; a cross-road just behind the main position enabled all arms to manœuvre freely, and the cavalry massed behind the British centre had facilities to advance from most points of the line.

I can only attempt a mere sketch of one of the most memorable battles of all time. The plan of Napoleon's attack, in which we perceive the last exhibition of his genius in war, was to turn Wellington's left—by many degrees the weakest point of the British position—and, simultaneously, to force his centre; success in this operation would not only separate the Duke's army completely from Blücher, but would cut off its retreat upon Brussels, and would force it into an intricate country where escape from a victorious foe would be difficult. This great effort was to be made by the corps of D'Erlon, supported by the fire of an array of batteries accumulated in front of La Haye Sainte, and thence as far as Papelotte and La Haye; and it was to be sustained by the Imperial Guard, by Lobau, and by a large reserve of cavalry; but it was to be masked by a feint against Wellington's right, in order to screen the decisive movement, and to draw the enemy's attention away from it. Napoleon gave the signal at 11.30 A.M., and part of Reille's corps on the Emperor's left advanced boldly against Hougoumont, in front, we have seen, of the right of the British position. The château and the adjoining grounds, composed of a wood, an orchard and walled enclosures, afforded an excellent centre of defence; and though the French surrounded the place in thousands—nearly all Reille's men became

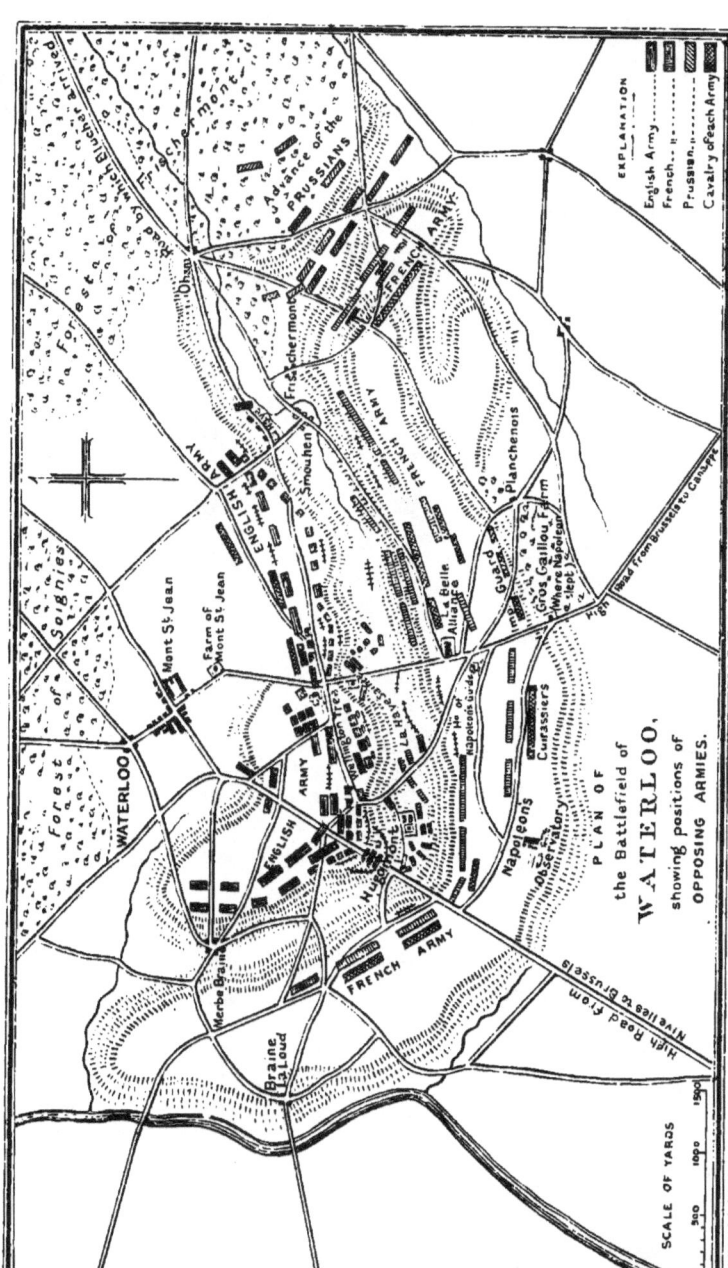

engaged—and captured most of the approaches to the house, and though some of the Duke's auxiliaries fled, the British Guards stubbornly clung to the spot, and made their resistance good to the last. The effect of this attack, in which we see precipitate haste on the part of the French—a defect in their tactics throughout the day—was to weaken most seriously the second corps, and to turn a diversion into a principal effort; and this admirably answered the Duke's purpose, for the force of his foe was broken on obstacles, and his own position was left intact.

It was now 1 P.M., and Napoleon was about to send an order to Ney for the grand attack, when he descried a body of troops on his right, at a considerable distance, near Chapelle St. Lambert, and he was soon apprised that this was the advance guard of Bülow's corps, 30,000 strong, already gathering menacingly on his flank. The Emperor detached Lobau, with 10,000 men, to the right, to hold this new foe in check, exclaiming that "Grouchy had lost him thirty chances"; and he instantly sent off a message to Grouchy, desiring the Marshal to approach Waterloo, and if possible, to fall on the rear of Bülow; some indication, perhaps, that Napoleon believed a part of Grouchy's force would be at once available, and possibly showing that the disputed order of the previous night may have been given. Meanwhile the batteries bearing on Wellington's line from La Haye Sainte to Papelotte and La Haye—a mass of from 70 to 80 guns, opposed by a much weaker artillery force—had been carrying destruction into the British ranks; and about 1.30 P.M. Ney was directed to carry the Duke's left, and to storm his centre. The assailants advanced in four huge columns of extraordinary depth, and with their flanks uncovered—this vicious formation has been acknowledged, but the author of it is not known—they moved slowly through the difficult ground; they swept away a Belgian division, which did not attempt to abide their onset; but they failed before Picton and his tenacious infantry, though they attained the crest of the British position. The Duke seized the occasion with perfect skill; and seeing that the French were already shaken, he launched against them a mass of heavy cavalry, which, in a few moments, carried all before it,

forced the enemy's columns in rout backwards, and clinging to
their unprotected sides, captured two eagles and 2,000 prisoners.
The horsemen, pressing the pursuit too far, were nearly destroyed
by a counter-attack of hostile cavalry from Napoleon's lines ; but
this magnificent charge completely defeated the first great effort
made by the Emperor, and had a marked effect on the fortunes of
the day.

It was nearly 3 P.M., and Napoleon's prospects, which had
appeared· so brilliant, had become clouded. Bülow had moved
forward from Chapelle St. Lambert ; Lobau, greatly out-numbered,
was falling back ; a messenger had arrived from Gembloux an-
nouncing that Grouchy was miles distant ; and Wellington had
completely maintained his position. It is difficult to determine
what, in this state of affairs, was the exact purpose formed by
Napoleon ; but he probably resolved to watch the movement of
Bülow ; and renouncing his attack on the Duke's left, which
would seriously endanger his own right, he turned against the
British centre, for the present suspending a decisive effort. Ney was
ordered to seize the advanced post of La Haye Sainte, and the place
was mastered at about 4 P.M.,* after a furious and well-contested
struggle, in which the French cavalry made their power manifest.
A gap was now opened in Wellington's front ; guns were brought up
to bear on his line ; a part of his troops fell back for shelter behind
the crest of his main position. Napoleon seems to have believed
in the beginning of a retreat, and he directed a large part of
his cavalry reserve, with Ney at their head, to advance on the
enemy, his purpose being, it seems probable, to sustain the
movement by the Imperial Guard. The French horsemen advanced in superb confidence ; carried the eminences held by the
hostile infantry, and sent terror into the hearts of the inferior
troops who crowded the ranks of the Duke's army, though checked
by the squares of the British and German footmen, who exhibited
the most heroic constancy. It seems now certain that Napoleon
meant to follow up this partial success, when a diversion caused

---

* I cannot accept General Shaw Kennedy's statement that La Haye Sainte was not
taken until 6 P.M.; it is contradicted by every other contemporaneous authority.

him to forego his purpose. Bülow had hesitated to make a serious attack; but Blücher had joined his halting lieutenant, and the fiery veteran, seeing how critical* was the situation of Wellington's army, ordered an immediate advance on Napoleon's flank. The Emperor was now fighting two battles; his attention was for some time engrossed in repelling Bülow's attack on his right; and this, indeed, became so formidable that a considerable part of the Imperial Guard was required to stem the enemy's progress. Ney, meanwhile, had been making desperate efforts with his cavalry to break the British centre; he employed the last reserve of this splendid force, undoubtedly against his master's wishes;† but though Wellington's line had been severely shaken, and thousands of fugitives covered his rear, and enormous gaps had been made in his army, the enemy's cavalry, unsupported by foot, were unable to force the British position, held by squares " rooted," it has been said, " in the earth."

The battle was undecided at 7 P.M.; but Bülow's attack had been repelled; Ney maintained his hold on the British front; the cannon of Grouchy were heard from Wavre, a pledge that he was keeping back the Prussians; and Reille and D'Erlon had made some progress in their efforts against the British right and centre. Napoleon thought his opportunity had come; a final stroke, he believed, would secure him victory, and forming the Guard into two great columns, supported by guns and the wreck of his cavalry, he directed one against the Duke's centre, holding the second in reserve to sustain the movement. Wellington's army had suffered immense losses; death, desertion, flight, had carried off thousands; undoubtedly he was in serious peril; and he now probably felt how grave had been the error of leaving 17,000 men at Hal. But, though " night or Blücher," significant words which fell from him,

---

* See on this point Blücher's official account of Waterloo, never contradicted by Wellington. English writers will not acknowledge the enormous importance of Bülow's attack.

† Napoleon, to the latest hour of his life, attributed to Ney the sacrifice of his last cavalry reserve, and declared it was one main cause of the rout of Waterloo. Ney acted recklessly on the 18th June; he had the hot fit and cold fit of a desperate man by turns in this campaign.

showed that he knew his danger, he had made everything ready to meet his foe; and drawing in his right wing behind his centre, he had even now a powerful reserve to oppose to Napoleon's supreme effort. The onset of the first column of the Guard for a time overbore all resistance; but it was arrested by the British Guards, by the renowned 52nd, and by a division of Dutchmen led by Chassé, and the defeated column swayed slowly backward, expecting the support of the approaching reserve. The needful assistance was never to come. Just at this moment part of the two corps of Ziethen and Pirch came into line. The French right was suddenly rent asunder, and a mass of British cavalry flooding the plain spread confusion and panic through the beaten army. The Duke now ordered a general advance; a terrible scene of ruin and disaster followed. The Imperial Guard fought nobly to the last; but the rest of Napoleon's routed troops became a mere chaos of dissolving fugitives, pursued with relentless hate by the Prussians, and scattered along the roads that lead across the Sambre. Not thirty thousand men of the perishing host were ever, probably, seen under arms again. The losses of the victors were not less than 22,000 or 23,000 men, and nearly 7,000 of these were Prussians.

Napoleon at Waterloo gave little proof of the energy and resource of Jena and Austerlitz. The plan of his attack was, indeed, perfect, and during the greater part of the day he was in a position of extreme difficulty, and he was badly seconded by his lieutenants, who displayed feverish impatience and great want of caution. But he did not prevent the waste of his troops round Hougoumont; he allowed Ney to engage a large part at least of his cavalry in a premature movement; he did not seize the occasion he perhaps had to attack in full force before Bülow's diversion. He was remiss and inactive throughout the battle; and this was due, there is now no doubt, to physical exhaustion * and long impaired health. The Duke, on the other hand, was the soul of

---

* Dorsey Gardoner, on the authority of two of Napoleon's staff officers, gives this account of the Emperor at Waterloo (p. 36): "he remained motionless, for long intervals, seated at a table, frequently sinking upon it."

the defence; he conducted the battle with wonderful skill, directing every movement at the right moment, making counter attacks when these were opportune, keeping a sufficient reserve for the supreme trial, and breathing into his men his stern sense of duty, his tenacity, and inflexible constancy. His management of the contest was so admirable that he held his ground, though he had expected Blücher in force on the field before midday, and though, humanly speaking, he must have lost the battle but for the intervention of the Prussian army—his composite force of 70,000 men, much weaker in guns, was not to be compared to the 72,000 troops under the Emperor's flag—still, I venture to think that even without this aid, he would not have suffered the crushing defeat on which Napoleon's hopes for the campaign rested. His one mistake, in fact, on this memorable day was the isolating 17,000 men at Hal; this certainly exposed him to real danger; but then this was a strategic not a tactical error. Nevertheless, Waterloo was decided by combinations outside the field; and we turn to the operations of Grouchy, the main cause, I believe, of Napoleon's overthrow.

The Marshal breaking up, we have seen, from Gembloux at least five or six hours too late, and marching with extraordinary slowness, reached Sart les Walhain at about 11·30—he was still eight or ten miles from Wavre—and at that place the thunder of cannon, far to the left, gave token of a great distant battle. Gérard, with true insight, at once urged Grouchy to cross the Dyle by Mousty and Ottignies, and to draw near the Emperor, known to be at Waterloo; for by so doing, Gérard justly argued, Wavre would be turned should it be attacked, and the French would attain the flank of Blücher, who, Gérard felt certain, was trying to join Wellington. Grouchy refused to listen to sagacious counsels, which, had they inspired him twelve hours before, would have perhaps changed the course of events in Europe, and which even now might have borne fruit; and he set off with his whole force for Wavre, where he expected to find the Prussian army. By this time Bülow was at Chapelle St. Lambert, but with a weak advanced guard only. Pirch and Ziethen were just breaking up from Wavre, and Thielmann was about to join them; but a great change took place in the Prussian movements when, at about 1 P.M., intelligence came that the enemy was approaching Wavre. Part of the corps of Pirch was ordered to fall back; the march of Ziethen was greatly retarded; and Thielmann was directed to remain at Wavre, and to make head against the scarcely expected foe. By 4 P.M., Grouchy was close to Wavre, having marched on the place, not across the Dyle towards the flank of Blücher, but along the river, thus striking Blücher's extreme rear, and pushing him, so to speak, on Wellington; the Marshal opened fire at once on the town, having just received Soult's letter of 10 A.M., which, no doubt, sanctioned an advance on Wavre, but ordered Grouchy to approach the Emperor. It is useless to follow the events of a combat of no importance to the result of the campaign; Thielmann, with only 18,000 men, contrived to hold Grouchy some hours in check; and meanwhile Bülow, completely free to act, and Pirch and Ziethen, all danger removed, succeeded in reaching Waterloo and in crushing Napoleon. Yet, bad as it was, the position of Grouchy made the Prussians cautious and kept them back; Pirch and Ziethen were only just up in time; and of an army of 90,000 men, not 50,000 made their way to Waterloo. By 7 P.M. Grouchy received the letter of 1 P.M., sent off from Napoleon's lines at the news of the apparition of Bülow; the Marshal crossed the Dyle, and tried to approach the Emperor; but the movement was now altogether too late; the French army and its chief had succumbed.

The junction of Blücher and Wellington, therefore, led to the overwhelming defeat of Waterloo; but for this, Napoleon would have won the battle—the chances, at least, were all in his favour—despite the tactical errors of the French, and the admirable defensive resource of Wellington. It follows that the great and capital question, as regards this part of the Campaign of 1815, is, Could Grouchy have prevented this junction, for, if he could, he must be held responsible for the catastrophe which befell the Emperor? The answer must largely depend on conjecture; but an impartial student of war, I think, especially if he can weigh evidence, will give it distinctly in the affirmative. Considerations,

·obvious and yet decisive, should have urged Grouchy, we have seen, to leave Gembloux in the early dawn of the 18th, to cross the Dyle at Mousty and Ottignies, and to approach Wavre as quickly as possible ; the idea, it will be observed, flashed on Gérard's mind the moment he heard the cannon of Waterloo. If the Marshal had taken this rational course, he would have been over the river at about 11 A.M.,* and, in that event, as affairs stood, he would have seriously menaced the flank of Bülow, toiling painfully, in long straggling columns, on the way from Wavre to Chapelle St. Lambert, and he would have been nearer Napoleon's lines than the corps of Ziethen, of Pirch, and of Thielmann, still near Wavre, and not on the march for Waterloo.

What, in these circumstances, would Blücher have done, giving him full credit for his daring and energy ? He would have been surprised in a perilous flank march, through a difficult and almost impassable country, for he had no conception that Grouchy would be near ; and his army would have been almost divided by an enemy threatening its separate parts. In this state of things I cannot doubt but that he would not have permitted Bülow to advance farther, or his three remaining corps to make a move towards Waterloo, until he had disposed of Grouchy ; he would have drawn the mass of his forces together. All this would have been an affair of hours. Grouchy could have made a prolonged resistance, and, meanwhile, Napoleon, free to bring the whole strength of his more powerful army against the Duke, would have triumphed over his much weaker enemy. The same results would have, perhaps, followed had Grouchy, without attempting to cross the Dyle, reached Wavre at 11 A.M., as he might have done ; Pirch, Ziethen, and Thielmann would not have moved ; Bülow, isolated, would not have dared to attack, and the French army would still have gained a victory. Even had Grouchy, at the eleventh hour, listened to the excellent advice of Gérard, and crossed the Dyle at Mousty and Ottignies, he might possibly have

---

* Grouchy might, I think, have been over the Dyle before 11 A.M. ; but I accept the time of Charras, who has made it as late as possible ; " before noon " is his exact phrase

averted a complete catastrophe. The movement could not have interfered with the attack of Bülow, but it might have arrested Pirch and Ziethen, and it was these chiefs who, at the last moment, dealt the French army the final mortal stroke.

It is impossible, therefore, to acquit Grouchy; he is mainly to blame for the result of Waterloo. This conclusion, however, has been assailed, with confidence, on two lines of argument. Napoleon, it is said, was not aware, from first to last, whither Blücher had gone; he despatched Grouchy from Sombreffe too late; Gembloux was not the true point on which the force of the Marshal should have been directed. Napoleon gave Grouchy no precise orders; he misled his lieutenant, and kept him in the dark; he approved, late on the 18th, the march on Wavre, and he has, therefore, to thank himself for his own overthrow. We may grant the premisses, yet they do not sustain the inference or exonerate Grouchy. Admitting that Napoleon believed that Blücher was falling back on his base after Ligny; that he should have sent Grouchy on his track much sooner; and that Gembloux was not the best place to be assigned for the restraining wing; still, it was the duty of Grouchy, knowing what he had learned on the 17th, to have left Gembloux at daybreak on the 18th, and marched rapidly on or towards Wavre; and had he done this, he would, I believe, have stopped the Prussians and averted Waterloo. As for Napoleon not having given directions to Grouchy of an exact kind, and having sanctioned the tardy advance on Wavre, the first statement assumes that Grouchy was not an independent general-in-chief, in command of a distinct army, and the second is opposed to the known evidence. Napoleon approved of the march to Wavre, but not at a late hour, or at a snail's pace; he certainly thought, and had a right to think, if a Prussian force existed at Wavre—the reader will recollect the letter of the 18th, pointing to his growing suspicion of the fact—that his lieutenant would be able to hold it in check, and this required an early and speedy march from Gembloux. This reasoning, in fact, errs in two respects; it ascribes to the mistakes Napoleon made results with which they are not chargeable; it assumes that Napoleon, in front of Wellington, was to instruct Grouchy, in front of Blücher, in his conduct, in the minutest details; it takes for granted that Grouchy, the head of the army, was a mere puppet to be directed in every operation he was to undertake, and that by his chief at a wide distance from him. The argument, when examined, falls to the ground; it cannot stand the test of impartial criticism.

The second contention, urged by Charras, rests on the fact that the army of Grouchy was very much weaker than that of Blücher; but though made with a parade of science, it does not mislead a true student of war. Grouchy, the argument runs, had but 34,000 men to oppose to the 90,000 of Blücher; the Prussian was an able, nay, a great soldier; and had Grouchy done all that man could do, he could not, his force was so inferior, have prevented the junction of Blücher and Wellington, and conjured away the disaster of Waterloo. Assume that Grouchy manœuvred rightly, had left Gembloux at the first possible moment, had marched rapidly, had seized Mousty and Ottignies, and had mastered the Dyle before mid-day, his adversary would have at once recognized, that the Prussians were nearly three to one to the French, and this would have determined Blücher's purpose. The Prussian marshal, aware of this fact, would have sent Pirch and Ziethen to hold Grouchy in check, and marched on Waterloo with Bülow and Thielmann; or he would have allowed Grouchy to draw near his flank, and, fending him off, would have moved on Wellington with three-fourths of his army at least; and in either case he would have joined the Duke, and both would have overwhelmed Napoleon.

This looks well on paper, and in mere theory; but is contradicted by the realities of war. Had Grouchy attained the Dyle by noon, he would have completely surprised Blücher, have caught him with an army far apart, on a flank march of the most critical kind; and in this position of affairs it is morally certain that Blücher would have reconnoitred and paused, would have waited to draw together his army, and would have fought a pitched battle with Grouchy, before he even thought of uniting with Wellington. In that event, inferior in numbers as he was, Grouchy would have detained the Prussians for hours; Blücher would have lost the chance of joining the Duke; and Waterloo would have been a French victory. The lessons of war, and the great authority of Jomini in this matter, confute the reasoning of a partizan censor, and the very incidents of the day point to the same conclusion. The mere apparition of Grouchy on the wrong bank of the Dyle, late as the hour was when he had approached Wavre, delayed the general movement of the Prussian army; and half of it never attained Waterloo. How different must the result have been had Grouchy crossed the Dyle at the true point, and gathered upon the flank of Blücher; in that case not even one Prussian division would, I think, have come to the aid of Wellington.

Grouchy, in short, was the Emperor's evil genius on the great and terrible day of Waterloo; Napoleon has written, with perfect truth, that he could no more foresee his lieutenant's conduct than he could assume that Grouchy would be swallowed up, with his army, by an unexpected earthquake. The Campaign of 1815 may be summed up in a few sentences. Striking at the extreme right, for the time isolated, of the hosts about to invade France, and screening the movement with wonderful skill, Napoleon collects an army of 128,000 men on the edge of France, running into Belgium, his object being to attack Blücher and Wellington, commanding about 224,000 men, but whose two armies were widely divided, in scattered groups, from Liège to Ghent and Charleroi. The Emperor, aiming at the allied centre, the weakest and most assailable point, begins the movement on the 15th of June; he does not, owing to a set of accidents, reach the strategic points of Quatre Bras and Sombreffe on the true line of junction of his antagonists, the lateral road from Nivelles to Namur; but his columns at nightfall are close to these, and his adversaries already are placed in danger. Blücher, meanwhile, acting as Napoleon had hoped, marches to Sombreffe with three-fourths of his army only; the Duke, fulfilling the expectations of his foe, lingers, hesitates, and delays his movements; and on the 16th Napoleon has a grand chance of reaching and beating his enemy in detail.

His plans, if formed on a false impression, are nevertheless so correct in principle, that had they been carried out ably the Prussian army must have been destroyed; but Ney, Reille, and D'Erlon failed: the Emperor is perhaps over-cautious in not pressing D'Erlon's advance on St. Amand; and Blücher escapes, through misadventures, which alone save him from complete ruin. Ligny, however, is a real French victory; and, meanwhile, Ney, though unequal to his task, fights an indecisive action at Quatre Bras; and though forced to fall back, he so far succeeds that he prevents Wellington from sending aid to his colleague, and, in fact, gains a strategic advantage. The close of the 16th sees Napoleon victorious upon the main scene of the contest, having only just failed to make Ligny a counterpart of the rout of Jena.

The 17th has come; the Allies, compelled to abandon their proper line of junction, retreat separately and in distant groups on a second line, between Wavre and Waterloo; they intend ultimately to unite on this; and this project, though crowned with success, was false strategy that might have proved their ruin. The French army, on this eventful day, makes a long halt not easy to explain; the retiring enemy is not pursued or watched; and this delay and remissness—utterly unlike the energy of Napoleon on the path of victory—and probably largely due to his declining health, save Blücher and Wellington from the gravest peril, and singularly aid their future projects. Napoleon does not move until noon from Ligny, his purpose being to attack Wellington, for several hours falling back on Waterloo; he has a noble army 72,000 strong to cope with 70,000 men of the Duke, more than a third of these being inferior troops; and he detaches Grouchy, with about 34,000, to pursue Blücher and to keep him away from Wellington. The Emperor follows the Duke from Quatre Bras, and finds his adversary in force near Waterloo; and meantime, though he remains convinced that Blücher is retiring on his base, he directs Grouchy to occupy Gembloux, having heard that Prussians were approaching that place. Grouchy reaches Gembloux by the night of the 17th; he informs his master that the Prussian army is in retreat in two great masses, one directed to Wavre, the other to Liège : and he shows that he understands his mission, and that he will endeavour "to separate Blücher and Wellington." This report perfectly reassures the Emperor ; he makes preparations for a decisive battle ; but the elements interfere to retard his purpose, and he does not attack the Duke until near noon on the 18th. Meanwhile Grouchy, whose plain duty it was to leave Gembloux early, and to march on Wavre across the Dyle on the flank of Blücher as rapidly as his troops could move, breaks up hours too late, proceeds with strange slowness, and reaches Wavre in the afternoon only, striking Blücher in the extreme rear, but still detaining a part of his army. During all this time the great fight of Waterloo has been raging with varying fortunes ; the French tactics are faulty, the Duke's admirable. In the afternoon Bülow reaches Napoleon ; the Emperor is engaged in a double battle. Ney recklessly squanders his master's cavalry, but Bülow is for a time repulsed ; and the Emperor makes a final effort to break Wellington's centre with the Guard. The attack fails, but all is not over until part of two fresh Prussian corps turns the scale decisively against the French, and Waterloo ends in a frightful rout. The Prussians, in fact, who might have been detained by Grouchy, were all but left free to advance on Waterloo ; they reached the field in the very nick of time. Grouchy kept back directly only 18,000 men ; and yet, miserable as his operations were, they indirectly retarded the Prussian army, a significant proof of what might have occurred had Grouchy been a capable chief.

Having reviewed the incidents of this great Campaign, let us disengage the permanent lessons it teaches an impartial student of war. Napoleon operated with too small an army : 128,000 men. could hardly overcome 224,000. He had a right to count on his transcendent genius ; he had no right to assume that the Allies would make the grave strategic mistakes they made, or would give him the opportunities they gave. In consequence of this numerical weakness he was compelled to divide his army into two masses not sufficiently connected by an intermediate body ; and this partly explains, though it does not excuse, the errors of Ney to the left on the 16th, and those of Grouchy to the right on the 18th. Had the Emperor had the 20,000 men he had intended to bring into the field, he would have had a force sufficient to fill this interval, and in that event he would have doubtless triumphed. The intellectual powers of Napoleon were splendidly exhibited in the contest; his plan for the Campaign is a masterpiece of art; his plan of attack at Waterloo defies criticism; his general ideas, though he made mistakes—for the greatest generals must necessarily err—reveal the wholly unrivalled strategist. His bodily strength, however, failed him : to this, I doubt not, we ought to ascribe the delays and carelessness of the 17th, and certainly this weakness had much to do with the inactivity and slackness he betrayed at Waterloo. It may well be, too, that his complete faith in himself had been diminished by recent events. Like Richard at Bosworth, he has recorded—

> I had not the alacrity of spirit,
> Or cheer of mind that I was wont to have ;

and the great player against Fate may, in this mighty hazard, have thrown his last die with a trembling hand. We may perhaps see hesitation, and even timidity, in his allowing D'Erlon to return to Quatre Bras, and in not pressing the movement on St. Amand home; and the same shortcomings may be possibly traced in his not seizing a real chance at Waterloo, when La Haye Sainte had been taken, and before Bülow had made a serious attack on his flank. Yet it was his lieutenants' errors that lost the campaign; on the 16th they failed on the left ; Grouchy, on the 18th was worse than useless ; and we can understand his bitter expression that victory was twice wrested from his hands through incomprehensible faults of subordinates. In this campaign, so to speak, the sun of Austerlitz seems about to break out in its old splendour; but malignant influences intercept its rays, and it sets at last in disastrous night.

To turn to the Allies, Blücher and Wellington were adversaries of a a very different kind from the Beaulieu and Colli of 1796. Both certainly, made great strategic mistakes; both were more than once in imminent peril; and we see in their conduct the divided counsels repeatedly fatal to a Coalition and its chiefs. But both, in different ways, were great soldiers; they cordially co-operated in a common design; and the heroism of Blücher, mastering defeat, and the tenacity and tactical skill of Wellington, are admirable specimens of great parts in war. Another cause of the ultimate success of the Allies should be carefully noted. Napoleon, in his last address to his troops, referred scornfully to the Prussians of Jena, and exclaimed "Are not we and they the same men?" and like many great chiefs he took no heed of national and patriotic passion. The Prussian army of 1815 was not, however, "the same men" as the Prussian army of 1806; it was fired with an intense hatred of France, and with an intense love of the Fatherland; and it was capable of very different efforts from those of the serf-like troops of Brunswick. Napoleon, relying on former experience, believed that the army defeated at Ligny would recoil on its base, and, beyond doubt, would not make a dangerous march on Waterloo; but the reasoning of strategy, as has often happened, was baffled by the ardour of a devoted soldiery; though had Grouchy been equal to his task all this energy would have come to nothing. In Spain and Russia Napoleon had suffered immense disasters from his inborn contempt of patriotic and popular sentiment; and this indifference had something to do with the final issue of the strife at Waterloo. But when all has been said, the Emperor's genius all but triumphed in the campaign of 1815; he was nearly successful although opposed to adversaries almost twofold in numbers; and victory was only wrested from him through the mistakes of others. Notwithstanding Zama, Hannibal remains the pre-eminent figure of ancient war; Napoleon is the great captain of modern times, though ruin overtook him on the plains of Belgium.

Printed by W. H. Allen & Co., Limited. 13, Waterloo Place, London, S.W.